ORDNA...

STREE...

Edinburgh

& East Central Scotland

Contents

IV *Key to maps*

VI *Administrative boundaries*

1 *Street maps*

232 *Index explanation and abbreviations*

233 *Index of towns, villages and rural localities*

234 *Index of street names*

PHILIP'S

First edition published 1995 by

Ordnance Survey   and   Philip's
Romsey Road   an imprint of Reed Books
Maybush   Michelin House, 81 Fulham Road, London, SW3 6RB
Southampton SO16 4GU   and Auckland, Melbourne, Singapore and Toronto

ISBN 0-540-06182-4 (Philip's, pocket edition)
ISBN 0-319-00800-2 (Ordnance Survey, pocket edition)

Printed in Great Britain by Cox and Wyman, Reading

Key to map symbols

⊕	British Rail station
🚂	Private railway station
●	Bus or coach station
Ⓗ	Heliport
◆	Police station (may not be open 24 hours)
✚	Hospital with casualty facilities (may not be open 24 hours)
☐	Post office
┿	Place of worship
◣	Important building
P	Parking
174	Adjoining page indicator
✕	No adjoining page
━━━	Motorway
━━━	Dual carriageway
───	Main or through road
A27	Road numbers (Department of Transport)
─┬─	Gate or obstruction to traffic (restrictions may not apply at all times or to all vehicles)
- - - -	All paths, bridleways, BOAT's, RUPP's, dismantled railways, etc.
═══	Track

The representation in this atlas of a road, track or path is no evidence of the existence of a right of way

Amb Sta	**Ambulance Station**	LC	**Level crossing**
Amb Dpo	**Ambulance Depot**	Liby	**Library**
Coll	**College**	Mus	**Museum**
FB	**Footbridge**	Acad	**Academy**
F Sta	**Fire Station**	Sch	**School**
Hospl	**Hospital**	TH	**Town Hall or Town House**

0	¼	½	¾	1 mile
0	250m 500m	250m	1 Kilometre	

The scale of the maps is approximately 2¹/₂ inches to 1 mile (1:25497)

The small numbers around the edges of the maps identify the 1 kilometre National Grid lines

Key to map pages

| 0 1 2 3 4 5 6 7 8 Km |
| 0   1   2   3   4   5 Miles |

Grange
Gauldry
A914
Balmullo
A92
Luchrie
Leuchars

NEWBURGH
A91
St Andrews Bay
ST ANDREWS
Moonzie
Strathkinness
Boarhills

Letham
A91
Springfield
CUPAR
Blebocraigs
Kingsbarns

Dunshalt
A914
LADYBANK
Pitscottie
Ceres
Stravithie
Fife Ness

Freuchie
A92
A916
Craigrothie
Peat Inn

Kingskettle
Montrave
Kirkton of
Largo
A915
Largoward
CRAIL

Langdyke
Star
Kennoway
Arncroach
KILRENNY
A917

Markinch
Colinsburgh
ANSTRUTHER

ROTHES
A92
Largo Bay
PITTENWEEM
ST MONANCE

Thornton
Methil
LEVEN
EARLSFERRY
ELIE
Isle of May

Cluny
A955
BUCKHAVEN
East Wemyss

West Wemyss

FIRTH OF FORTH

tertool
17 **18**
KIRKCALDY

35
A921
KINGHORN

BURNTISLAND
Inchkeith

NORTH BERWICK

51 **52** **53** **54** **55** **56**
Dirleton
Gullane
Kingston
Scoughall

Aberlady
A198
Drem
Whitekirk

70 **71** **72** **73** **74** **75** **76** **77** **78** **79**
Athelstaneford
EAST LINTON
DUNBAR
Thornonloch

INBURGH
Cockenzie &
Port Seton
Longniddry
A6137
A1

94 **95** **96** **97** **98** **99** **100** **101** **102** **103** **104** **105** **106** **107** **108** **109**
Elvingston
Stenton
Pitcox

Musselburgh
TRANENT
HADDINGTON
Halls
Innerwick

124 **125** **126** **127** **128** **129** **130** **131** **132** **133** **134** **135** **136** **137** **138** **139** **140**
Elphinstone
New Town
A6093
Bolton
Garvald
Oldhamstocks

Ormiston
Pencaitland
Carfrae
Ecclaw
A1

155 **156** **157** **158** **159** **160** **161** **162** **163** **164** **165** **166**
A720
Peastonbank
Gifford
Danskine

Bonnyrigg &
Lasswade
Peaston
Gilchriston
Longyester

Loanhead
181 **182** **183** **184** **185** **186** **187** **188** **189** **190**
A68
Humbie
Abbey
St Bathans

Roslin
Cranshaws

A701
A6094
Carrington
Gorebridge
Fala
Blegbie

205 **206** **207** **208** **209** **210** **211**
Ellemford

Howgate
Temple
Tynehead
Longformacus
A6112

Middleton
Gilston
Preston

224 **225** **226** **227** **228** **229**
Falahill
DUNS

eadburn
Heriot
Oxton
Gavinton
A6105

A7
Polwarth
Fogo

Fountainhall
Torquhan
Blythe
Westruther
Halliburton
Greenlaw
Leitholm

Kiliochyett
Houndslow
A697

LAUDER
Lambden
Eccles

PEEBLES
Stow
Nether
Blainslie
Gordon
Hume

A72
Walkerburn
Blackhaugh
Bowland
Langshaw
Earlston
Fans
A6089
Stichill

Eddleston
A68
A6105

Buckholm

Major administrative boundaries of Lothian

Legend:
- District Boundaries
- Region or Islands Area
- National Boundary

0 5 10 Kilometres

Regions:
- FIFE REGION
- TAYSIDE REGION
- CENTRAL REGION
- STRATHCLYDE REGION
- BORDERS REGION

CITY OF EDINBURGH
- QUEENSFERRY
- EDINBURGH

EAST LOTHIAN
- NORTH BERWICK
- EAST LINTON
- HADDINGTON
- DUNBAR
- COCKENZIE
- PRESTONPANS
- MUSSELBURGH

MIDLOTHIAN
- DALKEITH
- BONNYRIGG
- LASSWADE
- LOANHEAD
- PENICUIK

WEST LOTHIAN
- LINLITHGOW
- LIVINGSTON
- BATHGATE
- ARMADALE
- WHITBURN

VI

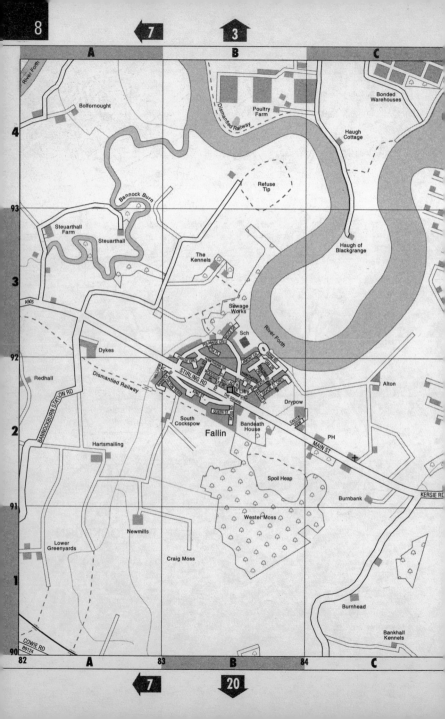

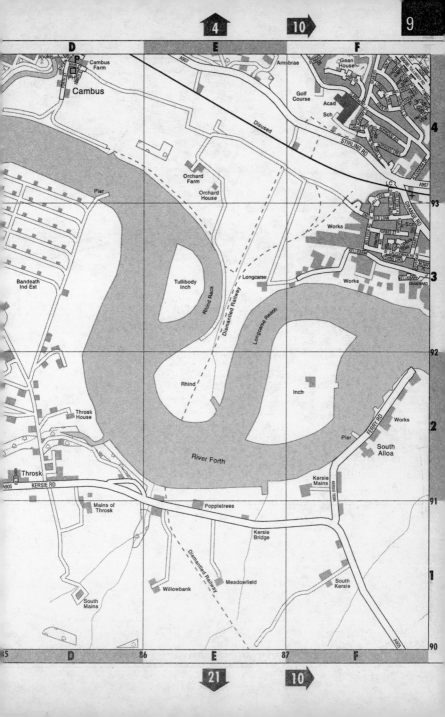

Cambus Farm
Arnsbrae
Gean House
Golf Course
Acad
Sch
STIRLING RD
Cambus
Disused
LC
A907

D E F

4

Orchard Farm
Orchard House
Pier
Works
Sch

93

Bandeath Ind Est
Tullibody Inch
Longcarse
Works

Rhind Rack
Dismantled Railway
Longcarse Reach

3

92

Rhind
Inch
Throsk House
FERRY RD
Works
Pier
South Alloa

2

River Forth
Throsk
KERSIE RD
Kersie Mains
KERSIE TERR

91

A905
Mains of Throsk
Poppletrees
Kersie Bridge

Dismantled Railway
Willowbank
Meadowfield
South Kersie

1

South Mains
A905

90

D 86 E 87 F

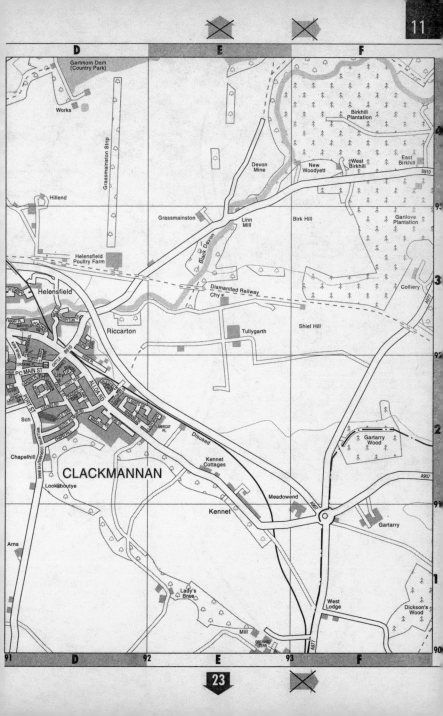

CLACKMANNAN

13

LOCHGELLY

1 FORRESTER CT
2 SOLAN SQ
3 DRYBURGH PL
4 KNOCKHILL CL

AUCHTERDERRAN RD B981

B981

STATION RD
DRUMMOND
Sch
MELGUND RD
P
STEWART CRES
Golf
Course
CH
Sch
BANK ST
Liby
MAIN ST
HIGH ST
Sch
DICKSON
CT
F Sta
LUMPHINNANS RD
B981
BRUCEFIELD TERR
THE AVENUE
Melgund
Lodge
Works
Mast
A92
B920
CH
Powguild
Lochen
Westerton
Loch Gelly
Lochgelly Burn
Colvin's
Knowe
Lochside
Plantation
Little
Raith
Easter
Lochhead
Wester Lochhead
Dismantled Railway
Dronachy Burn
Walton East
Strip
Walton East
Clump
Dronachy Burn
Walton
Raith
Hill
Chemical
Works
Cemy
Manse
B920

4
93
3
92
2
91
1
90
18   19   20
A   B   C

13   32

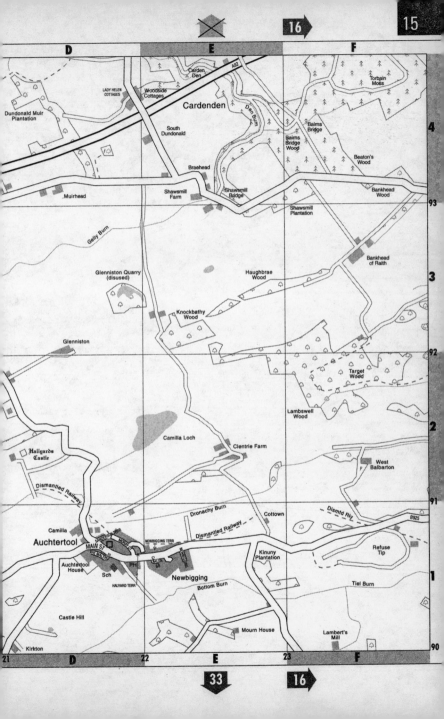

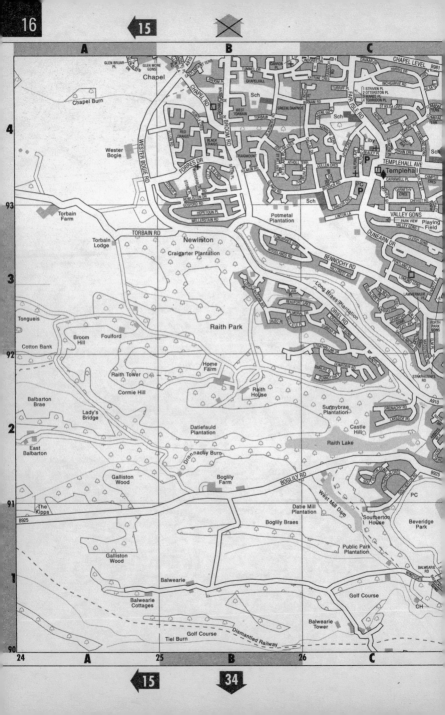

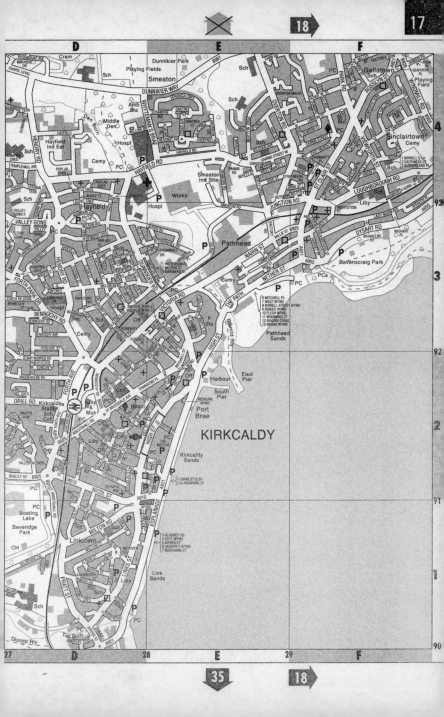

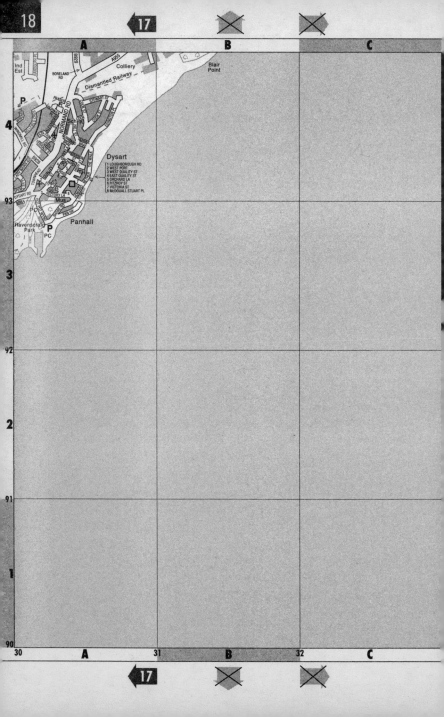

Ind
Est

Colliery

BORELAND
RD

Dismantled Railway

Blair
Point

P

NORMAND RD

4

Dysart

1 LOUGHBOROUGH RD
2 WEST PORT
3 WEST QUALITY ST
4 EAST QUALITY ST
5 ORCHARD LA
6 FITZROY ST
7 VICTORIA ST
8 McDOUALL STUART PL

93

Mus

DYSART RD

PAN TER

Ravenscraig
Park

P
PC

Panhall

3

92

2

91

1

90

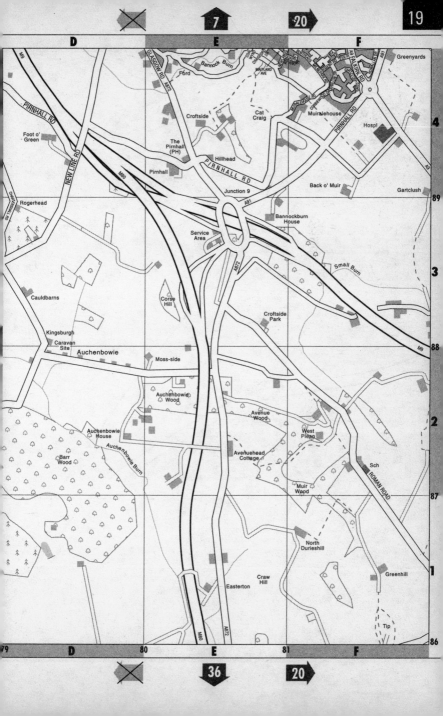

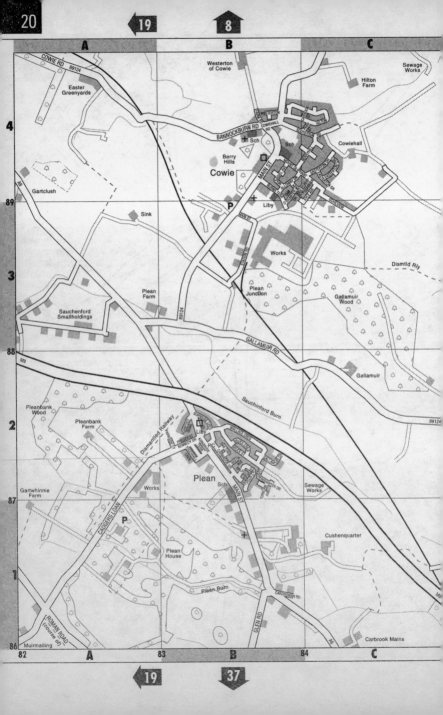

D   E   F

Mine

Sight Hill

Overton

West
Grange

Burrowine

Dismantled Railway

4

Blinkeerie

Middle
Grange

89

Launchout Burn

East
Grange

Balgownie
Mains

Bluther Burn

Oneford Burn

Righead

Thornyhaw

3

Balgownie Wood

Park
Plantation

88

Muirhead

Shires
Mill

Gallowridge

Blairhall

B9037

Kirkton Wood

Blairhall
Wood

2

PC

Couston
Wood

Keir Burn

Cemy

Kirkton

Blairhall
Mains

B9037

Ashes

87

Waes
Plantation

GALLOWS LOAN

A985

B9037

WOODHEAD FARM RD

Woodhead

1

Kirkbrae
Wood

B9037

Dean Burn

The Park

KIRK ST

MAIN ST

FORTHBANK

LOW CSWY

B9037

86

D   98   E   99   F

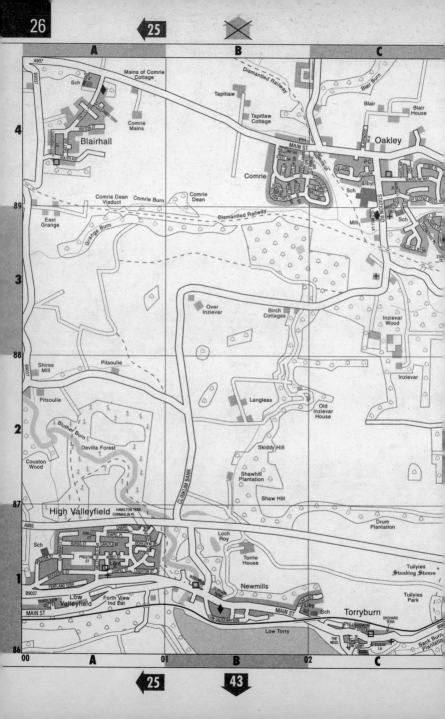

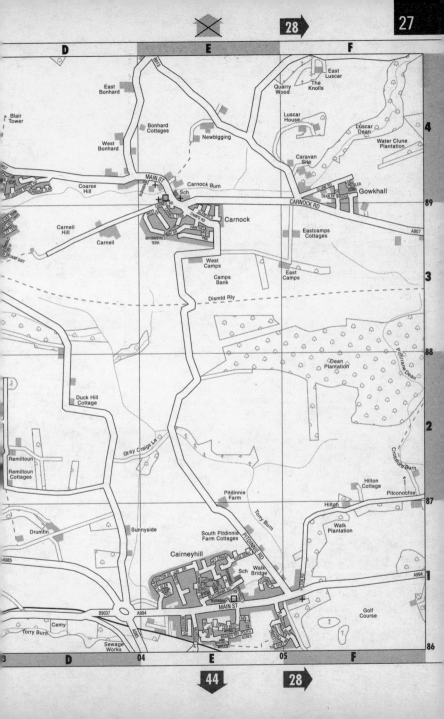

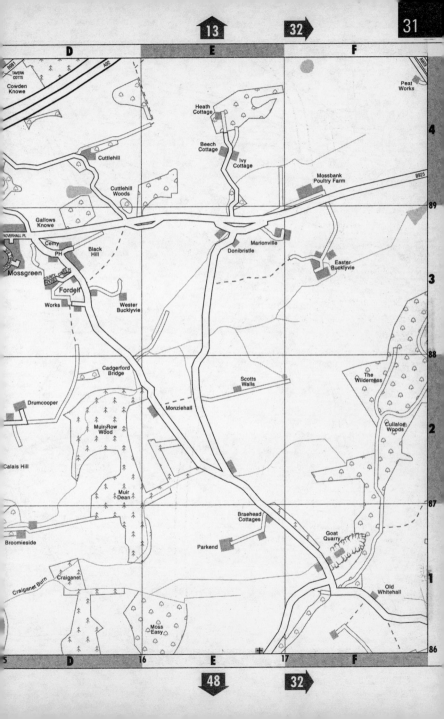

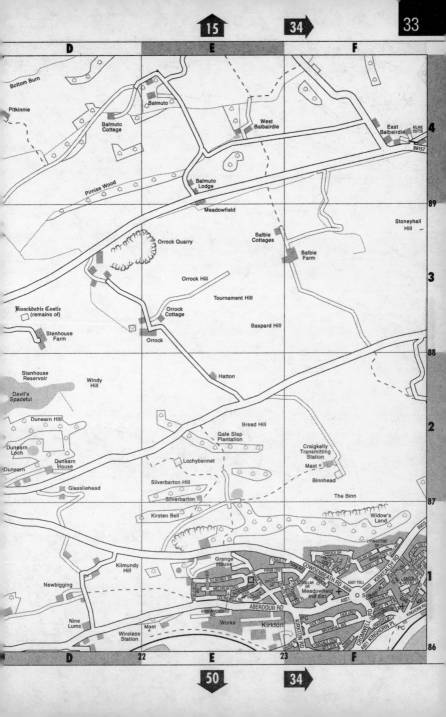

D
E
F

Bottom Burn

Pitkinnie

Balmuto

Balmuto Cottage

West Balbairdie

East Balbairdie

KILRIE COTTS

B9157

4

Pirniss Wood

Balmuto Lodge

89

Meadowfield

Stoneyhall Hill

Orrock Quarry

Balbie Cottages

Balbie Farm

Orrock Hill

3

Knockdavie Castle (remains of)

Orrock Cottage

Tournament Hill

Stenhouse Farm

Orrock

Baspard Hill

88

Stenhouse Reservoir

Windy Hill

Hatton

Devil's Spadeful

Dunearn Hill

Bread Hill

Dunearn Loch

Gale Slap Plantation

Craigkelly Transmitting Station

2

Dunearn

Dunearn House

Lochybennet

Mast

Binnhead

Glassliehead

Silverbarton Hill

The Binn

Silverbarton

87

Kirsten Bell

Widow's Land

LYNNASTONE

B923

Kilmundy Hill

Grange House

ORROCK DR

COWDENBEATH RD

KIRKCALDY RD

Newbigging

Meadowfield Ind Est

EAST TOLL

A921

School

1

Nine Lums

Mast

ABERDOUR RD

Wireless Station

Works

Kirkton

KIRKTON RD

CROMWELL RD

A921 KINGHORN PK

PC

86

D
22
E
23
F

D
E
F

INVERTIEL RD
89157
Factory
KINGHORN RD
JAVRANES RD

Tyrie

Tyrie Farm
Cottages

Seafield
House

Seafield
Tower

Vicar's
Grange

Linton
Court

Abden
Farm

ORCHARD CT

KINGHORN

IRB
Sta

1 GLOVER'S CT
2 BRUCE ST
3 ST LEONARD'S PL
4 ST LEONARD'S CT
5 SOUTH OVERGATE
6 TRONGATE
7 ABDEN CT
8 CHURCH WLK
9 HARBOUR RD

Kinghorn Ness

4

89

3

88

2

87

1

86

27
D
28
E
29
F

A   B   C

Boards Burn

Northfield Farm

4

Boards Quarry

Woodcockfauld

Northfield Quarry

Wellsfield Farm

Braes Wood

Dales Wood

85

Quarter Wood

High Quarter Farm

Quarter House

Braes

Old Quarter

3

Burnhouse

Low Quarter Mill

Croftfoot

Broomhill Farm

84

Rosebank

Bankend

Avon Burn

Sch

Denovan Mains

Drumelzier

Dunipace

Toptowie Hill

2

Sch

BARNEGO RD

Denovan Mains

Herbertshire Castle Park

Denny Bridge

Sch

Ind Est

Risk

River Carron

83

Mill

A883

STIRLING

P

Stoneywood

Sch

BROOMPARK SDNS

P

Lihy Church

ST JOHN'S GATE 1
ST JOHN'S GR 2

Drum

DUKE ST

A883

BROAD ST

STONEYWOOD PK

B818

NETHERMAINS RD

CUSTONHALL PL

East Boreland PL

ANDERSON PARK RD

1

Garth

Holehouse

TEMPLE DENNY RD

SINCLAIR CRES

SAVERS AVE

FERGUSON RD

ROSS TERR

Denny

1 THE VENNEL WAY
2 HALGRS WAY
3 DUNCARRON RD
4 VILLA BANK
5 KIRKENNEL PL
6 BANKSIDE CT

Castlerankine Burn

LANGHILL PL 3
GARVALD LA 4
DUNDAFF CT 5
RANDOLPH GDNS 6
CARNOCK WLK 2
GLEN TERR 8 1

SMITH PL

TOWN HOUSE ST

Sta

Easter Castlerankine

Sch

SHANKS AVE

Mydub

82

79   A   80   B   81   C

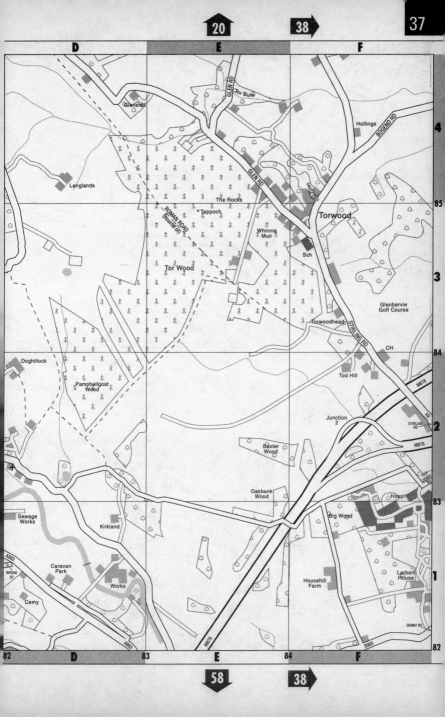

A   B   C

4   Blairs

Bogend

BOGEND RD

M9

Pow Burn

Kersebrock

Drum of Kinnaird

Hill of Kinnaird

85

North
Inches

M876

HAMILTON RD

Titlandhill

Junction 8

3   Glenbervie
Golf Course

Shiels Farm

Inches

Bellsdyke
Hospital

84

M876

Central Park
Business Park

North
Broomage

BELLSDYKE RD

Antonshill

STRATHMIGLO PL

2   STIRLING RD

M876

A88

STIRLING RD

BROOMAGE AVE

MUIRHALL RD

TRYST RD

Golf Course

Stenhousemuir

Cem'y

PC

KING ST

STENHOUSE RD

Larbert

LADYWELL CT

CH

Sch

Sch

Liby

P

PC

Crownest
Park

Carron
Hill
Sch

83   Hospl

BALQUIE CRES

MAIN ST

Main St

1   Lochside
House

STIRLING RD

FOUNDRY LOAN

F Sta

Works

Larbert
Station

P

Main St

Carron
Dams

Works

PRETORIA RD

Sch

South
Broomage

River Carron

82   B905   DENNY RD

River Carron

85   A   86   B   87   C

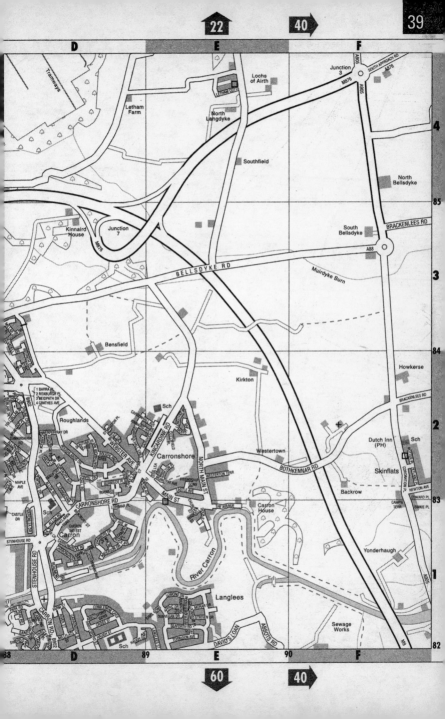

39
23

A
B
C

4

Greendyke

Powfoulis
Manor Hotel

Mains of
Powfoulis

Pocknave

Brackenlees

85

Hardlands

Stonehouse
Farm

3

Firth of Forth

BRACKENLEES RD

Orchardhead

84

Newton Mains
Farm

2

Skinflats

NEWTON AVE

NEWTON RD

83

Grangemouth Harbour
& Docks

North Shore Rd

Western Channel

River Carron

Sch

Carron Dock

CENTRAL DOCK RD

off

LC

1

Glensburgh

South Bridge St

STATION RD

1 YORK LA
2 YORK SQ
3 YORK ARC
4 LA PORTE PRE
TH

NELSON
GDNS

LC's

SOUTH SHORE RD

A984

PC

82

91
A
92
B
93
C

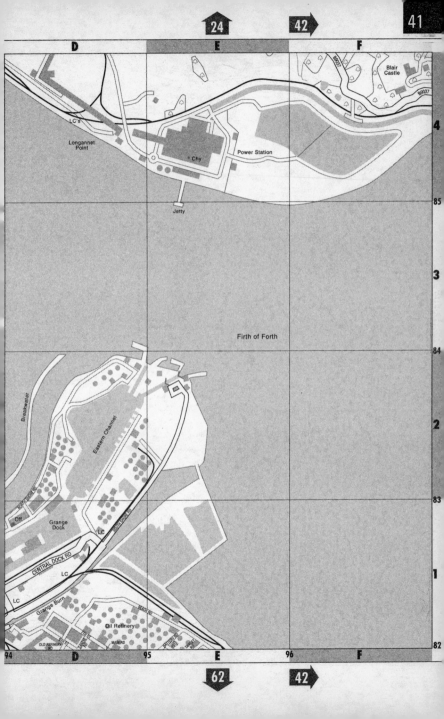

D
E
F

B9037

Blair
Castle

B9037

LC's

Longannet
Point

4

Chy

Power Station

85

Jetty

3

Firth of Forth

84

Breakwater

Eastern Channel

2

83

Off

Grange
Dock

LC

SOUTH SHORE RD

CENTRAL DOCK RD

1

LC

LC

Grange Burn

BEACH RD

Oil Refinery

82

OLD REFINERY
RD

FIRTH ST

CARRO

MAIN RD

PATTERSON
BR'G

GRANG
ST

94
D
95
E
96
F

A

B

C

Mus

Dunimarle
Castle

BALGOWNIE W

Sch

Mus

LOW CAUSEWAYSIDE

LC

Blairburn

PC

PH

Sch

1 FAIRHOUSE BRAE
2 MID CSWY
3 LITTLE CSWY

CULROSS

4

85

3

Firth of Forth

84

2

83

1

West Pier

82

97

A

98

B

99

C

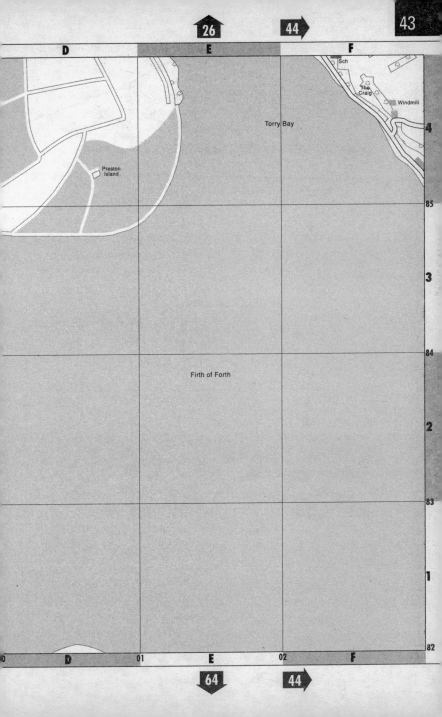

D

E

F

Sch

The
Craig

Windmill

Torry Bay

4

Preston
Island

85

3

84

Firth of Forth

2

83

1

82

D

01

E

02

F

B916

D

Dover Heights

Annfield
Cottage

Mid Duloch

Annfield

Old Duloch

Duloch Home
Farm

Pinkerton Burn

E

M90

B981

Castle Hill

Parniehall
Plantation

Strawberry Bank

Fordell Burn

F

Fordell
Castle

4

MASTERTON RD

SCEERBROOK

Mastertown

Middlebank

Middlebank
(Animal Welfare Centre)

B916

Balbougie Glen

Clockluine
Wood

Balbougie

CLOCKLUINE RD

Fordell
Glen

85

23 M

Junction 2

Dales Farm
Cottages

The Dales

Keathing Burn

Pargillis
Bridge

Cemetery

3

B916

A921

Inverkeithing
North
Junction

North Rd

East Junction

Hillend

HARBOUR RD

84

Letham

ADMIRALTY RD

Central
Junction

Bois
Bridge

Letham Hill
Wood

2

IMRALTY RD

BELLKNOWES
IND EST

PARK RD

HELLWOOD TERR

Junction 1

M90

Fairy Kirk

P

Inverkeithing
Station

Sch

HILLEND RD

THE SPENCE

SPENCERFIELD
STEADINGS

MARLINES RD

CHAPEL PL

BORELAND RD

ALMA ST

KING ST

St KING ST

HIGH ST

Lib

HOPE ST

HILL ST

TOWNHALL ST

Seafield
House

83

astlandhill

CASTLANDHILL RD

LOTHIANS VIEW

DUNFERMLINE WYND

MANSE PL

PAUL
VIEW

P

Offices

HAMILTON
TERR

Muckle
Hill

Mill

HILL ST

PRESTON PL

ELLINGTON PL.

COCHRANE

Preston
Hill

Quarry
(disused)

ROSEBERY CT
SEAFIELD PL
THE BRIDGES

St David's
Harbour

ROSEBERY

1

Cemetery

Little
Hill

GLEBE TERR

Inner Bay

Pier

Pier
East Ness

South Pier

Inverkeithing Bay

Whinny
Hill

B980

A90

FERRYHILL RD.

HOPE ST

CRUICKNESS RD

INVERKEITHING

West Ness

82

2

D

13

E

14

F

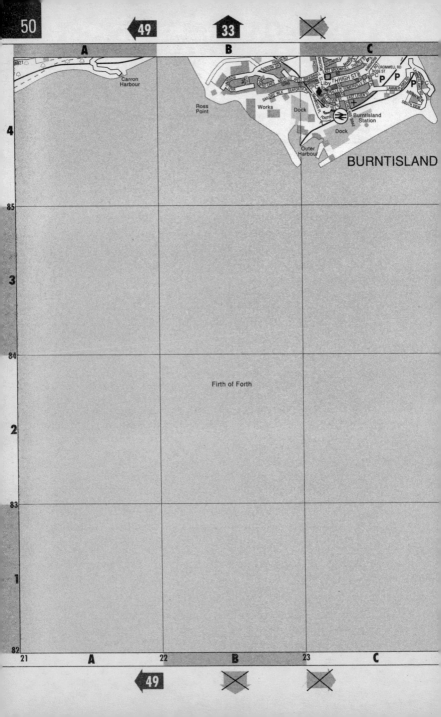

A   **B**   **C**

A921

Carron
Harbour

Ross
Point

Works

Dock

HIGH ST

CROMWELL RD
ROSE ST

P P P

Burntisland
Station

Dock

Outer
Harbour

BURNTISLAND

4

85

3

84

Firth of Forth

2

83

1

82

21   **A**   22   **B**   23   **C**

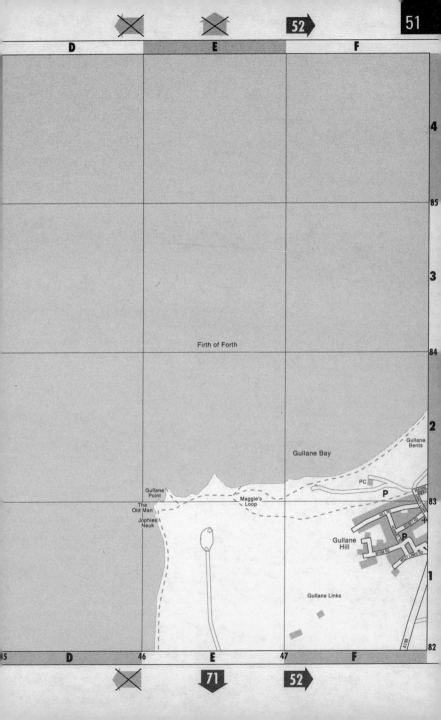

D

E

F

4

85

3

84

Firth of Forth

2

Gullane
Bents

Gullane Bay

PC

P

Gullane
Point

Maggie's
Loop

MAUDE
TERRACE

83

The
Old Man

HOLM RD

LECKIE RD

Jophies
Neuk

P

Gullane
Hill

WAIM RD

WEST LINKS RD

1

Gullane Links

A198

82

51

A
B

Marina
Villa

Hanging
Rocks

White Knowes

4
Firth of Forth

Eldbotle Wood

Sandy Knowe

North Links

Strabauchlinn Knowe

85
West Links

Eldbotle
Park

Duncan's
Plantation

3
Black Rocks

Freshwater
Haven

Rabbit
Warren

Mast

Broad Wood

Jamie's
Neuk

Yapin Hill

84
Archerfield

Golf Course

Home
Farm

West Strip

Halfmoon Plantation

CH

2
Gullane
Bents

Muirfield

A198

83
MAIN ST

MUIRFIELD
STEADING

Queenstonbank

B1345

PC

Liby

Sch

Gullane

1
A198

P

MARINE TER

Mill Burn

Saltcoats

82
48
A
49
B
50
C

A   B   C

Firth of Forth

**NORTH
BERWICK**

4

West Links

SPRINGFIELD CRES

North Berwick
Bay

Mus & Liby

Milsey Bay

CH

CROMWELL RD

FIDRA RD

STATION HILL

BEACH RD

WESTGATE

HIGH ST

MARINE PAR

DIRLETON AVE

A198

ABBEY RD

ST ANDREW ST

MARKET PL

PC

East Links

EAST RD

B1347

Castle
Hill

CH

PC's

QUIDENHAM CT

CLUNIE RD

Sta

KING'S KNOLL HOTEL

Hospl

ST BALDRED'S CRES

Caravan
Site

85

CLIFFORD RD

ST BALDRED'S RD

SEVERS PK

A198

Marly
Knowe

MACNAIR AVE

DUNCAS AVE

LAZY JANE AVE

COUPER AVE

DUNBAR RD

TANTALLON RD

Cemy

3

PC's
Caravan
Park

GRANGE RD

Schs

LOCHBRIDGE RD

Heugh

Gilsland

HADDINGTON RD

P

84

North Berwick
Law

Quarry
(dis)

Bonnington

Thorntree

2

Wamphray

Highfield

HIGHFIELD

83

Windmill

BALGONE BARNS
COTTS

Balgone
Barns

Balgone Heughs

1

Sch

Kingston

Balgone
House

Twr
(remains of)

B1347

Carperstane

82

54   A   55   B   56   C

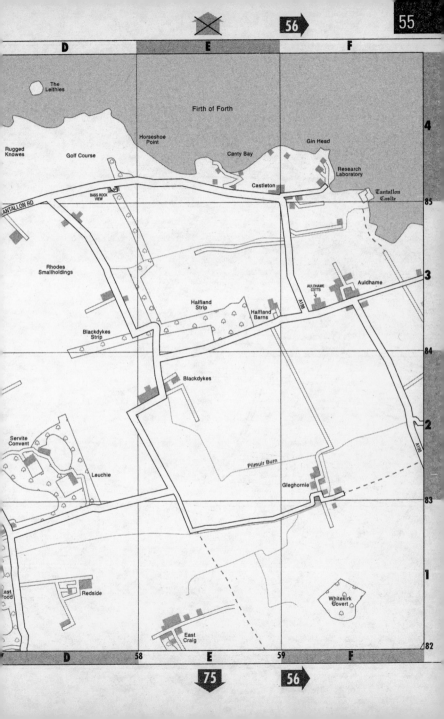

The Leithies

Firth of Forth

Horseshoe Point

Gin Head

Rugged Knowes

Golf Course

Canty Bay

Research Laboratory

Castleton

Tantallon Castle

BASS ROCK VIEW

TANTALLON RD

Rhodes Smallholdings

Auldhame

AULDHAME COTTS

Halfland Strip

Halfland Barns

A198

Blackdykes Strip

Blackdykes

Servite Convent

A198

Pilmuir Burn

Leuchie

Gleghornie

East Wood

Redside

Whitekirk Covert

East Craig

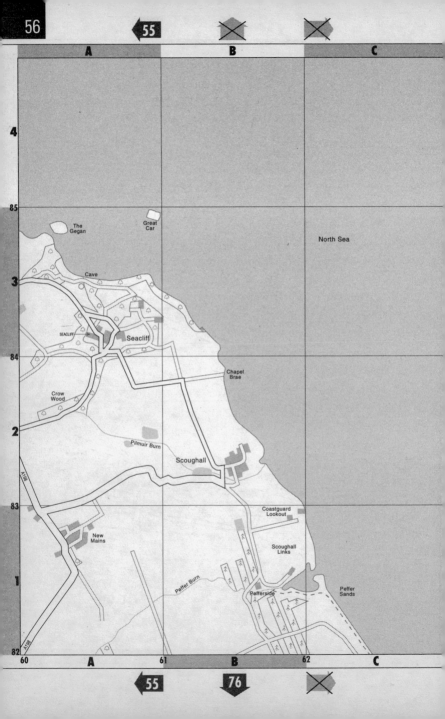

A   B   C

4

85

The
Gegan

Great
Car

North Sea

3

Cave

SEACLIFF

Seacliff

84

Chapel
Brae

Crow
Wood

2

Pilmuir Burn

Scoughall

A198

83

Coastguard
Lookout

New
Mains

Scoughall
Links

1

Peffer Burn

Pefferside

Peffer
Sands

A198

82

60   A   61   B   62   C

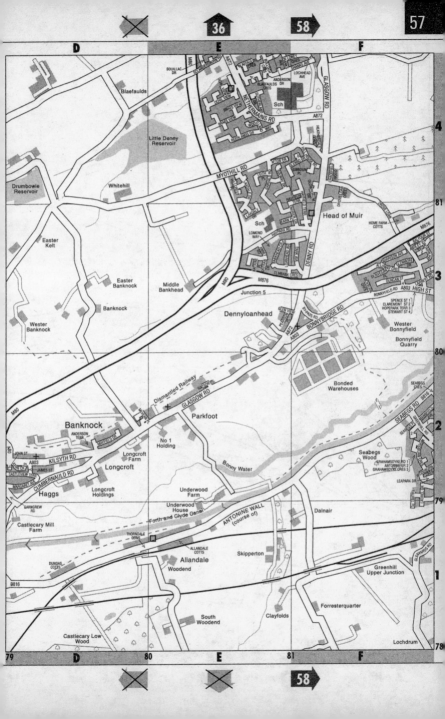

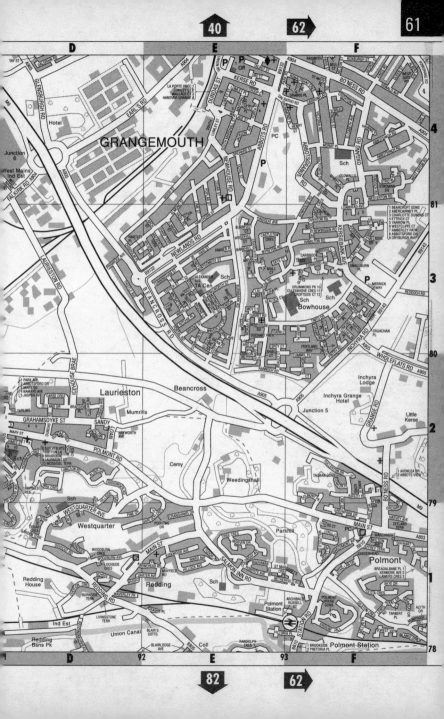

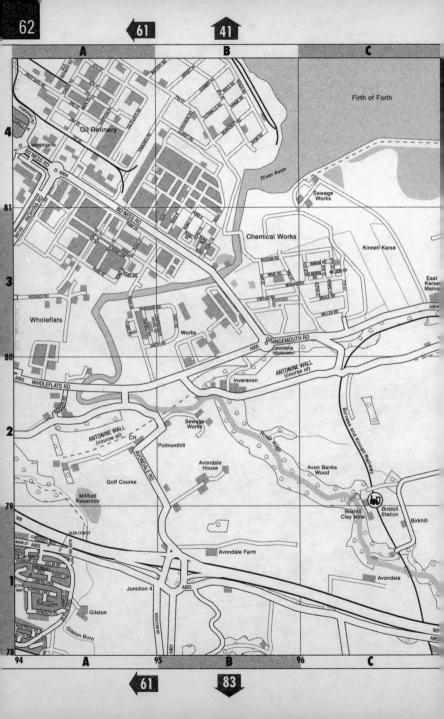

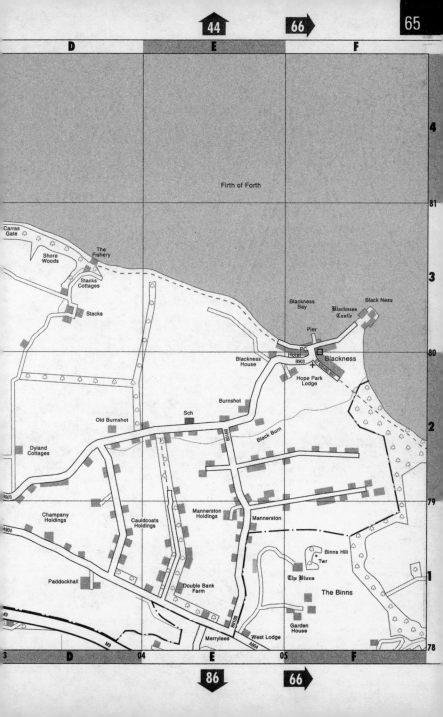

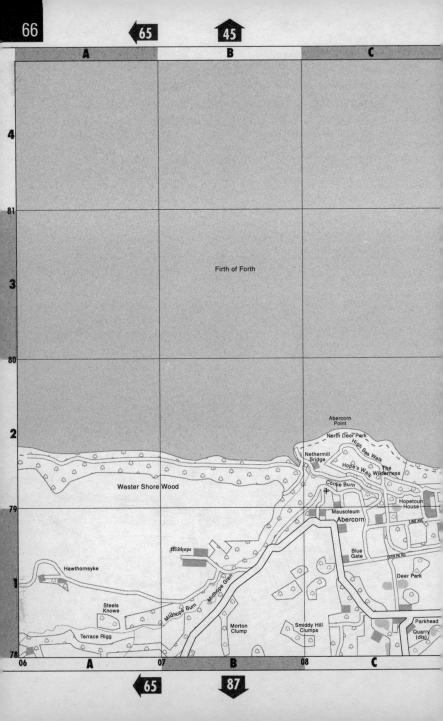

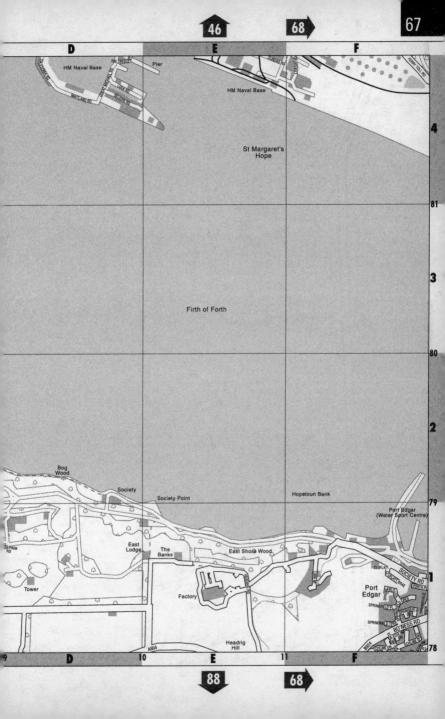

D
E
F

HM Naval Base

THE CRESCENT

Pier

DUNDAS RD

FERRY TOLL RD

DOCK RD

DRILL HALL RD

MATLAND RD

HM Naval Base

4

St Margaret's
Hope

81

3

Firth of Forth

80

2

Bog
Wood

Society

Society Point

Hopetoun Bank

79

Port Edgar
(Water Sport Centre)

ER PARK RD

East
Lodge

The
Banks

East Shore Wood

SOCIETY RD

CLUFLATS

1

Tower

Factory

Port
Edgar

SPRINGF

BO NESS RD

SPRINGFIELD TER

Headrig
Hill

A904

78

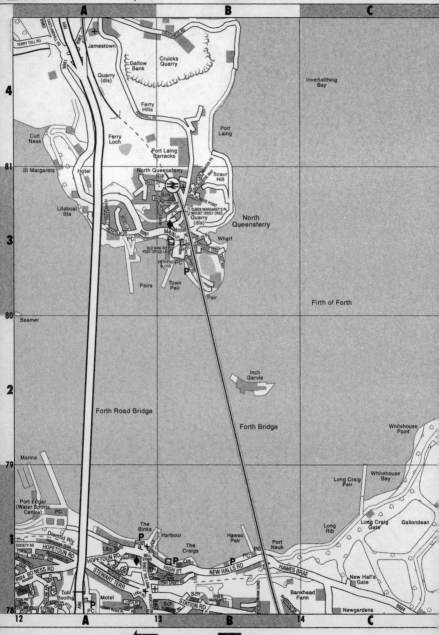

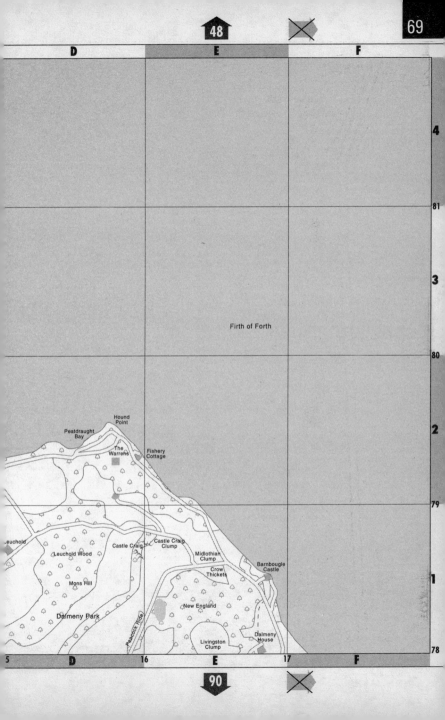

D

E

F

4

81

3

Firth of Forth

80

2

Hound
Point

Peatdraught
Bay

The
Warrens

Fishery
Cottage

79

Leuchold

Leuchold Wood

Castle Craig

Castle Craig
Clump

Midlothian
Clump

Barnbougle
Castle

Crow
Thickets

1

Mons Hill

New England

Dalmeny Park

Peacock Hide

Livingston
Clump

Dalmeny
House

78

5

D

16

E

17

F

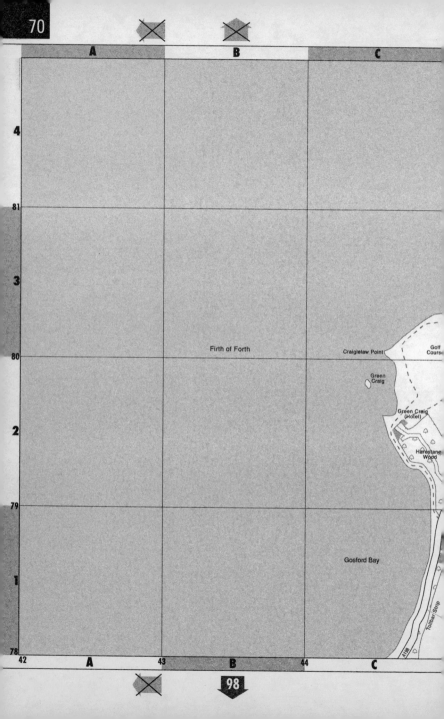

Firth of Forth

Craiglelaw Point

Golf
Course

Green
Craig

Green Craig
(Hotel)

Harestane
Wood

Gosford Bay

Tollbar Strip

A198

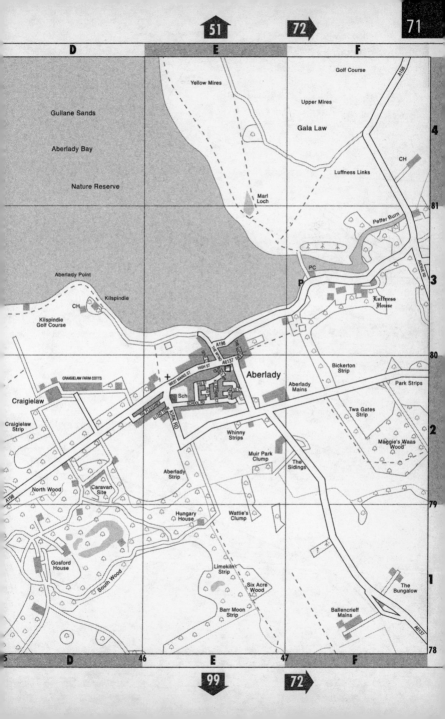

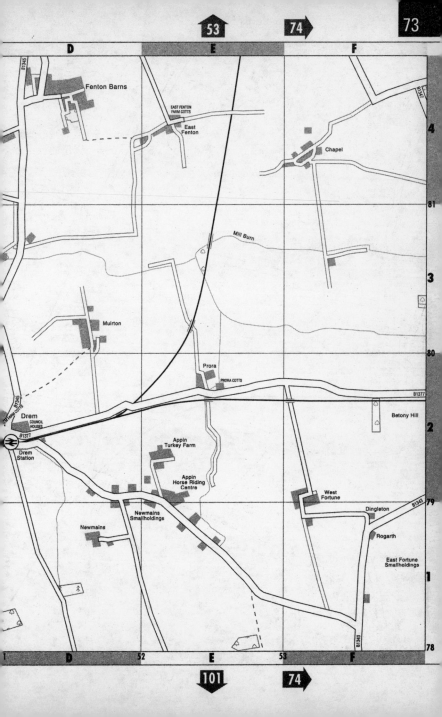

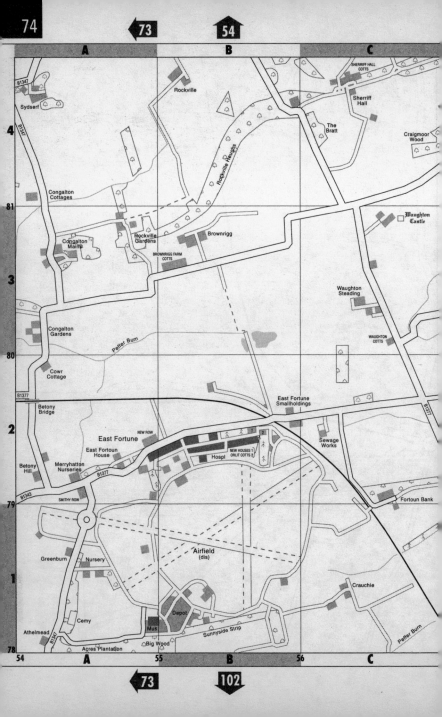

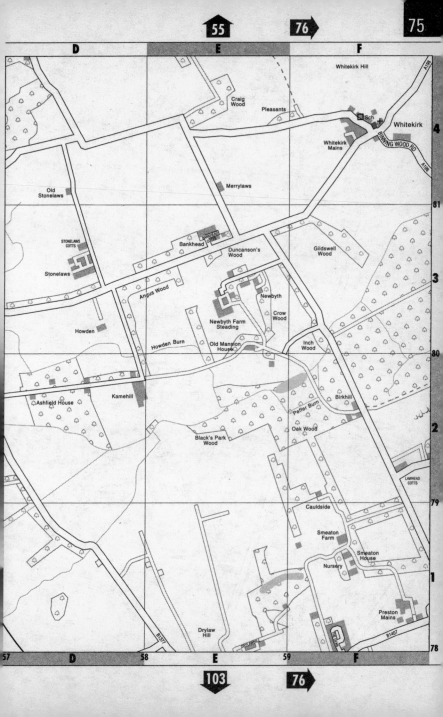

D   E   F

Whitekirk Hill

Craig
Wood

Pleasants

Sch   Whitekirk

4

Whitekirk
Mains

BINNING WOOD RD

A198

A198

Old
Stonelaws

Merrylaws

81

STONELAWS
COTTS

Bankhead

BANKHEAD
COTTS

Duncanson's
Wood

Gildswell
Wood

Stonelaws

Angus Wood

Newbyth

3

Howden

Newbyth Farm
Steading

Crow
Wood

Howden Burn

Old Mansion
House

Inch
Wood

80

Ashfield House

Kamehill

Birkhill

Peffer Burn

Black's Park
Wood

Oak Wood

2

LAWHEAD
COTTS

79

Cauldside

Smeaton
Farm

Smeaton
House

Nursery

1

Preston
Mains

B1347

Drylaw
Hill

B1407

57   D   58   E   59   F   78

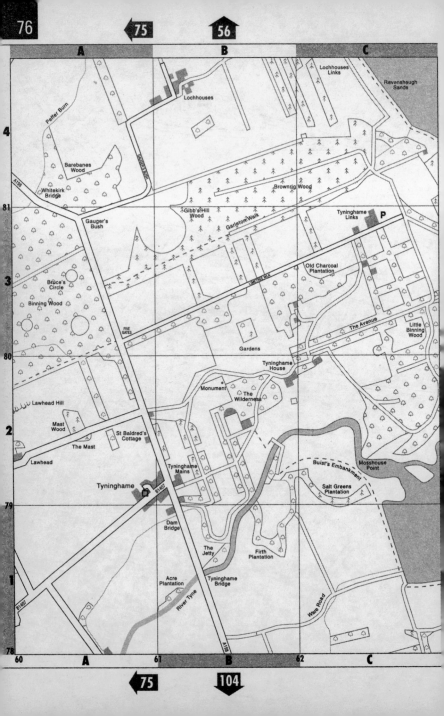

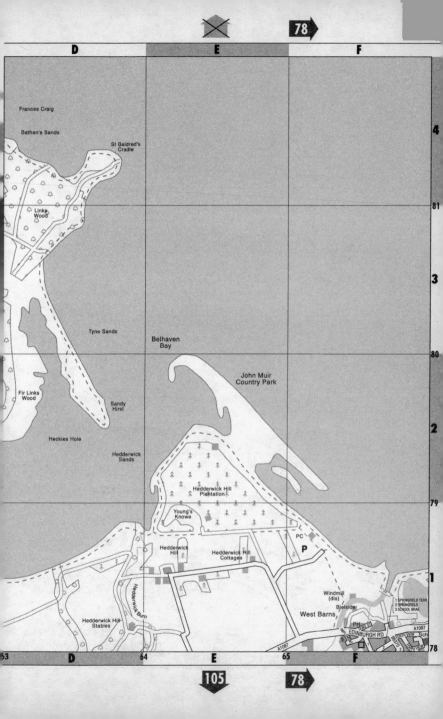

D E F

Frances Craig

Bathan's Sands

St Baldred's
Cradle

4

81

Links
Wood

3

Tyne Sands

Belhaven
Bay

80

John Muir
Country Park

Fir Links
Wood

Sandy
Hirst

2

Heckies Hole

Hedderwick
Sands

Hedderwick Hill
Plantation

79

Young's
Knowe

PC

P

Hedderwick
Hill

Hedderwick Hill
Cottages

1

Windmill
(dis)

Hedderwick Burn

Bielside

1 SPRINGFIELD TERR
2 SPRINGFIELD
3 SCHOOL BRAE

Hedderwick Hill
Stables

West Barns

PH

A1087

EDINBURGH RD

Sch

A1087

78

63 D 64 E 65 F

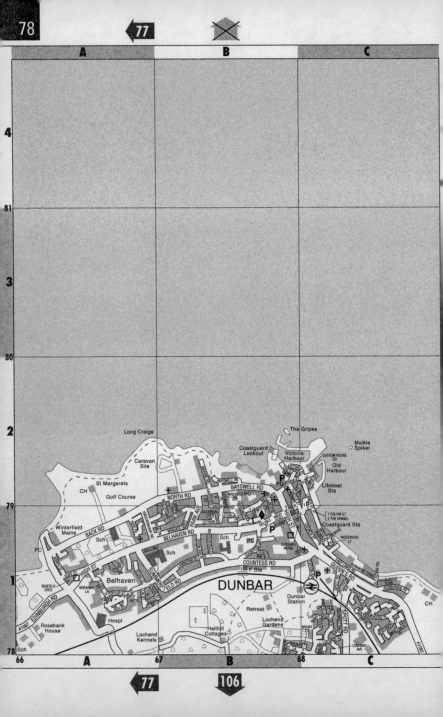

A   B   C

4

81

3

80

2

Long Craigs

The Gripes

Meikle
Spiker

Coastguard
Lookout

Caravan
Site

Victoria
Harbour

CUSTOM HOUSE
50

Old
Harbour

St Margarets

CH

Golf Course

BAYSWELL LN

BAYSWELL RD

NORTH RD

MAYVILLE PC

Lib

Lifeboat
Sta

79

Winterfield
Mains

BACK RD

Sch

PC

KNOCKENDALE RD

PARK AVE

GARDENER ST

BELHAVEN RD

VICTORIA ST

LITTLE ST

DELISLE ST

HIGH ST

BRIDGE ST WEST

1 COLVIN ST
2 THE VENNEL

Coastguard Sta

WOODBUSH
CT

Sch

Sch

GALA GN

Sch

PC

COSSARD WYND

1

SEAFIELD
CRES

HIGH ST

Belhaven

BREWERY
LA

POPLAR
CT

SUMMERFIELD RD

BAYLE ST

ELD RD

COUNTESS RD

F Sta

DUNBAR

Retreat

QUEEN'S RD

P

CH

EDINBURGH RD

A1087

Rosebank
House

Hospl

Lochend
Kennels

Hallhill
Cottages

Lochend
Gardens

Dunbar
Station

LATCH RD

BRUNT

SPOTT RD

LOCHEND
AVE

A1087

78 Sch

D   E   F

4

81

3

80

2

79

1

78

Lawrie's Den

The Vaults

Golf Course

West Links

Vaults Wood

Sports & Social Centre

9   D   70   E   71   F

107

A   B   C

4

Kilbean
Wood

Glenrig

Auchengean
Wood

Mast

Wester
Strip

Westerglen

Easter
Strip

Westerglen
Transmitting
Station

Masts

77

Auchengean

Rottenstocks

3

Barleyside

Greencraig

76

2

Darnrig
Moss

Masonfield
Works

High
Stanerig

Darnrig

75

Lochend

1

Strathavon

Nappiefaulds
House

Dismtd Rly

Dyke

74
85   A   86   B   87   C

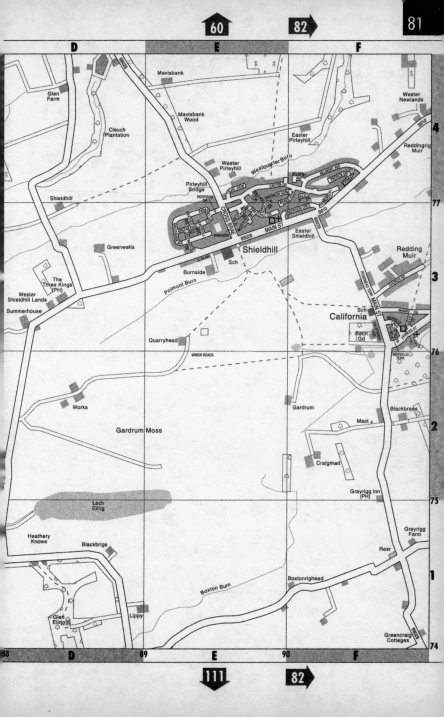

D E F

Mavisbank

Glen
Farm

Wester
Newlands

Cleuch
Plantation

Mavisbank
Wood

Easter
Pirleyhill

Reddingrig
Muir

Shieldhill

Wester
Pirleyhill

Westquarter Burn

Pirleyhill
Bridge

PATERSON

Redding
Muir

Greenwells

MAIN ST

Easter
Shieldhill

Shieldhill

Burnside

Sch

California

The Three Kings
(PH)

Polmont Burn

Sch

Wester
Shieldhill Lands

Recn
Gd

Summerhouse

MERVILLE
TERR

Quarryhead

MINOR ROADS

Blackbraes

Works

Gardrum

Mast

Gardrum Moss

Craigmad

Grayrigg Inn
(PH)

Loch
Ellrig

Greyrigg
Farm

Heathery
Knowe

Blackbrigs

Resr

Boxtonrighead

Boxton Burn

Glen
Ellrig

Lippy

Greencraig
Cottages

88 D 89 E 90 F

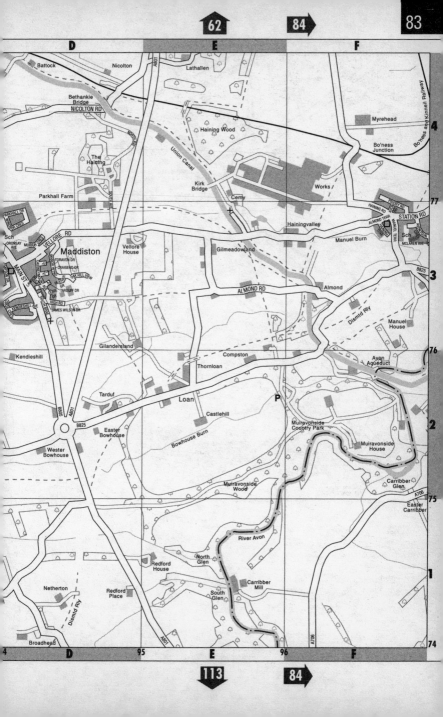

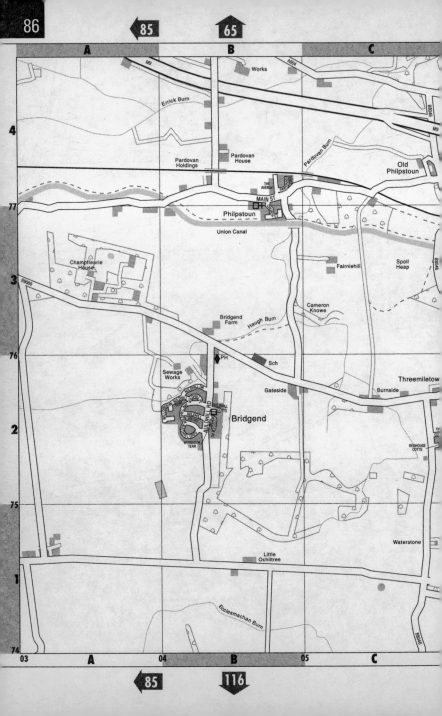

D
E
F

Philpstoun House

Hopetoun Wood

The Manse

Woodville

A904

B9020

4

Whitequarries Ind Est

Sch

Woodend

Woodend

East Philpstoun

Galascrook

Duntarvie

77

Philpstoun Mill

Craigton

Bailles Muir

Philpstoun Muir

Craigton House

Fawnspark

3

M9

Union Canal

Mounthooly

The Den

Myre

76

Trinlaymire

2

Garage

PC

Tippet Knowes

MAIN ST B9080

75

Lampinsdub

Glendevon

Schs

NIDDRY RD

Glendevon Cottages

Winchburgh

Cemy

Tippet Knowes

Millcraig

PC

1

Niddry Burn

Kirklands

Niddry

Fauchel Dean

B9020

74

D
E
F

07
08

87 67

A **B** **C**

A904

Icehouse Hill

A904

B924

BO NESS RD

BUILYEON RD

1 ECHLINE FARM COTTS
2 ECHLINE STEADINGS
3 ECHLINE PL

PH

MAIN ST

DUDDINGSTONE TERR

4 Newton

Duddingston

Lawflat

Duddingston Wood

Linn Mill Burn

White Gate

Echline Strip

Dundas Mains

Gallow Hill

77

Burn Craigs

Railway

Totleywells Cottages

Westfield

Chapel Acre

Dundas Castle

Dundas Hill

3 Duntarbie Castle (remains of)

Dismantled

Weftmuir Riding School

Barrancraig Wood

B9020

M9

Swineburn Wood

Swineburn

Dundas Loch

76

Swine Burn

Muiriehall Wood

Carmelhill Wood

Carmelhill Cottage

Humbie Reservoir

2

B9020

ROAD

Niddry Mains House

Beatlie Wood

Swine Burn

Humbie

Sch

Niddry Mains

75

B9080

MAIN ST

OAKBANK PL

NDOW VIEW CASTLE TERR

ABERCORN PL

MICROFT PL

CRANTON PL

Hawk Hill Wood

CH

Junction 1

Junction number due to change Summer 96

1 Cemy

Golf Course

Niddry Castle

Ross's Plantation

Charles's Bridge

Niddry Burn

Lindsay's Craigs

Union Canal

Overton

74

09 **A** 10 **B** 11 **C**

87 118

D   E   F

4

77

3

76

Firth of Forth

2

75

1

74

1 ELECTRA PL.
2 HILLCOAT LOAN
3 WESTBANK PL.
4 WESTBANK LOAN
5 HILLCOAT PL.
6 GREAT CANNON BANK

1 HARBOUR PL.
2 WILLIAM JAMESON PL.
3 BRICKFIELD
4 LAW PL.
5 THE POTTERY
6 SPA PL.
7 SHRUB MOUNT
8 AITCHISON'S PL.
9 WHINS PL.
10 RAMSAY PL.

NEW TOWER PL.

BATH PL.

REGENT PL.

KING'S

ROATS FORT/BEL LOTH/HIGH ST.

D   31   E   32   F

| A | B | C |

4

77

3

76

Firth of Forth

2

75

SIR WALTER SCOTT PEND 1
FOWLERS CT 2
PYPERS WYND 3
CEMETERY RD 4
HARLAWHILL GDNS 5

PRESTONPANS

1

HIGH ST
PC
Sch
Liby
TH
P
Cuthill
PRESTONGRANGE
RD
B 1348
INCHVIEW
BURNSIDE
Sch

74

| 36 | A | 37 | B | 38 | C |

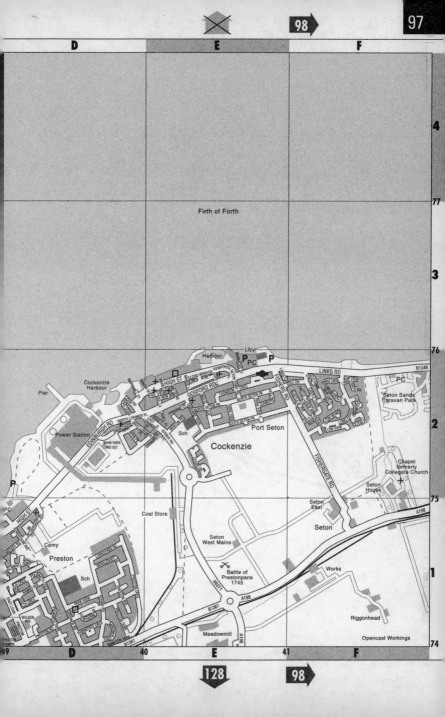

A B C

4

Firth of Forth

P
PC

Eventyr

Fernyness
Wood

77

LYARS RD

B1348

A198

P PC

CH

Golf Course

Liby

CHURCH GDNS

WEMYSS TERR

Sch

3

PC

P

B1377

Longniddry
Station

Longniddry Dean

P

MAIN ST

A198

Longniddry

Seton Sands

P

KINGS RD

76

Lorne
Bridge

Longniddry
Farm

B1348

Caravan
Park

Seton Dean

2

Cantyhall
Bridge

Canty Burn

Cantyhall

Redcoll

SETON
MAINS

St Germains
Crossing

75

A198

LC

Chesterhall

THE
STEADING

Southfield

St Germains

St Germains
Farm

1

Opencast
Workings

74

42 A 43 B 44 C

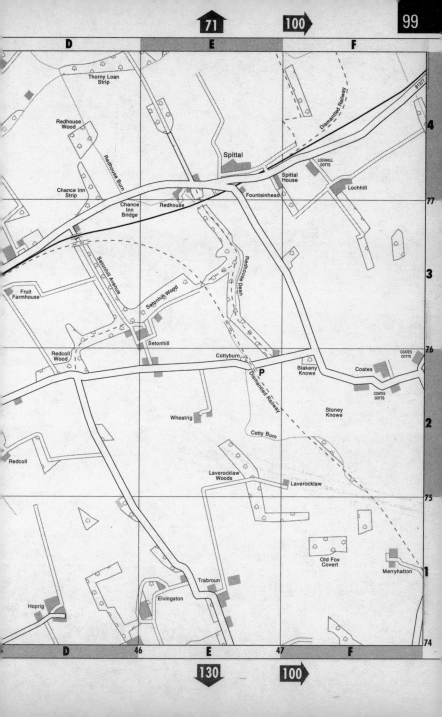

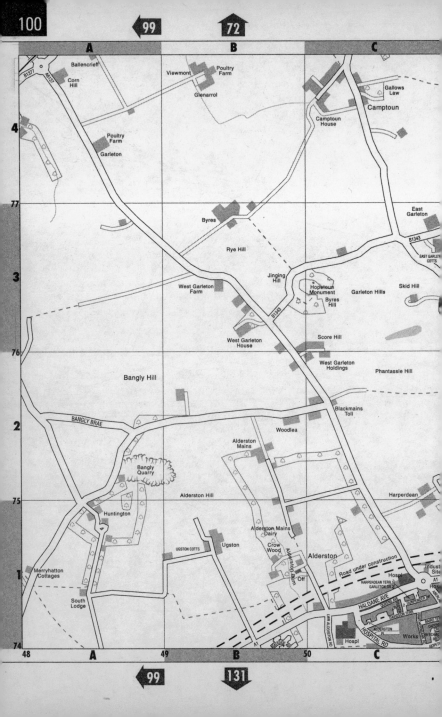

101
74

101
133

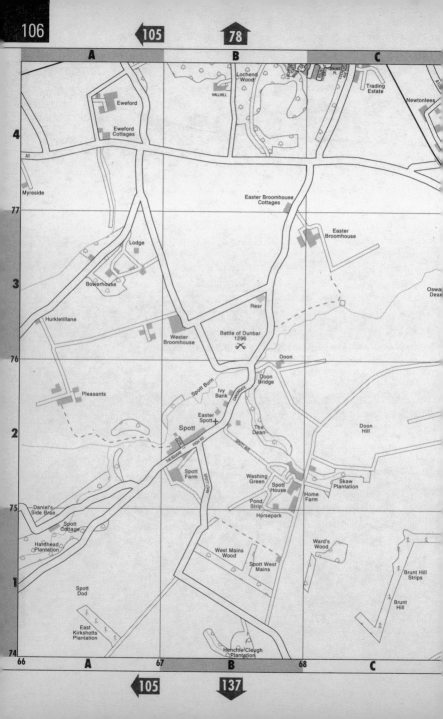

A   B   C

4
Eweford
Eweford
Cottages

Lochend
Wood
HALLHILL

Trading
Estate
Newtonlees

A1

Myreside

77
Easter Broomhouse
Cottages

Easter
Broomhouse

3
Lodge

Bowerhouse

Hurkletillane

Resr

Oswal
Dean

Wester
Broomhouse

Battle of Dunbar
1296

Doon

76
Doon
Bridge

Pleasants

Spott Burn

Ivy
Bank

Easter
Spott

CANONGATE

Doon
Hill

2
Spott

The
Dean

SPOTT AVE

THE SQUARE

HIGH RD

Spott
Farm

SPOTT LOAN

Washing
Green

Spott
House

Home
Farm

Skaw
Plantation

75
Daniel's
Side Brae

Spott
Cottage

Pond
Strip

Horsepark

Hardhead
Plantation

Ward's
Wood

Brunt Hill
Strips

West Mains
Wood

Spott West
Mains

Brunt
Hill

1
Spott
Dod

East
Kirkshotts
Plantation

Henchie/Cleugh
Plantation

74
66   A   67   B   68   C

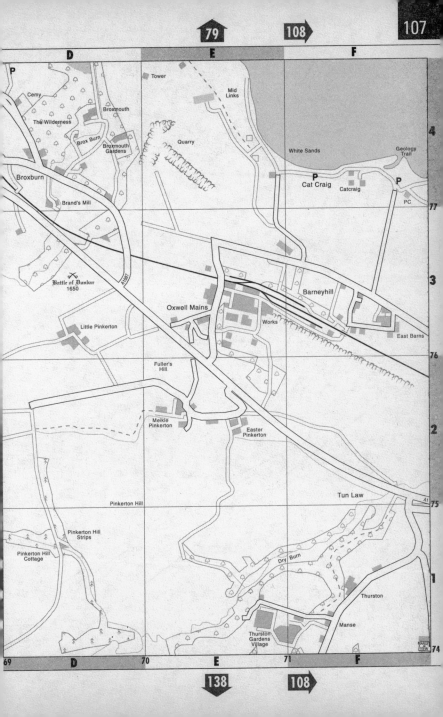

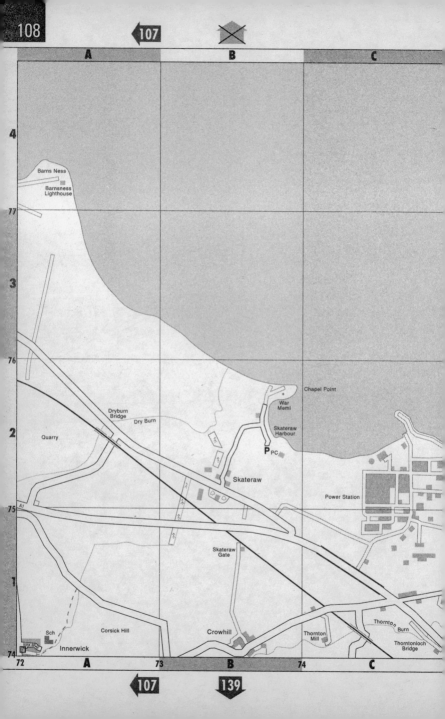

A B C

4

Barns Ness

Barnsness
Lighthouse

77

3

76

Chapel Point

Dryburn
Bridge
Dry Burn

War
Meml

Skateraw
Harbour

2

Quarry

P PC

Skateraw

Power Station

75

A1

Skateraw
Gate

1

Sch

Corsick Hill

Crowhill

Thornton
Mill

Thornton Burn

Thorntonloch
Bridge

Innerwick

74

D E F

4

77

3

76

2

Torness Point

75

1

Caravan
Park

P

Thorntonloch

74

75 D 76 E 77 F

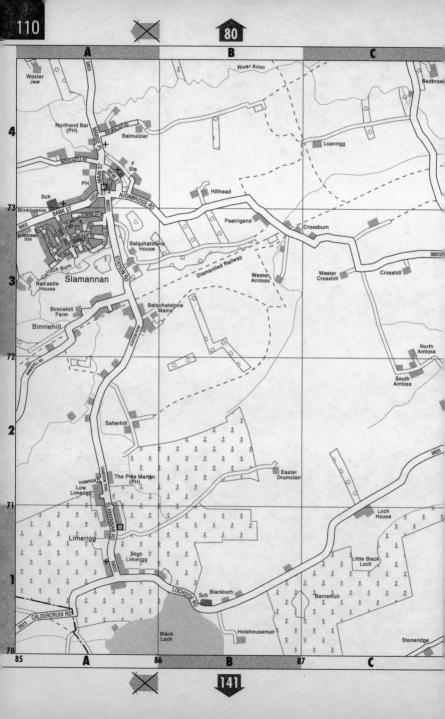

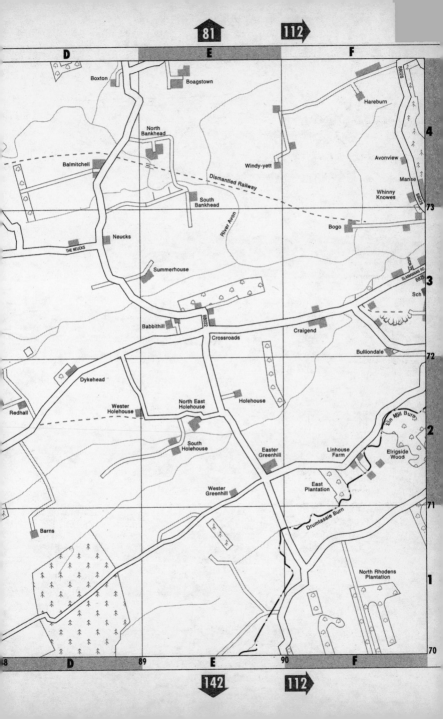

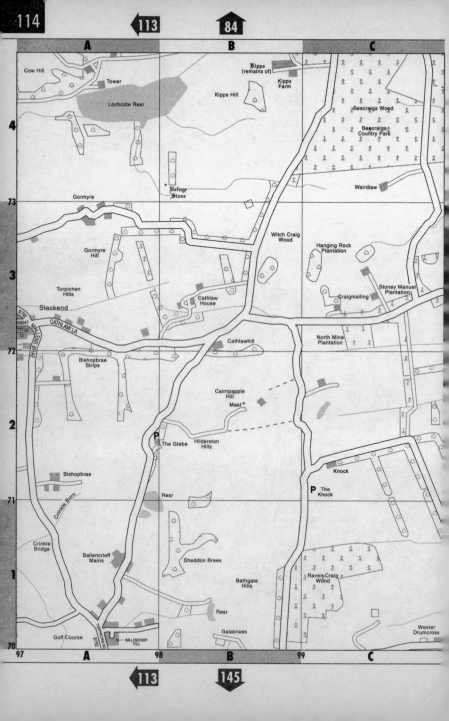

115
86

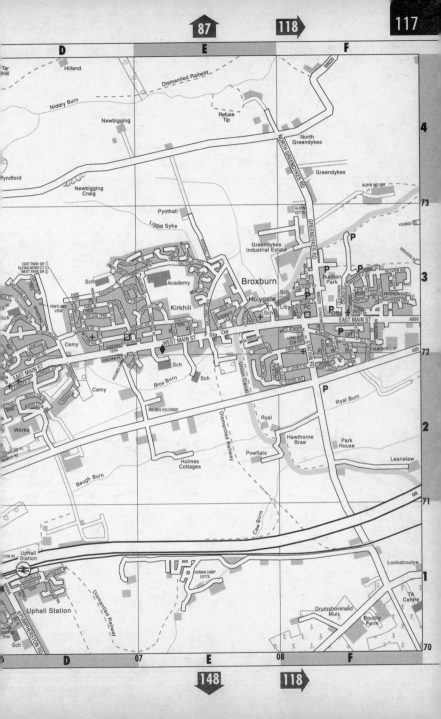

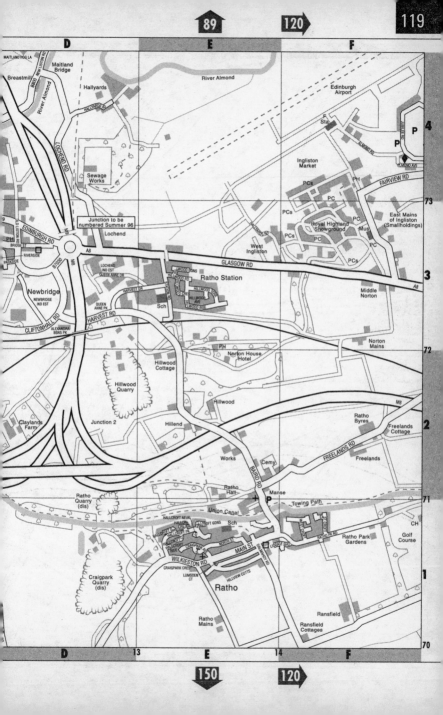

◄ 123

94 ▲

D
E
F

4

73

3

72

2

71

1

70

B1348
PRESTONGRANGE TERR
B1348
BELLFIELD SQ
PRESTONGRANGE RD
PRESTON RD
SOUTH GRANGE
B1361
Cuthill

PRESTON CT 1
TURRET GDNS 2
NORTHFIELD CT 3
WEST LOAN 4
WEST LOAN T'S

CH

Morrison's
Haven

Mining
Museum

Golf
Course

Caravan and Camping
Site

Rigley
Hill

LC

A1

Levenhall Links
Leisure Park

B1348

Drum-Mohr

Westpans

Dolphingstone
Farm

A199

RAVENSHAUGH RD

Goshen

Levenhall

Ravenshaugh Burn

Hotel

A199

A199

B1361

Pinkie
Braes

HADDINGTON RD

MACBETH MOIR RD

Wallyford
Station

FORTHVIEW DR

Sch

Wallyford

Wallyford
Ind
Est

ST CLEMENT'S CRES

SALTERS RD

Barbachlaw

Battle of Pinkie
1547

Rosehill
Villa

St Clement's
Wells

Whinny Loan

Mast

Myles
Farm

Falside
Hill

Crookston

Falside
Castle

West
Mains

Elphinstone Tower
Farm Cottages

B6414

46
D
37
E
38
F

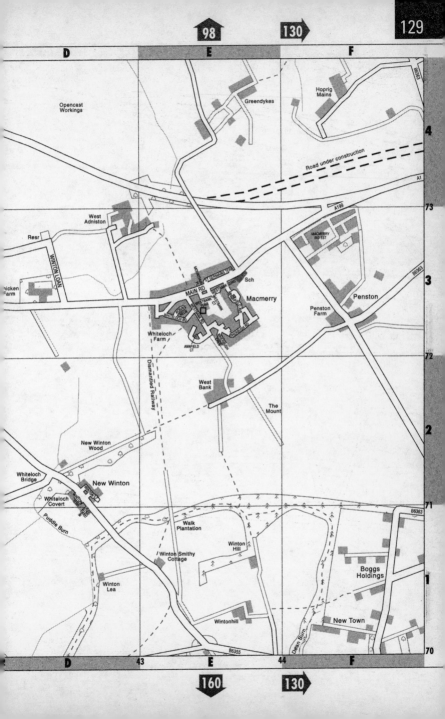

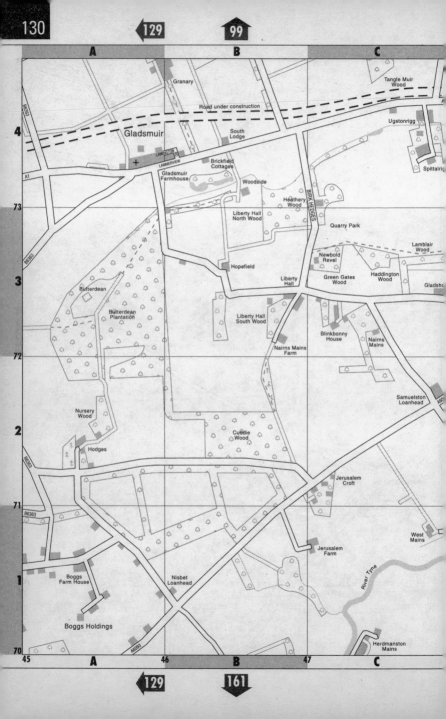

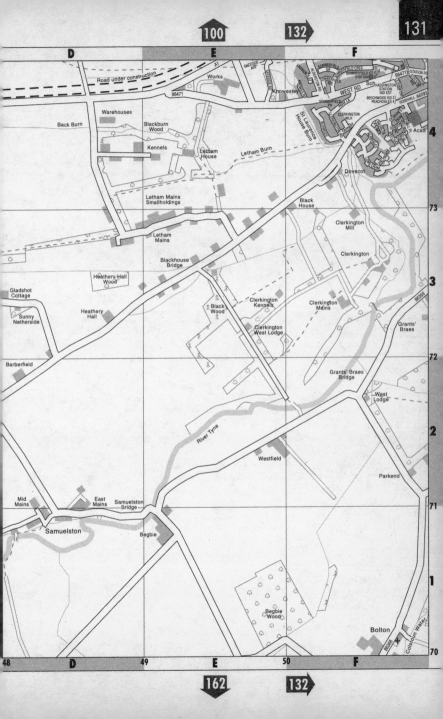

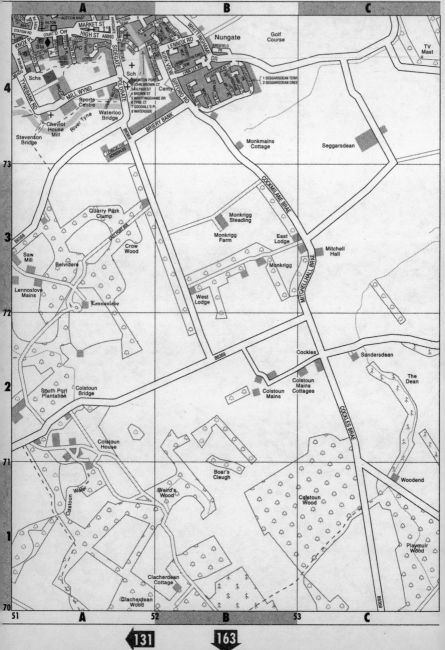

131

101

A

B

C

AUCTION MART
MARKET ST
HISTON
STATION RD
A6471
HIGH ST
COURT ST
A6093
VICTORIA
KNOX PL
St
PC
SIDEGATE
Off
ST MARTIN'S
Nungate
Golf
Course

TV
Mast

Schs
Sch
LENNOX RD
KIRK VIEW
NORTON PORT
JOHN BROWN CT
BROWN ST
WHITTINGEHAME DR
TYNE CT
GOODALL'S PL
WATERSIDE
Cemy
1 SEGGARSDEAN TERR
2 SEGGARSDEAN CRES

4

Cheviot
House
Mill

TYNEBANK RD
MILL WYND
Sports
Centre
Waterloo
Bridge
River Tyne
PALTDATE
BRIERY BANK

Stevenson
Bridge

B6093

LENNOXLOVE
HOSPITALS

Monkmains
Cottage

Seggarsdean

73

Quarry Park
Clump

Monkrigg
Steading

EASTPARK DR

Monkrigg
Farm

COCKMLANE BRAE

3

B6368

Saw
Mill

Crow
Wood

Belvidere

East
Lodge

Mitchell
Hall

Monkrigg

Lennoxlove
Mains

Lennoxlove

MITCHELLHALL BRAE

West
Lodge

72

B6369

Cockles

Sandersdean

South Port
Plantation

Colstoun
Bridge

Colstoun
Mains

Colstoun
Mains
Cottages

The
Dean

2

Colstoun
House

COCKLES BRAE

71

Colstoun
Water

Weird's
Wood

Boar's
Cleugh

Colstoun
Wood

Woodend

1

Playmuir
Wood

Clacherdean
Cottage

Clacherdean
Wood

B6369

70

51

A

52

B

53

C

131

163

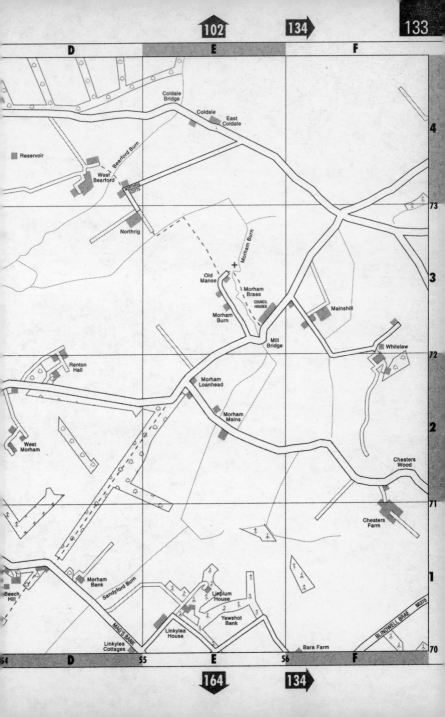

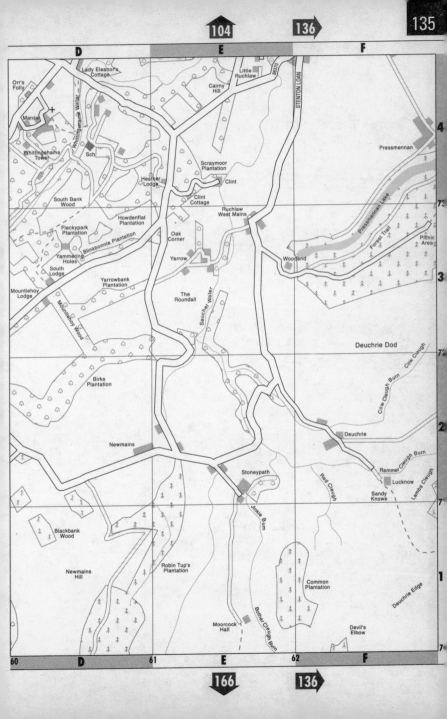

D
E
F

Orr's Folly

Lady Eleanor's Cottage

Little Ruchlaw

Cairny Hill

STENTON LOAN

B6370

Manse

Whittingehame Water

Whittingehame Tower

Sch

Pressmennan

4

Scraymoor Plantation

Heather Lodge

Clint

South Bank Wood

Clint Cottage

Ruchlaw West Mains

7½

Howdenflat Plantation

Fleckypark Plantation

Oak Corner

Woodend

Pressmennan Lake

Forest Trail

Picnic Area

Blinkbonnie Plantation

Yammering Holes

Yarrow

South Lodge

Mountlehoy Lodge

Yarrowbank Plantation

The Roundall

Saucher Water

3

Mountlehoy Wood

Deuchrie Dod

7½

Birks Plantation

Cow Cleugh Burn

Cow Cleugh

2

Deuchrie

Newmains

Rammel Cleugh Burn

Lambs Cleugh

Stoneypath

Red Cleugh

Lucknow

Sandy Knowe

7

Blackbank Wood

Jinkie Burn

Newmains Hill

Robin Tup's Plantation

Common Plantation

Deuchrie Edge

1

Moorcock Hall

Bother Cleugh Burn

Devil's Elbow

7

60
D
61
E
62
F

A

B

C

4

Bennet's Burn

Ford

Burnhead
Wood

Frizzels
Wood

Ice
Cleugh

Pressmennan
Wood

Channel
Wood

CHANNEL RD

73

The
Sneep

Pathhead

Staneshal
Wood

Halls

Cauld Burn

Gallows
Law

Gairly Burn

3

Well Hill

Rottenraw Burn

72

Hartside

Deuchrie
Wood

Rammer
Wood

Hartside
Burn

Hartside
Law

Lint Burn

Herring Road

Sleepy
Knowe

Mearns Cleugh

2

Halls Edge

Lothian Edge

Ox Cleugh

Redcar Burn

Rammer
Dodd

Rammer Cleugh

Herring Road

Rammer Cleugh Burn

Wester Hartside
Edge

71

Crow
Cleugh

Rammer Moss

1

Mosay Burn

Lodge Burn

Watch
Law

70

63

A

64

B

65

C

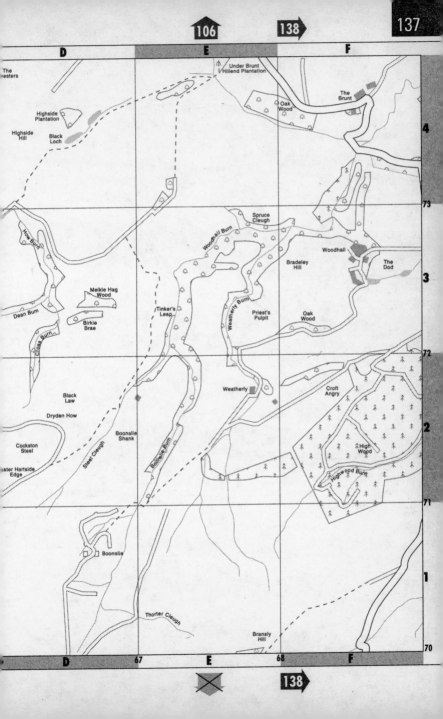

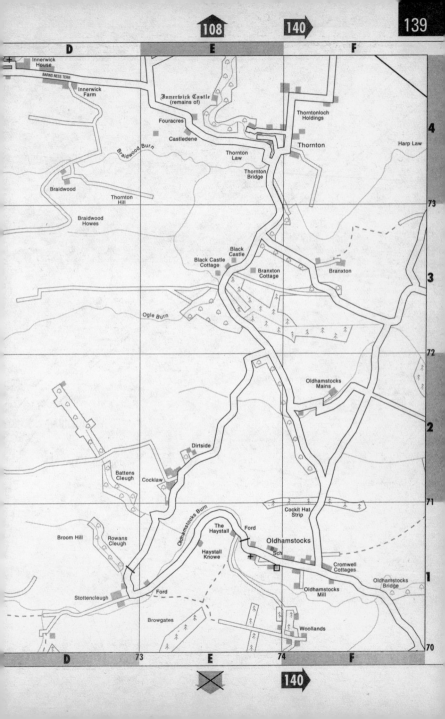

139
109

A   **B**   **C**

4

73   Lawfield

Bilsdean
Creek

The Linn

3   Birnieknowes   Bilsdean   Gutcher's
                  Clay   Hole
                  Knowe   PC
           Broomward   Bilsdean   Dunglass   Dunglass
                 Bridge   Bridge   Old Bridge

Braid Law   Rams
          Gallows Law   Dunglass   Heugh
         Plantation   New Bridge
                 Dunglass   Dunglass   Castle Dyke
                 Mains   Viaduct   Cottage

72   Gallows   Dunglass
      Law   Church   Deanberry
                                 Hole
Bilsdean   Dunglass   Killflat
Banks   Wood
           Forth Brae
                                             CG
                                             Sta
        Rules   Cov
        Law

2   Pathhead   Cats Ho
    Closehead   Gowdies   Belvidere   Eildbalks   Plantai
              Well   Wood   Wood
        Cati   **Cockburnspath**
        Heugh
Springfield   PC
          Dean Mill   Sch
           Bog   Hotel

71   Chapelhill
                        Braeside   Cotts
                        Cottage
                 Dovecot
                 Hall   Chapelhill
                       Cockburnspath Burn
                                            Hazeldean Burn

1   Kirklands   Sand
                                      Pit

    Berwick Burn   Neuk
                                  / Farm   Kinegar
70   Strip

75   **A**   76   **B**   77   **C**

139

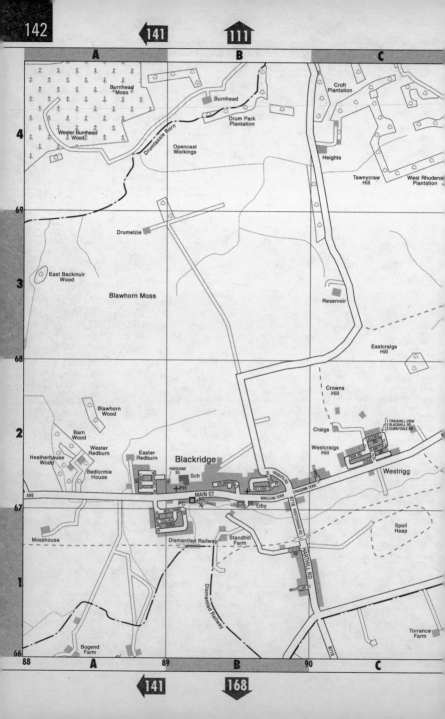

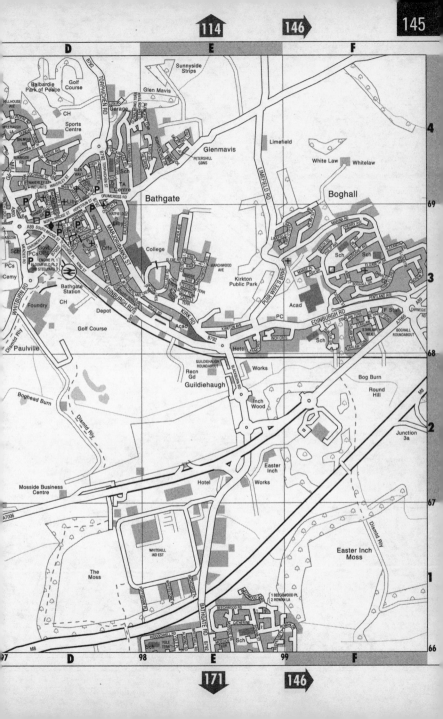

D E F

Sunnyside
Strips

Balbardie
Park of Peace
Golf Course

HILLHOUSE
AVE

Glen Mavis

Garage

Limefield

4

Sports
Centre

White Law   Whitelaw

Glenmavis

PETERSHILL
GDNS

Bathgate

Boghall

69

LIMEFIELD RD

TA
Centre

Libr

DRUMCROSS RD

College

MARCHWOOD
AVE

Sch   Sch

A89 SOUTH BRIDGE ST

Govt
PCs Offs

Kirkton
Public Park

Acad

Offs

PUIR WIFE'S BRAE

3

Cemy

PCs

Bathgate
Station

CH

Acad

F Sta

CARNEGIE
RD

Foundry

KIRK RD

PC

EDINBURGH RD

Boghall
ROUNDABOUT

Depot

EDINBURGH RD

Paulville

Golf Course

Acad

Sch

68

Hotel

GUILDIEHAUGH
ROUNDABOUT

Recn
Gd

Works

Bog Burn

Boghead Burn

Guildiehaugh

BLACKBURN RD

Round
Hill

Inch
Wood

M8

Junction
3a

2

Easter
Inch

Mosside Business
Centre

Hotel

Works

67

A7006

Easter
Inch
Moss

Dismtd Rly

WHITEHILL
IND EST

The
Moss

1

1 BEECHWOOD PL
2 ROWAN LA

BEECHWOOD RD

M8

BATHGATE RD B792

CATHERINE

Sch

66

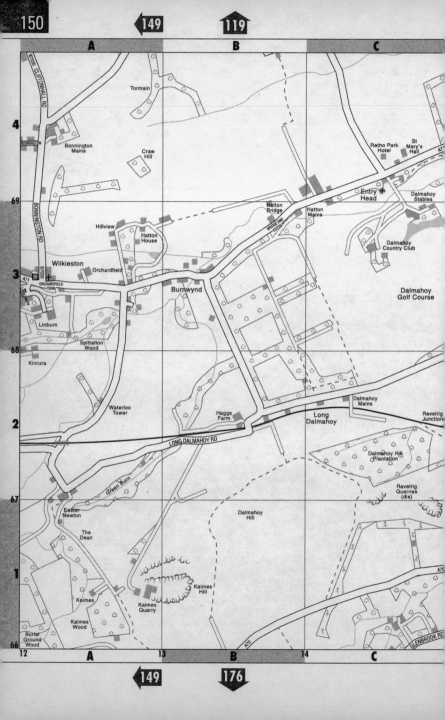

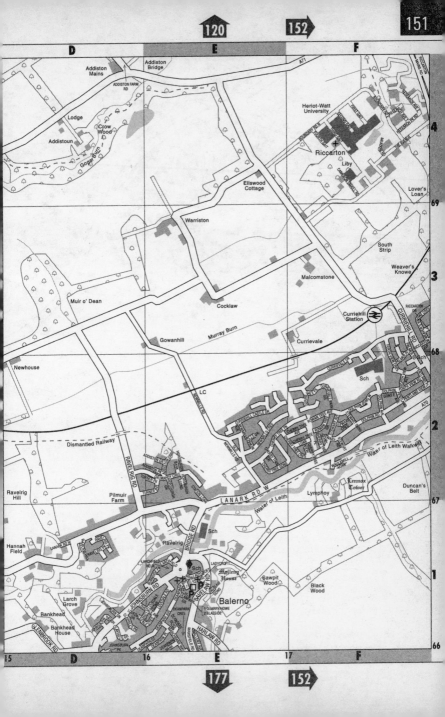

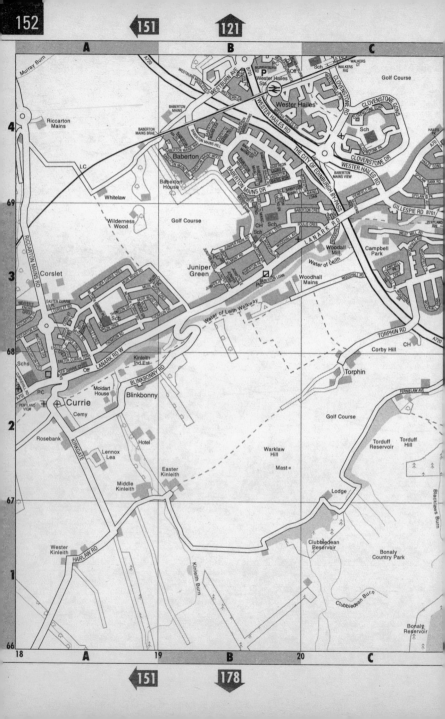

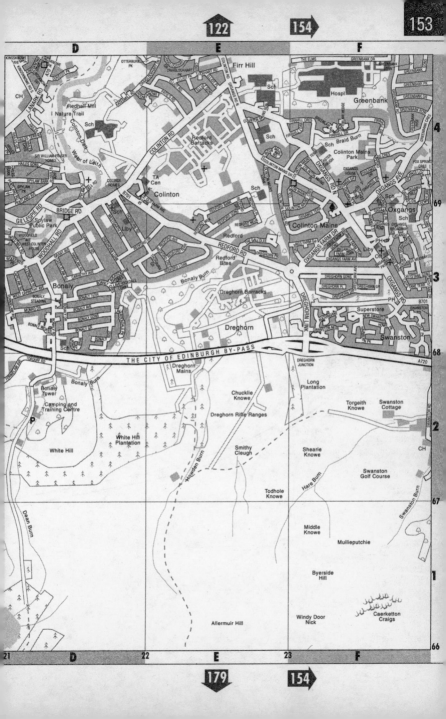

D E F

4

69

3

68

2

67

1

66

Newton

Newton
House

THE CITY OF EDINBURGH BY-PASS

A720

Castlesteads
Park

Castle
Steads

River Esk

Smeaton
Bridge

Home
Farm

A6094

Smeaton

A6124

DEANTOWN DR

Barons
Park

Cecil's
Field

Smeaton
Junction

Pickle
Dirt

Meeting of
the Waters

SALTER'S RD

Newfarm

Dismtd Rly

Lady's
Seat

Sandyriggs
Wood

Smeaton
Head

Howlands
Park

River North Esk

Old
Wood

Dalkeith
Park

Cat
Haugh

Langside

Langside

Laundry
House

Steel
Park

Laundry Bridge

Langside
Head

Lugton
Haugh

Montagu
Bridge

River South Esk

Cowden Cleugh

Cowden Cleugh
Cottage

Dalkeith
House

Sch

Nature
Trail

Park Walk

Thornybank
House

Thornybank
Industrial Estate

Long
Strip

Lugton

MUSSELBURGH RD

THORNY
BANK

A6094

B6414

Sch

Wester
Cowden

Brannies Pk
Ind Est

LANSBURY CT

ST ANDREW ST

HIGH ST

P

P

PC

P

Sch

EDINBURGH RD

BUCCLEUCH ST

LONDON RD

NEWMILLS RD

COWDEN GREEN

COWDEN
VIEW

ROBERT BURNS
MEWS

ROBERT BURNS LOAN

Sch

Adult Training
Centre

Caravan
Park

1 TAIT ST
2 ROBERTSON'S CL
3 WHITE'S CL
4 PETTIGREW'S CT
5 JARNAC CT
6 OLD EDINBURGH RD
7 WHITE HART ST
8 ESKDAILL CT
9 LAUDER LODGE

PENTLAND
VIEW

LAUDER RD

WATERSIDE WAY

Sch

ABBEY RD

NEWBATTLE RD

B703

F Sta

Benbught
Wood

CH

Maiden
Bridge

Golf Course

Lord
Ancrum's
Wood

Sch

PRIMROSE
TERR

Whitehill

Whitehill
Farm

DALKEITH

Newbattle
Abbey Hostel

Archbishop
Leighton's
House

Queen
Margaret's
Gate

KIPPIELAW MIDWAY

Kippielaw
Hatchery

Kippilaw

EASTHOUSES RD

B6482

Shaw's
Wood

Newbattle
Abbey

EASTHOUSES RD

33 D 34 E 35 F

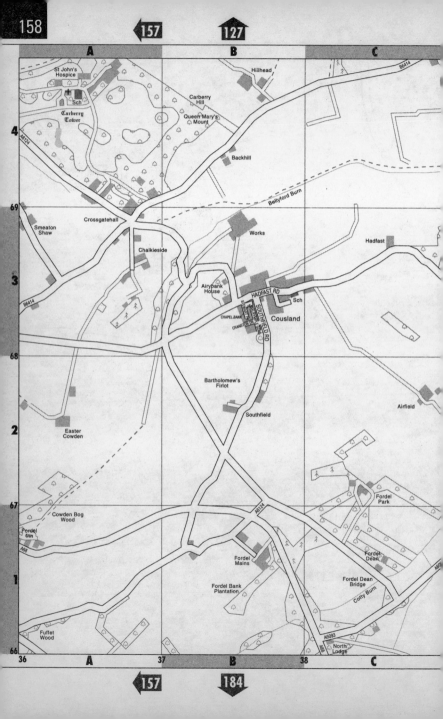

157
127

A   B   C

St John's Hospice
Sch
Hillhead
Carberry Hill
Carberry Tower
Queen Mary's Mount
B6414

4

Backhill

A6124

Ballyford Burn

69

Crossgatehall
Smeaton Shaw
Works
Hadfast

Chalkieside

3

Airypbank House
HADFAST RD
Sch
B6414
CHAPEL BANK
SOUTHFIELD RD
Cousland
CRANSTON RD

68

Bartholomew's Firlot
Airfield

Southfield

2

Easter Cowden

67

Cowden Bog Wood
A6124
Fordel Park

Fordel Inn
A68
Fordel Dean

Fordel Mains
Fordel Dean Bridge

1

Fordel Bank Plantation
Cotty Burn

Fuffet Wood
A6093
North Lodge
A68

66
36   A   37   B   38   C

157
184

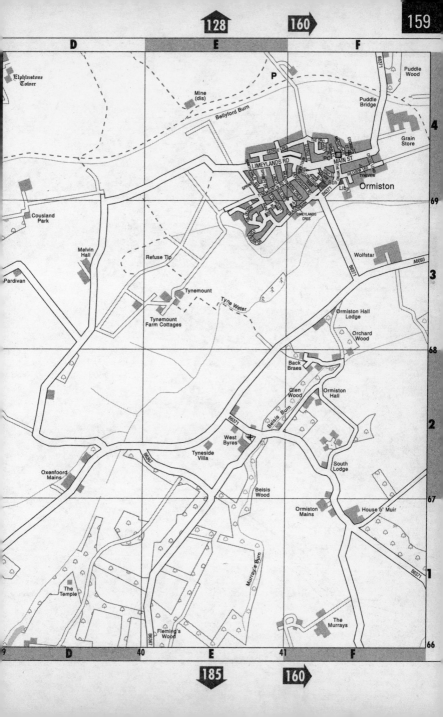

D E F

Elphinstone Tower

Mine (dis)

Bellyford Burn

P

Puddle Wood

Puddle Bridge

Grain Store

4

LIMEYLANDS RD

MAIN ST

PO

Liby

Ormiston

69

Cousland Park

LIMEYLANDS CRES

Melvin Hall

Refuse Tip

Wolfstar

A6093

Pardivan

Tynemount

Tyne Water

Ormiston Hall Lodge

3

Tynemount Farm Cottages

Orchard Wood

68

Back Braes

Glen Wood

Ormiston Hall

West Byres

Belsis Burn

2

B6371

Tyneside Villa

Oxenfoord Mains

South Lodge

Belsis Wood

67

Ormiston Mains

House o' Muir

Murray's Burn

1

The Temple

Fleming's Wood

The Murrays

66

9 D 40 E 41 F

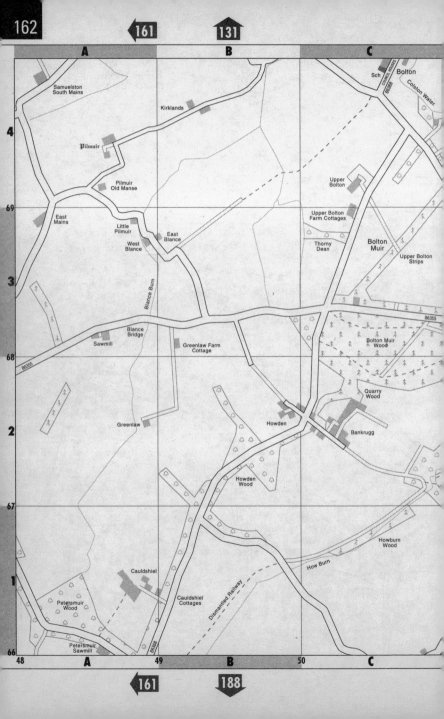

A　　　　　　　B　　　　　　　C

Samuelston
South Mains

Kirklands

4

Pilmuir

Sch
Bolton
Coldingham Walks
B6368
Coldstream Water

Upper
Bolton

69

Pilmuir
Old Manse

Upper Bolton
Farm Cottages

East
Mains

Little
Pilmuir

East
Blance

Thorny
Dean

Bolton
Muir

West
Blance

Upper Bolton
Strips

3

Blance Burn

B6355

Blance
Bridge

Sawmill

Greenlaw Farm
Cottage

Bolton Muir
Wood

68

B6355

Quarry
Wood

2

Greenlaw

Howden

Bankrugg

Howden
Wood

67

Howburn
Wood

Cauldshiel

1

Cauldshiel
Cottages

How Burn

Petersmuir
Wood

Dismantled Railway

B6368

Petersmuir
Sawmill

66

48　　　　A　　　　49　　　　B　　　50　　　C

163
133

A   **B**   **C**

Sandyford Burn

Bara Farm

Bara

B6370

Bara Wood

4

Sounding Burn

Bara Loch

69

Winding Law

3

Townhead

Townhead Wood

B6370

B6355

Duncanlaw

Cross Hill

68

Duncanlaw Strip

Sheriffside Roundall

Danskine Loch

Sunnyside

Sheriffside

Walden

2

Kailrig Wood

Sunnyside Strip

Danskine Lodge

Danskine

Sheriffside Clough

B6355

Thicket Wood

Walden Lea

Yester House

Duncan's Bog

Castle Wood

Danskine Burn

Hattie Braes

67

Gifford Water

Shank Lee Wood

Swallow Cleugh

Gamuelston Burn

Newlands Burn

Newlands

1

Black Basin

Hopes Water

Todlaw Bog Wood

Castle Mains House

Newlands Strip

Park

Castle Mains

66

54   **A**   **55**   **B**   **56**   **C**

163
190

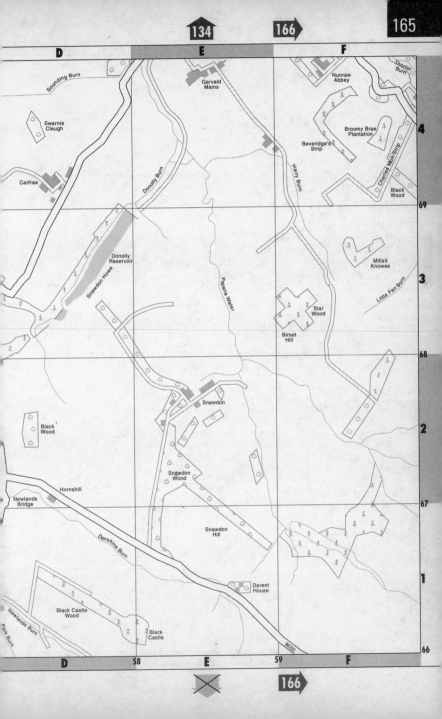

D E F

Thortel
Burn

Sounding Burn

Garvald
Mains

Nunraw
Abbey

Swarnie
Cleugh

Broomy Brae
Plantation

Beveridge's
Strip

4

Charlies Mair Strip

Carfrae

Donolly Burn

Hairy Burn

Black
Wood

69

Donolly Reservoir

Snawdon Howe

Papana Water

Millsit
Knowes

3

Little Fen Burn

Star
Wood

Birset
Hill

68

Black
Wood

Snawdon

2

Snawdon
Wood

Hornshill

Newlands
Bridge

67

Snawdon
Hill

Danskine Burn

Newlands Burn

Black Castle
Wood

Darent
House

1

Park Burn

Black
Castle

66

D 58 E 59 F

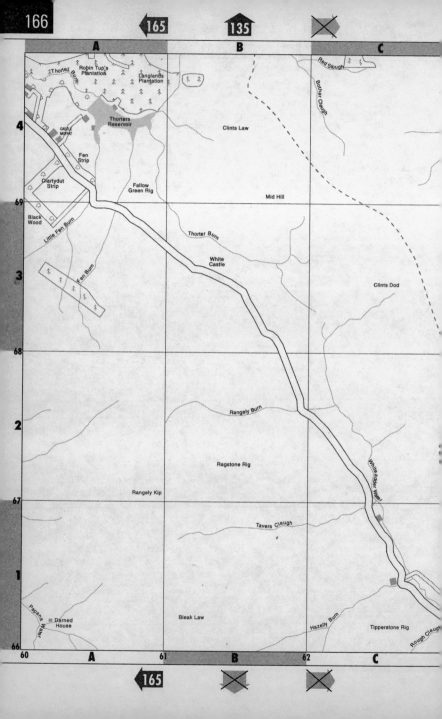

165
135

A   B   C

Thorter Burn
Robin Tup's Plantation
Langlands Plantation

Red Slough

Thorters Reservoir

Bother Cleugh

4

CASTLE MOFFAT

Clints Law

Fen Strip

Clartydut Strip

Fallow Green Rig

Mid Hill

69

Black Wood

Little Fen Burn

Thorter Burn

White Castle

3

Fen Burn

Clints Dod

68

Rangely Burn

2

Ragstone Rig

White Adder Water

67

Rangely Kip

Tavers Cleugh

1

Papana Water

Darned House

Bleak Law

Hazely Burn

Tipperstone Rig

Rough Cleugh

66

60   A   61   B   62   C

165

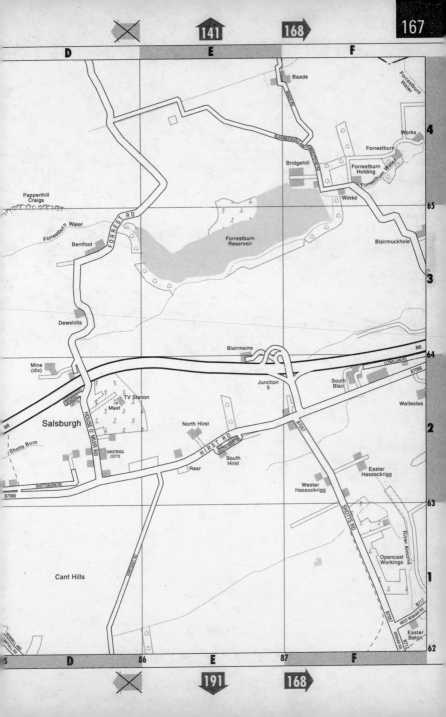

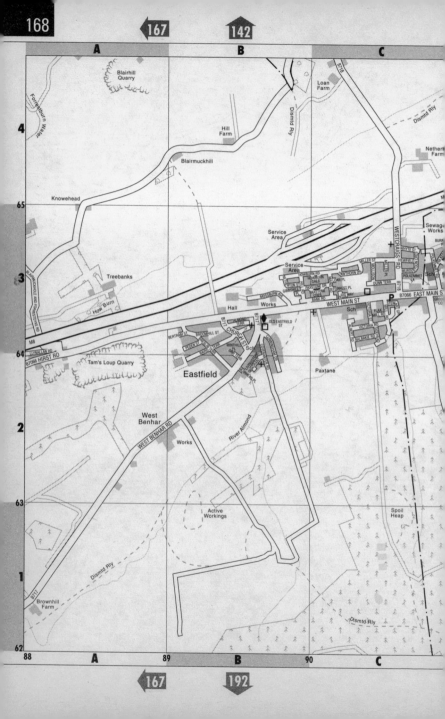

D E F

Sch
MARKET TERR
ROWAN RD
ROWAN PL
REDHOUSE PL

NELSON
RIDDOCHHILL
RIDDOCHHILL VIEW
BATHGATE RD
Liby ASH GR
P
SYCAMORE WLK
Blackburn
Training
Ctr
ELM GR
Acad
Sch
GRAHAM
Red
House
A705
REDHOUSE RD
SEAFIELD RD
REDHOUSE CT

Acad
Swinabbey
WEST MAIN ST
EAST MAIN ST
BATHGATE RD
MAIN ST
Ind-Est
River Almond
Latch Burn
Latchbrae

4

Mosshall

Blackburnhall
Holdings
BLACKBURNHALL
South-hill
Bickerton Burn
Grove
Mount
65

Spoil
Heap
Gardner's
Hall
3

Burnbrae

Mid
Foulshiels

Mid Seat of
Foulshiels
Foulshiels Burn
64

Dismantled Railway
B7015
2

Sch
B7015
Caravan
Park
Auchenhard

63
Cuthill
Cuthill
Bridge
Addiewell
B792
BLACKBURN RD
PH
MUCKHART TERR
HILL TERR
CRAIG VIEW
ELIZABETH ST
Hotel
MAIN ST
SUNNYSIDE
Stoneyburn
WILSON TERR
Sch
GLADSTONE
Stoneyburn
Farm
Breich Water
Sch
LIVINGSTONE ST
LODGE ST
RAEBURN
PL
Bents
MAIN ST
MEADOWHEAD PL
MEADOWHEAD GR
1
Loganlea
LOGANLEA RD
Skolie Burn
MEADOWHEAD RD
Addiebrownhill
MEADOWHEAD LOAN
Warehouses
A71
62

D 98 E 99 F

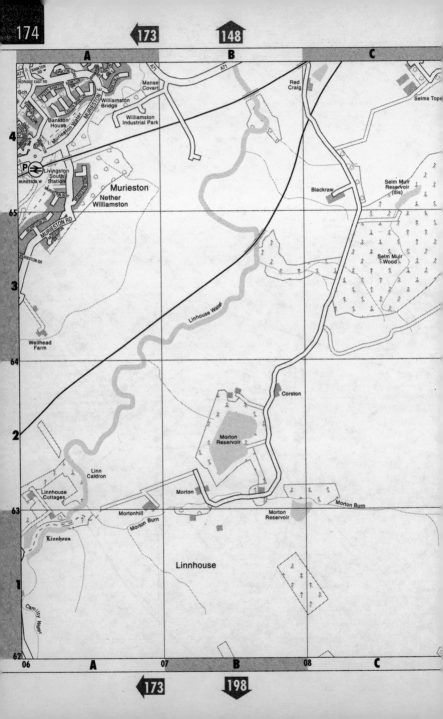

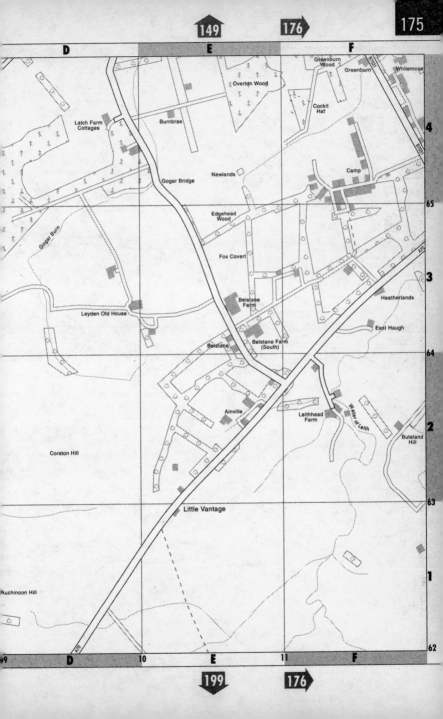

D E F

Greenburn Wood
Greenburn
Whitemoss
Cockit Hat
Overton Wood
Latch Farm Cottages
Burnbrae
Camp
Newlands
Gogar Bridge
Edgehead Wood
Fox Covert
Heatherlands
Gogar Burn
Belstane Farm
East Haugh
Leyden Old House
Belstane Farm (South)
Belstane
Ainville
Leithhead Farm
Water of Leith
Buteland Hill
Corston Hill
Little Vantage
Auchinoon Hill

A70
B7031

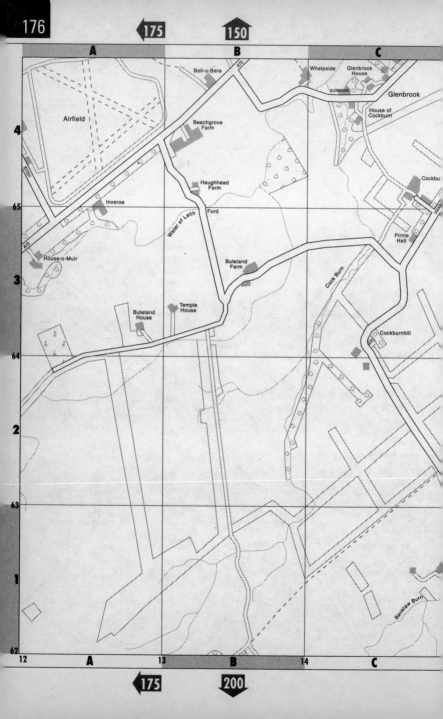

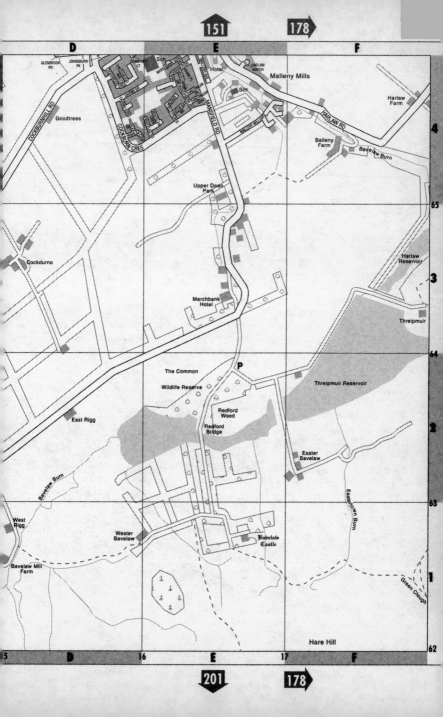

D   E   F

Malleny Mills

GLENBROOK
RD
JOHNSBURN
PK
TEAPNOE
CT
Sch
Hotel
HARLAW
MARCH

Harlaw
Farm

COCKBURNHILL RD

Goodtrees

GARDINE RD
COCKBURN CRES
MANSFIELD RD
MALLENY MILLS RD

Sch

HARLAW RD

Baileny
Farm

Bavelaw Burn

4

Upper Dean
Park

65

Cockdurno

Harlaw
Reservoir

3

Marchbank
Hotel

Threipmuir

64

P

The Common

Wildlife Reserve

Threipmuir Reservoir

East Rigg

Redford
Wood

Redford
Bridge

2

Easter
Bavelaw

63

Bavelaw Burn

West
Rigg

Wester
Bavelaw

Bavelaw
Castle

Eastertown Burn

Bavelaw Mill
Farm

1

Green Cleugh

Hare Hill

62

5   D   16   E   17   F

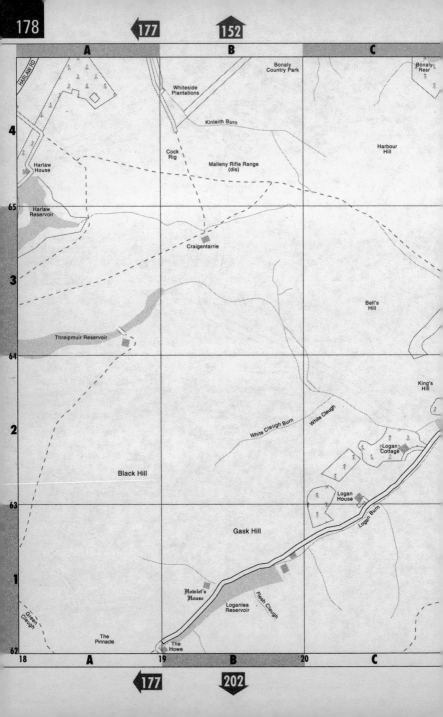

A　　　　　　　　B　　　　　　　　C

HARLAW RD

Bonaly
Country Park

Bonaly
Resr

Whiteside
Plantations

Kinleith Burn

4

Cock
Rig

Malleny Rifle Range
(dis)

Harbour
Hill

Harlaw
House

65

Harlaw
Reservoir

Craigentarrie

3

Bell's
Hill

Threipmuir Reservoir

64

King's
Hill

2

White Cleugh Burn

White Cleugh

Logan
Cottage

Black Hill

Logan
House

Logan Burn

63

Gask Hill

1

Green
Cleugh

Howlet's
House

Loganlea
Reservoir

Flesh Cleugh

The Pinnacle

62

The
Howe

18　　　　　A　　　　　19　　　　B　　　　20　　　C

D E F

Capelaw Hill

Caerketton Hill

Fala Knowe

Boghall Burn

4

Kirk Burn

Woodhouselee Hill

65

Castlelaw Hill

3

DANGER AREA

Knightfield Rig

Woodhouselee

Castlelaw Firing Ranges

Kirk Bridge

Castle Knowe

Easter Howgate

64

Kirkton

Glencorse Reservoir

Crosshouse

Breakwater

Castlelaw

Glen Cottage

2

The Glen

Visitor Centre P

Crawley Cottages

Glencorse Burn

Flotterstone Bridge

PH

63

Turnhouse Hill

House O' Muir Farm

Turnhouse

1666

Glencorse Mains

1

White Craig Heads

Rullion Green Cottage

BELWOOD RD

Bellwood House

Mauricewood Mains

Nursery

MAURICEWOOD RD

62

D   E   F

WADINGBURN RD

Ramsay   Hosp   Eskgrove
FOUNDRY LA
Sch   Offs   HUNTER AVE
MAYBERRY CR   Loanhead
HAWTHORN TERR   Farm
Liby
Sch   GLEN ST B702   LASSWADE RD   Riding   4
Leisure   Sch   Centre
Centre   P   H   Sch
PENTLAND RD   HIGH ST   LINDEN PL   Polton House   65
THE LOAN   Sch   MAYFIELD   DALHOUSIE AVE W 1
CT   DALHOUSIE PL 2
A768   Job Ctr   POLTON OR 3
NIVEN'S KNOWE RD HERD TERR   DRYDEN RD   Cemy   Dryden   Mavisbank   POLTON RD   Polton-
Bank   House   POLTON BANK   hall
LOANHEAD   POLTON RD W   Sch
Burghlee   GORDON AVE
Bilston   Bilston Burn   Polton
Wood   Bilston Wood   Springfield   3
Coal Store   River North Esk
Hewan Bank   The Maiden   CAMERON LOOP
Castle
Shinbanes Fields   Hewan Bog   Dalhousie
Kill Burn   Chesters
Animal Breeding   Midfield House   64
Research Centre
Mauntmarie
Poultry Research   Hawthornden   ROSEWELL RD
Centre
Hawthornden   2
Castle   Whitebog
Gortonlee   Farm
Cemy
Slatebarns   Wallace's   Gorton   Rosewell
Cave   House   Manse
PENICUIK RD   63
Sch   Parkneuk
GORTON RD   Sch
Rosewell   PG   1
Linn   Rosewell   DUKE ST   Sewage   The Glen
Mains   Works   Sch
Lee   The   Opencast   FORRNETHE ST   Shiel Burn   Hosp
Farm   Thicket   Workings   62
Road Under Construction
Dismantled Railway

27   D   28   E   29   F

A B C

View Bank
Golf Course
Works
Newbatt
ESKBANK ROAD ROUNDABOUT
CH
Broomieknowe
River North Esk
POLTON RD
Hardengreen
MILLHEAD
Sch
ESKBANK RD
Eldindean
Quarryhead
Sewage Works
HARDENGREEN JUNC
Leisure Centre
Dobbie's Knowe
P
P
P
Lady Lothian's Plantation
BONNYRIGG
Ott
LOTHIAN ST
DICKSON GDN
P
Liby
RD
DUNDAS ST
Dalhousie Dairy
Lothianbridg
Dalhousie Mains
Lothian Bridge
65
Sch
DALHOUSIE RD E
POLTON ST
Craigesk
Pittendriech Burn
Sch
COCKPEN RD
Parsonspool Bridge
POLTON AVENUE RD
Sch
Hopefield
1 WILLOW AVE
2 CHESTNUT DR
3 POPLAR TERR
SHERWOOD CT
SHERWOOD WLK
Dalhousie Courte
Sch
3
Poltonhall
ROSEWELL RD
4 SKELTIEMUIR CT
5 COCKPEN PL
6 COCKPEN DR
Grove Farm
Fancy Grove Wood
Catholes Wood
Cockpen Bridge
64
Burnbrae House
Little Wood
Dalhousie Grange
Cockpen Farm
Dalhousie Chesters
Castle Park
Cockpen Dean
Saw Mill
Dalhousie Castle
2
Chesters Bog Wood
Dalhousie Strip Wood
Anna Park
Blow Loun
River South Esk
RAMSAY
B70
Dalhousie Burn
Upper Dalhousie
63
Castle Dean Wood
Castle Dean Burn
Galladean Plantation
Young Bog Wood
1
Tore Hill Wood
Dalhousie Burn Plantation
Castle Dean Burn
Aikendean Glen
Kirkhill Hotel
Kirkhill Bank
62
30 A 31 B 32 C

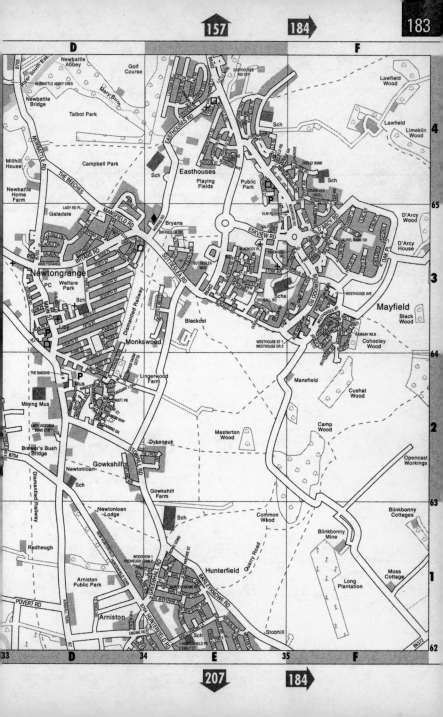

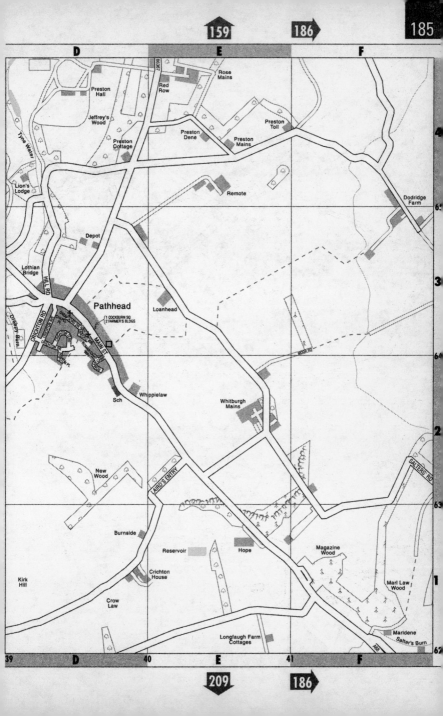

D E F

Preston Hall

Red Row

Rose Mains

Jeffrey's Wood

Preston Dene

Preston Toll

Preston Mains

4

Preston Cottage

Tyne Water

Lion's Lodge

Remote

Dodridge Farm

65

Depot

Lothian Bridge

3

Drospy Burn

HILL RD

Pathhead

Loanhead

MOOR RD

1 COCKBURN SQ
2 FARMER'S BLDGS

CRICHTON RD

MAIN ST

64

Whippielaw

Whitburgh Mains

Sch

2

New Wood

LAIRD'S ENTRY

SALTERS RD

63

Burnside

Reservoir

Hope

Magazine Wood

Kirk Hill

Crichton House

Marl Law Wood

1

Crow Law

Longfaugh Farm Cottages

Maridene

Salter's Burn

39 D 40 E 41 F 62

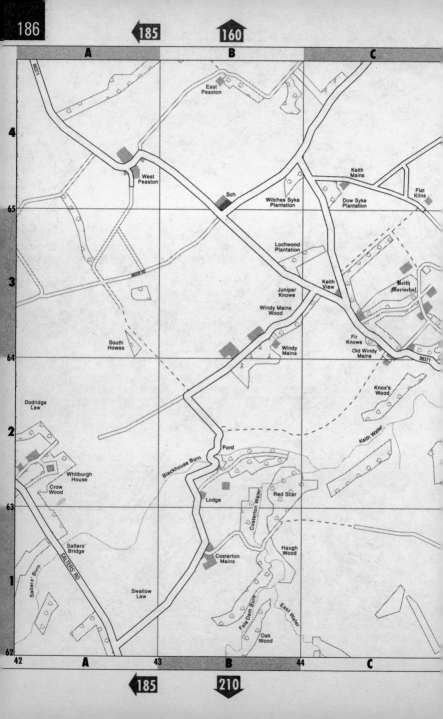

D **E** **F**

Old Duncrahilll

Duncrahill

Saltoun Forest

Masters Wood

Birns Water

Gilchriston

4

Humbie Wood

Keith Woods

65

Nether Keith

Highlea Wood

Highlea Cottages

BG598

Keith Glen

Highlea

3

Hut Wood

Bughtknowe

Keith Water

Humble Water

Church Wood

Humble House

64

Keith Bridge

New Mains

Manse

Leggate

Hattonhill

Kirk Bridge

The Roundle Wood

2

Lady Wood

Corsehope Plantation

Bankhead

Humble Mill

B6371

Humble Mill Bridge

63

Hazyhill

Johnstounburn Water

Humble Mains

Humbie

Sch

Blegbie Burn

Upper Keith

The Children's Village

1

pit ill

Sch

Muirpark Cottage

Scadlaw Wood

B6368

62

D 46 **E** 47 **F**

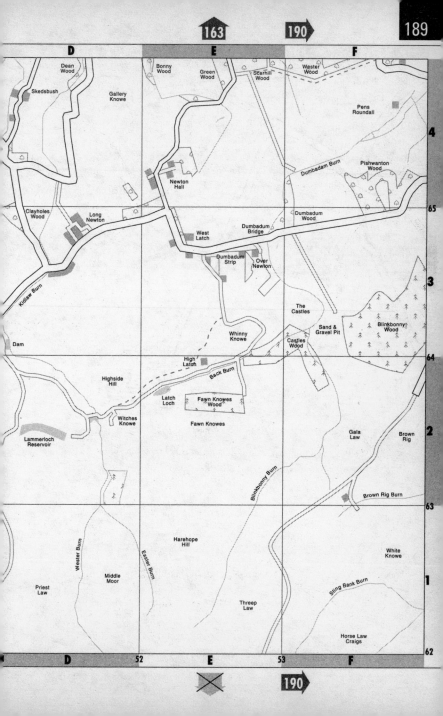

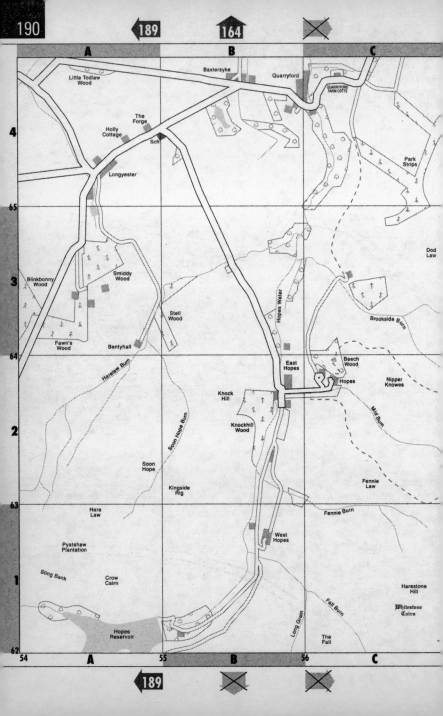

A   B   C

Little Todlaw Wood

Baxtersyke

Quarryford

QUARRYFORD FARM COTTS

The Forge

Holly Cottage

Sch

Park Strips

4

Longyester

65

Dod Law

Blinkbonny Wood

Smiddy Wood

3

Stell Wood

Hopes Water

Brookside Burn

Fawn's Wood

Bentyhall

East Hopes

Beech Wood

64

Hareiaw Burn

Hopes

Nipper Knowes

Knock Hill

Knockhill Wood

Soon Hope Burn

Mid Burn

2

Soon Hope

Kingside Rig

Fennie Law

63

Hare Law

Fennie Burn

Pyatshaw Plantation

West Hopes

Sting Bank

Crow Cairn

Harestone Hill

1

Whitestone Cairn

Long Grain

Fall Burn

Hopes Reservoir

The Fall

62

54   A   55   B   56   C

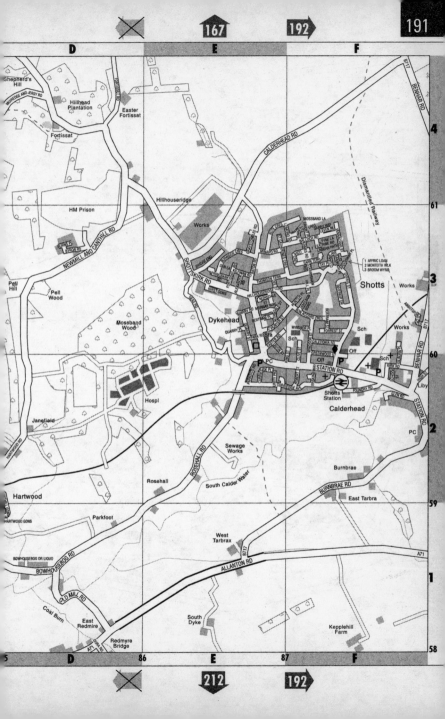

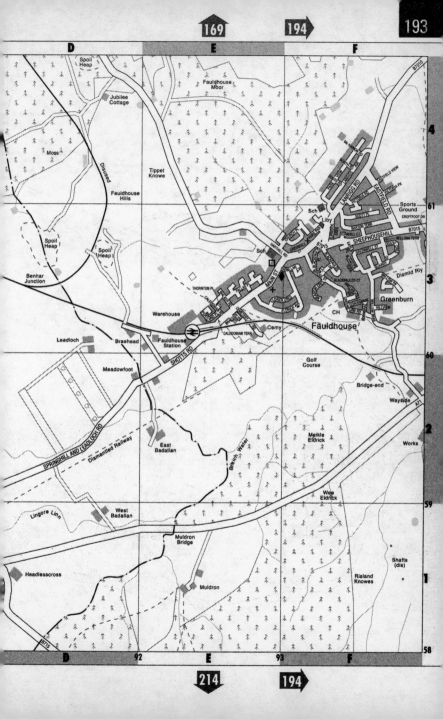

4

Spoil Heap

Jubilee Cottage

Fauldhouse Moor

B7010

Moss

Disused

Tippet Knowe

McMahons

61

Sports Ground

CROFTFIELD VIEW

LANRIGG RD

EASTFIELD RD

Sch

EASTFIELD PK

Fauldhouse Hills

Liby

CROFTFOOT DR

B7015

SHEEPHOUSEHILL

Sch

Spoil Heap

BARONS HILL CT

BELLORA TERR

Benhar Junction

Spoil Heap

B7715

Dismtd Rly

3

THORNTON PL

BLACKFAULDS CT

Greenburn

CH

Warehouse

Fauldhouse

Leadloch

Brachead

Fauldhouse Station

CALEDONIAN TERR

Cemy

60

Meadowfoot

Golf Course

Bridge-end

A71

Wayside

2

SPRINGHILL AND LEADLOCH RD

Dismantled Railway

East Badallan

Breich Water

Meikle Eldrick

Works

59

Lingore Linn

West Badallan

Muldron Bridge

Wee Eldrick

Shafts (dis)

1

B7715

Headlesscross

Muldron

Risland Knowes

58

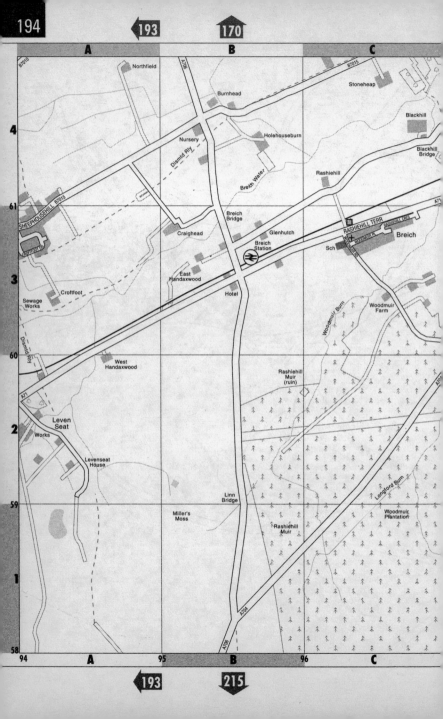

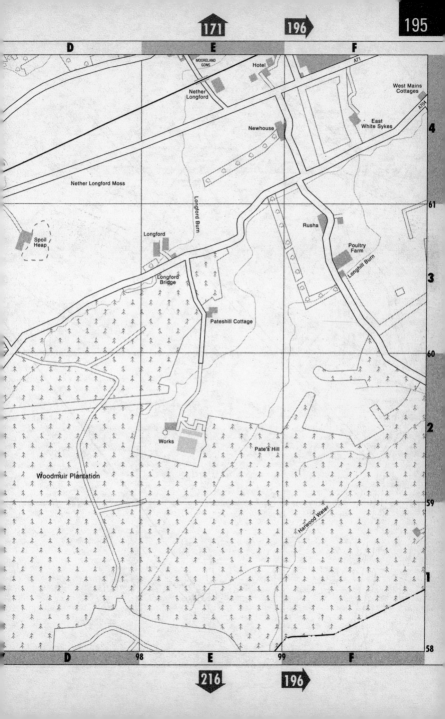

D   E   F

MOORELAND GDNS.

Hotel

Nether Longford

A71

West Mains Cottages

A704

Newhouse

East White Sykes

4

Nether Longford Moss

Longford Burn

61

Spoil Heap

Longford

Rusha

Poultry Farm

Longhill Burn

3

Longford Bridge

Pateshill Cottage

60

Works

Pate's Hill

2

Woodmuir Plantation

59

Harwood Water

1

58

195
172

A | B | C

A704

Cow Hill

Cairnview Mains

4

Little Harwood

Hartwood

West Mains

Hartwood Bridge

Hartwood Mains

Harwood Water

61

Mossend

Mid Hartwood

3

West Harwood

60

Bog Burn

Baadsmill

Baad's Mill Bridge

Vain Syke

2

Adie's Syke

Coal Burn

59

Pearie Law

Cobbinshaw Reservoir

1

Benry Bog

Benry Bridge

58

00 | A | 01 | B | 02 | C

195
217

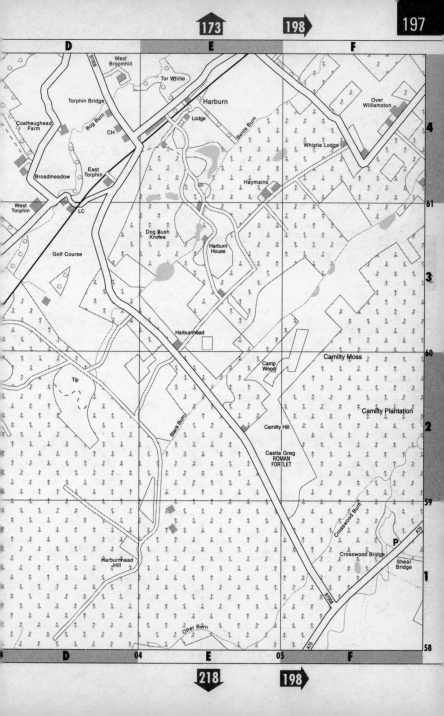

D
E
F

West Broomhill

Tor Whitie

Harburn

Torphin Bridge

Lodge

Bents Burn

Over Williamston

Coalheughead Farm

Bog Burn

CH

4

Whistle Lodge

Broadmeadow

East Torphin

Haymains

West Torphin

LC

61

Dog Bush Knowe

Harburn House

Golf Course

3

Harburnhead

60

Camp Wood

Camilty Moss

Tip

Camilty Plantation

Black Burn

2

Camilty Hill

Castle Greg ROMAN FORTLET

59

Crosswood Burn

P

A70

Harburnhead Hill

Crosswood Bridge

Shear Bridge

B7008

1

A70

Otter Burn

D
04
E
05
F
58

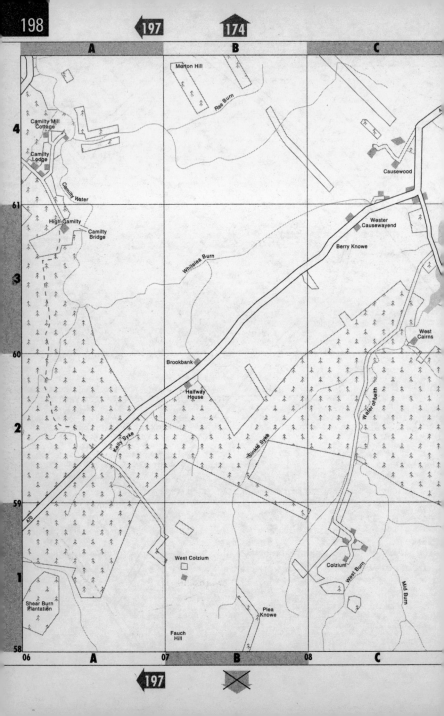

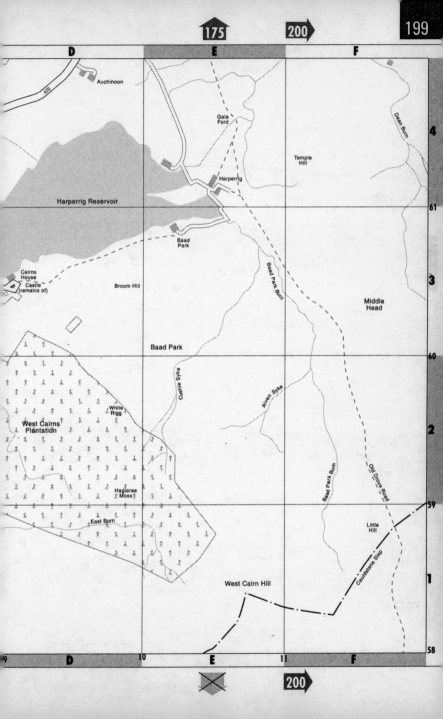

D E F

Auchinoon

A70

Gala
Ford

Temple
Hill

Dean Burn

Harperrig Reservoir

Harperrig

61

Baad
Park

Baad Park Burn

Cairns
House

Castle
(remains of)

Broom Hill

Middle
Head

3

Baad Park

60

Cuahie Syke

Alwan Syke

White
Rigg

West Cairns
Plantation

2

Hagierae
Moss

Baad Park Burn

Old Drove Road

59

East Burn

Little
Hill

Chauldstane Slap

West Cairn Hill

1

58

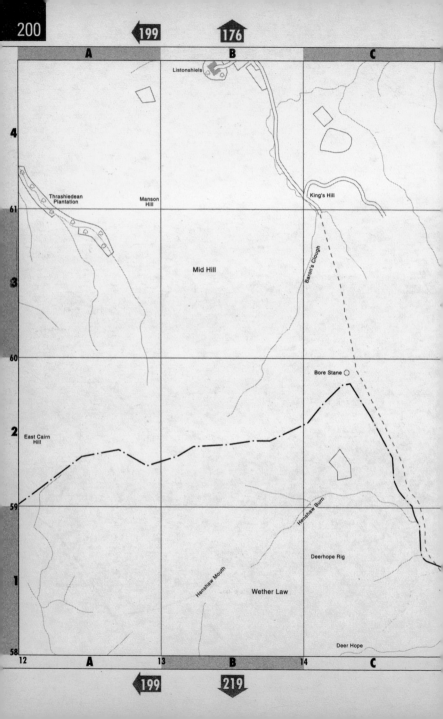

A   B   C

Listonshiels

4

Thrashiedean
Plantation

Manson
Hill

King's Hill

61

Mid Hill

Baron's Clough

3

60

Bore Stane

2

East Cairn
Hill

59

Henshaw Burn

Deerhope Rig

1

Henshaw Mouth

Wether Law

Deer Hope

58

12   A   13   B   14   C

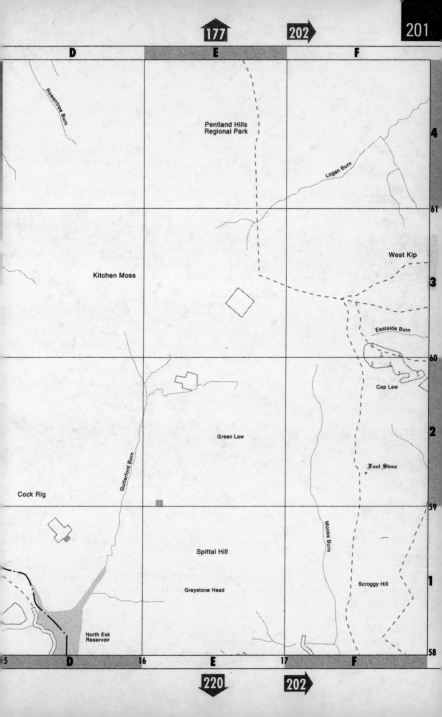

D   **E**   **F**

Rowantree Burn

4

Pentland Hills
Regional Park

Logan Burn

61

West Kip

Kitchen Moss

3

Eastside Burn

60

Cap Law

Green Law

2

Font Stone

Cock Rig

Gutterford Burn

59

Spittal Hill

Monks Burn

Greystone Head

Scroggy Hill

1

North Esk
Reservoir

5   **D**   16   **E**   17   **F**   58

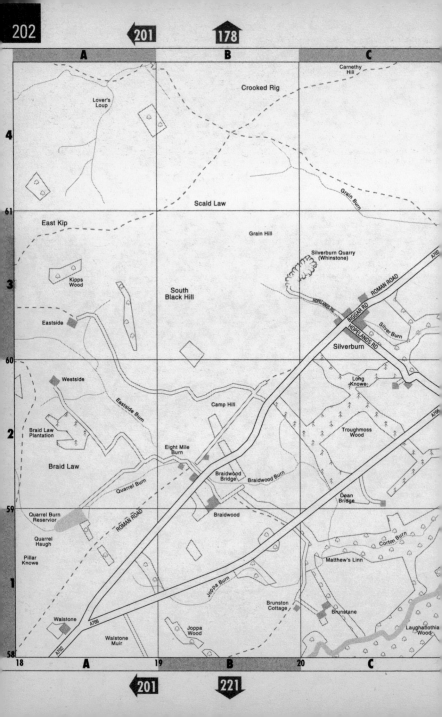

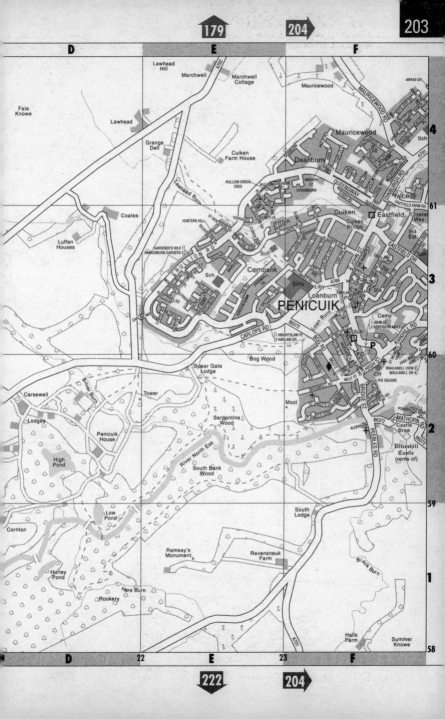

D
E
F

Dismd Rly

Rosedale

A6094

Hospl
St Mary's

4

GOURLAW
COTTS

Thornton

Gourlaw

Shiel Burn

Broachrigg
Farm

61

Highwood
House

Belmount Strip

3

Broadmeadows Strip

Newbigging

Shewington

Curling Pond

60

Refuse
Tip

Peter's Wood

Ladies Walk
Plantation

Cowie's Bank Strip

Edgelaw Moor

Edgelaw Moor Strip

2

Resr

59

Hosie Plantation

Wilkie
Strip

Cauldhall Moor

Edgelaw

1

Edgelaw
Reservoir

Whinny Plantation

Steelfoot
Bridge

Ancrielaw

Cauldhall

58

7
D
28
E
29
F

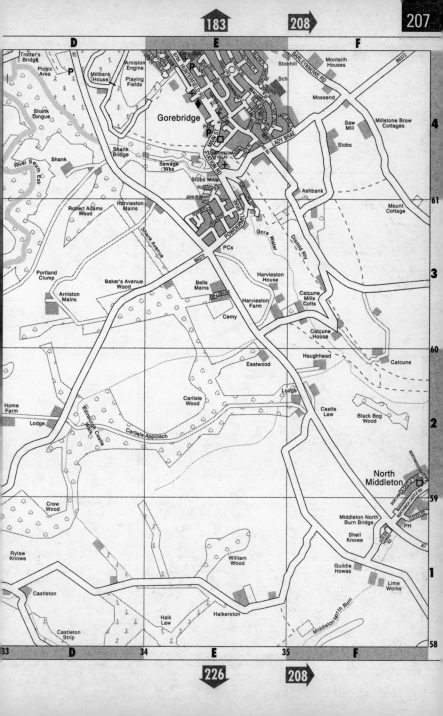

Trotter's Bridge

Pichic Area

P

Millbank House

Arniston Engine

Playing Fields

Stobhill

Monteith Houses

Barleyknowe Rd

B6372

Sch

Mossend

Gorebridge

Saw Mill

Millstone Brow Cottages

4

P

Lady Brae

Stobs

Shank Tongue

Shank Bridge

Shank

Sewage Wks

Harvieston Villas

Ashbank

Mount Cottage

61

River South Esk

Robert Adams Wood

Harvieston Mains

Stobs Mills

John Bernard Way

Powderhall Brae

Dismil Riv.

Gore Water

Shank Avenue

PCs

Harvieston House

Catcune Mills Cotts

3

Portland Clump

Arniston Mains

Baker's Avenue Wood

Bells Mains

Harvieston Farm

Cemy

Catcune House

B6372

Haughhead

Catcune

60

Eastwood

Lodge

Home Farm

Lodge

Carlisle Wood

Castle Law

Black Bog Wood

2

Edinburgh Castle Walk

Carlisle Approach

North Middleton

59

Crow Wood

Middleton North Burn Bridge

Sheil Knowe

PH

A7

Rylaw Knowe

William Wood

Guildie Howes

Lime Works

1

Castleton

Halkerston

Halk Law

Middleton North Burn

Castleton Strip

58

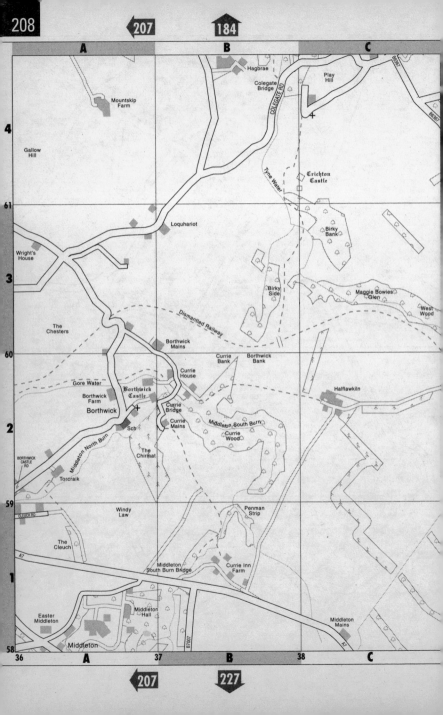

207
184

A   B   C

Hagbrae

Play Hill

Colegate Bridge

COLEGATE RD

B6367

4

Mountskip Farm

Gallow Hill

Tyne Water

Crichton Castle

61

Loquhariot

Birky Bank

Wright's House

3

Birky Side

Maggie Bowie's Glen

West Wood

The Chesters

Dismantled Railway

Borthwick Mains

60

Gore Water

Currie Bank

Borthwick Bank

Currie House

Halflawkiln

Borthwick Farm

Borthwick Castle

Currie Bridge

Middleton South Burn

Borthwick

Sch

Currie Mains

Currie Wood

2

BORTHWICK CASTLE RD

Middleton North Burn

The Chirmat

Torcraik

59

CLEUCH RD

Windy Law

Penman Strip

The Cleuch

A7

Middleton South Burn Bridge

Currie Inn Farm

1

Easter Middleton

Middleton Hall

B7007

Middleton Mains

58

Middleton

36   A   37   B   38   C

207
227

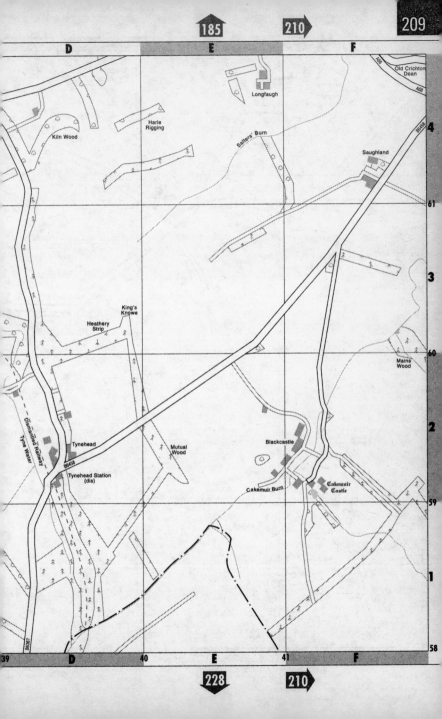

Old Crichton Dean

A68

B6458

Longfaugh

Salters' Burn

Saughland

4

61

Harle Rigging

Kiln Wood

3

King's Knowe

Heathery Strip

60

Mains Wood

Dismantled Railway

Tyne Water

Tynehead

B6458

Mutual Wood

Blackcastle

2

Tynehead Station (dis)

Cakemuir Burn

Cakemuir Castle

59

B6367

1

58

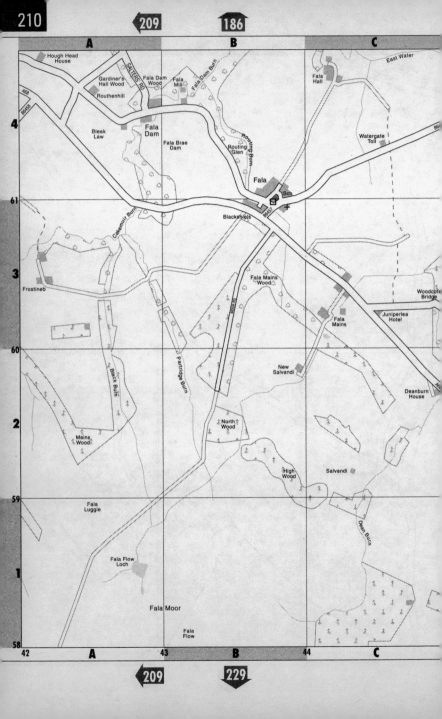

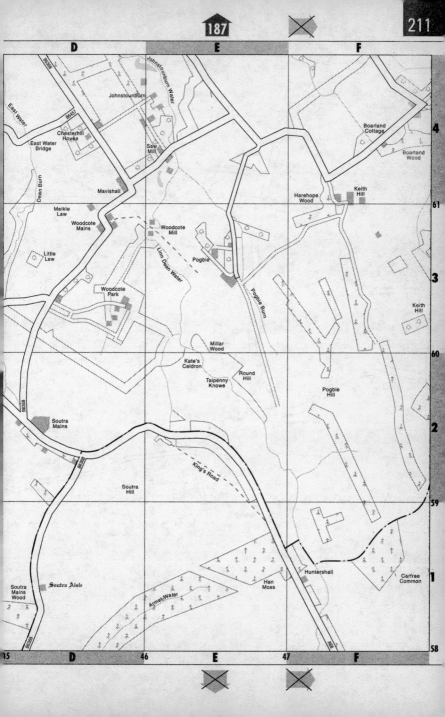

D

E

F

East Water

B6368

Johnstounburn

Johnstounburn Water

Boarland
Cottage

B6457

Chesterhill
House

East Water
Bridge

Saw
Mill

Boarland
Wood

4

Dean Burn

Mavishall

Harehope
Wood

Keith
Hill

61

Meikle
Law

Woodcote
Mains

Woodcote
Mill

Woodcote

Little
Law

Linn Dean Water

Pogbie

Keith
Hill

3

Woodcote
Park

Pogbie Burn

Millar
Wood

60

Kate's
Caldron

Round
Hill

Taipenny
Knowe

Pogbie
Hill

B6368

Soutra
Mains

2

B6368

King's Road

Soutra
Hill

59

Soutra
Mains
Wood

Soutra Aisle

Armet Water

Hen
Moss

Huntershall

Carfrae
Common

1

B6368

A68

15

46

47

58

D

E

F

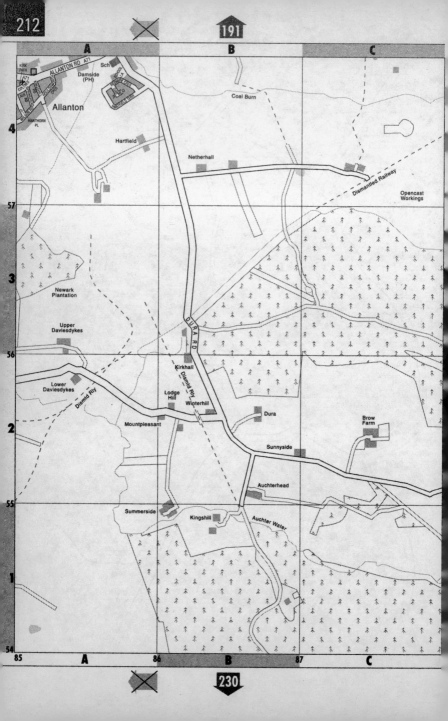

191

Allanton

ALLANTON RD A71

KIRK PATH

Sch

Damside (PH)

Hartfield

Netherhall

Coal Burn

Opencast Workings

Dismantled Railway

HAWTHORN PL.

Newark Plantation

Upper Daviesdykes

DURA RD

Kirkhall

Lower Daviesdykes

Dismtd Rly

Dismtd Rly

Lodge Hill

Winterhill

Dura

Brow Farm

Mountpleasant

Sunnyside

Auchterhead

Summerside

Kingshill

Auchter Water

230

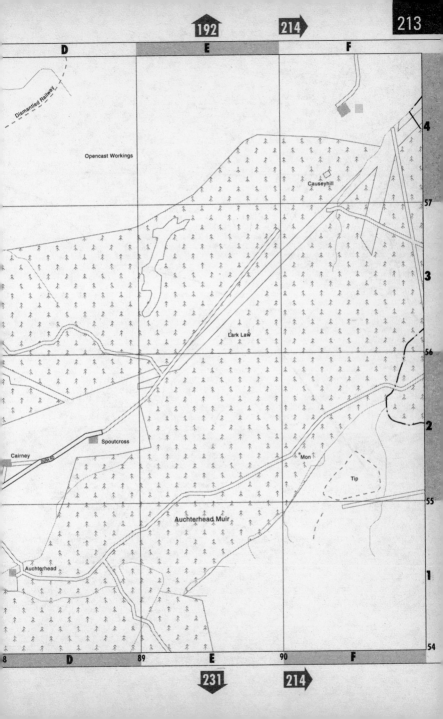

D
E
F

Dismantled Railway

4

Opencast Workings

Causeyhill

57

3

Lark Law

56

2

Spoutcross

Cairney

NURA 60

Mon

Tip

55

Auchterhead Muir

Auchterhead

1

54

8
D
89
E
90
F

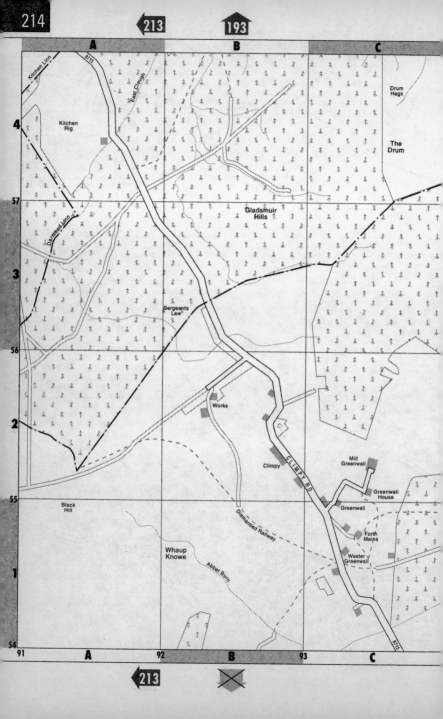

213
193

A

B

C

Kitchen Linn

B715

East Cleugh

Drum
Hags

4

Kitchen
Rig

The
Drum

57

Darmead Linn

Gladsmuir
Hills

3

Sergeants
Law

56

Works

2

Climpy

CLIMPY RD

Mid
Greenwall

Greenwall
House

55

Black
Hill

Greenwall

Dismantled Railway

Forth
Mains

Whaup
Knowe

Abbet Burn

Wester
Greenwall

1

54

91

A

92

B

93

C

B715

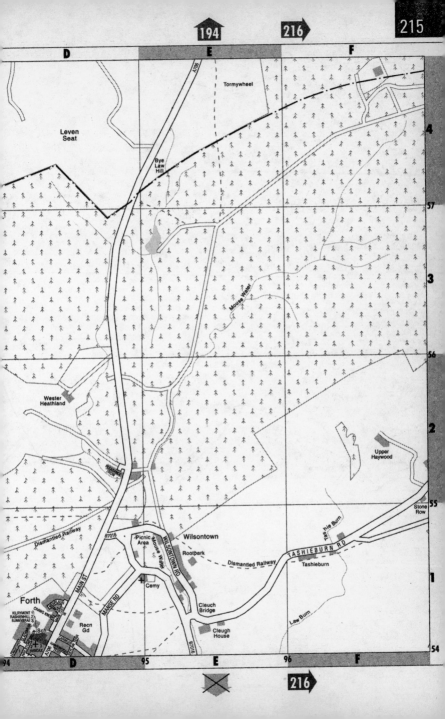

215
195

A   **B**   **C**

Hendry's Gorse

4

57

Wormlaw Burn

Mosshat Burn

3

Worm Law

Mountainblaw Farm

Easter Mosshat

56

Wester Mosshat

2

Burnfoot Poultry Farm

Bughtknowes

Old Manse

Burnfoot

Dippool Water

TASHIEBURN RD

55

Crooklands

Lawhead View

Pentland View

Haywood

Greenbank

Memorial

1

Auchengray Inn (PH)

Mid Auchengray

54

Auchengray

Hillhead of Auchengray

97   **A**   **98**   **B**   **99**   **C**

215

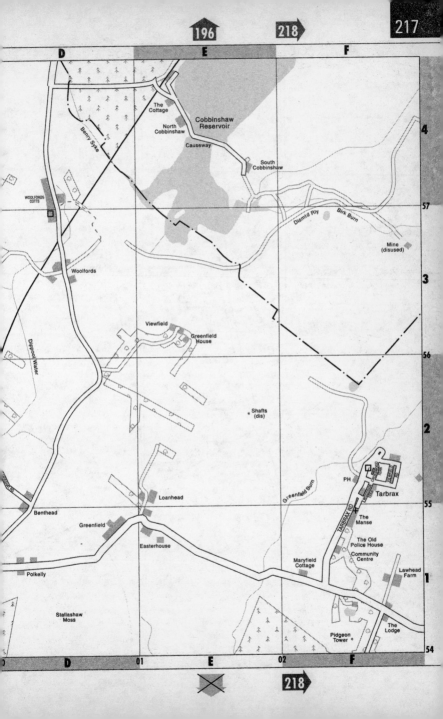

D   E   F

The Cottage

Cobbinshaw
Reservoir

North
Cobbinshaw

Causeway

South
Cobbinshaw

Berry Syke

Dismtd Rly

Birk Burn

WOOLFORDS
COTTS

Mine
(disused)

57

Woolfords

3

Dippool Water

Viewfield

Greenfield
House

56

Shafts
(dis)

2

Greenfield Burn

PH

Tarbrax

55

Loanhead

The Manse

Benthead

Greenfield

The Old
Police House

Community
Centre

Easterhouse

Maryfield
Cottage

Lawhead
Farm

Polkelly

1

TARBRAX RD

Stallashaw
Moss

Pidgeon
Tower

The
Lodge

54

D   01   E   02   F

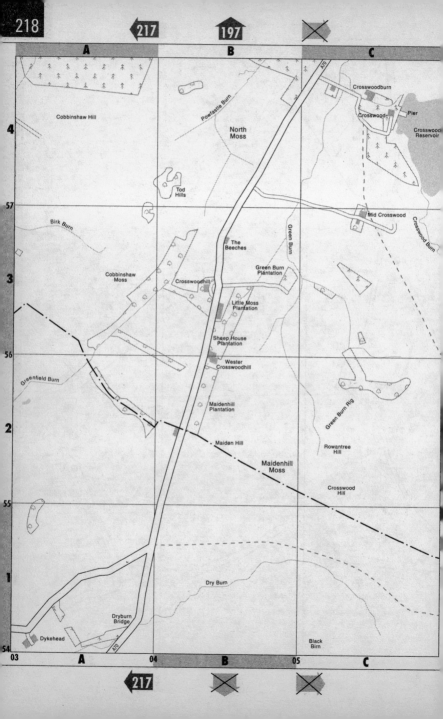

D
200
220
F

The Mount

Ravendean Burn
Lyne Water
Lynslie Burn

Cairn Muir

4

Little
Hill

Fairliehope Burn

Grain Heads

57

Hareshaw Sike

3

Petrifying
Spring

Glenmade Burn

56

Baddinsgill
Reservoir

Black Pots

Little
Knock

Mount Maw

Kennels

2

Baddinsgill Burn

Colin's Rig

55

Baddinsgill
House

Baddinsgill
Farm

Dipper
Wood

Lower Glen Ely
Wood

Glen Ely

Upper Glen Ely
Wood

Lyne Water

1

Faw Mount

Windy Gowl

ROMAN ROAD
(course of)

Wakefield

Cock
Rig

54

D
13
E
14
F

220

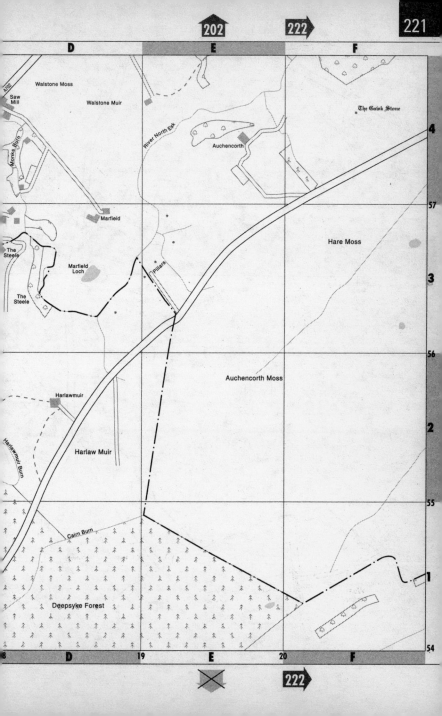

A   **B**   **C**

Dykeneuk

4

Hare Burn

Netherton

Glen Rosslyn
Mink Farm

57

Black Burn

Bowles

Sch

3

Auchencorth
Moss

Springfield

Ros
View

56

Springfield
Moss

Anne's Mill
Bridge

Newste

Woodend

Hotel

Leadburn
House

2

Rosemay

Lead Burn

Leadburn
Mains

Leadburn

55

Rosehill

Disznid Rly

1

Blaircochrane

Craigburn

Willow Burn

Mitchell
Hill

Blairburn

Disznid Rly

Whim Park
Cottage

Whim
Pond

54

21   **A**   22   **B**   23   **C**

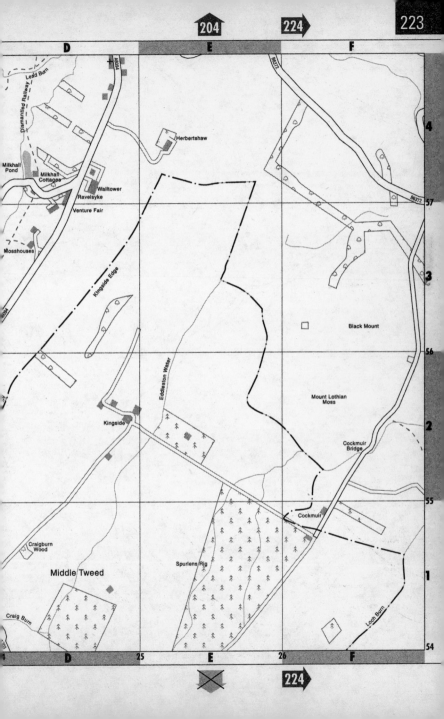

D   E   F

Ledd Burn

Dismantled Railway

Herbertshaw

Milkhall Pond

Milkhall Cottages

Walltower

Ravelsyke

Venture Fair

4

B6372

57

Mosshouses

Kingside Edge

3

Black Mount

56

Eddleston Water

Mount Lothian Moss

Kingside

2

Cockmuir Bridge

55

Cockmuir

Craigburn Wood

Middle Tweed

Spurlens Rig

1

Craig Burn

Loch Burn

54

D   25   E   26   F

223

205

A   B   C

4

Cauldhall Glen Plantation

Steelfoot Strip

Peter's Plantation

Pond Wood

Smithy Strip

Fullarton

57

B6372

Mount Lothian

Fullarton Water

Gillygub Dean

Fountainside

3

Side Plantation

Easter Wood

56

B6372

Upper Side

Allan Clump

2

Loch Burn

55

1

Toxsidehill Wood

Tweedale Burn

Stell Plantation

Toxsidehill

The Old Wood

Gladhouse Plantation

Toxside

54

27   A   28   B   29   C

223

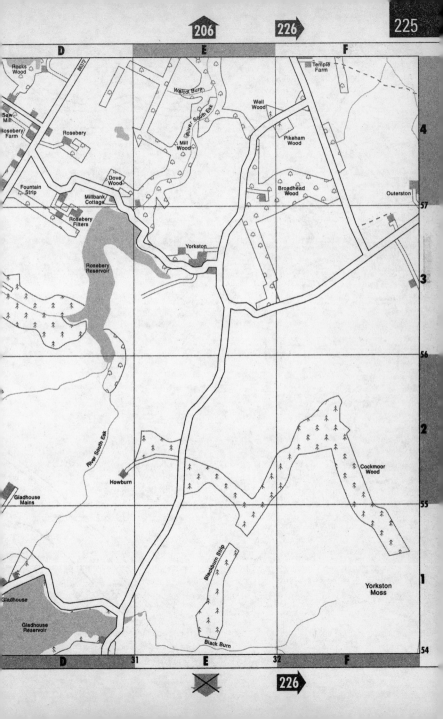

D E F

Rocks Wood

B6372

Saw Mill

Rosebery Farm

Rosebery

Walcot Burn

River South Esk

Mill Wood

Well Wood

Pikeham Wood

4

Temple Farm

Fountain Strip

Dove Wood

Millbank Cottage

Broadhead Wood

Outerston

57

Rosebery Filters

Yorkston

3

Rosebery Reservoir

56

River South Esk

2

Howburn

Cockmoor Wood

Gladhouse Mains

55

Gladhouse

Blackburn Strip

Yorkston Moss

1

Gladhouse Reservoir

Black Burn

54

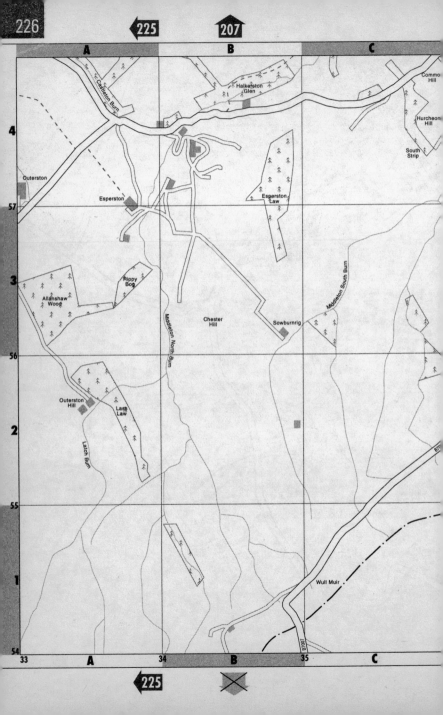

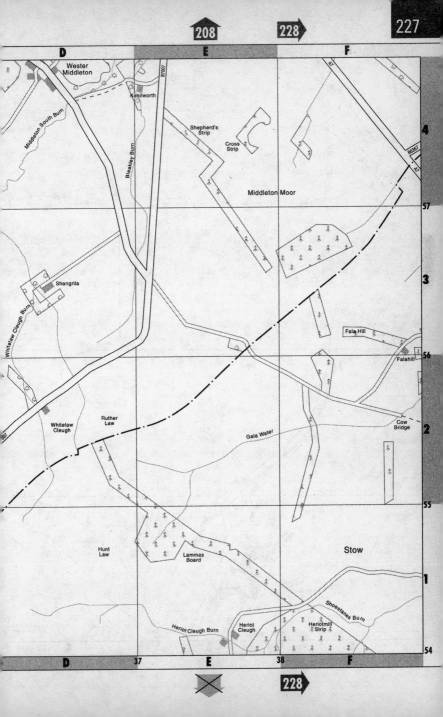

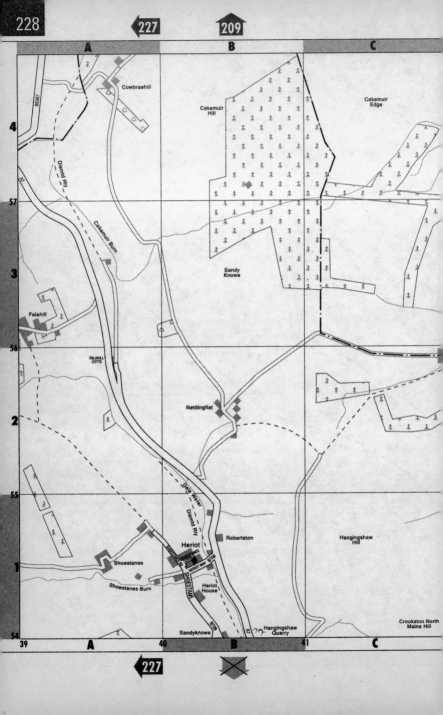

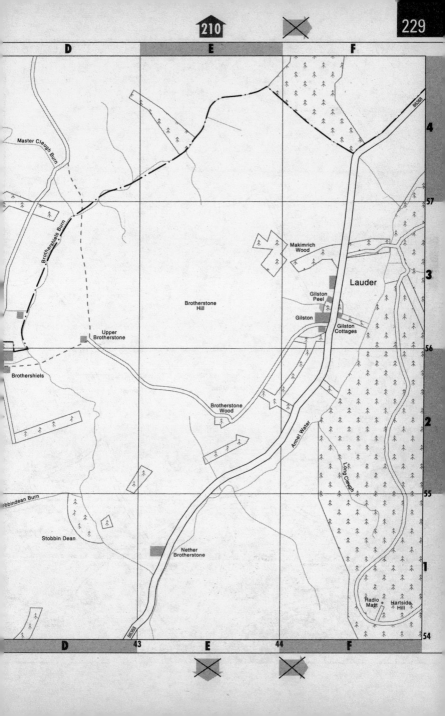

D   E   F

Master Cleugh Burn

4

57

Brothershiels Burn

Makimrich
Wood

3

Lauder

Gilston
Peel

Brotherstone
Hill

Gilston

Gilston
Cottages

Upper
Brotherstone

56

Brothershiels

Brotherstone
Wood

2

Armet Water

Long Cleugh

55

ebbindean Burn

Stobbin Dean

Nether
Brotherstone

1

Radio
Mast

Hartside
Hill

54

D   E   F

43   44

A   B   C

4

Gair
Reservoirs

Kingshill Plantation

Bowridge
Cottage

Bowridge Burn

King's Law

53

Bowridge

Gair

Gair Farm

3

Resr

52

Belstane Burn

Kingshaw Moss

Thorn

Under
Thorn

Belstane
Town
Farm

Honeybank
Bridge

ROMAN ROAD

Moss-side Burn

Dyke

Fairyknowe
View

Stonedyke Rd

Moss-side

Thornhome

West
Highcross

Albert
Cottage

51

Yieldshields Burn

B7056

Carluke

Hillhead

Equestrian
Centre

KING ST

Sch

Cauldron
Gill

West
Quarter

Yieldshields Rd

Yieldshields

1

A721

CARNWATH RD

Jock's Burn

Yieldshields
Farm

1 STRAEHOUSE WYND
2 MUIRLEE RD
3 CARLIN LA
4 CROSSEN LA
5 JOHNSTONE LA
6 KELLY'S LA
7 DAVIDSON LA
8 CANDIMILNE CT

ROMAN ROAD

Coldstream
Burn

GLENAFEOCH RD

KILNCADZOW RD

Croftfoot

WILTON RD

Hospl

Coldstream
Bridge

1 EASTFIELD RD
2 TARBET PL

50

85   A   86   B   87   C

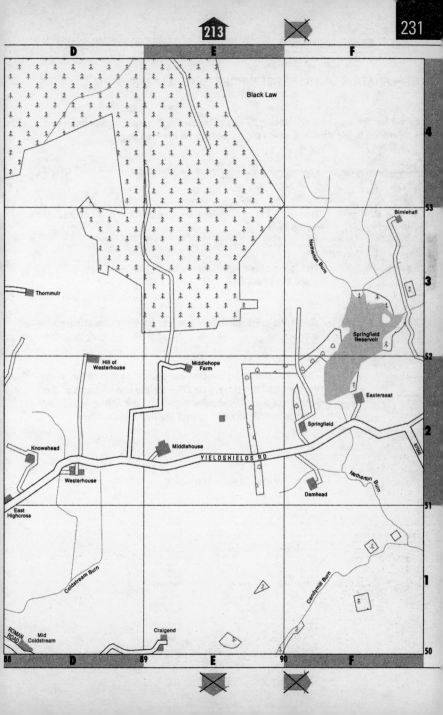

D   E   F

Black Law

Birniehall

Netherton Burn

4

53

Thornmuir

Springfield
Reservoir

3

52

Hill of
Westerhouse

Middlehope
Farm

Easterseat

Springfield

B7056

Knowehead

Middlehouse

YIELDSHIELDS RD

2

Westerhouse

Netherton Burn

East
Highcross

Damhead

51

Coldstream Burn

Caendymill Burn

1

ROMAN
ROAD

Mid
Coldstream

Craigend

50

88   D   89   E   90   F

EXPLANATION OF THE STREET INDEX REFERENCE SYSTEM

Street names are listed alphabetically and show the locality, the page number and a reference to the square in which the name falls on the map page.

Example: Melville Dr. Edin..123 E3

Melville Dr   This is the full street name, which may have been abbreviated on the map.

Edin   This is the abbreviation for the town, village or locality in which the street falls.

123   This is the page number of the map on which the street name appears.

E3   The letter and figure indicate the square on the map in which the centre of the street falls..The square can be found at the junction of the vertical column carrying the appropriate letter and the horizontal row carrying the appropriate figure.

ABBREVIATIONS USED IN THE INDEX
Road Names

Approach	App	Green	Gn
Arcade	Arc	Grove	Gr
Avenue	Ave	Heights	Hts
Boulevard	Bvd	Industrial Estate	Ind Est
Buildings	Bldgs	Junction	Junc
Business Park	Bsns Pk	Lane	La
Business Centre	Bsns Ctr	North	N
Broadway	Bwy	Orchard	Orch
Causeway	Cswy	Parade	Par
Centre	Ctr	Park	Pk
Circle	Circ	Passage	Pas
Circus	Cir	Place	Pl
Close	Cl	Precinct	Prec
Common	Comm	Promenade	Prom
Corner	Cnr	Retail Park	Ret Pk
Cottages	Cotts	Road	Rd
Court	Ct	South	S
Courtyard	Ctyd	Square	Sq
Crescent	Cres	Stairs	Strs
Drive	Dr	Steps	Stps
Drove	Dro	Street,Saint	St
East	E	Terrace	Terr
Embankment	Emb	Trading Estate	Trad Est
Esplanade	Espl	Walk	Wlk
Estate	Est	West	W
Gardens	Gdns	Yard	Yd

Key to abbreviations of Town, Village and Rural locality names used in the index of street names.

Aberdour	Abe	49	E4	Cockburnspath	Cock	140	C2	Halbeath	Hal	30	A3	Ormiston	Orm	159	F4

Aberdour .... Abe 49 E4
Aberlady .... Aber 71 E2
Addiewell .... Add 171 F1
Airth .... Air 22 B2
Allanton .... Alla 212 A4
Alloa .... All 10 B3
Alva .... Alva 5 D3
Armadale .... Arm 143 F3
Athelstaneford ..... Ath 101 F4
Auchendinny .... Auch 180 B1
Auchengray .... Auc 216 C1
Auchtertool .... Aucht 15 D1
Avonbridge .... Avon 112 A3
Balerno .... Bale 151 E1
Banknock .... Bank 57 D2
Bannockburn .... Bann 7 F1
Bathgate .... Bath 145 E4
Blackburn .... Black 171 E4
Blackridge .... Blac 142 B2
Blairhall .... Bla 26 A4
Bo'ness .... B'ness 63 F4
Boghall .... Bog 145 F4
Bonnybridge .... Bon 58 A3
Bonnyrigg .... Bonn 182 B4
Bridge of Allan .... B of A 2 A4
Bridgend .... Brid 86 B2
Broxburn .... Brox 117 E3
Burntisland .... Burn 50 C4
Caldercruix .... Cald 141 D3
California .... Cali 81 F3
Cambus .... Camb 9 D4
Cambusbarron .... Cam 6 B3
Cardenden .... Card 15 E4
Carluke .... Car 230 A1
Clackmannan .... Clack 11 D2

Cockburnspath ...... Cock 140 C2
Cockenzie .... Cocke 97 E2
Cowdenbeath .... Cow 13 F2
Cowie .... Cowie 20 B4
Crossford .... Crossf 28 A1
Crossgates .... Cross 30 C3
Culross .... Cul 42 B4
Currie .... Curr 152 A2
Dalgety Bay .... D Bay 48 B2
Dalkeith .... Dalk 157 D1
Dalmeny .... Dal 89 F4
Danderhall .... Dan 156 B4
Dechmont .... Dech 116 B1
Denny .... Den 36 C1
Dirleton .... Dir 53 D2
Dunbar .... Dunb 78 B1
Dunblane .... Dun 1 B4
Dunfermline .... Dunf 29 E2
Dunipace .... Duni 36 B2
East Calder .... E Cal 148 C2
East Linton .... E Lin 103 E4
Eastfield .... East 168 B2
Edinburgh .... Edin 123 E3
Elphinestone .... Elph 128 A1
Falkirk .... Falk 60 B3
Fallin .... Fall 8 B2
Fauldhouse .... Fau 193 F3
Fishcross .... Fish 5 F2
Forth .... For 215 D1
Gifford .... Giff 163 F2
Gladsmuir .... Glad 130 A4
Gorebridge .... Gore 207 E4
Grangemouth .... Gran 61 E4
Gullane .... Gull 52 A1
Haddington .... Hadd 101 E1

Halbeath .... Hal 30 A3
Harthill .... Hart 169 D3
High Valleyfield ... H Val 26 A1
Howgate .... How 204 A1
Humbie .... Hum 187 D1
Inverkeithing ...... Inver 47 E1
Kelty .... Kel 12 B4
Kincardine .... Kin 23 F2
Kinghorn .... King 35 D2
Kirkcaldy .... Kirk 17 E2
Kirkliston .... Kirkl 89 D1
Kirknewton .... Kir 149 F1
Larbert .... Lar 38 A2
Lauder .... Lau 229 F3
Laurieston .... Laur 61 D2
Limekilns .... Lime 45 F2
Linlithgow .... Lin 85 D3
Linnhouse .... Linn 174 B1
Livingston .... Liv 147 E3
Loanhead .... Loan 181 D4
Lochgelly .... Loch 14 B4
Longniddry .... Long 98 C3
Maddiston .... Madd 83 D3
Mayfield .... May 183 F3
Menstrie .... Men 3 F3
Middle Tweed .... M Twee 223 D1
Muirhouses .... Muir 64 B3
Murieston .... Muri 174 A4
Musselburgh .... Muss 126 B4
New Sauchie .... N Sau 5 E1
Newton .... New 88 A4
Newtongrange .... Newt 183 D3
North Berwick ...... N Ber 54 B4
North Middleton .... N Mid 207 F2
Oakley .... Oak 26 C4

Ormiston .... Orm 159 F4
Pathhead .... Path 185 D3
Pencaitland .... Pen 160 B4
Penicuik .... Peni 203 F3
Plean .... Plea 20 B2
Polmont .... Pol 61 F1
Prestonpans .... Pres 96 C1
Pumpherston .... Pump 148 A4
Queensferry .... Que 89 D4
Ratho .... Rat 119 E1
Rosewell .... Rose 181 E1
Roslin .... Rosl 180 C2
Rosyth .... Ros 46 C2
Salsburgh .... Sals 167 D2
Shieldhill .... Shi 81 E3
Shotts .... Shot 191 F3
Slamannan .... Slam 110 A3
Stenhousemuir ...... Sten 38 B2
Stirling .... Stir 7 E4
Stoneyburn .... Ston 171 E1
Stow .... Stow 227 F1
Tillicoultry .... Till 5 F4
Torphichen .... Torp 113 F3
Torryburn .... Torr 26 C1
Torwood .... Tor 37 F3
Tranent .... Tran 128 B4
Tullibody .... Tull 4 B2
Uphall .... Uph 116 C2
West Calder .... W Cal 172 B1
West Linton .... W Lin 220 A1
Westfield .... West 112 C3
Whitburn .... Whit 170 A4
Whitecraig .... White 126 C1
Winchburgh .... Winch 87 F1

1st St. Gran 62 A4
2nd St. B'ness 62 B3
2nd St. Gran 62 A4
3rd St. B'ness 62 B3
3rd St. Gran 62 A4
4th St. B'ness 62 C3
4th St. Gran 62 A4
5th St. B'ness 62 C3
5th St. Gran 62 A4
6th St. B'ness 62 C3
6th St. Gran 41 D1
7th St. B'ness 62 C3
7th St. Gran 62 B4
8th St. Gran 62 B4
Abbey Craig Rd. N Sau ... 5 D1
Abbey Cres. N Ber 54 A4
Abbey Ct. N Ber 54 A4
Abbey Mill. Stir 7 E4
Abbey Mains. Hadd 101 F2
Abbey Mews. N Ber 54 A4
Abbey Mill. Stir 7 E4
Abbey Park Pl. Dunf 29 D2
Abbey Rd. Dalk 157 D1
Abbey Rd. Dunb 78 B1
Abbey Rd. N Ber 54 A4
Abbey Rd Pl. Stir 7 E4
Abbey Rd. Stir 2 B1
Abbey St. Edin 94 A1
Abbey St. H Val 26 A1
Abbey Strand. Edin 123 F4
Abbey View. Crossf 28 B1
Abbey View. Dunf 29 F1
Abbeygrange. Newt 183 D3
Abbeyhill Cres. Edin 93 F1
Abbeyhill. Edin 93 F1
Abbeymount. Edin 93 F1
Abbot Rd. Bann 7 F2
Abbot St. Dunf 29 D2
Abbot's View. Hadd 101 D1
Abbots Cres. Falk 59 F4
Abbots Ct. Falk 60 B4
Abbots Mill. Kirk 17 D2
Abbots Moss Dr. Falk 59 F1
Abbots Rd. Falk 60 B4
Abbots Rd. Gran 61 E4
Abbots View. Pol 61 F2
Abbots Wlk. Kirk 16 C2
Abbotsford Cres. Edin ... 123 D2
Abbotsford Cres. Shot ... 191 F3
Abbotsford Ct. Edin 123 D2
Abbotsford Dr. Gran 61 F3
Abbotsford Dr. Laur 61 D2
Abbotsford Gdns. Falk ... 39 D1
Abbotsford Pk. Edin 123 D2
Abbotsford Pk. N Ber 53 F4
Abbotsford Pl. Stir 2 B1
Abbotsford Rd. N Ber 53 F4
Abbotsford Rise. Muri ... 148 A1
Abbotsford St. Falk 60 A4
Abbotsgrange Rd. Gran .. 61 F4
Abbotshall Rd. Kirk 17 D1
Abbotsinch Rd. Gran 61 F4
Abden Ave. King 35 D2
Abden Ct. King 35 D2
Abden Pl. King 35 D2
Abel Pl. Dunf 29 D1
Abercairney Cres. Madd .. 82 C3
Abercairney Pl. Gran 61 F4
Abercorn Ave. Edin 124 B4
Abercorn Cres. Edin 124 B3
Abercorn Ct. Edin 124 B4
Abercorn Dr. Edin 124 B4
Abercorn Gr. Edin 124 B4
Abercorn Pl. Winch 87 F1
Abercorn Rd. Edin 124 B4
Abercorn Terr. Edin 125 E4
Abercrombie Pl. Men 3 F3
Abercrombie St. Falk 59 F3
Abercromby Dr. B of A 2 A4
Abercromby Pl. Edin 93 E1
Abercromby Pl. Stir 7 D4
Abercromby Pl. Tull 4 A1
Aberdour Cres. Dunf 29 E1
Aberdour Pl. Dunf 29 E1
Aberdour Rd. Burn 33 E1
Aberdour Rd. Dunf 29 F1
Aberlady Rd. Hadd 100 C1
Aberlour St. Ros 46 C2
Abinger Gdns. Edin 122 B4
Abington Rd. Dunf 28 C1
Aboyne Ave. Stir 2 B2
Aboyne Gdns. Kirk 16 C4
Academy La. Loan 181 E4
Academy Pk. Edin 94 A2
Academy Rd. Pres 7 F1
Academy Rd. B'ness 64 A4
Academy Rd. Stir 7 D4
Academy Sq. Lime 45 E2
Academy St. All 9 F4
Academy St. Arm 143 F3
Academy St. Bath 145 D3
Academy St. Edin 94 A2
Acheson Dr. Pres 127 F4
Achray Ct. All 10 B3
Achray Dr. Stir 2 A2
Ackam Path. Loan 180 C4
Acorn Cres. Lar 38 B1
Acre Rd. Muir 64 B3

Acredale. Bath 145 D3
Acredale. Lin 85 D3
Acredales. Hadd 131 F4
Acredales Wlk. Hadd 131 F4
Adam Cres. Stan 38 C1
Adam Pl. Loth 14 A4
Adam Sq. Muri 173 E3
Adam St. Falk 60 B3
Adambrae Rd. Muri 173 E4
Adamson Ave. Kirk 17 D3
Adamson Cres. Dunf 29 E3
Adamson Pl. Stir 2 A2
Adamson Rd. Loch 14 A4
Addiston Cres. Bale 151 E2
Addiston Farm Rd. Rat .. 120 A1
Addiston Gr. Bale 151 E2
Addiston Pk. Bale 151 E2
Adelaide St. Liv 148 A3
Adelphi Gr. Edin 125 D4
Adelphi Pl. Edin 125 D4
Admiral Terr. Edin 123 D3
Admiralty Rd. Inver 47 E2
Admiralty Rd. Lime 46 B2
Admiralty Rd. Ros 46 B2
Admiralty St. Edin 93 F3
Affleck Ct. Edin 121 D4
Affric Dr. Falk 39 E1
Affric Loan. Shot 191 F3
Affric Way. Crossf 28 A1
Afton Ct. Dech 116 B1
Afton Ct. Stir 7 E3
Afton Dr. Bank 57 E4
Afton Dr. Dunf 29 F3
Afton Pl. Edin 93 D3
Afton Terr. Edin 93 D3
Agnew Terr. Edin 93 E3
Ailsa Gr. Kirk 16 C4
Ainslie Gdns. Pol 61 F2
Ainslie Pl. Edin 93 D1
Aird's Cl. Edin 123 E4
Airdrie Rd. Cald 141 D2
Airlie Dr. Pol 61 F1
Airth Dr. Stir 7 E2
Airthrey Ave. B of A 2 A4
Airthrey Dr. Sten 39 D2
Airthrey Rd. B of A 2 A3
Airthrey Rd. Stir 2 B3
Aitchison Dr. Lar 38 A2
Aitchison's Pl. Edin 95 D1
Aitken Cres. Stir 7 D1
Aitken Ct. Kirk 17 D1
Aitken Dr. Slam 110 A3
Aitken Dr. Whit 170 A4
Aitken Gdns. Stir 59 F3
Aitken Orr Dr. Brox 117 F3
Aitken Rd. Falk 59 F3
Aitken St. Edin 94 A1
Aitken Terr. Falk 59 E3
Akarit Rd. Sten 38 C1
Alan Breck Gdns. Edin ... 91 E1
Albany La. Edin 93 E1
Albany St. Dunf 29 D2
Albany St. Edin 93 E1
Albert Ave. Gran 61 F4
Albert Cl. Muss 127 D3
Albert Cres. Muss 127 D3
Albert Dr. Falk 59 F1
Albert Rd. East 168 C3
Albert Rd. Edin 94 A3
Albert Rd. Falk 60 A4
Albert St. Edin 93 F2
Albert St. Ros 46 C2
Albert Terr. Edin 123 D2
Albert Terr. Muss 126 C3
Alberta Ave. Liv 147 F2
Albion Pl. Edin 94 A1
Albion Rd. Edin 94 A1
Albion Terr. Edin 94 A1
Albyn Cofts. Brox 117 F3
Albyn Dr. Muri 173 E3
Albyn Ind Est. Brox 117 F4
Albyn Pl. Edin 93 D1
Albyn Terr. Brox 117 F3
Alder Gr. Dunf 29 E1
Alder Gr. Laur 61 D1
Alderbank Gdns. Edin ... 122 C2
Alderbank. Peni 203 F2
Alderbank Pl. Edin 122 C2
Alderbank Terr. Edin 122 C2
Alderston Dr. Dunf 29 E3
Alderston Pl. Hadd 100 C1
Alderston Rd. Hadd 131 F4
Alderstone Rd. Muri 173 E2
Aldersyde. Brid 86 C3
Aldhammer House. Pres . 96 C4
Alexander Ave. Falk 60 C3
Alexander Ave. Gran 61 E3
Alexander Dr. B of A 2 A4
Alexander Dr. Edin 122 B3
Alexander Dr. Pres 127 F4
Alexander Pk. Brox 117 F2
Alexander Pl. Ros 46 C3
Alexander Rd. Shot 191 E3
Alexander St. Cow 13 E3
Alexander St. Kirk 18 A4
Alexander St. Uph 117 D2
Alexander The Third St.

King 34 C1
Alexandra Bsns Pk. Kirkl . 119 D3
Alexandra Dr. All 9 F4
Alexandra Dr. Dog 145 F3
Alexandra Pl. Stir 2 B1
Alexandra St. Dunf 29 D3
Alexandra St. Kirk 17 E3
Alford Ave. Kirk 16 C4
Alfred Pl. Edin 123 F2
Alice Cox Wlk. Dunf 29 E1
Alice Gr. Cross 30 C3
Aline Ct. D Bay 48 A3
Alison Gr. Crossf 28 A1
Alison St. Kirk 17 D1
Allan Barr Ct. Falk 60 A1
Allan Cres. Dunf 29 F1
Allan Cres. Duni 36 B2
Allan Ct. Gran 40 C1
Allan Park Cres. Edin ... 122 B2
Allan Park Dr. Edin 122 B1
Allan Park Gdns. Edin .. 122 B1
Allan Park Loan. Edin ... 122 B1
Allan Park Rd. Edin 122 B1
Allan Pk. Cow 13 D1
Allan Pk. Kirkl 89 D1
Allan Pk. Stir 7 D4
Allan Rd. Whit 169 F3
Allan St. Edin 93 D1
Allan Terr. Dalk 157 D2
Allanbank Rd. Lar 38 B1
Allandale Cotts. Bon 57 E1
Allanfield. Edin 93 F1
Allanton Rd. Shot 191 E1
Allanvale Rd. B of A 1 C4
Allanwater Gdns. B of A .. 2 A4
Allanwood Ct. B of A 2 A4
Allen Gr. Bla 26 C4
Aller Pl. Liv 147 D2
Allermuir Ave. Rosl 180 C3
Allermuir Rd. Edin 153 D3
Allison Pl. Kirkl 89 D1
Alloa Pk. B of A 9 F3
Alloa Rd. Clack 11 D2
Alloa Rd. N Sau 5 E2
Alloa Rd. Sten 39 D2
Alloa St. Edin 93 D3
Alloway Cres. Bon 57 F3
Allowey Dr. Cowie 20 B4
Alma La. Falk 60 A3
Alma St. Falk 60 A3
Alma St. Inver 47 E2
Alma Terr. Falk 60 A3
Almond Ave. Kirkl 119 F4
Almond Bank Cotts. Edin 91 D3
Almond Cres. Bonn 182 A3
Almond Ct. Edin 124 C2
Almond Ct. Liv 148 B3
Almond Ct. Stir 7 E3
Almond Ct. Whit 170 C4
Almond E. Liv 148 A3
Almond Gn. Edin 121 D4
Almond Gr. E Cal 148 C3
Almond Gr. Que 89 E4
Almond Interchange. Liv 148 A2
Almond Pk. Liv 148 A3
Almond Pl. Kirk 17 E4
Almond Rd. Black 145 E1
Almond Rd. Dunf 29 F1
Almond Rd. Kirkl 119 F4
Almond Rd. Liv 148 A3
Almond Rd. Madd 83 E3
Almond S. Liv 148 B3
Almond Side. E Cal 148 B2
Almond Sq. Edin 121 D4
Almond Sq. Whit 170 C4
Almond St. Gran 61 E3
Almond Terr. East 168 B3
Almond Terr. Madd 83 F3
Almond View. Black 146 A1
Almond Vly Cal 148 A2
Almond West Rd. Liv 148 A2
Almondbank Terr. Edin . 122 C2
Almondell Ct. Brox 117 F3
Almondell Rd. Brox 117 F3
Almondell Terr. E Cal .. 148 C3
Almondhill Rd. Kirkl 89 D1
Almondside. Kirkl 89 D1
Almondside. Muri 147 F1
Almondvale Ave. Muri .. 147 F1
Almondvale Bvd. Muri .. 147 F1
Almondvale Dr. Muri ... 147 F1
Almondvale E. Muri 147 F1
Almondvale N. Muri 147 F1
Almondvale Parkway. Muri 147 F1
Almondvale Rd. Liv 147 F1
Almondvale Roundabout.
Muri 147 F1
Almondvale S. Liv 147 F1
Almondvale W. Muri 147 F1
Almondview. Muri 147 F1
Alness St. Dunf 28 C1
Alnwickhill Cres. Edin .. 154 C3
Alnwickhill Ct. Edin 154 C3
Alnwickhill Dr. Edin 154 C3
Alnwickhill Gdns. Edin . 154 C3
Alnwickhill Gr. Edin 154 C3
Alnwickhill Loan. Edin .. 154 C3

Alnwickhill Pk. Edin 155 D3
Alnwickhill Rd. Edin 155 D4
Alnwickhill Terr. Edin .. 154 C3
Alnwickhill View. Edin .. 154 C3
Alpha St. B'ness 62 C3
Alva Pl. Edin 94 A1
Alva St. Edin 123 D4
Alyth Dr. Pol 62 A1
Amberley Path. Gran 61 F3
Ambrose Rise. Muri 148 A1
Amisfield Pk. Hadd 132 B4
Amisfield Pl. Hadd 132 B4
Amisfield Pl. Long 98 C3
Amos Path. Loan 180 C4
Amulree Pl. B'ness 63 E4
Ancrum Bank. Dalk 156 C1
Ancrum Rd. Dalk 156 C1
Anderson Ave. Arm 143 F2
Anderson Ave. Crossf ... 28 A1
Anderson Ave. Newt ... 183 D3
Anderson Cres. Gail 81 F3
Anderson Dr. Cow 13 D1
Anderson Dr. Den 36 C1
Anderson Dr. Sten 39 D1
Anderson La. Kirk 17 D1
Anderson La. Kirk 23 F2
Anderson La. Ros 46 B3
Anderson Park Rd. Den .. 36 C1
Anderson Pl. Edin 93 F3
Anderson Pl. Stir 7 D2
Anderson St. Bon 58 A4
Anderson St. Kirk 18 A4
Anderson Terr. Bank 57 D2
Andrew Ave. Bog 145 F3
Andrew Cres. Sten 38 B2
Andrew Ct. Peni 203 F4
Andrew Dodd's Ave. May 183 F4
Andrew St. Loch 14 A3
Andrew Wood Ct. Edin .. 93 E3
Angle Park Terr. Edin ... 122 C3
Angres Ct. Dan 156 A4
Angus Rd. Car 230 A1
Angus St. B' ness 63 E3
Ann St. Edin 93 D1
Annabel Ct. Inver 47 E1
Annan Ct. Falk 60 A1
Annandale St. Edin 93 F1
Annandale Street La. Edin 93 F1
Anne Dr. B of A 2 A3
Anne Dr. Sten 38 C2
Anne St. Edin 93 D1
Anne St. Stir 2 A2
Anne St. Bog 145 F3
Anne St. Peni 203 F4
Annet Rd. Bank 57 E3
Annfield Ct. Glad 129 E3
Annfield Dr. Stir 7 E3
Annfield. Edin 93 E3
Annfield Gdns. Stir 7 E3
Annfield St. Edin 93 E3
Annfield. Tran 128 C3
Anson Ave. Falk 59 F2
Antigua St. Edin 93 F1
Antonine Ct. B' ness 63 E3
Antonine Gdns. Falk 59 E3
Antonine Gr. Bon 57 F2
Appin Cres. Dunf 29 E3
Appin Cres. Kirk 16 C4
Appin Gr. Pol 61 F2
Appin Terr. Edin 122 B2
Appin Terr. Shot 192 A2
Appleton Parkway. Liv .. 146 C2
Arboretum Ave. Edin 93 D1
Arboretum Pl. Edin 93 D2
Arboretum Rd. Edin 93 D2
Arbroath Cres. Stir 2 A2
Arbuthnot Rd. Loan 181 E4
Arbuthnot St. Falk 59 F3
Arcade. Liv 148 A3
Arcade. Stir 7 D4
Archers Ave. Stir 7 E2
Archers Cl. Gull 52 A1
Archibald Pl. Edin 123 E4
Archibald Russell Ct. Pol . 61 E3
Ard Ct. Gran 61 E3
Ardeer Pl. Dunf 29 E1
Arden St. Edin 123 E3
Ardgowan Pl. Shot 191 F3
Ardmillan Pl. Edin 122 C3
Ardmillan Terr. Edin 122 C3
Ardshiel Ave. Edin 91 E1
Ardvreck Pl. Sten 39 D2
Argyle Cres. Edin 125 E4
Argyle Park Terr. Edin .. 123 E3
Argyle Pl. Bonn 181 F3
Argyle Pl. Edin 123 E3
Argyll Ave. Falk 60 B3
Argyll Pk. W E Cal 148 B2
Argyll Pl. All 10 B4
Argyll St. All 10 B4
Arkaig Dr. Crossf 28 B1
Arkwright Ct. N Ber 54 A4
Armadale Rd. Whit 170 A4
Armine Pl. Peni 204 A4
Armour Ave. Cowie 20 B4
Arnot Pl. Pol 82 B4

Arnot St. Falk 60 B2
Arnothill Ct. Falk 59 F3
Arnothill. Falk 60 A2
Arnothill Gdns. Falk 60 A2
Arnothill La. Falk 60 A2
Arnothill Mews. Falk 60 A2
Arnott Gdns. Edin 122 A1
Arnprior Rd. Gore 207 D3
Arns Gr. All 9 F4
Arnswell. N Sau 5 E1
Aran Cres. Kirk 16 C4
Arran Ct. All 10 A3
Arran Ct. Gran 61 E3
Arran Pl. Edin 125 E2
Arran Pl. Edin 125 E2
Arran Terr. Falk 59 E3
Arras Gr. Auch 204 A4
Arrol Cres. All 10 B4
Arrol Pl. Que 89 E4
Arrol Sq. Liv 146 C3
Arthur Pl. Cow 13 E2
Arthur St. Cow 13 E2
Arthur St. Dunf 29 D3
Arthur St. Edin 93 F2
Arthur Street La. Edin ... 93 F2
Arthur View Cres. Dan .. 156 A4
Arthur View Terr. Dan .. 156 A4
Arthur's Dr. Sten 38 C1
Artillery Pk. Hadd 101 D1
Ash Braes. Kin 23 E2
Ash Gr. All 10 B3
Ash Gr. Black 171 E4
Ash Gr. Bog 145 F3
Ash Gr. Cow 13 D2
Ash Gr. Dunb 78 A1
Ash Gr. Dunf 46 B4
Ash Gr. Laur 61 D1
Ash Gr. Liv 148 A3
Ash Gr. Oak 27 E3
Ash Gr. Sten 38 C1
Ash La. Loan 180 C4
Ash Terr. Stir 6 C3
Ashbank Terr. E Cal 148 C2
Ashbrae Gdns. Stir 7 D1
Ashburnham Gdns. Que . 68 B3
Ashburnham Rd. Que 89 E4
Ashfield Ct. Dunb 78 C1
Ashfield Pl. Dunb 78 C1
Ashgrove. May 183 F4
Ashgrove. Muss 126 C3
Ashgrove Pl. Muss 126 C3
Ashgrove View. Muss ... 126 C3
Ashley Ct. Lin 84 C3
Ashley Dr. Edin 122 C2
Ashley Gdns. Edin 122 C2
Ashley Gr. Edin 122 C2
Ashley Hall Gdns. Lin ... 84 C3
Ashley Pl. Edin 93 F2
Ashley Rd. Pol 62 A1
Ashley St. Bon 57 F3
Ashley Terr. Edin 10 A4
Ashley Terr. Edin 122 C2
Ashton Gr. Edin 124 A1
Ashville Terr. Edin 94 A3
Asquith St. Kirk 17 D2
Assembly St. Edin 94 A3
Assynt Bank. Peni 204 A3
Atheling Gr. Que 89 E4
Athol Cres. Laur 61 D2
Athol Pl. Bath 145 D4
Athol Pl. Dunf 29 E2
Athol Terr. Bath 145 D4
Atholl Cres. Edin 123 D4
Atholl Crescent La. Edin 123 D4
Atholl Pl. Stir 1 C1
Atholl Terr. Kirk 16 B4
Attlee Cres. May 183 F3
Auchengray Rd. Auc 216 C1
Auchinbaird. N Sau 5 E1
Auchingane. Edin 153 F3
Auchinlec Ct. Edin 93 E3
Auchterderran Rd. Loch .. 14 A4
Auction Mart. Hadd 101 D1
Audenhard Terr. Ston ... 171 E1
Auld Orch. Bonn 182 B3
Auldgate. Kirkl 89 D1
Auldhame Cotts. E Lin .. 55 F3
Auldhill Ave. Brid 86 B2
Auldhill Cotts. Brid 86 B2
Auldhill Cres. Brid 86 B2
Auldhill Dr. Brid 86 B2
Auldhill Entry. Brid 86 B2
Auldhill Pl. Brid 86 B2
Auldhill Rd. Brid 86 B2
Auldhill Terr. Brid 86 B2
Ava St. Kirk 17 D1
Aven Dr. Laur 60 C2
Avenue Pk. B of A 1 C4
Avenue Pk. E Cal 148 B2
Avenue Pk. W E Cal 148 B2
Avenue Rd. Cocke 97 E2
Avenue Rd. Dalk 156 C1
Avenue The. B of A 2 A4
Avenue The. Brid 86 B4
Avenue The. Giff 163 F2
Avenue The. Gore 183 E3
Avenue The. Liv 147 F2
Avenue The. Loch 14 B4

nue The. Rat ... 151 F4
nue The. Sten ... 39 E1
nue The. Whit ... 170 A3
nue Villas. Edin ... 92 C1
ton. For ... 215 D1
n Ct. Falk ... 60 B1
n Dr. Lin ... 84 B4
r. Gr. Edin ... 91 D2
r. Gr. Peni ... 204 A3
r. Pl. B' ness ... 111 F3
n Pl. B' ness ... 63 F4
n Rd. Bath ... 91 D2
n Rd. Bath ... 145 D4
n Rd. Edin ... 91 D2
n Rd. Gran ... 62 B4
n Rd. Madd ... 83 F3
n St. Dunf ... 36 B2
n St. Gran ... 40 A1
m Terr. Avon ... 112 A3
nbank Ave. Gran ... 61 F3
bridge Rd. Slam ... 110 B4
ndale Cres. Arm ... 143 F3
ndale Dr. Arm ... 143 F3
ndale Pl. Edin ... 93 D1
ndale Rd. Pol ... 62 A2
nlea Ter Rd ... F2
rmill Rd. Lin ... 84 B4
rmill View. Lin ... 84 B4
nside Dr. Dunf ... 36 B3
ntoun Cres. Madd ... 84 A3
ntoun Pk. Lin ... 84 B3
s Wynd. Pres ... 96 C1
un Cres. Burn ... 33 F1
un Gr. Dunf ... 28 C3

Bakehouse Cl. Edin ... 123 F4
Baker St. B' ness ... 63 F3
Baker St. Stir ... 7 D4
Balantyne Pl. Lin ... 147 D2
Balbakie Rd. East ... 168 C3
Balbardie Ave. Bath ... 145 D4
Balbardie Cres. Bath ... 145 D4
Balbardie Rd. Bath ... 145 D3
Balbirnie Pl. Edin ... 122 C4
Balcarres Ct. Edin ... 123 D1
Balcarres Pl. Muss ... 126 B4
Balcarres Rd. Muss ... 126 B4
Balcarres St. Edin ... 123 D1
Balcastle Rd. Slam ... 110 A3
Balderston Gdns. Edin ... 124 A1
Balderstone's Wynd. N Ber .. 54 B4
Baldridgeburn. Dunf ... 28 C3
Baldwin Cres. Kirk ... 17 D3
Balfour Cres. Lar ... 38 B1
Balfour Cres. Plea ... 20 B2
Balfour Ct. Edin ... 91 D1
Balfour Pl. Edin ... 93 F2
Balfour St. All ... 10 B4
Balfour St. Bann ... 7 E1
Balfour St. Bon ... 57 F3
Balfour St. Edin ... 93 F2
Balfour St. Kirk ... 17 D3
Balfour St. N Ber ... 54 B4
Balfour St. Stir ... 1 C1
Balfour Terr. Auch ... 180 A1
Balfour's Sq. Tran ... 128 B3
Balfron Loan. Edin ... 91 E1
Balgone Barns Cotts. E Lin .. 54 B1
Balgreen Ave. Edin ... 122 A3
Balgreen Gdns. Edin ... 122 A3
Balgreen Pk. Edin ... 122 A3
Balgreen Rd. Edin ... 122 A3
Balgreen Rd. Edin ... 122 B2
Baliol St. King ... 34 C1
Ballantyne Rd. Edin ... 93 F3
Ballast Bank. Inver ... 47 E1
Ballater Dr. Stir ... 2 A1
Ballencrieff Toll. Bath ... 114 A1
Ballengeich Pass. Stir ... 2 A1
Ballengeich Rd. Stir ... 1 C1
Ballingry La. Loch ... 14 A4
Ballingry St. Loch ... 14 A4
Balloch Rd. Shot ... 191 F3
Balm Well Ave. Edin ... 155 D4
Balm Well Gr. Edin ... 155 D3
Balm Well Terr. Edin ... 155 D3
Balmoral Dr. Falk ... 59 F1
Balmoral Dr. Kirk ... 16 B3
Balmoral Gdns. Muri ... 173 D3
Balmoral Gdns. Pol ... 82 B4
Balmoral Pl. Edin ... 93 D1
Balmoral Pl. Stir ... 38 C2
Balmoral Pl. Stir ... 7 D4
Balmoral Rd. B'ness ... 62 C3
Balmoral St. Falk ... 59 F2
Balmuir Rd. Bath ... 144 C4
Balmulzier Rd. Slam ... 110 A4
Balnacraig. Crossf ... 28 A1
Balquhatstone Cres. Slam 110 A3
Balquhidderock. Stir ... 7 E2
Balsusney Rd. Kirk ... 17 D2
Baltic St. Edin ... 94 A3
Balure Cres. Fall ... 8 B2
Balvaird Pl. Dunf ... 29 D2
Balwearie Cres. Kirk ... 17 D1
Balwearie Gdns. Kirk ... 16 C1
Balwearie Rd. Kirk ... 17 D1
Banchory Cotts. King ... 34 C3
Banchory Pl. Tull ... 4 A2
Bancroft Ave. Liv ... 147 F2
Bandeath Rd. Fall ... 8 A1
Bandon Ave. Kirk ... 17 F4
Bangholm Ave. Edin ... 93 D3
Bangholm Bower Ave. Edin ... 93 D3
Bangholm Gr. Edin ... 93 D3
Bangholm Loan. Edin ... 93 D3
Bangholm Pk. Edin ... 93 D3
Bangholm Pl. Edin ... 93 D3
Bangholm Rd. Edin ... 93 D3
Bangholm Terr. Edin ... 93 D2
Bangholm View. Edin ... 93 D3
Bangly Brae. Ath ... 100 A2
Bangor Rd. Edin ... 93 F3
Bank Pk. E Lin ... 103 F4
Bank Rd. East ... 168 C3
Bank St. All ... 10 A3
Bank St. E Cal ... 148 B2
Bank St. Edin ... 123 E4
Bank St. Falk ... 60 A3
Bank St. Gran ... 40 A1
Bank St. Inver ... 47 E1
Bank St. Kirk ... 17 F4
Bank St. Loch ... 14 A4
Bank St. N Ber ... 54 B4
Bank St. Peni ... 203 F2
Bank St. Slam ... 110 A3
Bank St. Stir ... 7 D4
Bank St. Whit ... 170 A4
Bankhead Ave. Edin ... 121 D2
Bankhead Broadway. Edin 121 D2
Bankhead Cotts. E Lin ... 75 E3

Bankhead Cres. Bank ... 57 E3
Bankhead Crossway N. Edin ... 121 D2
Bankhead Crossway S. Edin ... 121 E1
Bankhead Dr. Edin ... 121 D2
Bankhead Gr. Dal ... 68 B1
Bankhead Ind Est. Edin ... 121 E2
Bankhead Medway. Edin ... 121 E2
Bankhead Pl. Edin ... 121 E1
Bankhead Rd. N Sau ... 5 E2
Bankhead St. Edin ... 121 E1
Bankhead Terr. Edin ... 121 D1
Bankhead Way. Edin ... 121 D1
Bankhill Ct. Gran ... 61 E3
Bankpark Brae. Tran ... 128 A4
Bankpark Cres. Tran ... 128 A4
Bankpark Gr. Tran ... 128 B4
Bankside Ct. Den ... 36 C1
Bankside. Falk ... 60 B4
Bankton Ct. Muri ... 174 A4
Bankton Dr. Muri ... 174 B4
Bankton Gdns. Muri ... 174 A4
Bankton Glade. Muri ... 174 A4
Bankton Gn. Muri ... 173 F4
Bankton Gr. Muri ... 174 A4
Bankton Pk E. Muri ... 173 F4
Bankton Pk W. Muri ... 148 A1
Bankton Rd. Muri ... 173 F4
Bankton Sq. Muri ... 173 F4
Bankton Terr. Pres ... 128 A4
Bankton Way. Muri ... 173 F4
Bankton Wlk. Muri ... 173 F4
Bannerman Ave. Inver ... 47 D2
Bannerman St. Dunf ... 29 D3
Bannoch Brae. Dunf ... 29 E2
Bannock Rd. Fall ... 8 B2
Bannockburn Rd. Cowie ... 20 B4
Bannockburn St. Stir ... 7 D3
Bannockburn Station Rd. Fall ... 8 A2
Bantaskine Dr. Falk ... 59 F2
Bantaskine Gdns. Falk ... 59 F2
Bantaskine Rd. Falk ... 59 F2
Bantaskine St. Falk ... 59 F2
Banton Pl. Bon ... 58 A2
Baptie Pl. B' ness ... 63 F3
Barassie Dr. Kirk ... 17 D4
Barbauchlaw Ave. Arm ... 143 F3
Barbour Ave. Stir ... 7 E3
Barbour Gr. Dunf ... 28 C3
Barclay Pl. Edin ... 123 D3
Barclay Rd. King ... 34 C2
Barclay St. Cow ... 13 D2
Barclay Terr. Edin ... 123 D3
Barclay Way. Liv ... 147 F4
Barham Rd. Ros ... 46 B1
Barharrow. Lin ... 84 C3
Barkly Ct. Kirk ... 17 E4
Barlaw Gdns. Arm ... 144 A3
Barleyhill. Bon ... 58 A4
Barleyknowe Cres. Gore ... 183 D1
Barleyknowe Gdns. Gore .. 183 D1
Barleyknowe La. Gore ... 183 D1
Barleyknowe Pl. Gore ... 183 D1
Barleyknowe Rd. Gore ... 183 D1
Barleyknowe St. Gore ... 183 D1
Barleyknowe Terr. Gore ... 183 D1
Barn Rd. Stir ... 7 D4
Barnbougle Ride. Dal ... 90 B4
Barnego Rd. Duni ... 36 B2
Barnes Gn. Liv ... 147 E4
Barnet Cres. Kirk ... 17 D1
Barnhill Dr. Tull ... 4 B2
Barnhill Pl. D Bay ... 48 B2
Barnhill Rd. D Bay ... 48 B2
Barns Court. Whit ... 170 C4
Barns Ness Terr. E Lin ... 139 D4
Barns Pk. D Bay ... 48 A1
Barnsdale Rd. Stir ... 7 D2
Barnshot Rd. Edin ... 153 D3
Barnton Ave. Edin ... 91 E3
Barnton Ave W. Edin ... 91 D2
Barnton Brae. Edin ... 91 D2
Barnton Ct. Edin ... 91 D2
Barnton Gdns. Edin ... 91 E2
Barnton Gr. Edin ... 91 D2
Barnton La. Falk ... 60 A2
Barnton Loan. Edin ... 91 E2
Barnton Park Ave. Edin ... 91 E2
Barnton Park Cres. Edin ... 91 E2
Barnton Park Dell. Edin ... 91 E2
Barnton Park Dr. Edin ... 91 E2
Barnton Park Gdns. Edin ... 91 E2
Barnton Park Gr. Edin ... 91 E2
Barnton Park Pl. Edin ... 91 E2
Barnton Park View. Edin ... 91 E2
Barnton Park Wood. Edin ... 91 D2
Barnton Pk. Edin ... 91 F2
Barnton St. Stir ... 7 D4
Barntongate Ave. Edin ... 91 D1
Barntongate Dr. Edin ... 91 D1
Barntongate Terr. Edin ... 91 D1
Barnwell Rd. Stir ... 2 B1
Barons Hill Ave. Lin ... 85 D4
Barons Hill Ct. Lin ... 85 D4
Baronscourt Rd. Edin ... 94 B1
Baronscourt Terr. Edin ... 124 B1

Barony Ct. B' ness ... 63 F3
Barony Pl. Edin ... 93 E1
Barony St. Edin ... 93 E1
Barony Terr. Edin ... 121 E4
Barr Cres. Inver ... 47 E1
Barra Pl. Sten ... 39 D2
Barracks Roundabout. Liv . 146 C3
Barracks St. Cocke ... 97 E2
Barrie Ct. Liv ... 148 B3
Barrie Pl. Dunf ... 28 C3
Barrie Pl. Gran ... 61 E3
Barrie Rd. Sten ... 38 C2
Barrie St. Dunf ... 28 C3
Barrie Terr. Bath ... 145 E3
Barton Rd. Ros ... 46 A1
Barton Terr. Fau ... 193 F3
Bass Rock View. N Ber ... 55 D4
Bastion Wynd. Stir ... 7 D4
Bath Pl. Edin ... 95 D1
Bath Rd. Edin ... 94 A3
Bath St. Edin ... 125 D4
Bath St La. Edin ... 125 D4
Bathfield. Edin ... 93 F3
Bathgate Rd. Black ... 171 E4
Bathgate Rd. Whit ... 170 C4
Bathville Bsns Ctr. Arm ... 144 A3
Baton Rd. Shot ... 191 E3
Battery Rd. Gran ... 62 B4
Battery Rd. Inver ... 68 B3
Battock Rd. Madd ... 62 C4
Bavelaw Cres. Peni ... 203 E3
Bavelaw Gdns. Bale ... 151 E1
Bavelaw Rd. Bale ... 151 E1
Baxter Cres. Den ... 36 B1
Baxter St. Fall ... 8 B2
Baxter's Pl. Edin ... 93 F1
Baxter's Wynd. Falk ... 60 A2
Bayne Gdns. Madd ... 84 A3
Bayside Dr. Stir ... 2 A1
Bayswell Pk. Dunb ... 78 B2
Bayswell Rd. Dunb ... 78 B2
Beach La. Edin ... 95 D1
Beach La. Muss ... 126 A4
Beach Rd. Gran ... 41 D1
Beach Rd. N Ber ... 54 A4
Beachmont Ct. Dunb ... 78 C1
Beachmont Pl. Dunb ... 78 C1
Bean Row. Falk ... 60 A2
Beancross Rd. Gran ... 61 E3
Bearcroft Gdns. Gran ... 61 F4
Bearcroft Rd. Gran ... 62 B4
Bearford Pl. Hadd ... 132 B4
Bearside Rd. Stir ... 7 D2
Beath View. Dunf ... 29 F2
Beath View Rd. Cow ... 13 D1
Beatlie Rd. Winch ... 88 A2
Beaton Ave. Bann ... 7 E1
Beatty Ave. Stir ... 2 B2
Beatty Cres. Kirk ... 17 E4
Beatty Pl. Dunf ... 29 D1
Beauchamp Gr. Edin ... 155 D4
Beauchamp Rd. Edin ... 155 D4
Beauclerc St. Alva ... 5 D4
Beaufort Dr. Sten ... 39 D2
Beaufort Dr. Sten ... 39 D2
Beaufort Rd. Edin ... 123 E2
Beauly Ct. Falk ... 60 B1
Beauly Ct. Gran ... 61 E2
Beauly Dr. Liv ... 148 A2
Beauly Pl. Kirk ... 16 C4
Beaumont Dr. Sten ... 39 D1
Beaverbank Pl. Edin ... 93 E2
Beaverhall Rd. Edin ... 93 E2
Beck Cres. Dunf ... 29 E3
Beda Pl. Fall ... 8 B3
Bedford Ct. All ... 10 A3
Bedford Ct. Edin ... 93 D1
Bedford Pl. All ... 10 A3
Bedford St. Edin ... 93 D1
Bedford Terr. Edin ... 125 E4
Bedlormie Dr. Blac ... 142 B1
Beech Ave. Abe ... 48 C3
Beech Ave. D Bay ... 48 C2
Beech Ave. E Cal ... 148 A1
Beech Ave. N Midd ... 206 C2
Beech Ave. Plea ... 20 B2
Beech Cres. Duni ... 36 B2
Beech Cres. Lar ... 59 E4
Beech Gr. Ave. Dalk ... 156 C1
Beech Gr. Dunf ... 46 B4
Beech Gr. Liv ... 148 A4
Beech Gr. Stir ... 170 B3
Beech Pl. Gran ... 61 E3
Beech Pl. Liv ... 147 E2
Beech Pl. Bog ... 145 F3
Beech Rd. B'ness ... 63 F3
Beech Terr. Pen ... 160 B3
Beech Way. D Bay ... 48 A3
Beechbank Cres. E Cal ... 148 C1
Beeches The. D Bay ... 48 A3
Beeches The. Gull ... 52 A1
Beeches The. Newt ... 183 D4
Beechgrove Rd. May ... 183 F3
Beechmount Cres. Edin ... 122 A4

Beechmount Ct. Shot ... 192 A1
Beechmount Pk. Edin ... 122 A3
Beechwood. Crossf ... 28 A1
Beechwood Gdns. Black .. 145 E1
Beechwood Gr. Pump ... 117 D1
Beechwood. Lin ... 85 D3
Beechwood Mains. Edin ... 122 A4
Beechwood N Sau ... 5 E1
Beechwood Pk. Liv ... 146 C4
Beechwood Pk. Newt ... 183 D3
Beechwood Pk. Pump ... 117 D1
Beechwood Pl. Black ... 145 E1
Beechwood Rd. Hadd ... 131 F4
Beechwood Terr. Edin ... 94 A2
Begbie Pl. Liv ... 147 D3
Begg Ave. Falk ... 59 F2
Beldormey Pl. Dunf ... 29 E3
Belfield Ct. Muss ... 126 A3
Belford Ave. Edin ... 122 C4
Belford Gdns. Edin ... 92 C1
Belford Pk. Edin ... 122 C4
Belford Pl. Edin ... 122 C4
Belford Rd. Edin ... 122 C4
Belgrave Cres. Edin ... 93 D1
Belgrave Crescent La. Edin 93 D1
Belgrave Gdns. Edin ... 121 F4
Belgrave Mews. Edin ... 92 C1
Belgrave Pl. Edin ... 92 C3
Belgrave Rd. Edin ... 121 F3
Belhaven Pl. Edin ... 123 D1
Belhaven Rd. Dunb ... 78 B1
Belhaven Terr. Edin ... 123 D1
Bell Ct. Gran ... 40 C1
Bell Pl. Edin ... 93 D1
Bell Rd. Ros ... 46 A1
Bell Sq. Muri ... 173 E3
Bell Stane. Que ... 68 A1
Bell's Mill Terr. Winch ... 87 F1
Bell's Mills. Edin ... 122 C4
Bell's Wynd. Falk ... 60 A2
Bellaknowes Ind Est. Inver .. 47 D2
Bellamond Cres. Whit ... 170 B4
Bellenden Gdns. Edin ... 124 B1
Bellevue Ave. Dunb ... 78 C1
Bellevue Cres. Edin ... 93 E1
Bellevue. Edin ... 93 E1
Bellevue Gdns. Edin ... 93 E2
Bellevue Gr. Edin ... 93 E1
Bellevue. Madd ... 82 C4
Bellevue Pl. Edin ... 93 E1
Bellevue Rd. All ... 9 F3
Bellevue Rd. Edin ... 93 E1
Bellevue St. Falk ... 60 B2
Bellevue St. Edin ... 93 E1
Bellfield Ave. Dalk ... 156 C1
Bellfield Ave. E Cal ... 148 C1
Bellfield Cres. Kirk ... 18 A4
Bellfield La. Edin ... 125 D4
Bellfield Rd. Bann ... 7 F1
Bellfield Rd. Stir ... 7 D3
Bellfield Sq. Pres ... 127 F4
Bellfield St. Edin ... 125 D4
Bellfield Terr. Edin ... 125 D4
Bellhouse Rd. Abe ... 49 D4
Bellman Way. D Bay ... 48 A3
Bellman's Rd. Peni ... 203 F3
Bellona Terr. Fau ... 193 F3
Bells Brae. Edin ... 123 D4
Bells Burn Ave. Lin ... 85 E4
Bellsdyke Rd. Air ... 39 E3
Bellsdyke Rd. Sten ... 38 B2
Bellsmains. N Mid ... 207 E3
Bellsmeadow Rd. Falk ... 60 B2
Bellsquarry S. Muri ... 173 F3
Bellyeoman La. Dunf ... 29 E3
Bellyeoman Rd. Dunf ... 29 E3
Bellyford Rd. Elph ... 128 A1
Belmont Ave. Edin ... 121 F4
Belmont Ave. Shi ... 81 F4
Belmont Cres. Edin ... 121 F4
Belmont Dr. Shot ... 192 A1
Belmont Gdns. Edin ... 121 F4
Belmont Pk. Edin ... 122 A4
Belmont Rd. Guri ... 152 B3
Belmont St. Falk ... 60 B2
Belmont Terr. Edin ... 122 A4
Belmont View. Edin ... 122 A4
Belstane Pk. Car ... 230 A2
Belstane Rd. Car ... 230 A2
Belsyde Ct. Lin ... 84 B3
Belvedere Pk. Edin ... 93 E3
Belvedere Rd. Bath ... 144 C4
Belwood Cres. Auch ... 180 A1
Ben Alder Pl. Kirk ... 16 C3
Ben Ledi Rd. Kirk ... 16 C3
Ben Nevis Pl. Kirk ... 16 C3
Ben Sayers Pk. N Ber ... 54 C3
Benarty St. Kirk ... 16 C3
Bendachin Dr. Dunf ... 29 F3
Bendameer Rd. Burn ... 33 E1

Benhar Rd. East 167 F1
Benhar Rd. Shot 192 A3
Benjamin Dr. B' ness 63 F3
Bennett Wood Terr. Winch .. 87 F2
Bennochy Ave. Kirk 17 D3
Bennochy Ct. Kirk 17 D3
Bennochy Gdns. Kirk 17 D3
Bennochy Rd. Kirk 16 C3
Bentheads. Bann 19 F4
Benview. Bann 7 E1
Benview Terr. Fish 5 F2
Beresford Ave. Edin 93 E3
Beresford Gdns. Edin 93 E3
Beresford Pl. Edin 93 D3
Beresford Rise. Muri 148 A1
Berkeley St. Stir 7 D2
Bernard Shaw St. Dunf 28 C3
Bernard St. Edin 94 A3
Bernard Terr. Edin 123 F3
Berry St. Loch 14 A4
Berryhill. Cowie 20 C4
Berryhill Cres. Gran 61 F3
Berryhill Pl. Shot 192 A1
Berrylaw Pl. Dunf 28 C2
Berrylaw Rd. Crossf 28 B2
Bertram Pl. Shot 191 E3
Bertram St. Shot 168 B3
Bertram St. Shot 191 F3
Bervie Dr. Muri 173 F3
Berwick Pl. Kirk 17 E3
Berwick Pl. Kirk 18 A4
Beulah. Muss 126 C3
Bevan Dr. Alva 5 E4
Bevan Pl. Ros 46 C2
Bevan Rd. May 183 E3
Bevan-lee Ct. Dalk 157 D2
Beveridge Ave. May 183 F3
Beveridge Cl. May 183 F3
Beveridge Rd. Kirk 17 D2
Beveridge Sq. Muri 147 F1
Beveridge St. Dunf 29 E1
Bickerton Terr. Whit 170 A3
Bickram Cres. Bla 26 B4
Biggar Rd. Edin 154 A2
Biggar Rd. Peni 202 C3
Biggin Wa's. Kirk 17 F4
Bingham Ave. Edin 124 C3
Bingham Broadway. Edin ... 125 D3
Bingham Cres. Edin 125 D3
Bingham Crossway. Edin ... 124 C3
Bingham Dr. Edin 125 D3
Bingham Medway. Edin 124 C3
Bingham Pl. Edin 124 C3
Bingham Way. Edin 124 C3
Binn Ave. Burn 33 F1
Binnie Pl. Gran 61 F3
Binniehill Rd. Slam 110 A3
Binning Rd. Inver 47 D2
Binning Wood Rd. E Lin 75 F4
Binny Park. Brid 116 C4
Birch Ave. Stir 6 C3
Birch Cres. Loan 180 C4
Birch Ct. Edin 91 D1
Birch Ct. Liv 147 E1
Birch Gr. Dunf 46 B4
Birchbank. Cow 13 D1
Birchwood. N Sau 5 E1
Birk Hedges. Hadd 130 C3
Birkdale Dr. Uph 116 C2
Birkenshaw Way. Arm 143 F3
Birkenside. Gore 207 E3
Birkfield Loan. Car 230 B1
Birkfield Pl. Car 230 B1
Birkhill Cres. B'ness 63 F3
Birkhill Rd. Cam 6 C3
Birkhill St. Edin 93 E3
Birkhill St. B'ness 63 F3
Birnam Ct. Falk 39 E1
Birnam Rd. Kirk 16 C4
Birnie Brae. Loch 14 A4
Birnie St. Loch 14 A4
Birniehill Ave. Bath 144 C2
Birniehill Cres. Bath 144 C2
Birniehill Rd. Bath 144 C2
Birniehill Terr. Bath 144 C2
Birniewell Rd. Slam 110 A3
Birrell Dr. Dunf 29 E1
Birrell Street Wynd. Kirk ... 17 E3
Birrell's La. Kirk 17 F4
Birsley Rd. Tran 128 B3
Bishops Pk. E Cal 148 A1
Bishops Pk. E Cal 148 A1
Bishops Rd. Lin 84 B1
Black Craigs. Kirk 16 B4
Blackbarony Rd. Edin 124 A1
Blackburn Ave. Dunf 28 B3
Blackburn Dr. Cow 13 D2
Blackburn Rd. Add 171 F1
Blackburn Rd. Bog 145 E2
Blackburnhall. Ston 171 E3
Blackchapel Cl. Edin 125 D2
Blackchapel Rd. Edin 125 D2
Blackcot Ave. May 183 E3
Blackcot Dr. May 183 E3
Blackcot Pl. May 183 E3
Blackcot Rd. May 183 E3
Blacket Ave. Edin 123 F3
Blacket Pl. Edin 123 F3
Blackfaulds Ct. Fau 193 F3

Blackfaulds Dr. Fau 193 F3
Blackfaulds Pl. Fau 193 F3
Blackford Ave. Edin 123 E2
Blackford Bank. Edin 123 E2
Blackford Gate. Edin 123 E2
Blackford Glen Rd. Edin ... 123 F1
Blackford Hill Gr. Edin 123 E1
Blackford Hill Rise. Edin .. 123 E1
Blackford Hill View. Edin .. 123 E1
Blackford Rd. Edin 123 E2
Blackfriars St. Edin 123 F4
Blackhall St. Shot 192 A2
Blackhill Rd. Blac 142 C2
Blackie Rd. Edin 94 A2
Blacklaw Rd. Dunf 29 E1
Blackmill Cres. Sten 39 D2
Blackmount Terr. Madd 82 C3
Blackmuir Pl. Tull 4 B2
Blackness Rd. Lin 84 A1
Blackston Rd. Avon 112 A3
Blackthorn Ct. Edin 91 D1
Blackwood Cres. Edin 123 F3
Blackwood Gn. Dunf 46 C4
Blaeberry Gdns. Edin 91 D1
Blaeberryhill Rd. Whit 170 B3
Blaefaulds Cres. Den 57 E4
Blair Ave. B' ness 63 F3
Blair Dr. Dunf 29 D3
Blair Dr. Kel 12 B4
Blair Pl. Kel 12 B4
Blair Pl. Kirk 16 B3
Blair St. Edin 123 E4
Blair St. Kel 12 B4
Blair Terr. Sten 39 D2
Blair's Cotts. Laur 61 E1
Blairdenon Cres. Falk 59 F2
Blairdenon Dr. N Sau 5 D1
Blairdenon Rd. Alva 4 C3
Blairforkie Dr. B of A 1 C4
Blairlodge Ave. Laur 82 B4
Blairlodge Ave. Pol 82 B4
Blairmore Rd. Kirk 16 C4
Blairmuckhole And Forrestdyke Rd.
  Sals 167 F4
Blairwood Wlk. Oak 26 C4
Blake St. Dunf 29 E3
Blamey Cres. Cow 13 D1
Blantyre Terr. Edin 123 D2
Blawearie Rd. Tran 128 B3
Bleachfield. Edin 93 D3
Bleachfield. Falk 60 A3
Blenheim Ct. Auch 204 C4
Blenheim Pl. Sten 38 C3
Blenheim Rd. Car 230 A1
Blindwell Brae. Giff 133 F1
Blindwells. Alva 4 A2
Blinkbonnie Terr. Slam 110 A3
Blinkbonny Ave. Edin 92 B1
Blinkbonny Cres. Edin 92 B1
Blinkbonny Gdns. Edin 92 B1
Blinkbonny Gr. Edin 92 B1
Blinkbonny Gr W. Edin 92 B1
Blinkbonny Rd. Curr 152 A2
Blinkbonny Terr. Falk 59 F2
Blinkbonny Terr. Edin 92 B1
Blinny Ct. Shot 192 A2
Bloom Ct. Liv 147 D2
Bloom Pl. Liv 147 D1
Bloom Roundabout. Liv 147 D2
Bloomfield Pl. Bath 145 D3
Blyth St. Kirk 17 F4
Bo'mains Rd. B' ness 63 F3
Bo'ness Rd. Gran 62 A3
Bo'ness Rd. Pol 61 F2
Bo'ness Rd. Que 67 F1
Boat Gn. Edin 93 E2
Bog Rd. Falk 60 A2
Bog Rd. Falk 60 C2
Bog Rd. Peni 203 F3
Bog Rd. Whit 170 A3
Bog The. B'ness 64 A4
Bogend Rd. Bann 19 F4
Bogend Rd. Lar 38 A4
Bogend Rd. Tor 37 F3
Boghall Dr. Bog 145 F3
Boghall Roundabout. Bog . 145 F3
Boghead Cres. Bath 144 C3
Bogie Wynd. Kirk 17 E3
Boglily Rd. Kirk 16 C2
Bogpark Rd. Muss 126 A3
Bogside Rd. Alla 122 A1
Bogwood Ct. May 183 E4
Bogwood Dr. Crossf 28 A1
Bogwood Rd. May 183 F3
Bohun Ct. Bann 7 E2
Bolam Ct. Burn 33 E3
Bolam Sq. Loch 14 A4
Bomar Ave. B'ness 63 F3
Bon Accord Cres. Shot 191 F3
Bonaly Ave. Edin 153 D3
Bonaly Brae. Edin 153 D3
Bonaly Cres. Edin 153 D3
Bonaly Dr. Edin 153 D3
Bonaly Gdns. Edin 153 D3
Bonaly Gr. Edin 153 D3
Bonaly Rd. Edin 153 D3
Bonaly Rise. Edin 153 D3
Bonaly Steading. Edin 153 D3
Bonaly Terr. Edin 153 D3

Bonaly Wester. Edin 153 D3
Bonar Pl. Edin 93 E3
Bonnar St. Dunf 29 D2
Bonnington Ave. Edin 93 E3
Bonnington Gr. Edin 93 E3
Bonnington Ind Est. Edin .. 93 F2
Bonnington. Rat 150 A4
Bonnington Rd. E Cal 150 A3
Bonnington Rd. Edin 93 F2
Bonnington Rd. Rat 150 A3
Bonnington Road La. Edin .. 93 F2
Bonnington Terr. Edin 93 E3
Bonnybank Ct. Gore 207 E4
Bonnybank Rd. Gore 207 E4
Bonnybridge Rd. Bon 57 F3
Bonnybridge Rd. Bon 57 F3
Bonnyfield Rd. Bon 57 F3
Bonnyhaugh. Edin 93 E2
Bonnyhaugh La. Edin 93 E2
Bonnyhill Rd. Bon 58 B2
Bonnyhill Rd. Falk 59 D2
Bonnyrigg Rd. Dalk 156 C1
Bonnyside Rd. Bon 58 A3
Bonnyton Pl. Dunf 29 E2
Bonnytoun Ave. Lin 85 E4
Bonnytoun Terr. Lin 85 E4
Bonnyview Gdns. Bon 58 A3
Bonnywood Ave. Bon 58 A4
Booth Ave. Ros 46 B2
Booth Pl. Falk 60 A2
Boothacre La. Edin 94 B2
Boreland Pk. Inver 47 E2
Boreland Rd. Inver 47 E2
Boreland Rd. Kirk 18 A4
Borestone Cres. Stir 7 D1
Borestone Ct. Stir 7 D1
Borestone Pl. Stir 7 D1
Boroughdales. Dunb 78 B1
Boroughloch La. Edin 123 F3
Boroughloch Sq. Edin 123 F3
Borrowlea Rd. Stir 7 E4
Borrowmeadow Rd. Stir 7 F4
Borrowstoun Cres. B'ness .. 63 F3
Borrowstoun Pl. B'ness 63 F3
Borrowstoun Rd. B'ness 64 A3
Borthwick Castle Pl.
  N Mid 207 F2
Borthwick Castle Rd.
  N Mid 207 F1
Borthwick Castle Terr.
  N Mid 207 F2
Borthwick Pl. Edin 122 C4
Boswall Ave. Edin 92 C3
Boswall Cres. Edin 92 C3
Boswall Dr. Edin 93 D3
Boswall Gdns. Edin 92 C3
Boswall Gn. Edin 93 D3
Boswall Gr. Edin 92 C3
Boswall Loan. Edin 92 C3
Boswall Parkway. Edin 92 C3
Boswall Pl. Edin 92 C3
Boswall Quadrant. Edin 92 C3
Boswall Rd. Edin 93 D3
Boswall Sq. Edin 92 C3
Boswall Terr. Edin 92 C3
Boswell St. King 35 D2
Boswell Dr. Oak 26 C3
Boswell Rd. Loch 14 A4
Bothkennar Rd. Air 39 F2
Bothkennar Rd. Sten 39 F2
Bothwell St. Dunf 29 D1
Bothwell St. Edin 94 A2
Boundary Rd E. Rat 151 F4
Boundary Rd N. Rat 151 F4
Boundary St. B'ness 64 A4
Bouprie Rise. D Bay 48 A2
Bourtree Gr. Bla 26 B4
Bow St. Stir 7 D4
Bowhill Terr. Edin 93 D3
Bowhouse Gdns. All 10 A3
Bowhouse Rd. All 10 A3
Bowhouse Rd. Gran 61 F3
Bowhouse Sq. Gran 61 E3
Bowhousebog Or Liquo.
  Shot 191 D1
Bowhousebog Rd. Shot ... 191 D1
Bowling Green Rd. Kirk 29 E3
Bowling Green Rd. Whit ... 170 A3
Bowling Green St. Cow 13 E2
Bowling Green The. Edin ... 93 E2
Bowmont Pl. Edin 123 F3
Bowmont Terr. Dunb 78 B1
Bowmore Wlk. Shot 192 A2
Bowyett. Torp 113 F3
Boyd Pl. Loch 14 A4
Boyd St. Falk 60 A3
Boyd St. Laur 61 D1
Boyd's Entry. Edin 123 F4
Boyd-Orr Dr. Auch 203 F4
Brackenlees Rd. Air 40 A3
Brackensbrae. Uph 117 D3
Bradbury St. Sten 39 D1
Brae Heads Loan. E Lin ... 103 E3
Brae Pk. Edin 91 D2
Brae Pk. Edin 91 D2
Brae Rd. B'ness 63 E3
Brae The. Auch 180 B1
Brae The. Bann 7 E1
Brae The. Cam 6 B3

Braefoot Gr. D Bay 48 A1
Braefoot Rd. B'ness 64 A3
Braefoot Terr. Edin 124 A1
Braehead. All 4 B1
Braehead. Alva 5 D4
Braehead Ave. Edin 91 D2
Braehead Ave. Lin 84 C3
Braehead Ave. Tull 4 B1
Braehead. B' ness 63 F4
Braehead Bank. Edin 91 D2
Braehead Cres. Edin 91 D2
Braehead Dr. Edin 91 D2
Braehead Loan. Edin 91 D2
Braehead Pk. Lin 84 C3
Braehead Pl. Lin 84 C3
Braehead Rd. Edin 91 D2
Braehead Rd. Lin 84 C3
Braehead Roundabout. Liv 147 E2
Braehead Row. Edin 91 D2
Braehead Terr. Lin 84 C3
Braehead View. Edin 91 D2
Braekirk Ave. Kir 149 E1
Braemar Cres. Car 230 A2
Braemar Cres. Falk 60 B3
Braemar Dr. Falk 59 F3
Braemar Gdns. Dunf 36 B2
Braemar Gdns. Pol 82 B4
Braemar Pl. Sten 39 D2
Braemount. Cow 13 D1
Braepark Rd. Edin 91 D2
Braes View. Den 57 E4
Braes View. Shi 81 F4
Braeside Cres. Fau 193 E3
Braeside Gdns. E Cal 148 A1
Braeside. N Sau 5 E1
Braeside Pk. E Cal 148 A2
Braeside Pl. Laur 61 D1
Braeside Rd. Laur 61 D2
Braeside Rd. Gore 207 E4
Braeside Rd. Loan 181 D4
Braeside Rd N. Gore 207 E4
Braeside Rd S. Gore 207 E4
Braeview. Shi 81 E3
Braeview. E Lin 103 E4
Braeview. Lar 38 B1
Braewell Gdns. Lin 84 B4
Braid Ave. Edin 123 D1
Braid Cres. Edin 123 D1
Braid Farm Rd. Edin 123 D1
Braid Hills App. Edin 154 A4
Braid Hills Ave. Edin 123 D1
Braid Hills Cres. Edin 154 A4
Braid Hills Dr. Edin 154 B4
Braid Hills Rd. Edin 154 A4
Braid Mount. Edin 154 A4
Braid Mount Crest. Edin .. 154 A4
Braid Mount Rise. Edin ... 154 A4
Braid Mount View. Edin ... 154 A4
Braidburn Cres. Edin 123 D1
Braidburn Terr. Edin 123 D1
Braidlaw Pk. Peni 203 E3
Braigh Gdns. Dunf 28 B3
Bramble Dr. Edin 91 D1
Bramdean Gr. Edin 154 A4
Bramdean Pl. Edin 154 A4
Bramdean Rise. Edin 154 A4
Bramdean View. Edin 154 A4
Brand Dr. Edin 125 E4
Brand Gdns. Edin 125 E4
Brandfield St. Edin 123 D3
Brandon St. Edin 93 E1
Brandon Terr. Edin 93 E2
Brands Row. Cross 30 C4
Brandy Riggs. Crossf 27 E1
Brandy Wells. Crossf 27 E1
Brandyhill. Fish 5 F2
Brankholm Brae. Ros 46 B2
Brankholm Cres. Ros 46 B3
Brankholm La. Ros 46 B3
Branning Ct. Kirk 17 F3
Branshill Rd. N Sau 10 A4
Bravo St. B'ness 62 C3
Bread St. Edin 123 D4
Bread Street La. Edin 123 D4
Breadalbane Pl. Pol 61 F1
Breadalbane St. Edin 93 F2
Breakers Way. D Bay 47 F1
Brechin Dr. Pol 62 A1
Brechin Terr. Auch 204 A4
Brentham Ave. Stir 7 D2
Brentham Cres. Stir 7 D2
Breslin Terr. East 168 B3
Breton Ct. Falk 60 B2
Brewery La. Dunb 78 A1
Brewery Pk. Hadd 132 A4
Brewlands Ave. B' ness 63 E3
Brewster Pl. Den 36 B1
Brewster Sq. Muri 173 E3
Briar Brae. Pol 82 B4

Briar Cotts. Ston 171
Briar Pl. Dunf 29
Briarbank. Liv 147
Briarbank Terr. Edin 122
Briarcliff St. Kirk 17
Briardene. Laur 61
Briarhill Ave. D Bay 48
Briars Rd. All 4
Briarton Pl. Edin 95
Brickworks Rd. Tran 128
Bridge Cres. Den 36
Bridge End Cotts. Rat 150
Bridge End. Edin 124
Bridge End. Shot 191
Bridge End. Whit 170
Bridge Pl. Brox 117
Bridge Pl. Den 36
Bridge Pl. Edin 93
Bridge Pl. Shot 192
Bridge Rd. Bale 151
Bridge Rd. Edin 153
Bridge St. Bon 58
Bridge St. Cow 13
Bridge St. Den 36
Bridge St. E Lin 103
Bridge St. Edin 95
Bridge St. Fau 193
Bridge St. Hadd 132
Bridge St. Kir 23
Bridge St. Kirk 17
Bridge St. Kirk 119
Bridge St La. Edin 95
Bridge St. Muss 126
Bridge St. Peni 203
Bridge St. Tran 128
Bridgecastle Cotts. West 112
Bridgecastle Rd. Arm 143
Bridgehaugh Rd. Stir 2
Bridgend Pl. Bath 144
Bridgend Rd. Arm 112
Bridgend Rd. Avon 112
Bridgeness Cres. B'ness .. 64
Bridgeness La. B'ness 64
Bridgeness Rd. B'ness 64
Bridges The. D Bay 48
Bridgeside Ave. Whit 170
Bridgeton Cotts. West ... 112
Brierbush Cres. Glad 33
Brierbush Rd. Glad 129
Briery Bank. Hadd 132
Briery Bauks. Edin 123
Brig-O-Doon Gr. Cowie 20
Bright's Cres. Edin 123
Brighton Pl. Edin 125
Brighton St. Edin 123
Brisbane St. Liv 148
Bristo Pl. Edin 123
Bristo Port. Edin 123
Britwell Cres. Edin 94
Broad St. All 10
Broad St. Cow 13
Broad St. Den 36
Broad St. Stir 7
Broad Wynd. Edin 94
Broad Wynd. Kirk 17
Broadgait. Gull 52
Broadgait. Gull 52
Broadhurst Rd. May 183
Broadleys Rd. Stir 7
Brock Pl. Stir 7
Brock St. Inver 68
Brocks Way. Brox 117
Brockwood Ave. Peni 203
Brodick Pl. Falk 59
Brodick Rd. Kirk 16
Brodie Ave. N Ber 54
Brodie St. Falk 60
Broich The. Alva 4
Bronte Pl. Sten 39
Brook St. Alva 5
Brook St. Men 3
Brookbank Terr. Car 230
Brooke La. Gran 61
Brooke St. Gran 61
Brookfield Pl. Alva 5
Brookfield Terr. Rosl 180
Brookside. Pol 61
Broom Gr. Dunf 29
Broom Pk. E. Men 4
Broom Pk. Men 4
Broom Pl. Kirk 16
Broom Rd. Kirk 16
Broom Rd. Stir 7
Broom Wlk. Liv 148
Broom Wynd. Shot 192
Broomage Ave. Lar 38
Broomage Cres. Lar 38
Broomage Dr. Lar 38
Broomage Pk. Lar 38
Broombank Terr. Edin 121
Broomfield Cres. Edin 121
Broomfield Dr. Dunf 29
Broomfield Rd. Cow 13
Broomfield Terr. Edin 121

237

3roomhall Ave. Edin

Candlemaker Row. Edin

3roomhall Ave. Edin ... 121 F2
3roomhall Bank. Edin ... 121 E3
3roomhall Cres. Edin ... 121 E3
3roomhall Dr. Edin ... 121 E3
3roomhall Gdns. Edin ... 121 E3
3roomhall Loan. Edin ... 121 E3
3roomhall Pk. Edin ... 121 E3
3roomhall Pl. Edin ... 121 E3
3roomhall Rd. Edin ... 121 E3
3roomhall Terr. Edin ... 121 E3
3roomhead Dr. Dunf ... 28 C3
3roomhead Pk. Dunf ... 28 C3
3roomhill Ave. Burn ... 33 F1
3roomhill Ave. Lar ... 38 A1
3roomhill Ave. Peni ... 203 F2
3roomhill. Burn ... 50 C4
3roomhill Dr. Dalk ... 156 C1
3roomhill Pk. Dalk ... 156 C1
3roomhill Pl. Duni ... 36 B2
3roomhill Pl. Stir ... 6 C3
3roomhill Rd. Bon ... 58 A2
3roomhill Rd. Peni ... 203 F2
3roomhill St. East ... 168 B3
3roomhouse Ave. Edin ... 121 E2
3roomhouse Bank. Edin ... 121 F2
3roomhouse Cres. Edin ... 121 F2
3roomhouse Ct. Edin ... 121 F2
3roomhouse Dr. Edin ... 121 F2
3roomhouse Gdns E. Edin 121 F2
3roomhouse Gdns W. Edin ... 121 E2
3roomhouse Gr. Edin ... 121 F2
3roomhouse Loan. Edin ... 121 F2
3roomhouse Market. Edin . 121 F2
3roomhouse Medway. Edin ... 121 F2
3roomhouse Path. Edin ... 121 F2
3roomhouse Pk. Edin ... 121 F2
3roomhouse Pl N. Edin ... 121 F2
3roomhouse Pl S. Edin ... 121 F2
3roomhouse Rd. Edin ... 121 E2
3roomhouse Row. Edin ... 121 F2
3roomhouse Sq. Edin ... 121 F2
3roomhouse St N. Edin ... 121 F2
3roomhouse St S. Edin ... 121 F1
3roomhouse Terr. Edin ... 121 F2
3roomhouse Way. Edin ... 121 F2
3roomhouse Wlk. Edin ... 121 F2
3roomhouse Wynd. Edin .. 121 F2
3roomieknowe. Bonn ... 182 A4
3roomieknowe. Dunf ... 29 E2
3roomieknowe Gdns. Bonn 182 A4
3roomieknowe Pk. Bonn ... 182 A4
3roomieknowe. Tull ... 4 B2
roomknowe Dr. Kin ... 23 E3
roomlea Cres. Edin ... 121 E3
roompark Gdns. Den ... 36 C1
roompark Gdns. E Cal ... 148 C2
roompark Rd. E Cal ... 148 C2
roompark Rd. Edin ... 121 F3
roompark View. E Cal ... 148 C2
roomridge Rd. Stir ... 7 E2
roomside. Kirk ... 16 B4
roomside Pl. Lar ... 38 B1
roomside Rd. Bon ... 58 A2
roomside Terr. Edin ... 121 F2
roomyknowe Dr. Liv ... 146 C3
roomyknowe. Edin ... 153 D4
rora Pl. Crossf ... 28 B1
rosdale Ct. Falk ... 60 A1
rougham Pl. Edin ... 123 E3
rougham St. Edin ... 123 D3
roughton Market. Edin ... 93 E1
roughton Pl. Edin ... 93 E1
roughton Place La. Edin ... 93 E1
roughton Rd. Edin ... 93 E2
roughton St. Edin ... 93 E1
roughton Street La. Edin ... 93 E1
rown Ave. All ... 4 C1
rown Ave. Stir ... 2 A1
rown St. Arm ... 143 F2
rown St. Edin ... 123 F4
rown St. Falk ... 59 E3
rown St. Hadd ... 132 A4
rown St. Shot ... 192 A2
rown St. Whit ... 170 A3
rown's Cl. Edin ... 123 F4
rown's Pl. E Lin ... 103 E4
rownrigg Farm Cotts. E Lin 74 B3
ruart Ave. Sten ... 38 C2
ruce Cres. Plea ... 20 B2
ruce Cres. Sten ... 39 D2
ruce Dr. Fall ... 8 B3
ruce Dr. Sten ... 38 C2
ruce Gdns. Dalk ... 157 D1
ruce Gdns. Pol ... 82 B4
ruce Gr. Pen ... 160 C3
ruce Pl. Gran ... 61 F4
ruce Rd. B'ness ... 62 C3
ruce Rd. Bath ... 145 E3
ruce St. All ... 10 B4
ruce St. Bann ... 7 F1
ruce St. Clack ... 11 D2
ruce St. Dunf ... 28 C2
ruce St. Edin ... 123 D1
ruce St. Falk ... 60 B3
ruce St. King ... 35 D2
ruce St. Plea ... 20 B2
Bruce St. Stir ... 2 A1
Bruce Terr. Cam ... 6 B3
Bruce Terr. King ... 35 D2
Brucefield Ave. Dunf ... 29 D1
Brucefield Cres. Clack ... 11 D2
Brucefield Dr. Whit ... 170 A3
Brucefield Feus. Dunf ... 29 E2
Brucefield Pk E. Muri ... 173 E3
Brucefield Pk N. Muri ... 173 E3
Brucefield Pk W. Muri ... 173 E3
Brucefield Terr. Loch ... 13 F3
Brucehaven Cres. Lime ... 45 F2
Brucehaven Rd. Lime ... 45 E2
Brunstane Bank. Edin ... 125 E3
Brunstane Cres. Edin ... 125 E3
Brunstane Dr. Edin ... 125 E3
Brunstane Gardens Mews. Edin ... 125 E4
Brunstane Gdns. Edin ... 125 E4
Brunstane Gdns. Peni ... 203 E3
Brunstane Rd. Edin ... 125 E4
Brunstane Rd N. Edin ... 125 E4
Brunstane Rd S. Edin ... 125 E3
Brunswick Rd. Edin ... 93 F1
Brunswick St. Edin ... 93 F1
Brunswick Street La. Edin ... 93 F1
Brunswick Terr. Edin ... 93 F1
Brunt Gr. Dunb ... 106 B4
Brunt La. Dunb ... 78 B1
Brunt Pl. Dunb ... 106 C4
Brunton Pl. Edin ... 93 F1
Brunton Terr. Edin ... 93 F1
Brunton's Cl. Dalk ... 157 D2
Bruntsfield Ave. Edin ... 123 D3
Bruntsfield Cres. Edin ... 123 D3
Bruntsfield Gdns. Edin ... 123 D3
Bruntsfield Pl. Edin ... 123 D3
Bruntsfield Terr. Edin ... 123 D3
Bryans Ave. Newt ... 183 D3
Bryans Rd. Newt ... 183 D3
Bryce Ave. Edin ... 94 C1
Bryce Ave. Sten ... 39 D1
Bryce Cres. Curr ... 152 A3
Bryce Gdns. Curr ... 152 A3
Bryce Gr. Edin ... 94 C1
Bryce Pl. Curr ... 152 A3
Bryce Rd. Curr ... 152 A3
Bryony The. Tull ... 4 A1
Bryson Rd. Edin ... 122 C3
Bryson St. Falk ... 60 A3
Buccleuch Pl. Edin ... 123 E3
Buccleuch St. Dalk ... 157 D2
Buccleuch St. Edin ... 123 F3
Buccleuch Terr. Edin ... 123 F3
Buchan La. Brox ... 117 F3
Buchan Pl. Gran ... 61 E3
Buchan Rd. B'ness ... 62 B3
Buchan Rd. Bath ... 144 C4
Buchan Rd. Brox ... 117 E3
Buchanan Ct. B' ness ... 63 F3
Buchanan Ct. Falk ... 60 A4
Buchanan Ct. Kirk ... 17 D1
Buchanan Dr. Stir ... 2 A2
Buchanan Gdns. Pol ... 61 E1
Buchanan St. Dunf ... 29 D2
Buchanan St. Edin ... 93 F2
Buckie Rd. May ... 183 F3
Buckingham Terr. Edin ... 93 D1
Buckstane Pk. Edin ... 154 A4
Buckstone Ave. Edin ... 154 A3
Buckstone Bank. Edin ... 154 A4
Buckstone Circ. Edin ... 154 B3
Buckstone Cl. Edin ... 154 B3
Buckstone Cres. Edin ... 154 A4
Buckstone Crook. Edin ... 154 B3
Buckstone Ct. Edin ... 154 A3
Buckstone Dell. Edin ... 154 A4
Buckstone Dr. Edin ... 154 A4
Buckstone Gate. Edin ... 154 B3
Buckstone Gdns. Edin ... 154 A3
Buckstone Gn. Edin ... 154 B3
Buckstone Gr. Edin ... 154 A4
Buckstone Hill. Edin ... 154 B4
Buckstone Howe. Edin ... 154 B3
Buckstone Lea. Edin ... 154 B3
Buckstone Loan E. Edin ... 154 B3
Buckstone Loan. Edin ... 154 B3
Buckstone Neuk. Edin ... 154 B4
Buckstone Pl. Edin ... 154 A3
Buckstone Rd. Edin ... 154 A3
Buckstone Rise. Edin ... 154 B3
Buckstone Row. Edin ... 154 B4
Buckstone Shaw. Edin ... 154 B3
Buckstone Terr. Edin ... 154 A3
Buckstone View. Edin ... 154 A4
Buckstone Way. Edin ... 154 A4
Buckstone Wood. Edin ... 154 A3
Buckstone Wynd. Edin ... 154 B3
Buffies Brae. Dunf ... 28 C2
Bughtknowes Dr. Bath ... 145 E4
Bughtlin Dr. Edin ... 91 D1
Bughtlin Gdns. Edin ... 121 D4
Bughtlin Gn. Edin ... 91 D1
Bughtlin Loan. Edin ... 121 D4
Bughtlin Pk. Edin ... 121 D4
Bughtlin Pl. Edin ... 91 D1
Builyeon Rd. Que ... 89 D4
Buller St. Loch ... 14 A4
Bullet Loan. Hadd ... 132 B4
Bulloch Cres. Den ... 36 B1
Buntine Cres. Stir ... 7 D2
Burdiehouse Ave. Edin ... 155 D2
Burdiehouse Cres. Edin ... 155 D2
Burdiehouse Crossway. Edin ... 155 D2
Burdiehouse Dr. Edin ... 155 D2
Burdiehouse Loan. Edin ... 155 D2
Burdiehouse Medway. Edin 155 D2
Burdiehouse Pl. Edin ... 155 D2
Burdiehouse Rd. Edin ... 155 D2
Burdiehouse Sq. Edin ... 155 D2
Burdiehouse St. Edin ... 155 D2
Burdiehouse Terr. Edin ... 155 D2
Burgess Hill. Lin ... 85 D3
Burgess Rd. Que ... 89 E4
Burgess St. Edin ... 94 A3
Burgess Terr. Edin ... 124 A2
Burgh Mews. All ... 10 A3
Burgh Mills La. Lin ... 84 B3
Burgh Rd. Cow ... 13 E2
Burghlee Cres. Loan ... 181 D4
Burghlee Cres. Loan ... 181 E4
Burghlee Terr. Loan ... 181 E4
Burghmuir Ct. Lin ... 85 E4
Burghmuir Rd. Stir ... 7 D3
Burghtoft. Edin ... 155 F3
Burleigh Cres. Inver ... 47 E2
Burleigh Way. All ... 10 B3
Burlington St. Edin ... 93 F3
Burn Dr. Stir ... 7 E2
Burnbank. Liv ... 147 E3
Burnbank. Oak ... 27 E4
Burnbank Rd. Falk ... 60 A4
Burnbank Rd. Gran ... 61 E3
Burnbrae. Edin ... 121 D4
Burnbrae. Fau ... 193 F3
Burnbrae Gdns. Alva ... 5 D3
Burnbrae Gdns. Falk ... 60 A3
Burnbrae. N Sau ... 10 B4
Burnbrae Pk. Kin ... 23 F2
Burnbrae Rd. Falk ... 60 A3
Burnbrae Rd. Hart ... 169 D3
Burnbrae Rd. Shot ... 191 F2
Burnbrae Rd. Ston ... 171 D1
Burnbrae Terr. Whit ... 170 B3
Burndene Dr. Edin ... 155 D1
Burnee. Fish ... 5 F2
Burney Pl. Ros ... 46 C2
Burnfield. Liv ... 147 D1
Burnfield Pl. Falk ... 60 B4
Burnfoot Ct. Gran ... 61 E3
Burnfoot La. Falk ... 60 A2
Burngrange Cotts. W Cal ... 172 B1
Burngrange Ct. W Cal ... 172 B1
Burngrange Gdns. W Cal .. 172 A1
Burnhead Cres. Edin ... 155 D3
Burnhead Gr. Edin ... 155 D3
Burnhead La. Falk ... 60 B2
Burnhead Loan. Edin ... 155 D3
Burnhead Path E. Edin ... 155 D3
Burnhead Path W. Edin ... 155 D3
Burnhead Rd. Lar ... 38 B2
Burnhouse Dr. Dech ... 116 B1
Burnhouse Dr. Whit ... 169 F3
Burnhouse Ind Est. Whit ... 169 F3
Burnhouse Rd. Dech ... 116 B2
Burnlea Dr. Ston ... 171 D1
Burnlea Pl. Ston ... 171 D1
Burns Ave. Arm ... 143 F3
Burns Ave. Gran ... 61 E3
Burns Cres. Hart ... 168 C3
Burns Cres. Laur ... 60 C2
Burns Cres. Whit ... 170 A3
Burns Ct. Liv ... 148 B3
Burns Pl. Shot ... 191 D3
Burns St. Dunf ... 28 C3
Burns St. Edin ... 94 A2
Burns St. H Val ... 26 A1
Burns St. Stir ... 2 A1
Burns Terr. Bath ... 145 E3
Burns Terr. Cowie ... 20 B4
Burnside Ave. Arm ... 143 E3
Burnside Ave. King ... 34 C2
Burnside Ave. May ... 183 E4
Burnside Ave. W Cal ... 172 C3
Burnside Cres. Clack ... 11 D3
Burnside Cres. Fau ... 193 F3
Burnside Cres. May ... 183 E4
Burnside Cres. Plea ... 20 B2
Burnside Cres. Ros ... 47 D3
Burnside Cres. Shot ... 191 E3
Burnside Ct. Giff ... 134 B1
Burnside. Dech ... 116 A1
Burnside. Edin ... 121 D4
Burnside. Hadd ... 131 F4
Burnside La. W Cal ... 172 C3
Burnside Pk. Bale ... 151 E1
Burnside Pl. Ros ... 47 D2
Burnside Pl. Sten ... 39 D2
Burnside. Pres ... 96 C1
Burnside Rd. Bath ... 144 C4
Burnside Rd. Gore ... 183 E1
Burnside Rd. Men ... 3 F3
Burnside Rd. Uph ... 117 D2
Burnside Rd. W Cal ... 172 C3
Burnside St. N Sau ... 5 E1
Burnside St. Ros ... 47 D3
Burnside St. Stir ... 7 E3
Burnside Terr. Cow ... 13 D1
Burnside Terr. E Cal ... 148 C3
Burnside Terr. Falk ... 59 F3
Burnside Terr. Fau ... 193 F3
Burnside Terr. Laur ... 61 D1
Burnside Terr. Oak ... 27 D4
Burnside Terr. W Cal ... 172 C3
Burnsknowe. Liv ... 146 C3
Burntisland Rd. King ... 34 C1
Burnvale. Brox ... 118 A2
Burnvale. Muri ... 147 F2
Burt Ave. King ... 34 C2
Burt Gr. Dunf ... 29 F1
Burt St. Dunf ... 29 D3
Bush St. Muss ... 126 A3
Bush Terr. Muss ... 126 A3
Bute Cres. Dunf ... 29 F2
Bute Cres. Shot ... 191 E3
Bute. Liv ... 146 C3
Bute Pl. Gran ... 61 E3
Bute St. Falk ... 60 A3
Bute Wynd. Kirk ... 17 D1
Butler's Pl. Liv ... 147 D2
Butlerfield Ind Est. Newt ... 183 D2
Butts The. Hadd ... 132 A4
Buxley Rd. Elph ... 128 A1
By-Pass Rd. Bank ... 57 F3
Byburn. Brid ... 116 C4
Byres The. Ros ... 46 B3
Byron Rd. Shot ... 191 D3
Cables Wynd. Edin ... 93 F3
Caddell's Row Cotts. Edin ... 91 D3
Cadell Dr. Sten ... 39 D3
Cadell Pl. Cocke ... 97 E2
Cadgers Loan. Plea ... 20 A1
Cadiz St. Edin ... 94 A3
Cadogan Rd. Edin ... 155 D4
Cadzow Ave. B' ness ... 63 F3
Cadzow Cres. B' ness ... 63 F4
Cadzow La. B' ness ... 63 F4
Cadzow Pl. Edin ... 94 A1
Caerketton Ave. Rosl ... 180 C3
Caerlaverock Ct. Edin ... 121 D4
Caesar Rd. Tran ... 128 B3
Caesar Way. Tran ... 128 B3
Caird's Row. Muss ... 126 A4
Cairn Gr. Crossf ... 28 B1
Cairn's La. B'ness ... 64 A4
Cairnbank Gdns. Peni ... 203 F2
Cairnbank Rd. Peni ... 203 F2
Cairncubie Rd. Dunf ... 29 E4
Cairneyhill Rd. Crossf ... 28 A1
Cairneymount Ave. Madd ... 83 D3
Cairneymount Rd. Car ... 230 A1
Cairngorm Cres. Kirk ... 16 C3
Cairngorm House. Edin ... 93 F3
Cairngorm Rd. Gran ... 61 F3
Cairnhill Ct. Car ... 230 A1
Cairnie Pl. Whit ... 170 A3
Cairnmuir Rd. Edin ... 121 F4
Cairnoch Way. Bann ... 7 F1
Cairnoch Wlk. Den ... 36 B1
Cairns Dr. Bale ... 177 D4
Cairns Gdns. Bale ... 177 D4
Cairns Street E. Kirk ... 17 F4
Cairns Street W. Kirk ... 17 E4
Cairns The. Lime ... 45 D2
Cairns The. Men ... 4 A3
Cairntows Cl. Edin ... 124 B2
Cairnwell Pl. Crossf ... 27 E1
Cairnwell Pl. Kirk ... 16 C4
Caithness Ct. Kirk ... 17 F4
Caithness Pl. Edin ... 93 D3
Caithness Pl. Kirk ... 17 F4
Caiyside. Edin ... 154 A2
Caiystane Ave. Edin ... 154 A3
Caiystane Cres. Edin ... 154 A3
Caiystane Dr. Edin ... 153 F3
Caiystane Gdns. Edin ... 154 A3
Caiystane Hill. Edin ... 154 A3
Caiystane Terr. Edin ... 154 A3
Caiystane View. Edin ... 154 A3
Calais View. Dunf ... 29 F1
Calaisburn Pl. Dunf ... 29 F1
Calder Cres. Arm ... 144 A3
Calder Cres. Edin ... 121 D1
Calder Ct. Edin ... 121 E1
Calder Ct. Stir ... 7 E3
Calder Dr. Edin ... 121 E1
Calder Dr. Shot ... 192 A2
Calder Gdns. Edin ... 121 E1
Calder Gr. Edin ... 121 E1
Calder House Rd. E Cal ... 148 A2
Calder Park Rd. E Cal ... 148 A1
Calder Pk. Edin ... 121 E1
Calder Pl. D Bay ... 48 A2
Calder Pl. Edin ... 121 E1
Calder Pl. Falk ... 60 B1
Calder Rd. Edin ... 121 E1
Calder Rd Gdns. Edin ... 122 A2
Calder Rd. Muri ... 173 E3
Calder Rd. Rat ... 121 D1
Calder View. Edin ... 121 D1
Calder's Lawn. Hadd ... 101 D1
Calderburn Rd. W Cal ... 173 D3
Caldercruix Rd. Cald ... 110 A1
Calderhall Ave. E Cal ... 148 C2
Calderhall Cres. E Cal ... 148 C2
Calderhall Terr. E Cal ... 148 C2
Calderhead Rd. Shot ... 191 E4
Caledonia Rd. Ros ... 46 A1
Caledonia Rd. Shot ... 191 F3
Caledonia Way. Ros ... 46 A2
Caledonian Cres. Edin ... 123 D3
Caledonian Gdns. All ... 9 F3
Caledonian Pl. Edin ... 123 D3
Caledonian Rd. All ... 9 F3
Caledonian Rd. Edin ... 123 D3
Caledonian Rd. Fau ... 193 E3
Caledonian Terr. Fau ... 193 E3
Calgary Ave. Liv ... 147 F2
California Rd. Madd ... 82 C3
California Terr. Cali ... 81 F3
Callander Dr. Lar ... 59 E4
Callander Pl. Cock ... 140 C2
Callendar Ave. Falk ... 60 A1
Callendar Rd. Falk ... 60 B2
Callendar Riggs. Falk ... 60 B2
Callender Bsns Pk. Falk ... 60 C2
Calliope Rd. Ros ... 46 A1
Calton Cres. Stir ... 7 D2
Calton Hill. Edin ... 93 F1
Calton Rd. Edin ... 123 F4
Calum Macdonald Ct. Ros .. 46 C2
Cambridge Ave. Edin ... 93 F2
Cambridge Gdns. Edin ... 93 F2
Cambridge St. Edin ... 123 D4
Cambusnethan St. Edin ... 94 A1
Camdean Cres. Ros ... 46 B3
Camdean La. Ros ... 46 B3
Camelon Rd. Falk ... 59 F3
Cameron Cres. Bonn ... 181 F3
Cameron Cres. Edin ... 124 A2
Cameron Gr. Inver ... 47 D2
Cameron House Ave. Edin 124 A2
Cameron March. Edin ... 124 A2
Cameron Pk. Edin ... 124 A2
Cameron Pl. Sten ... 39 D1
Cameron Smaill Rd. Rat ... 151 F4
Cameron St. Dunf ... 28 C2
Cameron Terr. Edin ... 124 A2
Cameron Terr. Slam ... 110 A2
Cameron Toll. Edin ... 124 A2
Cameron Toll Gdns. Edin .. 124 A2
Cameron Way. Liv ... 147 F4
Cameronian Dr. Car ... 230 A1
Cameronian St. Stir ... 7 D4
Camilla Gr. Aucht ... 15 E1
Cammo Bank. Edin ... 91 D1
Cammo Brae. Edin ... 91 D1
Cammo Gdns. Edin ... 91 D1
Cammo Hill. Edin ... 90 C1
Cammo Parkway. Edin ... 91 D1
Cammo Pl. Edin ... 91 D1
Cammo Rd. Edin ... 90 C1
Cammo Wlk. Edin ... 90 C1
Camp Rd. Lime ... 44 B3
Camp Rd. May ... 183 F4
Camp Wood View. May ... 183 F3
Campbell Ave. Edin ... 122 B4
Campbell Cres. Laur ... 60 C2
Campbell Cres. Loch ... 14 A4
Campbell Ct. Long ... 98 B3
Campbell Ct. Stir ... 6 C2
Campbell Dr. Lar ... 38 A1
Campbell Pk Cres. Edin ... 152 C3
Campbell Pk Dr. Edin ... 152 C3
Campbell Rd. Edin ... 122 B4
Campbell Rd. Long ... 98 B3
Campbell St. Dunf ... 29 D2
Campbell's Cl. Edin ... 123 F4
Camperdown Rd. Ros ... 46 B1
Campfield St. Falk ... 60 A3
Campie Gdns. Muss ... 126 A3
Campie La. Muss ... 126 A3
Campie Rd. Muss ... 126 A3
Campie Terr. Gran ... 39 F1
Camps Rd. Oak ... 27 E3
Camps Rigg. Liv ... 147 D4
Campsie Cres. Kirk ... 16 C4
Campsie Rd. Gran ... 61 F3
Campus Roundabout. Muri 147 E1
Campview Ave. Dan ... 156 A4
Campview Cres. Dan ... 156 B4
Campview. Dan ... 156 A4
Campview Gdns. Dan ... 156 A4
Campview Gr. Dan ... 156 B4
Campview Rd. Bonn ... 182 A3
Campview Terr. Dan ... 156 A4
Camus Ave. Edin ... 154 A3
Camus Pk. Edin ... 154 A3
Camus Pl E. Edin ... 154 A3
Camus Rd E. Edin ... 154 A3
Camus Rd W. Edin ... 154 A3
Canaan La. Edin ... 123 D2
Canal St. Falk ... 59 E3
Canal St. Falk ... 60 A4
Canavan Ct. Stir ... 7 E2
Canberra St. Liv ... 148 A3
Candie Cres. Gran ... 61 F3
Candie Rd. Gran ... 62 A4
Candimilne Ct. Car ... 230 A1
Candlemaker Row. Edin ... 123 E4

Candlemaker's Cres. Edin 155 F3
Candlemaker's Pk. Edin 155 F3
Candleriggs. All 10 A3
Caneluk Ave. Car 230 A1
Canmore Dr. Sten 38 C2
Canmore Gr. Dunf 29 D3
Canmore St. Dunf 29 D2
Canmore St. King 34 C1
Canmore St. Que 89 D4
Canmore Terr. Dunf 29 D4
Canning St. Edin 123 D4
Canning Street La. Edin 123 D4
Cannon Wynd. Edin 93 F3
Cannons Way. Falk 39 D1
Cannop Cres. Ston 170 C1
Canon La. Edin 93 E1
Canon Lynch Ct. Dunf 28 C2
Canon St. Edin 93 E1
Canongate. Edin 123 F4
Canonmills. Edin 93 E2
Canthill Gdns. Shot 191 D2
Cantlie Pl. Ros 46 C2
Cantsdam Rd. Kel 12 C4
Canty Gr. Long 98 B2
Capelaw Rd. Edin 153 D3
Caplaw Way. Peni 203 E3
Caponfiat Cres. Hadd 100 C1
Caponhall Ct. Tran 128 B3
Caponhall Dr. Tran 128 B3
Caponhall Rd. Tran 128 B3
Cappers Ct. Arm 143 F2
Captain's Dr. Edin 155 D3
Captain's Loan. Edin 155 D3
Captain's Rd. Edin 155 D3
Captain's Row. Edin 155 D3
Capuchall Rd. Liv 146 B3
Carberry Ct. White 157 F4
Carberry Mains Cotts. White 127 D1
Carberry Pl. Edin 122 C4
Carberry Rd. Muss 126 C2
Carbrook Dr. Plea 20 B2
Carbrook Pl. Gran 61 F3
Carcraig Pl. D Bay 48 A2
Cardross Ave. Uph 117 D3
Cardross Cres. Brox 117 E3
Cardross Rd. Brox 117 E3
Cardrowan Rd. Plea 20 B1
Carfrae Gdns. Edin 92 A1
Carfrae Gr. Edin 92 A1
Carfrae Pk. Edin 92 A1
Carfrae Rd. Edin 92 A1
Cargil Terr. Edin 93 D3
Carhowden Rd. Laur 61 D2
Carlaverock Ave. Tran 128 B3
Carlaverock Cres. Tran 128 B3
Carlaverock Ct. Tran 128 C3
Carlaverock Dr. Tran 128 B3
Carlaverock Gr. Tran 128 B3
Carlaverock Terr. Tran 128 C2
Carlaverock View. Tran 128 B3
Carlaverock Wlk. Tran 128 B3
Carledubs Ave. Uph 117 D3
Carledubs Cres. Uph 117 D3
Carlie Ave. B of A 2 A3
Carlin Craig. King 34 C1
Carlin Cres. King 34 C1
Carlin La. Car 230 A1
Carlingnose Pk. Inver 68 B3
Carlingnose Point. Inver 68 B3
Carlingnose Way. Inver 68 B3
Carlops Ave. Peni 203 E3
Carlops Cres. Peni 203 F3
Carlops Rd. Peni 203 E3
Carlowrie Ave. Dal 89 F4
Carlowrie Cres. Dal 89 F4
Carlowrie Pl. Gore 207 E4
Carlton St. Edin 93 D1
Carlton Terr. Edin 93 F1
Carlton Terrace La. Edin 93 F1
Carlton Terrace Mews. Edin 93 F1
Carlyle Ct. Hadd 132 A4
Carlyle Ct. Liv 148 B3
Carlyle Gdns. Hadd 101 D1
Carlyle Pl. Edin 94 A1
Carlyle Pl. Muss 126 B3
Carlyle Rd. Kirk 17 D2
Carlyle St. H Val 26 A1
Carlyle Terr. Bath 145 E3
Carmel Ave. Kirk 89 D1
Carmel Rd. Kirk 89 D1
Carmelaws. Lin 85 D3
Carmelite Rd. Que 89 D4
Carmondean Centre Rd. Liv 147 D3
Carmuir. Pol 215 D1
Carmuirs Ave. Falk 59 E3
Carmuirs Dr. Falk 59 E3
Carmuirs St. Falk 59 E3
Carnaughton Pl. Alva 4 C3
Carnbee Pl. Dunf 29 E2
Carnegie Ave. Dunf 46 C4
Carnegie Dr. Falk 59 E3
Carnegie Rd. Bog 146 A3
Carnegie St. Edin 123 F4
Carneil Rd. Oak 27 E4

Carneil Terr. Oak 27 E3
Carnethie St. Rose 181 F1
Carnethy Ave. Edin 153 D3
Carnethy Ave. Peni 203 F3
Carnethy Cres. Kirk 16 C4
Carnethy Ct. Peni 203 F3
Carnock Rd. Dunf 28 A3
Carnock Rd. Oak 27 F3
Carnock St. Cowie 20 C4
Carnwath Rd. Car 230 A1
Caroline Gdns. Alva 4 C3
Caroline Gdns. E Cal 148 A1
Caroline Gdns. Edin 121 F4
Caroline Park Gr. Edin 92 B3
Caroline Pk. E Cal 148 A1
Caroline Pl. Edin 121 F4
Caroline Terr. Edin 121 E4
Carpet La. Edin 94 A3
Carradale Ave. Falk 59 E2
Carriber Ave. Madd 84 A3
Carrick Cres. May 183 E4
Carrick Dr. Stir 7 D4
Carrick Dr. D Bay 48 A2
Carrick Gdns. Muri 173 F3
Carrick Gr. D Bay 48 A2
Carrick Knowe Ave. Edin 121 F3
Carrick Knowe Dr. Edin 121 F3
Carrick Knowe Gdns. Edin 121 F3
Carrick Knowe Gr. Edin 121 F3
Carrick Knowe Hill. Edin 121 F3
Carrick Knowe Loan. Edin 121 F3
Carrick Knowe Parkway. Edin 121 F3
Carrick Knowe Pl. Edin 121 F3
Carrick Knowe Rd. Edin 121 F2
Carrick Knowe Terr. Edin 121 F3
Carrick Pl. Falk 59 E2
Carrick Pl. Gran 59 D2
Carriden Brae. Muir 64 B3
Carriden Glade. B'ness 64 B4
Carrington Cres. Edin 92 C2
Carrington Mains Cotts. Newt 206 B3
Carrington Rd. Edin 92 C1
Carron Ind Est. Sten 39 D1
Carron La. Dunf 29 F2
Carron Pl. Edin 94 A3
Carron Pl. Gran 61 E2
Carron Pl. Kirk 16 C4
Carron Pl. Stir 7 D1
Carron Rd. Falk 60 A4
Carron Terr. Madd 82 C4
Carron View. Madd 82 C4
Carron Wlk. Liv 148 A2
Carronbank Ave. Sten 39 D1
Carronbank Cres. Den 36 C2
Carronbank Ct. Sten 39 D1
Carronflats Rd. Gran 61 F4
Carrongrove Ave. Sten 39 D1
Carrongrove Rd. Sten 39 D1
Carronhall Ave. Sten 39 D1
Carronlea Dr. Sten 39 D1
Carronshore Rd. Sten 39 D1
Carronside St. Falk 60 A4
Carronside Pl. Falk 60 A4
Carronvale Ave. Lar 38 B1
Carronvale Rd. Lar 38 B1
Carronview. Lar 38 B1
Carse Cres. Laur 61 D2
Carse Knowe. Lin 85 E4
Carse Terr. Air 22 C2
Carse View. Air 22 C2
Carse View. B'ness 63 E3
Carsebridge Rd. N Sau 10 B3
Carseview. Bann 7 F1
Carseview. Tull 4 A1
Carson Pl. Ros 46 B3
Carswell Pl. Dunf 28 C3
Cartmore Rd. Loch 14 A4
Cassel's La. Edin 93 F2
Cassels St. Edin 93 F2
Cast The. Rose 181 E3
Castings Ave. Falk 60 A4
Castings Ct. Falk 60 A4
Castings Dr. Falk 60 A3
Castings Rd. Falk 60 C3
Castings The. Dunf 28 B3
Castlandhill Rd. Ros 47 D1
Castle Ave. Cocke 97 F2
Castle Ave. Edin 121 E3
Castle Ave. Sten 39 E2
Castle Cres. Den 36 B1
Castle Cres. E Cal 148 C1
Castle Cres. Falk 60 A4
Castle Cres. Tor 37 F4
Castle Ct. Falk 60 B4
Castle Ct. Men 3 F3
Castle Ct. Stir 7 D4
Castle Dr. Den 36 C1
Castle Gate. Dunf 78 B2
Castle Moffat. Giff 166 A4
Castle Pk. Dir 53 D2
Castle Pl. Dunb 78 B2
Castle Pl. Falk 60 B4
Castle St. Cocke 97 F2

Castle Rd. Falk 60 B4
Castle Rd. Men 3 F3
Castle Rd. Ros 46 C1
Castle Rd. Stir 2 B2
Castle Rd. Winch 88 A1
Castle Row. Dunf 28 B3
Castle St. All 10 A3
Castle St. Clack 11 D2
Castle St. Dunb 78 B2
Castle St. Edin 123 D4
Castle Terr. Clack 11 D2
Castle Terr. Cocke 97 F2
Castle Terr. Den 36 B1
Castle Terr. Edin 123 E4
Castle Terr. Winch 88 A1
Castle View. Cocke 97 F2
Castle View. Fall 8 B2
Castle View. Pen 160 B3
Castle Wlk. Cocke 97 F2
Castle Wynd. Stir 7 D4
Castlebiair. Dunf 28 C2
Castlebiair La. Dunf 28 C3
Castlebiair Mews. Dunf 28 C3
Castlebiair Pk. Dunf 28 C3
Castlegait. Stir 7 D4
Castlehill Ave. Slam 110 A3
Castlehill. B'ness 63 E4
Castlehill. Edin 123 E4
Castlelaurie St. Falk 60 B4
Castlelaw Cres. Rosl 180 C3
Castlelaw Ct. Pen 160 B3
Castlelaw Rd. Edin 153 D3
Castlemains Pl. Dir 53 E3
Castlemount Terr. Kirk 16 B4
Castlepark. Kin 23 E3
Castleray. King 34 C1
Castle View Cres. Gran 61 E3
Castleview. B of A 2 A2
Castleview Dr. B of A 2 A4
Castleview Terr. Bank 57 D2
Cathcart Pl. Edin 122 C3
Cathedral La. Edin 93 E1
Catherine St. Bann 7 E1
Catherine Terr. Black 145 E1
Cathlaw La. Torp 114 A3
Cathrine Gr. B'ness 64 A3
Catriona Terr. Auch 180 A1
Cattle Market. Clack 11 D3
Cauldhame Cres. Cam 6 B3
Causeway The. B of A 2 B3
Causeway The. Stir 2 B3
Causewayend. Edin 93 F3
Causewayside. Edin 123 F3
Causeyside Pl. Stir 7 D4
Cavalry Park Dr. Edin 124 B3
Cawder Gdns. B of A 1 C4
Cawder Rd. B of A 1 C4
Cawdor Cres. Kirk 16 C3
Cecil St. Stir 7 D3
Cedar Ave. Kirk 17 E4
Cedar Ave. Stir 6 C3
Cedar Cres. Laur 61 D1
Cedar Cres. Loch 13 E3
Cedar Cres. Whit 170 B3
Cedar Dr. Cocke 97 F2
Cedar Gr. Dunf 46 B4
Cedar Gr. Laur 61 D1
Cedar Gr. Sten 38 B1
Cedar Rd. Loan 180 C4
Cedar St. Dunb 78 A1
Cedar St. Gran 61 E4
Cedarbank. Liv 147 F3
Cedars The. Tull 4 A1
Cedric Rise. Muri 148 A1
Cemetery Rd. Dalk 156 C1
Cemetery Rd. Fau 193 E3
Cemetery Rd. Pres 96 C1
Cemetery Rd. Shot 192 A2
Central Ave. Gran 61 F3
Central Dr. Sten 38 C2
Central Dock Rd. Gran 40 C1
Central Way. D Bay 48 B3
Centre Interchange. E Cal 148 A1
Centre Rd N. Liv 147 F1
Centre Rd S. Muri 147 E1
Chacefield St. Bon 58 A3
Chacefield Wood. Bank 57 F4
Chalmers Cres. Edin 123 E3
Chalmers Sq. Liv 146 B3
Chalmers St. Dunf 28 C3
Chalmers St. Edin 123 E3
Chalmerston Rd. Cam 1 A2
Chalton Rd. B of A 2 A4
Chalybeate. Hadd 131 F4
Chamberfield Rd. Dunf 29 E3
Chamberlain Rd. Edin 123 D2
Chambers Dr. Sten 39 D1
Chambers St. Edin 123 E4
Champigny Ct. Muss 126 C3
Chancelot Cres. Edin 93 E3
Chancelot Gr. Edin 93 E3
Chancelot Terr. Edin 93 E3
Chapel Ct. Edin 124 C2
Chapel Dr. Sten 38 C2
Chapel La. Edin 94 A3
Chapel La. Falk 60 A3

Chapel Level. Kirk 16 C4
Chapel Loan. Rosl 181 D2
Chapel Pl. H Val 26 A1
Chapel Pl. Inver 47 E2
Chapel Pl. Inver 68 B3
Chapel Pl. Kirk 16 B4
Chapel Pl. Path 185 D3
Chapel Rd. Kirk 16 B4
Chapel St. Cow 13 E2
Chapel St. Dunf 28 C2
Chapel St. Edin 123 F3
Chapel St. H Val 26 A1
Chapel St. Kin 23 F2
Chapel St. Loch 14 A4
Chapel Villas. D Bay 48 A1
Chapelhill Gdn. Dunf 29 F2
Chapelhill. Clack 11 D2
Chapelhill. Dir 53 D2
Chapelhill St. Kin 23 E3
Chapelton Ave. W Cal 172 C2
Chapelton Dr. W Cal 172 C2
Chapelton Gdns. W Cal 172 C2
Chapelton Gr. W Cal 172 C2
Chapelton Pl. W Cal 173 D2
Chapelton Terr. W Cal 172 C3
Charing Cross. Gran 40 C1
Charles Ave. B of A 2 A3
Charles Cres. Bog 145 F3
Charles Cres. Car 230 A1
Charles Ct. Lime 45 F2
Charles St. Alva 5 D4
Charles St. All 9 F4
Charles St. Dunf 29 D1
Charles St. Edin 123 E3
Charles St. Pen 203 F4
Charles St. Shot 192 A2
Charles St La. Edin 123 E3
Charles Way. Lime 45 F2
Charles Way S. Lime 45 F2
Charlesfield La. Liv 147 D1
Charlotte Dundas Ct. Gran 61 F3
Charlotte La. Edin 123 D4
Charlotte Sq. Edin 123 D4
Charlotte St. Kirk 17 D2
Charlotte Sq. Pol 82 B4
Charlotte St. Shot 192 A2
Charlton Gr. Rosl 180 C2
Charter St. Stir 7 D2
Charterhall Gr. Edin 123 E2
Charterhall Rd. Edin 123 E1
Charteris Ct. Long 98 B3
Charteris Pk. Long 98 B3
Charteris Rd. Long 98 B3
Chartershall Rd. Bann 7 D1
Chartershall Rd. Bann 19 D3
Chattan Ave. Stir 2 A2
Cherry Ave. Stir 6 C3
Cherry Rd. Bonn 182 A3
Cherry La. May 183 F3
Cherry Pl. Cow 13 E2
Cherry Pl. Dunf 46 B4
Cherry Tree Ave. Curr 151 F2
Cherry Tree Cres. Curr 151 E2
Cherry Tree Gdns. Curr 151 E2
Cherry Tree Gr. Curr 151 E2
Cherry Tree Loan. Curr 151 F2
Cherry Tree Pk. Curr 151 E2
Cherry Tree Pl. Curr 151 F2
Cherry Tree View. Curr 151 F2
Cherrybank. Dunf 29 E3
Cherryton Dr. Clack 11 D3
Chesser Ave. Edin 122 B2
Chesser Cres. Edin 122 B2
Chesser Gdns. Edin 122 A2
Chesser Gr. Edin 122 A2
Chesser Loan. Edin 122 A2
Chester Dr. May 183 E3
Chester Gr. Bonn 182 A3
Chester St. Edin 123 D4
Chester View. May 183 E3
Chasters View. Bonn 182 A3
Chestnut Ave. Kirk 17 E4
Chestnut Ave. Whit 170 B3
Chestnut Cres. Dunf 36 B2
Chestnut Gr. B' ness 63 E3
Chestnut Gr. Bonn 182 A3
Chestnut Gr. Dunf 46 C4
Chestnut Gr. Liv 148 A3
Chestnut St. Edin 38 C2
Chestnut Gr. Winch 87 F1
Chestnut St. Edin 93 D4
Cheviot Pl. Gran 61 F3
Cheviot Rd. Kirk 16 C4
Cheyne St. Edin 93 D1
Chisholm Ave. Stir 2 A2
Chisholm Cres. Loch 14 A4
Chisholm Pl. Gran 61 F3
Chisholm St. Dunf 29 E4
Chisholm Terr. Peni 203 F4
Christian Cres. Edin 125 E4
Christian Gr. Edin 125 D4
Christie Pl. Kirk 17 E4
Christie St. Dunf 29 D3

Christiemiller Ave. Edin 94
Christiemiller Gr. Edin 94
Christiemiller Pl. Edin 94
Church Ct. Bird 86
Church Gdns. Long 98
Church Gr. Burn 33
Church Gr. N Sau 5
Church Hill. Edin 123
Church Hill Pl. Edin 123
Church La. Duni 36
Church La. Kirk 17
Church La. Lime 45
Church Pl. Bath 144
Church Pl. Arm 144
Church Pl. Cross 30
Church Pl. Fau 170
Church Pl. Fau 193
Church Rd. B' ness 63
Church Rd. Bonn 155
Church Rd. Call 81
Church Rd. N Ber 54
Church St. All 10
Church St. Bon 58
Church St. Brox 117
Church St. Clack 11
Church St. Cow 13
Church St. Dunb 78
Church St. East 168
Church St. Hadd 132
Church St. Hal 12
Church St. Inver 47
Church St. Kirk 17
Church St. Lime 45
Church St. Loan 181
Church St. Loch 14
Church St. Sten 39
Church St. Sten 39
Church St. Tran 128
Church Wlk. Den 36
Church Wlk. King 35
Church Wynd. B' ness 63
Churchhill Dr. Edin 123
Churchill Dr. B of A 2
Churchill Pl. Ros 46
Churchill St. All 4
Churchill Way. Kirk 149
Churchway. Long 98
Cinderhall Pl. Eiph 128
Circle The. Dan 156
Circus Gdns. Edin 93
Circus La. Edin 93
Circus Pl. Edin 93
Citadel Pl. Edin 93
Citadel St. Edin 93
City Of Edinburgh By-Pass The. Dan 156
City Of Edinburgh By-Pass The. Edin 154
City Of Edinburgh By-Pass The. Kirkl 120
City Of Edinburgh By-Pass The. Rat 121
City Of Edinburgh By-Pass The. White 126
Clackmae Gr. Edin 154
Clackmae Rd. Edin 154
Clackmannan Rd. All 10
Clare Ct. N Ber 54
Clarebank Cres. Edin 94
Claremont. All 10
Claremont Bank. Edin 93
Claremont Cres. Edin 93
Claremont Ct. Edin 93
Claremont Dr. B of A 2
Claremont Gdns. Edin 94
Claremont Gr. Edin 93
Claremont Pk. Edin 94
Claremont Rd. Edin 94
Claremont St. Bon 57
Clarence St. Edin 93
Clarendon Cres. Edin 93
Clarendon Cres. Lin 85
Clarendon Pl. Stir 7
Clarendon Rd. Lin 85
Clarendon Rd. Stir 7
Claret Rd. Gran 61
Claret Rd. Gran 62
Clarinda Ave. Falk 59
Clarinda Gdns. Dalk 157
Clarinda Terr. Edin 155
Clark Ave. Edin 93
Clark Pl. Edin 93
Clark Pl. Kirk 16
Clark Rd. Inver 47
Clark St. Stir 2
Claverhouse Dr. Edin 155
Clayhills Gr. Bale 151
Clayhills Pk. Bale 151
Clayknowes Ave. Muss 126
Clayknowes Cres. Muss 126
Clayknowes Ct. Muss 126
Clayknowes Dr. Muss 126
Clayknowes Pl. Muss 126
Clayknowes Way. Muss 126

Claymore Dr. Bann 7 E2
Cleariburn Cres. Edin 124 A2
Clearburn Gdns. Edin 124 A2
Clearburn Rd. Edin 124 A2
Clearburn Rd. Gore 183 D1
Cleaves The. Tull 4 A1
Cleekim Dr. Edin 125 D2
Cleekim Rd. Edin 125 D2
Cleghorn Dr. Uph 117 D3
Cleikiminrig. Edin 125 D2
Cleish Gdns. Kirk 16 C3
Cleish Pl. Dunf 29 F1
Cleish Rd. Dunf 29 F1
Cleland St. Whit 170 A4
Clement Rise. Muri 148 A1
Clerics Hill. Kirk 89 D1
Clerk Gr. Dunf 29 F1
Clerk Rd. Peni 203 E3
Clerk St. Edin 123 F3
Clerk St. Loan 181 A1
Clerkington Rd. Hadd 131 F4
Clerkington Wlk. Hadd 131 F4
Clermiston Ave. Edin 91 E1
Clermiston Cres. Edin 91 F1
Clermiston Gdns. Edin 91 E1
Clermiston Gn. Edin 91 E1
Clermiston Gr. Edin 91 E1
Clermiston Hill. Edin 91 F1
Clermiston Loan. Edin 91 E1
Clermiston Medway. Edin . 91 E1
Clermiston Pk. Edin 91 E1
Clermiston Pl. Edin 91 E1
Clermiston Rd. Edin 121 E4
Clermiston Rd N. Edin 91 F1
Clermiston Terr. Edin 121 E4
Clermiston View. Edin 91 F1
Clerwood Bank. Edin 121 E4
Clerwood Gdns. Edin 121 E4
Clerwood Gr. Edin 121 E4
Clerwood Loan. Edin 121 E4
Clerwood Pk. Edin 121 E4
Clerwood Pl. Edin 121 E4
Clerwood Row. Edin 121 E4
Clerwood Terr. Edin 121 E4
Clerwood View. Edin 121 E4
Cleuch Ave. Tull 4 A1
Cleuch Dr. Alva 4 C4
Cleuch Rd. N Mid 207 F1
Cleuchbrae. W Cal 172 B2
Cleveland Dr. Inver 47 D1
Clifford Rd. N Ber 54 B3
Clifford Rd. Shir 7 D3
Clifton Rd. Rat 118 C1
Clifton View. Brox 118 A3
Cliftonhall Rd. Kirkl 119 D3
Climpy Rd. For 214 B2
Clinkum Bank. Torr 26 B2
Clinton Rd. Edin 123 D2
Clive St. Shot 191 F3
Cloanden Pl. Kirk 17 D2
Clockhill La. Edin 94 A1
Clockluine Rd. D Bay 47 F2
Close The. Ros 46 B1
Clova Dr. Muri 173 F3
Clovenstone Dr. Edin 152 C4
Clovenstone Gdns. Edin .. 152 C4
Clovenstone Pk. Edin 152 C4
Clovenstone Rd. Edin 152 C4
Cloverbank. Liv 147 F3
Cloves The. Men 4 A3
Clunie Ave. Shot 191 F3
Clufast Brae. Que 67 F1
Clune Rd. Oak 27 F4
Clunie Rd. Dunf 29 F2
Clunivar St. Dunf 28 B3
Cluny Ave. Edin 123 D1
Cluny Dr. Edin 123 D1
Cluny Dr. Sten 38 C2
Cluny Gdns. Edin 123 E1
Cluny Pl. Edin 123 E2
Cluny Terr. Edin 123 D1
Clyde Cres. Dunf 29 F1
Clyde Cres. Lar 38 A2
Clyde Dr. Liv 148 A2
Clyde Dr. Shot 192 A2
Clyde St. Edin 93 E1
Clyde St. Falk 59 F3
Clyde St. Gran 40 A1
Clydesdale St. B' ness 63 F3
Clydevale Pl. Pump 117 D1
Coal Neuk. Tran 128 B3
Coal Rd. Fur 28 C1
Coal Wynd. Bann 7 D1
Coal Wynd. Kirk 17 E2
Coalgate. All 10 A3
Coalgate Ave. Tran 128 C4
Coalgate Rd. Tran 128 C4
Coalhill. Edin 93 F3
Coalpots Way. Fish 5 F2
Coates Cotts. All 99 F2
Coates Cres. Edin 123 D4
Coates Gdns. Edin 123 D4
Coatfield La. Edin 94 A3
Cobblebrae Cres. Falk 39 E1
Cobden Cres. Edin 123 F2

Cobden Rd. Edin 123 F2
Cobden St. Alva 5 D3
Coblecrook Gdns. Alva 4 C3
Coblecrook La. Alva 4 C3
Coblecrook Pl. Alva 4 C3
Coburg St. Edin 93 F3
Cochran Pl. Edin 93 E1
Cochrane Ave. Falk 60 A2
Cochrane Ave. Inver 47 E1
Cochrane Cres. Alva 4 C4
Cochrane Pl. Edin 94 A2
Cochrane Rd. Ros 46 A1
Cochrane Sq. Muri 173 E3
Cochrane St. Bath 145 D4
Cochrane St. Falk 60 A2
Cochrane Terr. Edin 93 E1
Cochrane Way. D Bay 48 A3
Cochrane Wlk. Dunf 29 F2
Cochrans The. Alva 5 D4
Cochrie Pl. Tull 4 B1
Cochrina Pl. Rose 181 E1
Cockburn Cres. Bale 177 D4
Cockburn St. Madd 84 A3
Cockburn Cr. Orm 159 F4
Cockburn Dr. Orm 159 E3
Cockburn Sq. Path 185 D3
Cockburn St. Edin 123 E4
Cockburn St. Falk 60 A2
Cockburnhill Rd. Bale 177 D4
Cocklaw St. Kel 12 C4
Cockles Brae. Giff 132 C2
Cockmylane. Edin 153 F4
Cockpen Ave. Bonn 182 A3
Cockpen Cres. Bonn 182 A3
Cockpen Dr. Bonn 182 A3
Cockpen Pl. Bonn 182 A3
Cockpen Rd. Bonn 182 A3
Cockpen Terr. Bonn 182 A3
Cockpen View. Bonn 182 A3
Coilesdene Gr. Edin 125 E4
Coilesdene Ave. Edin 125 E4
Coilesdene Cres. Edin 125 E4
Coilesdene Dr. Edin 125 E4
Coilesdene Gdns. Edin ... 125 E4
Coilesdene Loan. Edin ... 125 E4
Coire Loan. Shot 192 A2
Coldingham Pl. Dunf 29 E2
Colegate Rd. Path 208 B4
Coles Pl. Cross 31 D3
Colinshiel Ave. Bath 144 C4
Colinshiel St. Bath 144 C4
Colinshiel View. Arm 143 F4
Colinswell Rd. Burn 33 E1
Colinton Gr. Edin 122 B1
Colinton Gr W. Edin 122 B1
Colinton Mains Cres. Edin 153 F3
Colinton Mains Dr. Edin . 153 F3
Colinton Mains Gdns. Edin 153 E3
Colinton Mains Gn. Edin . 153 E4
Colinton Mains Gr. Edin . 153 F3
Colinton Mains Loan. Edin 153 E3
Colinton Mains Pl. Edin .. 153 F3
Colinton Mains Rd. Edin . 153 E3
Colinton Mains Terr. Edin 153 F3
Colinton Rd. Edin 122 C2
Coll Pl. Gran 61 E3
College Cres. Falk 60 B4
College Wynd. Edin 123 E4
Collingwood Ct. Falk 59 F3
Collins Pl. Edin 93 D1
Collision Rd. Dunf 29 E3
Collyland Rd. N Sau 5 E2
Colmestone Gate. Edin ... 154 A3
Colonsay Ave. Pol 61 F1
Colonsay Terr. Falk 60 A1
Colquhoun St. Stir 7 E3
Colsnaur. Men 4 A3
Coltbridge Ave. Edin 122 B4
Coltbridge Gdns. Edin 122 C4
Coltbridge Terr. Edin 122 B4
Coltbridge Vale. Edin 122 C4
Coltness Ave. Alla 212 A4
Columba Ave. Edin 92 A1
Columba Rd. Edin 92 A1
Colvin St. Dunb 78 B1
Combfoot Cottages. E Cal 148 B2
Comely Bank Ave. Edin 93 D1
Comely Bank. Edin 93 D1
Comely Bank Gr. Edin 92 C1
Comely Bank Pl. Edin 93 D1
Comely Bank Place Mews.
  Edin 93 D1
Comely Bank Rd. Edin 93 D1
Comely Bank Row. Edin 93 D1
Comely Bank St. Edin 92 C1
Comely Bank Terr. Edin 93 D1
Comely Green Cres. Edin .. 94 A1
Comely Green Pl. Edin 94 A1
Comely Park La. Dunf 29 D2
Comely Park Terr. Falk 60 A2
Comely Pk. Dunf 29 D2
Comely Pl. Falk 60 A2
Comely Pl. Pol 82 C4
Comiston Dr. Edin 123 D1
Comiston Gdns. Edin 123 D1

Comiston Gr. Edin 154 A4
Comiston Pl. Edin 123 D1
Comiston Rd. Edin 154 A4
Comiston Rise. Edin 154 A4
Comiston Springs Ave.
  Edin 154 A4
Comiston Terr. Edin 123 D1
Comiston View. Edin 154 A4
Commercial La. Kirk 17 E3
Commercial Rd. Inver 47 E1
Commercial School La.
  Dunf 29 D2
Commercial St. Edin 93 F3
Commercial St. Kirk 17 E3
Commissioner St. B'ness ... 64 A4
Commodores Wlk. Ros 46 B1
Compressor House Rd.
  B'ness 62 B3
Compton Rd. Gran 61 E3
Comrie Terr. B'ness 63 F3
Comyn Dr. Pol 82 B4
Comyn St. Shi 82 A4
Concorde Way. Inver 47 E2
Coneyhill Rd. B of A 2 A4
Coneypark. Stir 6 C3
Conifer Rd. May 183 F4
Coningsby Pl. All 10 A3
Connaught Pl. Edin 93 E3
Conner Ave. Falk 60 A4
Considine Gdns. Edin 94 B1
Considine Terr. Edin 94 B1
Constable Rd. Stir 7 D3
Constitution Pl. Edin 94 A3
Constitution St. Edin 94 A3
Conway Ct. Falk 59 F2
Cook Cres. May 183 E3
Cook Pl. Kirk 18 A4
Cook Sq. Loch 14 A4
Cook St. Kirk 18 A4
Cooper's La. Kin 23 F2
Cooperage La. Falk 60 A3
Cope La. Cocke 97 E2
Copeland Cres. Cow 13 D1
Copland Pl. Alva 4 C4
Copper Beech Wynd.
  Crossf 27 E1
Corbett Pl. Dunf 29 F1
Corbiehall. B'ness 63 F4
Corbiehill Ave. Edin 92 A2
Corbiehill Cres. Edin 91 F2
Corbiehill Gdns. Edin 92 A2
Corbiehill Gr. Edin 92 A2
Corbiehill Pl. Edin 91 F2
Corbiehill Rd. Edin 91 F2
Corbiehill Terr. Edin 91 F2
Corbieshot. Edin 125 D3
Corbiewood Dr. Bann 59 F3
Corentin Ct. Falk 60 B2
Corlevoe Ave. Falk 60 A3
Corn Exchange Rd. Stir 7 D4
Cornhill Cres. Stir 7 D2
Cornhill Terr. Edin 94 A2
Cornton Cres. B of A 2 A3
Cornton Rd. B of A 2 A2
Cornton Rd. Stir 2 A2
Cornwall St. Edin 93 E1
Cornwallis Pl. Edin 93 E1
Coronation Pl. Gran 39 F2
Coronation Pl. May 183 E4
Corpach Dr. Dunf 28 C1
Corporation St. Falk 60 B3
Corrennie Dr. Edin 123 D1
Corrennie Gdns. Edin 123 D1
Corrie Ave. Sten 38 C2
Corrie Ct. Newt 183 D2
Corrie Pl. Falk 60 A1
Corruna Ct. Car 230 A1
Corslet Cres. Curr 152 A3
Corslet Pl. Curr 152 A3
Corslet Rd. Curr 152 A3
Corston Pk. Liv 148 A2
Corstorphine Bank Ave.
  Edin 121 E4
Corstorphine Bank Dr.
  Edin 121 E4
Corstorphine Bank Terr.
  Edin 121 E4
Corstorphine High St.
  Edin 121 E3
Corstorphine Hill Ave.
  Edin 121 F4
Corstorphine Hill Cres.
  Edin 121 F4
Corstorphine Hill Gdns.
  Edin 121 F4
Corstorphine Hill Rd.
  Edin 121 F4
Corstorphine House Ave.
  Edin 121 F3
Corstorphine Park Gdns.
  Edin 121 F3
Corstorphine Rd. Edin 122 A4
Cortachy Ave. Sten 39 D2
Cortleferry Dr. Dalk 156 C1
Cortleferry Gr. Dalk 156 C1
Cortleferry Pk. Dalk 156 C1
Cortleferry Terr. Dalk 156 C1
Corunna Pl. Edin 93 F3
Corunna Terr. Auch 204 A3

Cossars Wynd. Dunb 78 B1
Cotburn Cres. Burn 33 F1
Cotlands Ave. Long 98 B2
Cotlands Pk. Long 98 B2
Cotlaws. Kirkl 89 D1
Cottage Cres. Falk 59 F3
Cottage Gn. Edin 91 D2
Cottage Homes. Edin 153 D4
Cottage La. Muss 126 C3
Cottage Pk. Edin 92 A1
Cotton La. Laur 61 D2
Cotts The. Winch 86 C2
Coulport Pl. Dunf 28 C1
Council Houses. Ath 101 F4
Council Houses. Giff 133 E3
Council Houses. Gull 52 A1
Council Houses. Kir 162 C4
Countess Ave. Dunb 78 B1
Countess Cres. Dunb 78 B1
Countess Rd. Dunb 78 B1
County Houses. Cross 31 D3
County Rd. Pres 96 C1
County Sq. Pres 96 C1
Couper Ave. N Ber 54 B3
Couper Gr. Dunf 29 F1
Couper St. Edin 93 F3
Court St. Hadd 132 A4
Courthill. Alva 5 D4
Cousin's La. Dunf 28 C2
Cousland Cres. Black 146 A1
Cousland Interchange. Liv 147 F3
Cousland Rd. Liv 147 E2
Cousland Terr. Black 146 A1
Couston Dr. D Bay 48 A2
Couston Pl. D Bay 48 A2
Couston Rd. D Bay 48 A2
Couston St. Dunf 29 D2
Cove Cres. Shot 191 F3
Covenanter Rd. East 168 B2
Coville Pl. Edin 93 D1
Cow Wynd. Falk 60 A2
Cowan Rd. Edin 122 C2
Cowan St. Bog 145 F3
Cowan St. Bon 58 A3
Cowan Terr. Peni 203 F4
Cowan's Cl. Edin 123 F3
Cowane St. Stir 2 A1
Cowden Cres. Dalk 157 E2
Cowden Gr. Dalk 157 E2
Cowden La. Dalk 157 E2
Cowden Pk. Dalk 157 E2
Cowden Terr. Dalk 157 E2
Cowden View. Dalk 157 E2
Cowdenbeath Rd. Burn 33 F1
Cowdenhill Rd. B'ness 64 A4
Cowgate. Edin 123 E4
Cowgatehead. Edin 123 E4
Cowie Rd. Bann 20 A4
Cowiehall Rd. Cowie 20 B4
Cowpits Ford Rd. Muss 126 B2
Cowpits Rd. White 126 B1
Coxfield. Edin 122 B2
Coxithill Rd. Stir 6 C2
Craig Ave. Hadd 101 D1
Craig Ave. Whit 169 F3
Craig Cres. Stir 2 B2
Craig Ct. B of A 2 A3
Craig Ct. Burn 33 E1
Craig St. Blac 142 C2
Craig St. Ros 47 D2
Craigbank. Crossf 28 B1
Craigbank. N Sau 5 E1
Craigbank Rd. Avon 112 A3
Craigbeath Ct. Cow 13 D3
Craigburn Ct. Falk 59 F1
Craigcrook Ave. Edin 92 A1
Craigcrook Gdns. Edin 92 A1
Craigcrook Gr. Edin 92 A1
Craigcrook Pl. Edin 92 A1
Craigcrook Rd. Edin 92 A1
Craigcrook Sq. Edin 92 A1
Craigcrook Terr. Edin 92 A1
Craigend Dr. O Bay 48 A1
Craigend Dr. Madd 83 D3
Craigend Pk. Edin 124 B1
Craigend Rd. Stir 7 D2
Craigentinny Ave. Edin 94 C1
Craigentinny Avenue N.
  Edin 94 B2
Craigentinny Cres. Edin 94 C1
Craigentinny Gr. Edin 94 C1
Craigentinny Pl. Edin 94 C1
Craigentinny Rd. Edin 94 B1
Craighall Bank. Edin 93 D3
Craighall Cres. Edin 93 D3
Craighall Gdns. Edin 93 D3
Craighall Rd. Edin 93 E3
Craighall St. Stir 1 C1
Craighall Terr. Edin 93 D3
Craighall Terr. Muss 126 C3
Craighill Gdns. Edin 122 C1
Craighill View. Blac 142 C2
Craighlaw. Dech 116 B1
Craighorn. Men 4 A3
Craighorn. Alva 4 C3

Craighouse Ave. Edin 122 C1
Craighouse Gdns. Edin ... 122 C1
Craighouse Pk. Edin 122 C1
Craighouse Rd. Edin 122 C1
Craighouse Terr. Edin 122 C1
Craigie Ct. Lar 38 A1
Craiglebield Cres. Peni ... 203 F2
Craiglaw Farm Cotts. Aber 71 D2
Craigievar Ave. Sten 39 D2
Craigievar Gdns. Kirk 16 C3
Craigievar Sq. Edin 121 D4
Craigievar Wynd. Edin 121 D4
Craiginn Terr. Blac 142 B2
Craigkennochie Terr. Burn . 33 F1
Craiglaw. Dech 116 B1
Craiglea Dr. Edin 123 D1
Craiglea Pl. Edin 122 C1
Craigleith Ave. Falk 59 F1
Craigleith Ave. N Ber 54 B3
Craigleith Ave N. Edin 122 B4
Craigleith Ave S. Edin 122 B4
Craigleith Bank. Edin 92 B1
Craigleith Cres. Edin 92 B1
Craigleith Dr. Edin 92 B1
Craigleith. Fish 5 F2
Craigleith Gdns. Edin 92 B1
Craigleith Gr. Edin 92 B1
Craigleith Hill. Edin 92 B1
Craigleith Hill Ave. Edin 92 B1
Craigleith Hill Cres. Edin ... 92 C1
Craigleith Hill Gdns. Edin .. 92 C1
Craigleith Hill Gn. Edin 92 B1
Craigleith Hill Gr. Edin 92 B1
Craigleith Hill Loan. Edin ... 92 B1
Craigleith Hill Pk. Edin 92 B1
Craigleith Hill Row. Edin ... 92 B1
Craigleith Ind Est. Edin 92 B1
Craigleith Rd. Edin 92 C1
Craigleith Rise. Edin 121 F4
Craigleith Rd. Gran 61 E3
Craigleith Terr. Edin 121 F4
Craigleith View. Edin 122 B4
Craigleith Hill Cres. Edin ... 92 C1
Craiglockhart Ave. Edin .. 122 B1
Craiglockhart Bank. Edin . 122 B1
Craiglockhart Cres. Edin . 122 B1
Craiglockhart Dell Rd. Edin 122 B1
Craiglockhart Dr N. Edin . 122 B1
Craiglockhart Dr S. Edin . 122 B1
Craiglockhart Gdns. Edin . 122 B1
Craiglockhart Gr. Edin 122 B1
Craiglockhart Gr. Edin 153 E4
Craiglockhart Loan. Edin . 122 B1
Craiglockhart Pk. Edin 122 B1
Craiglockhart Pl. Edin 122 B1
Craiglockhart Quadrant.
  Edin 122 B1
Craiglockhart Rd. Edin 122 B1
Craiglockhart Rd N. Edin . 122 B1
Craiglockhart Terr. Edin .. 122 C2
Craiglockhart View. Edin . 122 B1
Craigluscar Ct. Oak 28 A4
Craigluscar Rd. Oak 28 A4
Craigmillar Castle Ave.
  Edin 124 C2
Craigmillar Castle Gdns.
  Edin 124 B2
Craigmillar Castle Gr.
  Edin 124 B2
Craigmillar Castle Loan.
  Edin 124 C2
Craigmillar Castle Rd.
  Edin 124 B1
Craigmillar Castle Terr.
  Edin 124 C2
Craigmillar Pk. Edin 124 A2
Craigmillar Pl. Sten 38 C2
Craigmore Gdns. Torr 26 C1
Craigmount App. Edin 121 E4
Craigmount Ave. Edin 121 E4
Craigmount Ave N. Edin ... 91 D1
Craigmount Bank. Edin 91 D1
Craigmount Bank W. Edin .. 91 D1
Craigmount Brae. Edin 91 D1
Craigmount Cres. Edin 121 E4
Craigmount Ct. Edin 91 D1
Craigmount Dr. Edin 121 D4
Craigmount Gdns. Edin ... 121 E4
Craigmount Gr. Edin 121 D4
Craigmount Gr N. Edin 121 D4
Craigmount Hill. Edin 91 D1
Craigmount. Kirk 16 A4
Craigmount Loan. Edin ... 121 D4
Craigmount Pk. Edin 121 D4
Craigmount Pl. Edin 121 E4
Craigmount Terr. Edin 121 E4
Craigmount View. Edin ... 121 D4
Craigmount Way. Edin 91 E3
Craigmyle St. Dunf 29 E3
Craigomus Cres. Men 3 F3
Craigour Ave. Edin 155 E4
Craigour Cres. Edin 155 F4
Craigour Dr. Edin 155 F4
Craigour Gdns. Edin 155 F4
Craigour Gr. Edin 155 F4
Craigour Loan. Edin 155 F4
Craigour Pl. Edin 155 F4
Craigour Terr. Edin 155 F4
Craigpark Ave. Rat 119 E1
Craigpark Cres. Rat 119 E1

240

Craigpark. Torp

Dovehill. A

Craigpark. Torp 113 F3
Craigridge Pl. D Bay 48 B3
Craigrie Terr. Clack 11 D2
Craigrigg Cotts. West 112 C2
Craigs Ave. Edin 121 E3
Craigs Bank. Edin 121 D4
Craigs Chalet Pk. Torp 84 A2
Craigs Cres. Edin 121 E4
Craigs Ct. Torp 113 F3
Craigs Dr. Edin 121 D4
Craigs Gdns. Edin 121 D4
Craigs Gr. Edin 121 E4
Craigs Loan. Edin 121 E4
Craigs Pk. Edin 121 D4
Craigs Rd. Edin 121 D4
Craigs Terr. Madd 82 C4
Craigseaton. Uph 117 D3
Craigshill E. Liv 148 A3
Craigshill Rd. Liv 148 A3
Craigshill St. Liv 148 A3
Craigston Dr. Dunf 29 E3
Craigswood. Liv 148 A3
Craigton Cres. Alva 4 C3
Craigton Pl. Cow 13 E1
Craigview. N Sau 5 E1
Craigward. All 10 A3
Craigwell Path. Lime 44 B4
Crame Terr. Dalk 156 C1
Cramond Ave. Edin 91 E3
Cramond Bank. Edin 91 D3
Cramond Brig Toll. Dal 90 C2
Cramond Cres. Edin 91 D3
Cramond Ct. Falk 60 A1
Cramond Gdns. Edin 91 D3
Cramond Gdns. Kirk 16 C4
Cramond Glebe Gdns. Edin 91 E3
Cramond Glebe Rd. Edin 91 D3
Cramond Glebe Terr. Edin 91 D3
Cramond Gn. Edin 91 D3
Cramond Gr. Edin 91 D3
Cramond Pk. Edin 91 D3
Cramond Pl. D Bay 48 B2
Cramond Pl. Edin 91 E3
Cramond Rd N. Edin 91 E3
Cramond Rd S. Edin 91 F2
Cramond Regis. Edin 91 D2
Cramond Terr. Edin 91 D3
Cramond Vale. Edin 91 D3
Cramond Village. Edin 91 D4
Cranshaws Dr. Laur 61 E1
Cranston Dr. Path 158 B3
Cranston St. Edin 123 F4
Cranston St. Peni 203 F3
Crarae Ave. Edin 122 B4
Crathes Ave. Sten 39 D2
Crathes Gdns. Muri 173 F3
Crathie Dr. Duni 36 B2
Craufurdland. Edin 91 D2
Crawfield Ave. B' ness 63 F3
Crawfield La. B' ness 63 F3
Crawfield Rd. B' ness 63 F2
Crawford Dr. Shi 82 A4
Crawford Pl. Dunf 29 E4
Crawford Sq. Air 22 B2
Crawfurd Rd. Edin 124 A2
Crawlees Cres. May 183 F3
Craws Knowe. For 215 D1
Creel Ct. N Ber 54 B4
Creran Dr. Bank 57 E3
Crescent The. Edin 123 D1
Crescent The. Gore 183 E2
Crescent The. Ros 46 A1
Creteil Pl. Gran 61 E4
Crewe Bank. Edin 92 C3
Crewe Cres. Edin 92 C3
Crewe Gr. Edin 92 C3
Crewe Loan. Edin 92 B3
Crewe Pl. Edin 92 B3
Crewe Rd N. Edin 92 B3
Crewe Rd S. Edin 92 C2
Crewe Rd W. Edin 92 B3
Crewe Road Gdns. Edin 92 B3
Crewe Terr. Edin 92 C3
Crewe Toll. Edin 92 B2
Crichton Ave. Path 185 D3
Crichton Dr. Gran 61 F4
Crichton Dr. Path 185 D3
Crichton Rd. Path 185 D3
Crichton St. Edin 123 E4
Crichton Terr. Path 185 D3
Crighton Pl. Edin 93 F2
Crimond Pl. Shi 81 F4
Cringate Gdns. Bann 7 F1
Crockett Gdns. Peni 203 E3
Croft An Righ. King 35 D2
Croft Pl. Liv 147 E3
Croft St. Dalk 157 D2
Croft St. Peni 203 F2
Croft's Rd. Tull 4 A2
Croft-An-Righ. Edin 93 F1
Crofters Way. Ston 170 C3
Croftfoot Dr. Fau 194 A3
Croftfoot Pl. Duni 36 B2
Crofthead Ct. Stir 2 A1
Crofthead Ctr. Muri 173 E4
Crofthead Interchange. Muri 173 F4
Crofthead Rd. Stir 2 A1
Crofthead Rd. Ston 171 D1
Croftmalloch Rd. Whit 170 A3
Crofts Rd. Cock 140 C1
Crofts The. E Lin 104 C1
Croftsacre. Cock 140 C1
Croftshaw Rd. Alva 5 D4
Croftside Ct. Gran 61 F3
Cromarty Pl. Kirk 17 F4
Cromwell Dr. Falk 60 B2
Cromwell Pl. Edin 93 F3
Cromwell Rd. Burn 33 F1
Cromwell Rd. Falk 60 B2
Cromwell Rd. N Ber 54 A4
Cromwell Rd. Ros 46 C3
Cromwell Rd W. Falk 60 B2
Crookston Rd. Muss 126 C2
Crophill. N Sau 5 E1
Cross Brae. Shi 81 E3
Cross Loan. Orm 159 F4
Cross Row. Lime 45 D2
Cross St. Falk 39 D1
Cross St. Kirk 18 A4
Cross The. Lin 85 D4
Cross Way. D Bay 48 B3
Cross Wynd. Dunf 29 D2
Crossen La. Car 230 A1
Crossgatehead Rd. Pol 82 B4
Crossgreen Dr. Uph 117 D3
Crossgreen Pl. Uph 117 D3
Crosshill Dr. B' ness 63 F3
Crosshill Dr. Bath 145 E3
Crossroads Pl. Ros 46 C2
Crosswood Ave. Bale 177 D4
Crosswood Cres. Bale 177 D4
Crosswood Terr. Auc 217 F2
Crowhill Rd. D Bay 48 B2
Crown Gdns. All 9 F4
Crown Pl. Edin 93 F2
Crown St. Edin 93 F2
Crownest Loan. Lar 38 C1
Cruachan Ave. Stir 2 A2
Cruachan Ct. Falk 60 B1
Cruachan Ct. Peni 204 A3
Cruachan Pl. Gran 61 F3
Cruickness Rd. Inver 68 B4
Cruickshank Dr. Shi 81 E3
Cruikshank's Ct. Den 36 C1
Crum Cres. Stir 7 E1
Crusader Dr. Rosl 180 C2
Crusader Rise. Muri 148 A1
Cuddy La. Edin 123 D2
Cuddyhouse Rd. Cow 12 B2
Cuddyhouse Rd. Hal 12 B2
Cuffabouts. B'ness 64 B4
Cuguen Pl. Bonn 156 A1
Cuiken Ave. Peni 203 F3
Cuiken Bank. Peni 203 E3
Cuiken Terr. Peni 203 F3
Cuikenburn. Peni 203 F4
Cuil Gr. Dunf 28 B3
Cuillin Ct. Falk 60 B1
Cuillin Pl. Gran 61 F3
Cullalo Cres. Abe 49 E4
Cullaloe Ct. D Bay 48 B2
Cullaloe View. Cow 13 E1
Cullen Cres. Kirk 16 C4
Culloch Rd. Slam 110 A3
Culmore Pl. Falk 60 C1
Cultenhove Cres. Gran 61 F3
Cultenhove Cres. Stir 6 C2
Cultenhove Pl. Stir 7 D2
Cultenhove Rd. Stir 7 D2
Cultins Rd. Edin 121 D1
Cultrig Dr. Whit 170 A3
Culvain Pl. Falk 60 B1
Culzean Cres. Kirk 16 B4
Culzean Pl. Sten 38 C2
Cumberland St. Edin 93 E1
Cumbernauld Rd. Bank 57 D2
Cumbrae Ct. Kirk 17 D4
Cumbrae Dr. Falk 59 E2
Cumbrae Terr. Kirk 17 D4
Cumin Pl. Edin 123 F2
Cumlodden Ave. Edin 122 B4
Cumnor Cres. Edin 124 A1
Cunnigar Gdns. E Cal 148 B2
Cunnigar Hill View. Liv 148 B2
Cunningham Ct. Long 98 B2
Cunningham Ct. N Ber 54 A3
Cunningham Dr. East 168 B3
Cunningham Gdns. Falk 60 C3
Cunningham Rd. Ros 46 B1
Cunningham Rd. Sten 39 D2
Cunningham Rd. Stir 7 E4
Cunningham St. Gran 61 E3
Curran Cres. Brox 117 F3
Curriehill Castle Dr. Curr 151 E2
Curriehill Rd. Curr 151 F3
Currieside Ave. Shot 191 F2
Currieside Pl. Shot 191 E2
Currievale Dr. Curr 151 F2
Currievale Park Gr. Curr 151 F2
Currievale Pk. Curr 151 F2
Cushenquarter Dr. Plea 20 B2
Custom House Sq. Dunb 78 C2
Custonhall Pl. Den 36 B1
Cuthill Cres. Ston 171 E1
Cuthill Terr. Ston 171 E1
Cuttyfield Pl. Sten 39 E2
Cypress Gr. Dunf 46 B4
D'arcy Rd. May 183 F3
Daiches Braes. Edin 125 E3
Dairy Cotts. Dir 53 D1
Daisy Terr. Edin 122 C2
Dalachy Cotts. Abe 32 C1
Dalbeath Cres. Cow 13 D1
Dalbeath Gdns. Cow 12 C1
Dalcross Way. Dunf 29 F3
Dalderse Ave. Falk 60 A3
Dalgety Ave. Edin 94 A1
Dalgety Gdns. D Bay 48 B3
Dalgety House View. D Bay 48 B3
Dalgety Rd. Edin 94 A1
Dalgety St. Edin 94 A1
Dalgleish Ct. Stir 7 D4
Dalgrain Rd. Gran 40 A1
Dalhousie Ave. Bonn 182 A3
Dalhousie Ave W. Bonn 182 A3
Dalhousie Dr. Bonn 182 A3
Dalhousie Gdns. Bonn 182 A3
Dalhousie Rd. Dalk 156 C1
Dalhousie Rd E. Bonn 182 A3
Dalhousie Rd W. Bonn 182 A3
Dalhousie Terr. Edin 123 D1
Dalkeith Rd. Edin 123 F3
Dalkeith St. Edin 125 E4
Dallas Ave. Burn 33 F1
Dallas Dr. Kirk 16 C4
Dalling Rd. Bath 144 C3
Dalmahoy Cres. Bale 151 E2
Dalmahoy Rd. Rat 119 E1
Dalmeny Rd. Edin 93 E3
Dalmeny St. Edin 93 F2
Dalmeny View. D Bay 48 B2
Dalmore Dr. Alva 4 C3
Dalmorglen Pk. Stir 6 C3
Dalratho Rd. Gran 61 F4
Dalry Pl. Edin 123 D4
Dalry Rd. Edin 122 C4
Dalrymple Cres. Edin 123 F2
Dalrymple Cres. Muss 126 A3
Dalrymple Gdns. Path 158 B3
Dalrymple Loan. Muss 126 B3
Dalton Ct. May 183 F3
Dalum Ct. Loan 181 D4
Dalum Dr. Loan 181 D4
Dalum Gr. Loan 181 D4
Dalum Loan. Loan 181 D4
Dalziel Pl. Edin 94 A1
Damhead Holdings Scheme. Rosl 154 B1
Damside. Edin 123 D4
Danderhall Cres. Dan 156 A4
Daniel Pl. Ros 46 B3
Danube St. Edin 93 D1
Dargai Pl. Uph 117 D3
Darian La. B' ness 63 F4
Darmeid Pl. Alla 212 A4
Darnaway St. Edin 93 D1
Darnell Rd. Edin 93 D3
Darney Terr. King 34 C1
Darnley St. Stir 7 D4
Darrach Dr. Duni 36 A1
Darwin St. Liv 148 A3
Davaar Dr. Kirk 16 C4
Davarr Pl. Falk 59 E2
Davenport Pl. Ros 46 C2
David Millar Pl. Dunf 28 C3
David Scott Ave. May 183 F4
David St. Dunf 29 D3
David St. Kirk 17 D2
David St. Loch 14 A4
David The First St. King 34 C1
David's Loan. Falk 39 E1
Davidson Gdns. Edin 92 A2
Davidson La. Car 230 A1
Davidson Pk. Edin 92 C2
Davidson Rd. Edin 92 C2
Davidson St. Bann 7 E1
Davidson Terr. Hadd 100 C1
Davidson Way. Liv 147 F4
Davie St. Edin 123 F4
Daviot Rd. Dunf 29 F3
Dawson Ave. All 9 F4
Dawson Ave. Liv 147 F3
Dawson Pl. B' ness 63 F3
Dawson St. Falk 60 A4
De Quincey Path. Bonn 181 F3
De Quincey Rd. Bonn 181 F3
Deacons Ct. Lin 85 D3
Dean Bank La. Edin 93 D1
Dean Cres. Stir 2 B1
Dean Ct. Long 98 B2
Dean Dr. Crossf 28 A1
Dean Gr. Crossf 28 A1
Dean Park Cres. Edin 93 D1
Dean Park Mews. Edin 93 D1
Dean Path. Edin 92 C1
Dean Pk. Long 98 B2
Dean Pk. Newt 183 D3
Dean Pk. Oak 27 F4
Dean Pk Pl. Newt 183 D3
Dean Pk St. Edin 93 D1
Dean Pl. Black 146 A1
Dean Pl. Peni 203 E3
Dean Rd. B' ness 63 F3
Dean Rd. Kirk 17 D2
Dean Rd. Long 98 B2
Dean Rd. Peni 203 E3
Dean Ridge. Oak 27 F4
Dean St. Edin 93 D1
Dean St. Whit 170 A4
Dean Terr. Edin 93 D1
Dean The. E Lin 75 F1
Deanburn Gr. B' ness 63 E3
Deanburn. Peni 203 F4
Deanburn Pk. Lin 84 C3
Deanburn Rd. Lin 84 C3
Deanburn Wlk. B' ness 63 E3
Deanery Cl. Edin 94 B1
Deanfield Cres. B' ness 63 F4
Deanfield Dr. B' ness 63 F3
Deanfield Pl. B' ness 63 F4
Deanfield Rd. B' ness 63 F4
Deanfield Terr. B' ness 63 F3
Deangate Gdns. B' ness 63 E3
Deanhaugh St. Edin 93 D1
Deanpark Ave. Bale 151 E1
Deanpark Bank. Bale 151 E1
Deanpark Brae. Bale 151 E1
Deanpark Cres. Bale 151 E1
Deanpark Ct. Bale 151 D1
Deanpark Gdns. Bale 151 E1
Deanpark Gr. Bale 151 E1
Deanpark Pl. Bale 151 E1
Deans N. Liv 146 C3
Deans Rd. Liv 146 B3
Deans Roundabout. Liv 146 B3
Deans S. Liv 146 C3
Deans Service Units. Liv 146 C3
Deanswood Pk. Liv 146 C3
Deantown Ave. White 157 F4
Deantown Dr. White 126 C1
Deantown Path. White 126 C1
Deas Rd. Inver 47 D1
Deas Rd. Shot 191 E3
Dechmont Rd. Edin 121 D3
Dedridge East Rd. Muri 148 A1
Dedridge North Rd. Muri 147 F1
Dedridge Nursery Units. Muri 148 A1
Dedridge West Rd. Muri 173 F4
Dee Dr. Liv 148 A3
Dee Pl. Dunf 29 F1
Dee St. Shot 191 E3
Deer Pk Rd. New 66 C1
Deerhill. Dech 116 B1
Deerpark. N Sau 5 F1
Deeside Dr. Car 230 A2
Delisle St. Dunb 78 B1
Dell Ave. Arm 143 F3
Dell Rd. Edin 153 D4
Delph Rd. Tull 4 B1
Delphwood Cres. Tull 4 B1
Delta Ave. Muss 127 D3
Delta Cres. Muss 127 D3
Delta Dr. Muss 127 D3
Delta Gdns. Muss 127 D3
Delta Pl. Muss 126 B2
Delta Rd. Muss 127 D3
Delta View. Muss 127 D3
Dempster Pl. Dunf 28 C3
Den La. Shot 191 E3
Den Rd. Kirk 17 E3
Denburn Pl. Kirk 17 E3
Denburn Rd. Kirk 17 E4
Denend Cres. Kirk 17 D3
Denham Green Ave. Edin 93 D3
Denham Green Pl. Edin 93 D3
Denham Green Terr. Edin 93 D3
Denholm Gr. Arm 143 F4
Denholm Rd. Muss 125 F3
Denholm Way. Muss 125 F3
Denny Rd. Bank 57 F3
Denny Rd. Lar 38 A1
Denovan Rd. Duni 36 C2
Denovan Rd. Tor 36 C2
Dequincey Wlk. Tran 128 B3
Derby St. Edin 93 E3
Deroran Pl. Stir 6 C3
Derwent Ave. Falk 59 F2
Devon Ct. Tull 4 A1
Devon Dr. Men 4 C2
Devon Pl. Camb 4 A1
Devon Pl. Edin 122 C4
Devon Rd. All 10 B3
Devon St. Gran 40 A1
Devon Terr. Dunf 29 F1
Devon Village. Fish 5 F2
Devonbank. Fish 5 F2
Devonway. Clack 11 D3
Dewar Ave. Kin 23 F2
Dewar Pl. Edin 123 D4
Dewar Place La. Edin 123 D4
Dewar Sq. Liv 146 B3
Dewar St. Dunf 28 C2
Dewar St. Loch 14 A4
Dewshill Cotts. Sals 167 D2
Dick Cres. Burn 33 F1
Dick Gdns. Whit 169 F3
Dick Pl. Edin 123 E2
Dick Pl. Ros 46 C3
Dick Pl. Ston 171 E1
Dick St. Dunf 29 E
Dick Terr. Peni 203 F
Dickburn Cres. Bon 57 F
Dickies Wells. Alva 5 E
Dickson Ct. Loch 14 A
Dickson St. Dunf 29 D
Dickson St. Edin 93 F
Dickson St. W Cal 172 B
Dicksons Gr. Bonn 182 A
Dinmont Dr. Edin 124 A
Dirleton Ave. N Ber 54 A
Dirleton Gdns. All 9 F
Dirleton La. All 9 F
Dirleton Rd. Dir 53 D
Dirleton Rd. N Ber 53 F
Distillery La. Edin 122 C
Diverswell. N Sau 5 E
Dixon Terr. Whit 170 A
Dobbie Ave. Lar 38 B
Dobbie's Rd. Bonn 182 A4
Dobson's Pl. Hadd 131 F4
Dobson's View. Hadd 131 F4
Dobson's Wlk. Hadd 131 F4
Dochart Cres. Pol 61 F1
Dochart Dr. Edin 91 E1
Dochart Path. Gran 61 E3
Dochart Pl. Falk 60 B
Dock Pl. Edin 93 F3
Dock Rd. Gran 40 B
Dock St. B'ness 64 A
Dock St. Edin 93 F3
Dock St. Sten 39 E1
Doctor's Row. Kirk 17 F4
Dog Well Wynd. Lin 85 D4
Dollar Ave. Falk 60 A4
Dollar Cres. Kirk 16 B4
Dollar Ct. Dunf 28 C3
Dollar Gdns. Falk 60 A4
Dollar Gr. Burn 33 F1
Dollar Rd. Burn 33 F1
Dolphin Ave. Curr 151 F2
Dolphin Gdns E. Curr 151 F2
Dolphin Gdns W. Curr 151 F2
Dolphin Rd. Curr 151 F2
Don Dr. Liv 148 A3
Don Rd. Dunf 29 F1
Don St. Gran 40 A1
Donald St. Dunf 29 E3
Donaldson Ct. Kin 23 F2
Donaldson Pl. Cam 6 B3
Donibristle Gdns. D Bay 48 A1
Doo'cot Brae. All 10 A4
Doocot Brae. B'ness 64 A4
Doon Ave. Dunb 78 B1
Doon Wlk. Liv 148 A2
Dornie Wynd. Shot 192 A2
Dorrator Rd. Falk 59 F3
Dorset Pl. Edin 123 D3
Double Dykes. Muss 126 B2
Double Hedges Pk. Edin 124 A1
Double Hedges Rd. Edin 124 A1
Double Row. Lime 45 D2
Dougall Ct. May 183 E3
Dougall Pl. May 183 E3
Dougall Rd. May 183 E3
Douglas Ave. Crossf 28 A1
Douglas Ave. Gran 61 F3
Douglas Ave. Lin 84 C3
Douglas Ave. Pol 82 B4
Douglas Cres. Bonn 182 A4
Douglas Cres. Edin 122 C4
Douglas Cres. Long 98 C3
Douglas Dr. B' ness 63 F3
Douglas Dr. Dunf 28 C3
Douglas Dr. Stir 7 E2
Douglas Gdns. Edin 122 C4
Douglas Gdns Mews. Edin 122 C4
Douglas Pk. Dunf 28 C3
Douglas Pl. B' ness 63 F3
Douglas Pl. Lin 84 C3
Douglas Pl. Sten 38 C2
Douglas Rd. B' ness 63 F3
Douglas Rd. Long 98 C3
Douglas Rd. Ros 46 B1
Douglas St. Bann 7 F1
Douglas St. Dunf 29 D2
Douglas St. Kirk 17 D2
Douglas St. Stir 2 A1
Douglas Terr. B' ness 63 F3
Douglas Terr. Stir 6 C3
Douglaswynd. Uph 117 D3
Doune Cres. Sten 39 D2
Doune Pk. D Bay 48 B2
Doune Terr. Edin 93 D1
Dovecot Brae. Tran 128 B4
Dovecot Gr. Edin 122 A1
Dovecot Loan. Edin 122 A1
Dovecot Pk. Abe 49 D3
Dovecot Pk. Edin 153 D4
Dovecot Pk. Lin 85 E4
Dovecot Pk. Pen 160 C3
Dovecot Pl. Tull 4 A2
Dovecot Rd. Edin 121 E3
Dovecot Rd. Laur 61 D1
Dovecot Rd. Tull 4 A2
Dovecot Way. Pen 160 C4
Dovecote Pl. Liv 147 E2
Dovehill. All 10 A4

owan Pl. Stir 6 C3
wer Cres. B'ness 64 A4
wie's Mill La. Edin 90 C2
wnfield. Cow 13 E3
wnfield Pl. Edin 122 C3
wnie Dr. Edin 121 F3
wnie Pl. Muss 126 B3
wning Point. D.Bay 48 A1
wns Cres. All 9 F3
eghorn Ave. Edin 153 F3
eghorn Cr. Edin 153 F3
eghorn Gdns. Edin 153 F3
eghorn Gr. Edin 153 F3
eghorn Junc. Edin 153 F3
eghorn Loan. Edin 153 F3
eghorn Loan. Edin 153 D3
eghorn Pk. Edin 153 E3
eghorn Pl. Edin 153 F3
em Farm Cotts. Gull 73 D2
ip Rd. Stir 1 C1
onachy Rd. Kirk 16 C2
ossie Rd. Falk 60 A2
ove Loan. Bon 57 F4
ove Loan Cres. Bank 57 F4
ove Loan. Den 57 F3
ove Rd. Arm 143 F4
overhall Ave. Cross 31 D3
overhall Pl. Cross 31 D3
overs Rd. Brox 118 A3
um Ave. Edin 155 F3
um Brae Ave. Edin 121 E4
um Brae Cres. Edin 91 E1
um Brae Dr. Edin 91 E1
um Brae Gdns. Edin 121 E4
um Brae Gr. Edin 91 E1
um Brae Neuk. Edin 121 E4
um Brae Park App. Edin 121 E4
um Brae Pl. Edin 121 E4
um Brae S. Edin 121 E4
um Brae Ter. Edin 91 E1
um Brae Wlk. Edin 91 D1
um Cotts. Edin 155 F3
um Cres. Edin 155 F3
um Pl. Edin 155 F3
um Rd. Whit 170 C4
um Rd. Dunf 29 E1
um Rd. Muir 64 B3
um St. Edin 155 F3
um Ter. Edin 94 A1
urum View. Dan 156 A4
urumacre Rd. B'ness 64 A3
urumclair Ave. Slam 110 A3
urumcross Rd. Bath 145 D4
urumdryan St. Edin 123 D3
urumlanrig Pl. Sten 38 C2
urummor Ave. Muss 127 D3
urummohr Gdns. Muss 127 D3
urumpark St. Stir 7 D3
urummond La. Stir 7 D3
urummond Pk. Gran 61 F3
urummond Pl. Bac 142 B2
urummond Pl. Bon 58 A4
urummond Pl. Dunf 29 E3
urummond Pl. Edin 93 E1
urummond Pl. Gran 61 F4
urummond Pl. Stir 7 D3
urummond Place La. Stir 7 D3
urummond Rd. Muir 173 E3
urummore Dr. Pres 127 F4
urummormie Rd. Crosrf 27 E1
urummond Sq. Loch 14 A4
urumpark Ave. B'ness 64 A3
urumpark St. B'ness 64 A3
urumshaugh Gdns. Edin 123 D4
urumshoreland Ave.
 Pump 148 A4
urumshoreland Cres.
 Pump 148 A4
urumshoreland Pl. Pump 148 A4
urumshoreland Rd. Pump 148 A4
urumside Terr. B'ness 64 A4
ryburgh Ave. Den 36 B1
ryburgh Pl. Loch 14 A4
ryburgh Way. Gran 61 F3
ryden Ave. Loan 181 D4
ryden Cres. Loan 181 D4
ryden Gdns. Edin 93 F2
ryden Glen. Loan 180 C4
ryden Gr. Rosl 181 D2
ryden Pl. Edin 93 F3
ryden Rd. Loan 180 C4
ryden St. Edin 93 F2
ryden Terr. Edin 93 F2
ryden Terr. Loan 181 D4
ryden View. Loan 181 D4
rylaw Cres. Edin 92 B1
rylaw Cres. Edin 92 A1
rylaw Gdns. E.Lin 103 E4
rylaw Gdns. Edin 92 A1
rylaw Gr. Edin 92 A1
rylaw House Gdn. Edin 92 A2
rylaw House Paddock.
 Edin 92 A2
rylaw Terr. E.Lin 103 E4
rylawhill. E.Lin 75 E1
ryrie St. Cow 13 D2

Drysdale Ave. Whit 170 A4
Drysdale St. All 10 A3
Duart Cres. Edin 91 E1
Dublin Meuse. Edin 93 E1
Dublin St. Edin 93 E1
Dublin Street La N. Edin 93 E1
Dublin Street La S. Edin 93 E1
Duddingston Ave. Edin 124 C4
Duddingston Cres. New 88 A4
Duddingston Gdns S. Edin 124 C3
Duddingston Gr E. Edin 124 C3
Duddingston Gr W. Edin 124 C3
Duddingston Loan. Edin 124 C3
Duddingston Mills. Edin 124 C4
Duddingston Pk. Edin 125 D4
Duddingston Pk S. Edin 125 E3
Duddingston Rd. Edin 124 C4
Duddingston Rd W. Edin 124 B3
Duddingston Rise. Edin 124 C3
Duddingston Row. Edin 124 C3
Duddingston Sq E. Edin 124 C3
Duddingston Sq W. Edin 124 C3
Duddingston View. Edin 124 C3
Duddingston Yards. Edin 125 D3
Duddingstone Terr. New 88 A4
Duddingston Gdns. N. Edin 124 C3
Dudgeon Pl. Kirk 89 D1
Dudley Ave. Edin 93 E3
Dudley Ave S. Edin 93 E3
Dudley Bank. Edin 93 E3
Dudley Cres. Edin 93 E3
Dudley Gdns. Edin 93 E3
Dudley Gr. Edin 93 E3
Dudley Terr. Edin 93 E3
Duff Cres. Stir 1 C1
Duff Ct. N.Ber 54 A4
Duff St. Edin 122 C3
Duff Street La. Edin 122 C3
Duffy Pl. Ros 46 C2
Dugald Stewart Ave. B'ness 64 A4
Duglas Rise. Muri 148 A1
Duke Pl. Edin 94 A2
Duke St. Alva 5 D4
Duke St. Bann 7 E1
Duke St. Clack 11 D2
Duke St. Dalk 157 D2
Duke St. Den 36 B1
Duke St. Dunb 78 B1
Duke St. Dunb 78 A1
Duke St. Edin 94 A2
Duke St. Gran 61 E3
Duke St. Rose 181 E1
Duke's Wlk. Edin 94 A1
Dumbarton Rd. Stir 6 C4
Dumbarton Rd. Stir 7 D4
Dumbiedykes Rd. Edin 123 F4
Dumbryden Dr. Edin 121 F1
Dumbryden Gdns. Edin 121 F1
Dumbryden Gr. Edin 121 F1
Dumyat Ave. Tull 4 A1
Dumyat Dr. Falk 59 F2
Dumyat Rd. Alva 4 C3
Dumyat Rd. Men 3 F3
Dumyat Rd. Stir 2 B2
Dumyat St. All 4 C1
Dunard Gdn. Edin 123 E2
Dunbar Ave. Sten 38 C2
Dunbar Gate. Duni 36 C2
Dunbar Pl. Kirk 16 C3
Dunbar Rd. Hadd 101 D1
Dunbar Rd. N.Ber 54 C3
Dunbar St. Edin 123 D3
Duncairn Ave. Bon 57 F3
Duncan Ave. Sten 39 D2
Duncan Cres. Dunf 29 F1
Duncan Ct. N.Ber 54 A3
Duncan Gdns. Tran 128 B4
Duncan Gr. Liv 147 D4
Duncan Pl. Edin 94 A2
Duncan St. Bon 57 F3
Duncan St. Edin 123 F2
Duncan St. Kirk 17 D2
Duncanson Ave. All 10 A4
Duncanson Dr. Muri 34 A1
Duncarron Pl. Den 36 C1
Duncur Rd. Gull 52 B2
Dundaff Ct. Den 36 B1
Dundarroch St. Lar 38 A1
Dundas Ave. N.Ber 54 B3
Dundas Ave. Que 89 E4
Dundas Cotts. Bon 57 D1
Dundas Cres. Clack 11 D3
Dundas Cres. Dalk 156 C1
Dundas Cres. Laur 61 D2
Dundas Gr. Dalk 156 C1
Dundas Pk. Bonn 182 B4
Dundas Pl. Kirkl 89 D1
Dundas Rd. Dalk 156 C1
Dundas Rd. Laur 61 D2
Dundas Rd. N.Ber 54 B3
Dundas Rd. Ros 67 E4
Dundas St. Bonn 182 A2
Dundas St. Bath 145 D4
Dundas St. Dunf 29 E4
Dundas St. Edin 93 E1

Dundas St. Gran 61 E4
Dundas St. Loch 14 A4
Dundee Pl. Falk 60 A4
Dundee St. Edin 122 C3
Dundonald Rd. Ros 46 B2
Dundonald St. Edin 93 E1
Dundrennan Cotts. Edin 124 B1
Dunearn Bank. Burn 33 E1
Dunearn Dr. Kirk 16 C3
Dunearn St. Edin 93 E2
Dunfermline Rd. Cross 30 C3
Dunfermline Rd. Lime 45 F2
Dunfermline Wynd. Inver 47 D1
Dunimarle St. H.Val 26 A1
Dunkeld Pl. Falk 39 E1
Dunlop Sq. Liv 146 B3
Dunlop Terr. Peni 204 A3
Dunmar Cres. All 4 C1
Dunn Cres. Dunf 29 F2
Dunn Pl. Winch 87 F1
Dunn St. Uph 117 D3
Dunn Terr. East 168 C3
Dunnet Way. Brox 118 A3
Dunnikier Rd. Kirk 17 E3
Dunnikier Way. Kirk 17 E4
Dunning Pl. Falk 39 E1
Dunnottar Dr. Sten 38 A2
Dunnottar Pl. Kirk 16 C2
Dunollie Ct. Edin 121 D4
Dunollie Gdns. Hadd 132 B4
Dunpender Dr. Hadd 100 C1
Dunpender Rd. E.Lin 103 E4
Dunrobin Ave. Sten 38 C3
Dunrobin Pl. Edin 93 D1
Dunrobin Rd. Kirk 16 C2
Duns Rd. Giff 163 F3
Dunsire St. Kirk 17 F4
Dunsmuir Ct. Edin 121 E3
Dunster Rd. Stir 2 B2
Dunure Cres. Bon 58 A3
Dunure Pl. Kirk 16 C2
Dunure St. Bon 58 A3
Dunvegan Ave. Kirk 16 B3
Dunvegan Ave. Sten 38 C2
Dunvegan Ct. All 10 A4
Dunvegan Ct. Crossf 28 A1
Dunvegan Ct. Edin 91 D2
Dunvegan Dr. Falk 39 E1
Dunvegan Dr. Stir 2 A2
Dunvegan Gdns. Muri 173 F3
Dunvegan Pl. Bon 57 F3
Dunvegan Pl. Pol 62 A1
Dura Rd. Alla 212 B3
Durar Dr. Edin 91 E1
Durham Ave. Bath 144 C3
Durham Bank. Bonn 182 B3
Durham Dr. Bath 144 C3
Durham Dr. Bath 144 C4
Durham Gdns N. Edin 125 D4
Durham Gdns S. Edin 125 D3
Durham Gr. Bonn 182 B3
Durham Gr. Edin 125 D4
Durham Pl. Bonn 182 B3
Durham Pl E. Edin 125 D4
Durham Pl W. Edin 124 C4
Durham Place La. Edin 125 D4
Durham Rd. Edin 125 D4
Durham Rd S. Edin 125 D4
Durham Sq. Edin 125 D4
Durham Terr. Edin 124 C4
Durham Terr. Torr 26 B3
Durie Pk. Burn 50 B4
Durie's Pk. Elph 128 A1
Durward Rise. Muri 148 A1
Durwood Gr. Edin 124 A1
Dyfrig St. Shot 191 F3
Dyke Brow. Hart 169 D3
Dyke Rd. Hart 169 D3
Dykes Rd. Peni 203 F4
Dykeside Rd. Bath 144 C4
Dymond Gr. Dunf 46 C4
Dysart Rd. Kirk 17 F3

East Barnton Ave. Edin 91 F2
East Barnton Gdns. Edin 91 F2
East Bay. Inver 68 B3
East Boreland Pl. Den 36 C1
East Bridge St. Falk 60 B2
East Brighton Cres. Edin 125 D4
East Broomhill Rd. Burn 50 C4
East Caiystane Pl. Edin 154 A3
East Caiystane Rd. Edin 154 A3
East Campbell Ct. Long 98 B3
East Castle Rd. Edin 123 D3
East Castle St. All 10 A3
East Champanyie. Edin 123 F2
East Clapperfield. Edin 124 A1
East Claremont St. Edin 93 E2
East Comiston. Edin 154 A3
East Croft. Rat 119 F1
East Cromwell St. Edin 93 F3
East Crosscauseway. Edin 123 F3
East Ct. Edin 92 B1
East Ct. Edin 124 C2
East Dr. Lar 38 B1
East End. W.Cal 172 B2
East Farm Of Gilmerton.
 Edin 155 F3
East Fenton Farm Cotts. Dir 73 E4
East Fergus Pl. Kirk 17 D2
East Fettes Ave. Edin 92 C2
East Fountainbridge. Edin 123 D4
East Garleton Cotts. Athl 100 C3
East Glen Ave. Liv 146 C3
East Harbour Rd. Lime 45 D2
East Hermitage Pl. Edin 94 A2
East Leven St. Burn 50 C4
East Lillypot. Edin 93 D3
East Link Rd. B of A 2 B3
East Links Rd. Dunb 78 C1
East Links Rd. Gull 52 A1
East Linton Station Ind Est.
 E.Lin 103 F4
East Loan. Pres 97 D1
East London St. Edin 93 E1
East Lorimer Pl. Cocke 97 E2
East Main St. Arm 144 A3
East Main St. Black 171 F3
East Main St. Blcox 117 F3
East Main St. Hart 168 C3
East Main St. Uph 117 D2
East Main St. Whit 170 A4
East Mains. Men 4 A3
East March St. Kirk 17 F4
East Market St. Edin 123 F4
East Mayfield. Edin 123 F2
East Montgomery Pl. Edin 93 F1
East Murrayfield. Bann 7 F1
East Newington Pl. Edin 123 F3
East Norton Pl. Edin 93 F1
East Park Gr. Uph 117 D3
East Parkside. Edin 123 F3
East Pier St. B'ness 63 F4
East Port. Dunf 29 D2
East Port. Dunf 29 D2
East Preston St. Edin 123 F3
East Preston Street La.
 Edin 123 F3
East Quality St. Kirk 18 A4
East Queensway. Peni 203 F3
East Rd. B'ness 62 B3
East Rd. N.Ber 54 B4
East Restalrig Terr. Edin 94 A2
East Savile Rd. Edin 123 F2
East Sciennes St. Edin 123 F3
East Scotland Street La.
 Edin 93 E1
East Silvermills La. Edin 93 D1
East Stirling St. Alva 5 D4
East Suffolk Rd. Edin 124 A2
East Telferton. Edin 94 C1
East Terr. Que 68 B1
East Toll. Burn 33 F1
East Trinity Rd. Edin 93 E3
East Vennel. All 10 A3
East Way. D.Bay 48 B3
Eastburn Dr. Falk 60 B2
Eastcroft Dr. Pol 62 A1
Eastcroft St. Lar 38 A1
Easter Bankton. Muri 174 A4
Easter Belmont Rd. Edin 122 A3
Easter Cornton Rd. Stir 2 A2
Easter Currie Cres. Curr 152 A3
Easter Currie Ct. Curr 152 A3
Easter Currie Pl. Curr 152 A3
Easter Currie Terr. Curr 152 A3
Easter Drylaw Ave. Edin 92 B2
Easter Drylaw Bank. Edin 92 B2
Easter Drylaw Dr. Edin 92 B2
Easter Drylaw Gdns. Edin 92 B2
Easter Drylaw Gr. Edin 92 B2
Easter Drylaw Loan. Edin 92 B2
Easter Drylaw Pl. Edin 92 B2
Easter Drylaw View. Edin 92 B2
Easter Drylaw Way. Edin 92 B2
Easter Ferrygate Pl. N.Ber 53 F4
Easter Haugh. Edin 153 F3
Easter Livilands. Stir 7 E2
Easter Park Dr. Edin 91 F2
Easter Rd. Brox 117 F3

Easter Rd. Dunf 94 A2
Easter Rd. Shot 191 E3
Easter Warriston. Edin 93 E2
Easterfield Ct. Liv 147 E2
Eastern Ind Est. Edin 125 E2
Easterton Cres. Cowie 20 C4
Easterton Dr. Cowie 20 C4
Easterton Gr. Cowie 20 C4
Eastertoun Gdns. Arm 143 F3
Eastfield Dr. Peni 203 F3
Eastfield Farm Rd. Peni 203 F4
Eastfield Gdns. Edin 125 F4
Eastfield Park Rd. Peni 203 F3
Eastfield Pl. Edin 125 F4
Eastfield Rd. Cal 230 A1
Eastfield Rd. Fau 193 F4
Eastfield Rd. Kirkl 120 A3
Eastfield Rd. N.Ber 54 B3
Eastfield View. Fau 193 F4
Easthouses Ct. May 183 E4
Easthouses Ind Est. May 183 E4
Easthouses Pl. May 157 E1
Easthouses Rd. Dalk 157 E1
Easthouses Rd. May 183 E4
Easthouses Way. May 157 E1
Easton Ct. Stir 2 A1
Easton Dr. Shi 81 E4
Easton Rd. Bath 144 C4
Eastwood Pk. Liv 147 D4
Ebenezer Pl. Cal 81 F3
Ecclesmachan Rd. Uph 116 C3
Echline Ave. Que 89 D4
Echline Dr. Que 88 C4
Echline Farm Cotts. Que 88 C4
Echline Gdns. Que 67 F1
Echline Gr. Que 67 F1
Echline Pk. Que 88 C4
Echline Pl. Que 88 C4
Echline Rigg. Que 88 C4
Echline Steadings. Que 88 C4
Echline Terr. Que 89 D4
Echline View. Que 89 D4
Echobank. Inver 47 D1
Eden Dr. Liv 148 A2
Eden La. Edin 123 D2
Eden Rd. All 9 F3
Eden Rd. Dunf 29 F1
Edenhall Bank. Muss 126 C3
Edenhall Cres. Muss 126 C3
Edenhall Rd. Muss 126 C3
Edgefield Ind Est. Loan 155 E1
Edgefield Pl. Loan 181 E4
Edgefield Rd. Loan 155 E1
Edgehead Rd. Path 184 B4
Edina Pl. Edin 94 A1
Edina St. Edin 93 F1
Edinburgh Rd. Auch 204 A4
Edinburgh Rd. Bog 145 E3
Edinburgh Rd. Cocke 97 D2
Edinburgh Rd. Dalk 157 D2
Edinburgh Rd. Dunb 77 F1
Edinburgh Rd. B'ness 168 B3
Edinburgh Rd. Kirkl 119 D3
Edinburgh Rd. Lin 85 D3
Edinburgh Rd. Muss 126 A3
Edinburgh Pl. W.Lin 220 A1
Edinburgh Rd. Bath 145 D3
Edington Pl. Kirk 18 A4
Edmonstone Ave. Dan 156 A4
Edmonstone Dr. Dan 156 A4
Edmonstone Rd. Dan 156 A4
Edmonstone Terr. Dan 156 A4
Edmonton Ave. Liv 147 F2
Edward Ave. Sten 38 C2
Edward Ave. Pl 2 B1
Edward Ct. Dunf 39 F2
Edward Rd. Stir 2 A1
Edward St. Dunf 29 D3
Edward St. Kirk 17 D4
Eglington Pl. Inver 47 E1
Eglingtoun Dr. Dunf 28 C3
Eglinton Cres. Edin 122 C4
Eighth St. Newt 183 D3
Eildon St. Edin 93 E2
Eildon Terr. Edin 93 E2
Eilean La. Torr 26 C1
Elam Terr. B'ness 63 F4
Elbe St. Edin 94 A3
Elcho Ct. Long 98 C3
Elcho Pl. Cocke 97 E2
Elcho Rd. Long 98 C4
Elcho Terr. Aber 71 E2
Elcho Terr. Edin 125 E4
Elcho Terr. Long 98 C3
Elder Pl. Ros 46 C3
Elder St. Dunb 78 A1
Elder St E. Edin 93 E1
Elder St. Edin 93 E1
Elder St. Tran 128 B4
Elderslie Dr. Shi 82 A4
Eldindean Pl. Bonn 182 A4
Eldindean Rd. Bonn 182 B4
Eldindean Terr. Bonn 182 B4
Eldrick Ave. Fau 193 F3
Eldrick Cres. Fau 193 F3
Electra Pl. Edin 95 D1
Elgin Ct. Dunf 29 D1

Elgin Dr. Stir

Elgin Dr. Stir 7 E2
Elgin Pl. Falk 60 B2
Elgin Rd. Cow 13 E2
Elgin St. Dunf 29 D1
Elgin St. Edin 93 F1
Elgin St. Kirk 17 D3
Elgin St N. Edin 93 F1
Elgin Terr. Edin 93 F1
Eilburn North Interchange.
  Liv 147 D3
Eilburn Rd. Liv 147 D2
Eilburn South Rd. Liv 147 E2
Elie Ave. Liv 146 C3
Elizabeth Ave. Gran 61 F4
Elizabeth Ave. Lar 38 B1
Elizabeth Cres. Falk 59 D3
Elizabeth Dr. Bog 145 F3
Elizabeth Gdns. Ston 171 D1
Elizabeth La. Bog 145 F3
Elizabeth St. Dunf 29 E1
Elizabeth St. Stir 2 C3
Elizafield. Edin 93 F2
Ellaleen Gr. Crossf 28 A1
Ellangowan Terr. Edin 124 B1
Ellen St. Whit 170 A4
Ellen's Glen Loan. Edin 155 E4
Ellen's Glen Rd. Edin 155 E4
Ellersly Rd. Edin 122 B4
Elliot Gdns. Edin 153 E4
Elliot Pk. Edin 153 E4
Elliot Rd. Edin 153 E4
Elliot Rd. Edin 153 E4
Elliot St. Edin 93 F1
Elliot Terr. Falk 60 A4
Elliothill St. Dunf 29 D1
Elm Dr. Lph 117 D3
Elm Dr. Laur 61 D1
Elm Dr. Shi 81 A1
Elm Gr. All 10 B3
Elm Gr. Black 171 F4
Elm Gr. Dunf 46 B4
Elm Gr. Lar 38 B1
Elm Gr. Liv 148 A3
Elm Pk. Black 171 F4
Elm Pl. Edin 94 A2
Elm Pl. Kirk 16 C3
Elm Pl. May 183 E3
Elm Rd. Bog 145 F3
Elm Row. Bonn 156 A1
Elm Row. Edin 93 F1
Elm St. Whit 170 B3
Elm St. Dunb 78 A1
Elm St. Stir 1 C1
Elmbank Cres. Bank 57 E3
Elmbank. Men 4 A3
Elmbank Rd. Stir 2 D2
Elmbank St. Gran 61 E3
Elmfield Ct. Dalk 157 D2
Elmfield Pk. Dalk 157 D2
Elmfield Rd. Dalk 157 D2
Elms The. Edin 153 F4
Elmwood Pk. Liv 146 C4
Elmwood Rd. Shot 192 A1
Elmwood Terr. Edin 94 A2
Elphinstone Cres. Air 22 C2
Elphinstone Rd. Tran 128 A3
Elphinstone St. Kin 23 F2
Elphinstone Wlk. Tran 128 B3
Eltringham Gdns. Edin 122 B2
Eltringham Gr. Edin 122 B2
Eltringham Terr. Edin 122 B2
Emily Ct. Gore 183 E1
Emily Pl. Gore 183 E1
Empire St. Whit 170 A4
Endrick Dr. Bank 57 F3
Endrick Pl. Stir 7 D2
Engelen Dr. All 10 A3
Engine La. Bath 145 D3
Engine Pl. Bath 145 D3
Engine Rd. Gore 183 D1
Engine Rd. Loan 181 E4
Ennis Pk. W Cal 172 C3
Epplestane Rd. Whit 170 B3
Epworth Gdns. Shi 82 A4
Erbach Ave. Laur 61 D2
Ercall Rd. Pol 82 C4
Erica Gr. Dunf 46 C4
Ericht Pl. Shot 191 F3
Ernest Pl. Dunf 29 D1
Erngath Rd. B'ness 64 A4
Erskine Brae. Cul 25 E1
Erskine Hill. Pol 61 F1
Erskine Loan. Gull 52 A2
Erskine Pl. Clack 11 D3
Erskine Pl. Pump 148 B3
Erskine Rd. Brox 117 E3
Erskine Rd. Gull 52 A2
Erskine Sq. Edin 29 E1
Erskine St. All 10 A4
Erskine St. Alva 5 D4
Erskine St. Loch 14 A3
Erskine Way. Liv 147 E4
Erskine Way. Shot 191 F2
Erskine Wynd. Oak 27 D4
Esk Dr. Liv 148 A2
Esk Glades. Dalk 157 D2

Esk Pl. Dalk 156 C2
Eskbank Rd. Bonn 182 B4
Eskbank Rd. Dalk 156 C1
Eskbank Road Roundabout.
  Dalk 156 B1
Eskbank Terr. Dalk 156 C1
Eskdaill Ct. Dalk 157 D2
Eskdaill St. Dalk 157 D2
Eskdale Ct. Bonn 182 A4
Eskdale Dr. Bonn 182 A4
Eskdale Mews. Muss 126 B3
Eskdale Terr. Bonn 182 A4
Eskgrove Dr. Rosl 180 C3
Eskhill. Peni 203 F3
Eskmill Rd. Peni 204 A3
Eskside E. Muss 126 B3
Eskside W. Muss 126 B3
Eskvale Cres. Peni 204 A3
Eskvale Dr. Peni 204 A3
Eskview Ave. Muss 126 A3
Eskview Cres. Muss 126 A3
Eskview Gr. Dalk 156 C1
Eskview Gr. Muss 126 A3
Eskview Rd. May 183 E3
Eskview Rd. Muss 126 A3
Eskview Terr. Muss 126 A3
Eskview Villas. Dalk 156 C1
Esmonde Ct. Ros 46 C1
Esplanade. Edin 123 E4
Esplanade. Falk 17 E1
Esplanade Terr. Edin 125 E4
Essendean Pl. Edin 91 E1
Essendean Terr. Edin 91 E1
Essex Brae. Edin 91 D2
Essex Pk. Edin 91 D2
Essex Rd. Edin 91 D2
Esslemont Rd. Edin 124 A1
Estate Ave. Falk 60 A1
Ethel Terr. Edin 123 D1
Etive Pl. D Bay 48 A1
Etive Pl. Stir 2 A2
Etive Way. Pol 62 A1
Etive Way. Shot 192 A2
Etive Wlk. Liv 148 A2
Etna Rd. Falk 60 B4
Eton Terr. Edin 93 D1
Ettrick Cres. D Bay 48 A2
Ettrick Ct. Falk 60 B1
Ettrick Ct. Gran 61 F3
Ettrick Dr. Liv 148 A3
Ettrick Gr. Edin 123 D3
Ettrick Gr. Edin 122 C2
Ettrickdale Pl. Edin 93 D2
Eva Pl. Edin 123 E1
Evans Gdns. Bonn 182 B4
Evans St. Lar 38 B2
Evelyn Terr. Auch 180 B1
Everard Rise. Muri 148 A1
Evershed Ct. Dunf 29 F1
Evershed Dr. Dunf 29 F1
Ewart Ave. Arm 144 A3
Ewart Gr. B'ness 63 F3
Ewerland. Edin 91 D2
Ewing Ave. Falk 60 A4
Ewing Ct. Stir 7 E2
Ewing Pl. Falk 60 A4
Ewing Rd. Auch 203 F4
Ewing St. Cow 13 D1
Ewing St. Loch 14 A3
Excise La. Kin 23 F2
Excise St. Kin 23 F2
Exmouth St. Liv 148 A3
Eyre Cres. Edin 93 E1
Eyre Pl. Edin 93 E1
Eyre Terr. Edin 93 E1

Fa'side Ave N. Muss 127 D2
Fa'side Ave S. Muss 127 D2
Fa'side Ave. Tran 128 B3
Fa'side Avenue Ct. Muss 127 D2
Fa'side Bldgs. Muss 127 D2
Fa'side Cres. Muss 127 D2
Fa'side Cres. Tran 128 B3
Fa'side Dr. Muss 127 D2
Fa'side Gdns. Muss 127 D2
Fa'side Rd. Tran 128 B3
Fa'side Terr. Muss 127 D2
Factory Rd. Bath 144 C2
Factory Rd. Cow 13 E2
Factory Rd. Kirk 16 C4
Fair Pl. Inver 47 D2
Fair-a-Far Cotts. Edin 91 D3
Fair-a-Far. Edin 91 D3
Fairbairn Rd. Liv 147 E2
Fairfax Ct. Burn 33 F1
Fairfield Ave. Bon 58 A3
Fairfield. N Sau 5 E1
Fairfield Pl. Falk 60 B3
Fairford Gdns. Edin 124 A1
Fairgreen Pl. Bann 19 F4
Fairhaven Terr. Shi 82 A4
Fairhill Rd. Stir 7 D1
Fairinsfell. Uph 117 D3
Fairley Ct. Crossf 27 E1
Fairlie Gdns. Falk 59 E3
Fairlie Rd. Falk 59 E3

Fairlie St. Falk 59 E3
Fairmile Ave. Edin 154 A3
Fairmont Pk. Whit 169 F3
Fairmount Dr. N Sau 5 D1
Fairspark Terr. B'ness 63 E3
Fairview Rd. Kirk 119 F4
Fairview Terr. Shi 82 A4
Fairway. Hadd 131 F4
Fairway The. Kirk 17 F4
Fairways Ave. Madd 82 C3
Fairways Dr. Madd 82 C3
Fairways Pl. Bon 58 A4
Fairy Fa' Cres. Cross 30 C3
Fairyburn Rd. All 9 F4
Fairykirk Rd. Ros 47 D2
Falahill Cotts. Stow 228 A2
Falcon Ave. Edin 123 D2
Falcon Brae. Liv 147 E3
Falcon Ct. Edin 123 D2
Falcon Dr. Lar 38 A2
Falcon Gdns. Edin 123 D2
Falcon Rd. Edin 123 D2
Falcon Rd W. Edin 123 D2
Falconer Ct. Stir 7 E2
Falconer Rise. Muri 147 F1
Falcons The. Gull 52 A2
Falkirk Rd. Bann 19 F4
Falkirk Rd. Bon 58 B3
Falkirk Rd. Falk 60 A1
Falkirk Rd. Gran 61 D4
Falkirk Rd. Lar 38 A1
Falkirk Rd. Lar 38 A3
Falkirk Rd. Lin 84 C4
Falkland Gdns. Edin 91 F1
Falkland Pl. Sten 38 C2
Fallas Pl. Fau 193 E3
Fallodon Cres. Kirk 17 D2
Falside Cres. Bath 144 C3
Falside Dr. Bath 144 C3
Falside Terr. Bath 144 C3
Faraday Pl. Add 171 F1
Farm Ave. Bonn 181 F3
Farm Cotts. Muss 127 E3
Farm Cotts. Pen 160 B3
Farm Rd. Cowie 20 B4
Farm Rd. Falk 8 B3
Farm Rd. Lime 44 B4
Farm Rd. Rose 204 C3
Farm St. Falk 39 D1
Farmer's Bldgs. Path 185 D3
Farne Ct. Kirk 16 C4
Farquhar Sq. Blac 142 B2
Farquhar Terr. Que 68 A1
Farrer Gr. Edin 94 C1
Farrer Terr. Edin 94 C1
Fauldburn. Edin 91 D1
Fauldburn Pk. Edin 91 D1
Fauldhouse Rd. Fau 170 A1
Featherhall Ave. Edin 121 E3
Featherhall Cres. Edin 121 E3
Featherhall Cres N. Edin 121 E3
Featherhall Cres S. Edin 121 E3
Featherhall Pl. Edin 121 E3
Featherhall Rd. Edin 121 E3
Featherhall Terr. Edin 121 E3
Feil's Rd. W Cal 172 C3
Fells Rigg. Liv 147 D4
Fendoch Rd. Gran 61 F3
Fenton St. All 10 A4
Fentoun Gait. Gull 52 B1
Fere Gait. Kin 23 F2
Fergus Ave. Liv 147 F2
Fergus Pl. Dunf 29 E1
Fergus Wynd. Kirk 17 D1
Ferguson Ct. Muss 126 B3
Ferguson Dr. Den 36 B1
Ferguson Dr. Muss 126 A2
Ferguson Dr. Sten 38 C3
Ferguson Gdns. Muss 126 B2
Ferguson Gn. Muss 126 A2
Ferguson Gr. Bon 58 A3
Ferguson Pl. Burn 33 F1
Ferguson St. Stir 1 C2
Ferguson View. Muss 126 A2
Ferguson Way. Liv 147 E4
Ferguson Way. Newt 183 D2
Fergusson Rd. Brox 117 F3
Fern Lea Gr. Sten 39 E2
Fernbank. Liv 147 E3
Fernie Pl. Dunf 28 C3
Ferniehill Ave. Edin 155 F3
Ferniehill Dr. Edin 155 F3
Ferniehill Gdns. Edin 155 F4
Ferniehill Gr. Edin 155 F4
Ferniehill Pl. Edin 155 F3
Ferniehill Rd. Edin 155 F3
Ferniehill Sq. Edin 155 F3
Ferniehill St. Edin 155 F3
Ferniehill Terr. Edin 155 F3
Ferniehill Way. Edin 155 F4
Fernielaw Ave. Edin 152 C2
Fernielaw Ave. Edin 153 D3
Fernieside Ave. Edin 155 F4
Fernieside Cres. Edin 155 F4
Fernieside Dr. Edin 155 F4

Fernieside Gdns. Edin 155 F4
Fernieside Gr. Edin 155 F4
Fernlea. Uph 116 C3
Ferrard Rd. Kirk 17 D2
Ferrier Cres. Arm 144 A3
Ferry Way. D Bay 48 A2
Ferry La. Inver 68 A3
Ferry Muir Gait. Que 89 D4
Ferry Orch. Stir 2 B1
Ferry Rd. Air 9 F2
Ferry Rd. Edin 92 B2
Ferry Rd. Stir 2 B1
Ferry Road Ave. Edin 92 B2
Ferry Road Dr. Edin 92 B3
Ferry Road Gdns. Edin 92 B2
Ferry Road Gr. Edin 92 B3
Ferry Road Pl. Edin 92 B2
Ferry Toll Pl. Ros 46 C1
Ferry Toll Rd. Ros 46 C1
Ferrybarns Ct. Inver 68 A3
Ferryburn Gn. Que 89 E4
Ferryfield. Edin 93 D3
Ferrygate Cottages. Dir 53 E3
Ferryhill Rd. Inver 68 B4
Ferryhill St. Air 22 B3
Ferrymuir La. Que 89 D4
Fetteresk Cotts. Peni 203 F2
Fettes Ave. Edin 92 C1
Fettes Rise. Edin 92 C2
Fettes Row. Edin 93 E1
Fidra Ave. Dir 53 D3
Fidra Ct. N Ber 53 F3
Fidra Rd. N Ber 54 A4
Fife Pl. Ros 46 A1
Fifth St. Newt 183 D3
Figgate Bank. Edin 95 D1
Figgate La. Edin 95 D1
Figgate St. Edin 95 D1
Fillyside Ave. Edin 94 C1
Fillyside Rd. Edin 94 C2
Fillyside Terr. Edin 94 C2
Finches The. Gull 52 A2
Findhorn Pl. Edin 123 F2
Findhorn Pl. Falk 60 B1
Findhorn Pl. Kirk 16 C4
Findlay Ave. Edin 94 A2
Findlay Cotts. Edin 94 B2
Findlay Cres. Ros 46 B2
Findlay Gdns. Edin 94 B2
Findlay Gr. Edin 94 B2
Findlay Medway. Edin 94 B2
Findlay St. Ros 46 C2
Fingal Pl. Edin 123 E3
Fingzies Pl. Edin 94 A2
Finistere Ave. Falk 60 A2
Finlaggan Ct. Edin 121 D1
Finlarig Ct. Sten 38 C2
Finlay Ave. E Cal 148 C2
Finlay Pl. May 183 F3
Fintry Rd. Gran 61 F3
Fir Gr. Dunf 46 C4
Fir Gr. Laur 61 D1
Fir Gr. Liv 148 A3
Fir La. Lar 38 B1
Firbank Gr. E Cal 148 C2
Firpark Terr. Cam 6 B3
Firrhill Cres. Edin 153 F4
Firrhill Dr. Edin 153 F4
Firrhill Loan. Edin 153 F4
Firs Cres. Bann 7 E1
Firs Entry. Bann 7 E1
Firs Rd. Tul 4 B1
Firs St. Falk 60 B3
Firs The. Bann 7 E1
Firs The. D Bay 48 A1
First Gait. Rat 151 F4
First St. Newt 183 D2
Firth Cres. Auch 180 B1
Firth Rd. Auch 180 B1
Firth Rd. Liv 147 F4
Firth Rd. Rose 204 C3
Firwood Dr. B'ness 63 E3
Fishergate Rd. Cocke 97 F2
Fishermne Ind Est. Muss 126 A4
Fishers' Rd. B'ness 63 F3
Fishers Rd. Cocke 97 E2
Fishers Wynd. Muss 126 A3
Fishmarket Sq. Edin 93 E4
Fishwives' Cswy. Edin 94 C1
Fitzgerald Pl. Torp 113 F3
Fitzroy Sq. Kirk 18 A4
Fitzroy St. Kirk 18 A4
Five Gates. E Lin 76 A3
Flare Rd. B'ness 62 C3
Flax Mill Rd. East 168 C3
Fleets Gr. Tran 128 B3
Fleets Rd. Tran 128 B3
Fleets View. Tran 128 B2
Fleming Dr. Sten 39 D2
Fleming Gdns. Falk 59 F3
Fleming Pl. Blac 142 C2
Fleming Rd. Liv 146 C1
Fleming Way. Bum 33 F1
Flemington Gdns. Whit 169 F3
Flesh Wynd. Kirk 17 E3
Fletcher Gr. Auch 203 F4
Floors Pl. Kirk 16 B3
Floors Terr. Dunb 78 B1
Florabank Rd. Hadd 101 D1

Flower Pl. Kel 12 C4
Fod St. Hal 30 A3
Fodbank View. Dunf 29 F2
Foot Pl. Ros 46 C2
Foote St. Loch 14 A3
Forbes Cres. Lar 38 A1
Forbes Ct. Falk 60 C3
Forbes Rd. Edin 123 D3
Forbes Rd. Falk 60 B2
Forbes Rd. Ros 46 B1
Forbes St. All 10 B4
Forbes St. Edin 123 F3
Forbes St. Falk 60 B2
Forbeslea Gdns. Oak 27 F4
Ford Rd. Bon 58 A3
Ford Rd. Hadd 132 B4
Ford View. Crossf 27 E1
Ford's Rd. Edin 122 A2
Fordell Bank. D Bay 48 B2
Fordell Way. Inver 47 E1
Forebraes. All 10 A4
Foredale Terr. B'ness 64 B3
Forest Kirk. Car 230 A1
Forest Pl. Dunf 29 E4
Forest Pl. Dunf 29 E4
Forest View. Pol 61 F1
Forestbank. Liv 147 F3
Forester Gr. All 4 C1
Forester's Lea Cres. Dunf 29 F2
Forester's View. Tran 128 B3
Forfar Pl. Pol 62 A1
Forgie Cres. Madd 83 D3
Forglen Cres. B of A 2 A3
Forglen Rd. B of A 2 A3
Forker Ave. Ros 46 B2
Forkneuk Rd. Uph 116 C2
Forman Gr. Dunf 29 F1
Forres Dr. Kirk 16 B4
Forres St. Edin 93 D1
Forrest Hill. Edin 123 E4
Forrest Rd. Cald 141 D1
Forrest Rd. Edin 123 E4
Forrest Rd. Sals 167 D3
Forrest St. Shot 191 F3
Forrest Wlk. Uph 116 C2
Forrester Ct. Loch 14 A4
Forrester Park Ave. Edin 121 E2
Forrester Park Ct. Edin 121 E2
Forrester Park Gdns. Edin 121 E2
Forrester Park Gn. Edin 121 E2
Forrester Park Gr. Edin 121 E2
Forrester Park Loan. Edin 121 E2
Forrester Park Rd. Edin 121 E2
Forrester Pl. Air 22 B2
Forrester Rd. Arm 143 F4
Forrestfield Rd. Cald 141 D3
Fort House. Edin 93 F3
Forth Ave. Kirk 17 D2
Forth Cres. D Bay 48 A3
Forth Cres. H Val 26 A1
Forth Cres. Stir 1 B2
Forth Ct. D Bay 48 A3
Forth Dr. Liv 148 A3
Forth Gdns. Cocke 97 F2
Forth Gdns. Oak 26 C3
Forth Gr. Cocke 97 F2
Forth Park Dr. Kirk 17 D3
Forth Park Gdns. Kirk 17 D3
Forth Pk. B of A 2 A2
Forth Pl. Burn 50 C4
Forth Pl. Que 58 A1
Forth Pl. Ros 46 A1
Forth St. Camb 19 D3
Forth St. Dunf 29 D1
Forth St. Edin 93 E1
Forth St. Fall 8 B2
Forth St. Gran 61 E4
Forth St. St. La N Ber 54 B4
Forth St. Stir 2 A1
Forth Terr. Que 89 E4
Forth View. Aber 71 E2
Forth View Cotts. H Val 26 A1
Forth View Cres. Curr 151 F2
Forth View Cres. Dan 156 A4
Forth View. Dunf 29 F2
Forth View. Inver 47 D1
Forth View Rd. Curr 151 F2
Forth Wynd. Cocke 97 F2
Forthbank Pl. Cul 25 F1
Forthside Terr. Inver 68 B3
Forthvale. Men 4 A3
Forthview Ave. Muss 127 D2
Forthview. Bann 7 E1
Forthview Cres. B'ness 63 E3
Forthview Cres. Muss 127 D3
Forthview Ct. Falk 59 F1

Forthview Ct. Falk

Forthview Dr. Muss 127 D3
Forthview Gdns. Shi 82 B4
Forthview Rd. Edin 92 B1
Forthview Rd. Long 98 C3
Forthview Terr. Edin 92 A1
Forthview Terr. Muss 127 D3
Forthview Terr. Shi 82 A4
Forties Rd. B'ness 62 B3
Fortingall Cres. Pol 62 A3
Fortissat Ave. Shot 191 E3
Fortissat Rd. Sals 167 D1
Fortune Ave. Hadd 101 D1
Foulden Pl. Dunf 29 E2
Foulford Pl. Cow 13 D3
Foulford Rd. Cow 13 D2
Foulford St. Cow 13 D2
Foulis Cres. Curr 152 C3
Foulshiels Rd. Ston 171 E1
Foundry La. Loan 155 E1
Foundry Loan. Lar 38 A1
Foundry Rd. Bon 58 A3
Foundry Rd. Shot 191 F2
Foundry St. Dunf 29 D2
Foundry St. Falk 60 A4
Fountain Pl. Loan 181 E4
Fountain Rd. B of A 2 A4
Fountainbridge. Edin 123 D3
Fountainhall Rd. Edin 123 E2
Fountainhead Rd. Bath 145 D4
Fountainpark Cres. B'ness .. 64 B4
Fourth Gait. Rat 151 F4
Fourth St. Newt 183 D3
Fowler Cres. Loan 181 E4
Fowler Pl. Pol 61 F1
Fowler St. Tran 128 B4
Fowler Terr. Edin 122 C3
Fowlers Ct. Pres 96 C1
Fox Covert Ave. Edin 91 F1
Fox Covert Gr. Edin 91 F1
Fox Spring Cres. Edin 154 A4
Fox Spring Rise. Edin 154 A4
Fox St. Edin 94 A3
Foxknowe Pl. Liv 147 D2
Franchi Dr. Sten 38 C3
Francis Ct. Dunf 28 B3
Francis St. Loch 14 A4
Frankfield Pl. D Bay 48 B2
Frankfield Rd. D Bay 48 B2
Fraser Ave. Edin 93 D3
Fraser Ave. Inver 47 E1
Fraser Cres. Edin 93 D3
Fraser Dr. Loch 14 A4
Fraser Gdns. Edin 93 D3
Fraser Gr. Edin 93 D3
Fraser Pl. Gran 61 E3
Fraser Pl. Kirk 18 A4
Fraser Pl. Stir 2 A2
Fraser Rd. Liv 146 C1
Frederick St. Edin 123 E4
Freeland Ave. Uph 117 D3
Freelands Rd. Kirkl 120 A2
Freelands Rd. Rat 119 F2
Fremantle St. Liv 148 A3
Freskyn Pl. Brox 118 A3
Frew Ct. Dunf 29 E1
Friars Brae. Lin 85 D3
Friars Loan. Lin 85 D3
Friars St. Stir 7 D4
Friars Way. Lin 85 D3
Friarton Gdns. Peni 203 E3
Friendship Gdns. Sten 39 E2
Frobisher Ave. Falk 59 F2
Frogston Ave. Edin 154 A3
Frogston Brae. Edin 154 C2
Frogston Gdns. Edin 154 B3
Frogston Gr. Edin 154 B3
Frogston Rd E. Edin 154 C3
Frogston Rd W. Edin 154 B2
Frogston Terr. Edin 154 B3
Fullerton Dr. Pol 61 F2
Fulmar Brae. Liv 147 E3
Fulmar Way. D Bay 48 A2
Furnace La. B'ness 64 B4
Furnace Pl. Loch 13 E3
Furniss Ave. Ros 46 B3
Fyne La. Shot 191 F3

Gaberston Ave. All 10 B4
Gagarin Way. Loch 13 D3
Gair Cres. Car 230 A2
Gair Rd. Car 230 A3
Gair Wynd. Shot 192 A2
Gairdoch Dr. Sten 39 E2
Gairdoch St. Falk 60 B4
Gala Gdns. Cres. Laur 61 E1
Gala Gn. Dunb 78 A1
Galabraes Cres. Bath 145 E4
Galachlawshot. Edin 154 B3
Galachlawside. Edin 154 B3
Galadale Cres. Newt 183 D3
Galadale Dr. Newt 183 D3
Galadale. Newt 183 D3
Gallacher Pl. Loch 13 F3
Gallamuir Dr. Plea 20 B2
Gallamuir Rd. Plea 20 B3
Galloe The. Edin 153 E3

Galloway Cres. Brox 117 E3
Galloway St. Falk 60 A3
Gallows Loan. Cul 25 E1
Galmeilen. Uph 117 E3
Gait Ave. Muss 127 D3
Gait Cres. Muss 127 D3
Gait Dr. Muss 127 D3
Gait Rd. Muss 127 D3
Gait Terr. Muss 127 D3
Gamekeeper's Loan. Edin .. 91 D3
Gamekeeper's Pk. Edin 91 D3
Gamekeeper's Rd. Edin 91 D3
Garden City. Ston 171 D1
Garden Ct. Dunf 29 E4
Garden Pl. Clack 11 D2
Garden Pl. Crossf 27 E1
Garden Pl. Dunf 29 E4
Garden Pl. Liv 147 E2
Garden St. Falk 60 B3
Garden Terr. Clack 11 D2
Garden Terr. Edin 91 F2
Garden Terr. Falk 60 B3
Garden Terr. Laur 61 D1
Gardener Rd. Dunb 78 B1
Gardener St. Dunf 29 D2
Gardener's Wlk. Peni 203 E3
Gardeners Ct. Dunf 29 D2
Gardeners' St. Dunf 29 D2
Gardenhead. Pol 61 F1
Gardens The. Aber 71 E3
Gardens The. Dir 53 D3
Gardiner Cres. Pres 97 D1
Gardiner Gr. Edin 92 A1
Gardiner Pl. Cow 13 D1
Gardiner Pl. Newt 183 D3
Gardiner Rd. Dow 13 E1
Gardiner Rd. Edin 92 A1
Gardiner Rd. Pres 97 D1
Gardiner St. Loch 14 A4
Gardiner Terr. Edin 92 A1
Gardiner Terr. Pres 128 C3
Gardiner Cres. Whit 169 F3
Gardner Terr. Ston 171 D1
Gardner's Cres. Edin 123 D4
Gardners La. Bath 145 D3
Gardrum Gdns. Shi 81 E4
Gardrum Pl. Madd 82 B4
Gareloch Way. Whit 170 B4
Garleton Ct. Gull 52 A1
Garleton Dr. Hadd 100 C1
Gamgrew Rd. Bank 57 D2
Garrison Pl. Falk 60 A3
Garry Pl. Falk 60 B1
Garry Pl. Gran 61 F3
Garry St. Loch 14 A4
Garry Way. Shot 191 F3
Garry Wlk. Liv 148 A2
Garscube Terr. Edin 122 B4
Gartclush Gdns. Bann 19 F4
Gartcows Ave. Falk 60 A2
Gartcows Cres. Falk 60 A2
Gartcows Dr. Falk 60 A2
Gartcows Gdns. Falk 60 A2
Gartcows Pl. Falk 60 A2
Gartcows Rd. Falk 60 A2
Garten Dr. Shot 192 A2
Garthill Gdns. Falk 60 A2
Garthill La. Falk 60 A2
Gartmorn Rd. N Sau 5 E1
Garvald La. Den 36 B1
Garvald Rd. Bank 57 E4
Garvally Cres. All 10 A4
Garvock Bank. Dunf 29 F2
Garvock Hill. Dunf 29 F2
Garvock Terr. Dunf 29 E2
Gas Wynd. Kirk 17 D1
Gasworks La. N Ber 53 F3
Gasworks La. Whit 170 A4
Gateshead Rd. Kirkl 88 C1
Gateside Ave. Bon 58 B3
Gateside Ave. Hadd 100 B1
Gateside Ct. Cow 13 D2
Gateside Rd. Hadd 131 E4
Gateside Rd. Kirkl 89 D1
Gateside Rd. Stir 7 D2
Gateside Rd. Whit 169 F3
Gauger's Bush. E Lin 76 A4
Gauze Pl. B'ness 64 A3
Gauze Rd. B'ness 64 A3
Gavin Pl. Liv 147 D3
Gavins Rd. All 4 C1
Gayfield Cl. Edin 93 F1
Gayfield Place La. Edin 93 F1
Gayfield Sq. Edin 93 F1
Gayfield St. Edin 93 F1
Gayfield Street La. Edin 93 E1
Gaymor Ave. Loan 181 D4
Gean Rd. All 9 F4
Gellatly Rd. Dunf 29 D1
Gelnorchy Terr. Edin 123 F2
George Ave. Loan 181 D4
George Cres. Loan 181 D4
George Cres. Orm 159 E4
George Dr. Loan 181 E4
George IV Bridge. Edin 123 E4
George Sq. Edin 123 E3
George Square La. Edin 123 E3
George St. Alva 5 D3

George St. Arm 143 F3
George St. B'ness 63 F3
George St. Bath 145 D3
George St. Cow 13 D2
George St. Dunf 29 D1
George St. Edin 123 E4
George St. Falk 60 A3
George St. Gran 61 F4
George St. Kirk 23 D2
George St. Lar 38 B2
George St. Laur 60 C2
George St. Orm 159 F4
George Terr. Loan 181 D4
George Way. Tran 128 B3
George Wlk. Tran 128 B3
Gerald Terr. Sten 38 C2
Gib Gr. Dunf 29 F1
Gibbdun Pl. Bank 57 F4
Gibbs Entry. Edin 123 F4
Gibbshill Pl. East 168 B3
Gibraltar Ct. Dalk 157 D2
Gibraltar Gdns. Dalk 157 D2
Gibraltar Rd. Dalk 157 D2
Gibraltar Terr. Dalk 157 D2
Gibson Dr. Dalk 157 E2
Gibson St. Edin 93 F2
Gibson Terr. Edin 123 D3
Gibsongray St. Falk 60 A4
Gideon Ct. Bath 145 D4
Gideon St. Bath 145 D4
Gifford Pk. Edin 123 F3
Gifford Rd. Hadd 132 B4
Giffordgate. Hadd 132 A4
Gilberstoun. Edin 125 E3
Gilberstoun Pl. Edin 125 E3
Gilbert Ave. N Ber 54 B3
Gilburn Pl. B' ness 63 E3
Gilburn Pl. Shot 191 F2
Gilchrist Cres. Whit 170 A3
Gilchrist Dr. Falk 59 D3
Giles St. Edin 93 F3
Gillespie Cres. Edin 123 D3
Gillespie Gr. Bra 26 C4
Gillespie Pl. Bann 7 D1
Gillespie Pl. Edin 123 D3
Gillespie Rd. Edin 152 C3
Gillespie St. Edin 123 D3
Gillies St. Stir 7 E2
Gillies Hill. Cam 6 B3
Gillsland Rd. Edin 122 C2
Gilmerton Dykes Ave. Edin ..155 E3
Gilmerton Dykes Cres.
  Edin 155 E3
Gilmerton Dykes Dr. Edin .. 155 E3
Gilmerton Dykes Gr. Edin .. 155 E3
Gilmerton Dykes Loan.
  Edin 155 E3
Gilmerton Dykes Pl. Edin .. 155 E3
Gilmerton Dykes Rd. Edin .. 155 E3
Gilmerton Dykes St. Edin .. 155 E3
Gilmerton Dykes Terr.
  Edin 155 E3
Gilmerton Dykes View.
  Edin 155 E3
Gilmerton Pl. Edin 155 E3
Gilmerton Rd. Edin 124 A1
Gilmerton Rd. Edin 156 A2
Gilmerton Road Roundabout.
  Dalk 156 B2
Gilmerton Station Rd. Edin . 155 F2
Gilmore Pk. Edin 123 D3
Gilmore Pl. Edin 123 D3
Gilmour Rd. Edin 123 F2
Gilmour St. Cow 13 E3
Gilmour St. Edin 123 F4
Gilsay Ct. Falk 60 B1
Gilston Cres. Pol 62 A1
Gladney Sq. Kirk 17 D1
Gladsmuir. For 215 D1
Gladstone Pl. Dunf 29 D3
Gladstone Pl. Edin 94 A2
Gladstone Pl. Stir 2 B1
Gladstone Rd. Sten 38 B2
Gladstone Terr. Edin 123 F3
Glaive Ave. Bann 7 E2
Glamis Gdns. D Bay 48 A2
Glamis Gdns. Pol 61 F1
Glamis Pl. D Bay 48 A2
Glamis Rd. King 34 C2
Glamis Rd. Kirk 16 B4
Glamis Terr. King 34 C2
Glasclune Gdns. N Ber 54 B4
Glasgow Rd. Bank 57 E2
Glasgow Rd. Bann 19 E3
Glasgow Rd. Bath 144 C3
Glasgow Rd. Den 36 B1
Glasgow Rd. Edin 121 D3
Glasgow Rd. Falk 59 E3
Glasgow Rd. Kirkl 119 E3
Glasgow Rd. Stir 7 D1
Glashill Terr. Peni 203 F3
Glass Cres. Winch 87 F1

Glass Pl. Winch 87 F1
Glass Rd. Winch 87 F1
Glassel Pk Rd. Long 98 B2
Glasshouse Loan. All 10 A3
Glasswork St. Kirk 17 D1
Glebe Ave. Stir 7 D4
Glebe Ave. Uph 117 D2
Glebe Cres. Alva 5 D4
Glebe Cres. Ath 101 F4
Glebe Cres. Stir 7 D4
Glebe Gdns. Edin 121 E3
Glebe Gdns. Edin 121 E3
Glebe Gr. Edin 121 E3
Glebe Pk. Inver 47 D1
Glebe Pk. Kirk 17 E3
Glebe Pl. Bonn 155 F1
Glebe Pl. Burn 33 F1
Glebe Pl. King 34 C2
Glebe Rd. Edin 145 E3
Glebe Rd. Edin 121 E3
Glebe Rd. Kin 23 F3
Glebe Rd. Uph 117 D2
Glebe Rd. W Cal 172 B1
Glebe Rd. Whit 170 A3
Glebe St. Dalk 157 D2
Glebe St. Dunf 36 C1
Glebe St. Falk 60 A3
Glebe Terr. All 10 A3
Glebe Terr. Edin 121 E3
Glebe The. Clack 11 D2
Glebe The. E Lin 103 F4
Glebe The. Hadd 131 F4
Glebe The. Kirkl 89 D1
Glebe The. Lin 85 D3
Glebe The. Pen 160 C4
Glebe The. Pen 161 F2
Glebe The. W Cal 172 B1
Gledhill Ave. Muir 64 B3
Glen Albyn Dr. Kirk 16 A4
Glen Artney Gr. Dunf 29 E1
Glen Avon Pl. Madd 82 C4
Glen Beasdale Ct. Dunf 29 E1
Glen Brae. Falk 60 A2
Glen Bridge. Dunf 28 C2
Glen Bruar Pl. Kirk 16 A4
Glen Clova Cres. Crossf 27 E1
Glen Cres. Falk 60 A1
Glen Ct. Liv 146 C3
Glen Ct. Liv 146 B3
Glen Fruin Gr. Dunf 29 E1
Glen Gdns. Falk 60 A2
Glen Isla Gr. Dunf 29 E1
Glen Isla Rd. Kirk 16 A4
Glen Lyon Ct. Pol 62 A1
Glen Moriston Dr. Crossf 27 E1
Glen Nevis Dr. Dunf 29 E1
Glen Ogle Ct. Pol 62 A1
Glen Pl. Peni 203 F3
Glen Rd. Bath 143 D4
Glen Rd. Bath 145 D4
Glen Rd. Liv 146 C3
Glen Rd. Plea 37 D1
Glen Rd. Shot 191 F2
Glen Rd. Tor 37 D1
Glen St. Edin 123 E3
Glen Terr. Den 36 B1
Glen Terr. Liv 146 C3
Glen View. B' ness 63 E2
Glen View Cres. Gore 207 E4
Glen View Ct. Gore 207 E4
Glen View Rd. Gore 207 E4
Glen Way. Bath 145 D4
Glenafeoch Rd. Car 230 A1
Glenallan Dr. Edin 124 A1
Glenallan Loan. Edin 124 A1
Glenalmond Cl. Uph 117 D3
Glenalmond Ct. Whit 170 B3
Glenalmond Terr. Bath 145 D4
Glenalmond. Whit 170 B3
Glenard View. Muir 64 B3
Glenavon Dr. Crossf 27 E1
Glenavon Terr. Bath 145 D4
Glenbank. Falk 60 A1
Glenbervie Ave. Lar 38 A2
Glenbervie Cres. Lar 38 A2
Glenbervie Dr. Lar 38 A2
Glenbervie Gr. Dunf 29 E1
Glenbervie Rd. Gran 61 F3
Glenbo Dr. Bank 57 F4
Glenbrae Ct. Falk 59 F2
Glenbridge Ct. Dunf 28 C2
Glenbrook. Bale 176 C4
Glenburn Gdns. Whit 170 B3
Glenburn Gr. Blu 26 C4
Glenburn Rd. Falk 60 B1
Glenburn Rd. N Ber 53 F4
Glencairn Cres. Edin 122 C4
Glencairn St. Stir 7 D2
Glencairn Terr. Bath 145 D4
Glencoe Rd. Car 230 A1
Glencoe Rd. Stir 2 A1
Glencorse Pk. Auch 204 B4

Glencoul Ave. D Bay 48 A3
Glencross Gdns. Peni 203 E3
Glendevon Ave. Edin 122 A3
Glendevon Dr. Stir 1 C1
Glendevon Gdns. Edin 122 A3
Glendevon Gr. Edin 122 A3
Glendevon Pk. Edin 122 A3
Glendevon Pk. Winch 87 F1
Glendevon Pl. Edin 122 A3
Glendevon Pl. Kirk 122 A3
Glendevon Rd. Edin 122 A3
Glendevon Terr. Edin 122 A3
Glendinning Cres. Edin 155 D4
Gleneagles Ct. Whit 170 B3
Gleneagles Way. Liv 146 B3
Glenesk Cres. Dalk 156 C1
Glenfield Cres. Cow 13 E3
Glenfield Cres. Cow 13 E3
Glenfield Ct. Cow 13 E3
Glenfield Gdns. Cow 13 E3
Glenfield. Liv 147 D2
Glenfield Rd. Cow 13 E3
Glenfinlas St. Edin 123 D4
Glenfuir Rd. Falk 59 F3
Glenfuir St. Falk 59 E3
Glengairn Wlk. Dunf 29 E1
Glengyle Terr. Edin 123 E3
Glenisla Gardens La. Edin .. 123 E2
Glenisla Gdns. Edin 123 E2
Glenlee Ave. Edin 124 B4
Glenlee Gdns. Edin 124 B4
Glenlockhart Bank. Edin 122 B1
Glenlockhart Rd. Edin 122 C2
Glenlockhart Valley. Edin .. 122 B1
Glenmavis Cres. Car 230 A1
Glenmavis Dr. Bath 145 D4
Glenmore Dr. Bon 57 F3
Glenmore. Whit 170 B3
Glennie Gdns. Tran 128 B3
Glenochil Pk. Men 4 C2
Glenochil Rd. Falk 60 A2
Glenochil Terr. Men 4 C2
Glenogle House. Edin 93 D1
Glenogle Pl. Edin 93 D1
Glenogle Rd. Edin 93 D1
Glenogle Terr. Edin 93 D2
Glenorchy Rd. N Ber 54 A3
Glenorchy Terr. Edin 123 F2
Glensburgh Rd. Gran 61 D4
Glenshiel Gr. Dunf 29 E1
Glenside Ct. Arm 143 F3
Glenside Gr. Edin 61 F3
Glenside Gdns. Arm 143 F3
Glentye Gdns. Falk 59 F1
Glenure Loan. Edin 91 E1
Glenvarloch Cres. Edin 155 D4
Glenview Cres. Ston 171 D1
Glenview Dr. Falk 59 F1
Glenview. Dunf 36 A2
Glenview. Men 4 A3
Glenview Rd. Ston 171 D1
Glenwinnel Rd. Alva 4 C4
Glenwood Dr. Arm 143 E3
Glenyards Rd. Bon 58 A3
Gloag Pl. W Cal 172 B2
Globe Rd. Ros 46 B1
Gloucester La. Edin 93 D1
Gloucester Pl. Edin 93 D1
Gloucester Sq. Edin 93 D1
Gloucester St. Edin 93 D1
Glover's Ct. King 35 D2
Glowrorum Dr. Bank 57 F4
Glynwed Ct. Falk 60 B4
Godfrey Ave. Den 36 B1
Godfrey Cres. Lar 38 B1
Goff Ave. Edin 94 C1
Gogar Loan. B of A 3 E3
Gogar Pl. Stir 2 A1
Gogar Station Rd. Edin 121 D1
Gogar Station Rd. Kirkl 120 C2
Gogar Station Rd. Rat 120 C2
Gogarbank Farm. Rat 120 B1
Gogarloch Haugh. Edin 121 D3
Gogarloch Muir. Edin 121 D3
Gogarloch Rd. Edin 121 D3
Gogarloch Syke. Edin 121 D3
Gogarstone Rd. Kirkl 120 A3
Goldenacre Terr. Edin 93 E2
Goldenstones Ave. Dunb 78 C1
Golf Course Rd. Bonn 182 A4
Golf Course Rd. Liv 147 D4
Golf Ct. Aber 71 E2
Golf Dr. Cocke 97 F2
Golf House Rd. Dunb 78 C2
Goldtrum St. Dunf 28 C2
Goodall Cres. Dech 116 B1
Goodall Pl. Dech 116 B1
Goodall's Pl. Hadd 132 B4
Goodman Pl. Madd 82 C4
Goose Green Ave. Muss 126 B4
Goose Green Cres. Muss 126 B4
Goose Green Pl. Muss 126 B4
Goose Green Rd. Gull 52 A1
Goose Green Rd. Muss 126 B4
Goosecroft Rd. Stir 7 D4
Gordon Ave. Bath 145 D4

Gordon Ave. Bonn ... 181 F3
Gordon Cres. B of A ... 2 A4
Gordon Cres. Stir ... 1 C1
Gordon Dr. All ... 10 B4
Gordon Loan. Edin ... 121 F4
Gordon Pl. Falk ... 59 F3
Gordon Rd. Edin ... 121 F4
Gordon Rd. Ros ... 46 A1
Gordon St. Cow ... 13 E3
Gordon St. Edin ... 94 A2
Gordon St. Loch ... 14 A4
Gordon St. May ... 183 E4
Gordon Terr. Dunf ... 29 D1
Gordon Terr. Edin ... 124 A1
Gordon Way. Liv ... 147 E4
Gore Ave. Gore ... 207 E4
Goremire Rd. Car ... 230 B1
Gorgie Rd. Edin ... 122 B2
Gorrie St. Den ... 36 B1
Gorrie St. Dunf ... 29 E1
Gorsebank. Liv ... 147 F3
Gort Pl. Gran ... 61 E3
Gorton Loan. Rose ... 181 E1
Gorton Pl. Rose ... 181 E1
Gorton Rd. Rose ... 181 E1
Goschen Pl. Uph ... 117 D3
Goschen Terr. Uph ... 117 D3
Gosford Pl. Edin ... 93 E3
Gosford Rd. Cocke ... 97 E2
Gosford Rd. Kirk ... 16 B4
Gosford Rd. Long ... 98 C3
Gote La. Que ... 68 A1
Gourlaw Cotts. Rose ... 205 D4
Gourlay St. Kirk ... 17 D2
Gourlaybank. Hadd ... 101 D1
Gow Cres. Kirk ... 17 D2
Gowan Ave. Falk ... 60 A3
Gowan La. Falk ... 60 A3
Gowanbank. Liv ... 147 E3
Gowanbrae Dr. Dunf ... 29 E2
Gowanbrae. Fau ... 193 F3
Gowanbrae Pl. Dunf ... 29 E2
Gowanbrae Terr. Dunf ... 29 E2
Gowanhill Gdns. Stir ... 1 C1
Gowanlea Dr. Slam ... 110 A3
Grace St. Loch ... 14 B4
Gracefield Ct. Muss ... 126 A3
Gracemount Ave. Edin ... 155 D3
Gracemount Dr. Edin ... 155 D3
Gracemount Pl. Edin ... 155 D3
Gracemount Rd. Edin ... 155 D3
Gracemount Sq. Edin ... 155 D3
Gracie Cres. Ratf ... 8 B2
Gracie's Wynd. Arm ... 144 A3
Gradion Pl. Falk ... 60 A2
Graeme Pl. Falk ... 59 F1
Graham Ave. Lar ... 38 A2
Graham Ave. Stir ... 2 B2
Graham Cres. B'ness ... 64 A4
Graham Ct. Black ... 171 F4
Graham St. B of A ... 2 A4
Graham St. Edin ... 93 F3
Graham Terr. Air ... 22 B2
Graham Way. Liv ... 147 E4
Graham's Rd. Auch ... 204 B4
Grahams Rd. Falk ... 60 A3
Grahamsdyke Ave. B'ness ... 64 A4
Grahamsdyke Cres. Bon ... 58 A2
Grahamsdyke La. B'ness ... 64 A4
Grahamsdyke Rd. B'ness ... 64 A4
Grahamsdyke Rd. Bon ... 58 A2
Grahamsdyke Rd. Muir ... 64 B3
Grahamsdyke St. Laur ... 61 D2
Grahamsdyke Terr. B'ness ... 64 A4
Graiglaw Pl. Dech ... 116 B2
Graigleith View. Tull ... 4 B2
Grainger St. Loch ... 14 A4
Grampian Cres. Gran ... 61 F3
Grampian Ct. Ros ... 46 C1
Grampian Gdns. Edin ... 153 F4
Grampian House. Edin ... 93 F3
Grampian Pl. Ros ... 46 C1
Grampian Rd. Roe ... 46 C1
Grampian Rd. Stir ... 6 C3
Grampion Ct. Muri ... 147 F1
Granary Rd. Falk ... 60 A4
Granary Sq. Falk ... 60 A4
Granby Ave. Liv ... 147 F2
Granby Rd. Edin ... 123 D2
Grandfield. Edin ... 93 E3
Grandville. Edin ... 93 E3
Grange Ave. Falk ... 60 A4
Grange Cotts. King ... 34 C3
Grange Cres E. Pres ... 96 C1
Grange Cres. Edin ... 123 D2
Grange Cres W. Pres ... 127 F4
Grange Dr. Dunf ... 46 B4
Grange Gdns. B of A ... 2 B4
Grange Gr. Pres ... 96 C1
Grange La. Gran ... 40 B1
Grange Loan. B'ness ... 64 A4
Grange Loan. Edin ... 123 E2
Grange Loan. Edin ... 123 E2
Grange Pl. Gran ... 40 B1
Grange Pl. Laur ... 61 E1
Grange Rd. All ... 9 F3
Grange Rd. B of A ... 2 B3

Grange Rd. Brox ... 117 F2
Grange Rd. Burn ... 33 E1
Grange Rd. Dunf ... 46 B3
Grange Rd. Edin ... 123 E3
Grange Rd. Liv ... 148 A4
Grange Rd. N Ber ... 54 A3
Grange Rd. Pol ... 61 F2
Grange Rd. Pres ... 96 C1
Grange Rd. Ros ... 46 A3
Grange Terr. B'ness ... 64 A4
Grange Terr. Edin ... 123 E2
Grange Tha. Pol ... 82 C4
Grange View. Lin ... 85 E4
Grangeburn Rd. Gran ... 40 C1
Grangemouth Rd. Falk ... 60 C3
Grangepans. B'ness ... 64 A4
Grangeview. Lar ... 38 C1
Grant Ave. Edin ... 153 D3
Grant Pl. Stir ... 2 A2
Grant St. All ... 9 F3
Grantham's Well Ave. Falk ... 59 F2
Granton Cres. Edin ... 92 C3
Granton Gdns. Edin ... 92 C3
Granton Gr. Edin ... 92 C3
Granton Mains Ave. Edin ... 92 B3
Granton Mains Brae. Edin ... 92 B3
Granton Mains Ct. Edin ... 92 B3
Granton Mains Gait. Edin ... 92 B3
Granton Mains Vale. Edin ... 92 B3
Granton Mains Wynd. Edin ... 92 B3
Granton Medway. Edin ... 92 C3
Granton Park Ave. Edin ... 92 C4
Granton Pl. Edin ... 92 C3
Granton Rd. Edin ... 93 D3
Granton Sq. Edin ... 92 C4
Granton View. D Bay ... 47 F1
Granton View. Edin ... 92 C3
Grants Bank. Dunf ... 29 D2
Grantully Pl. Edin ... 123 F2
Granville Terr. Edin ... 123 D3
Granville Way. Ros ... 46 C2
Grassmarket. Edin ... 123 E4
Gray Pk. Cow ... 13 E3
Gray Pl. Inver ... 47 F2
Gray St. Shot ... 192 A2
Gray's Loan. Edin ... 123 D2
Graystale Rd. Stir ... 7 D2
Graystonelee Rd. Shot ... 191 E3
Great Cannon Bank. Edin ... 95 D1
Great Carleton Sq. Edin ... 125 D2
Great Junction St. Edin ... 93 F3
Great King St. Edin ... 93 E1
Great Michael Cl. Edin ... 93 E4
Great Michael Rd. Ros ... 46 A3
Great Michael Rise. Edin ... 93 E3
Great Michael Sq. Edin ... 93 E4
Great Stuart St. Edin ... 93 D1
Great Stuart St. Edin ... 123 D4
Green Apron Pk. N Ber ... 54 A4
Green La. Bonn ... 181 F4
Green St. Dunf ... 29 E4
Green St. Edin ... 93 E1
Green The. Alva ... 5 D4
Green The. Edin ... 145 E4
Green The. Pen ... 191 F2
Green The. Pen ... 160 C3
Green Tree La. B'ness ... 63 E3
Greenacre Ct. Bann ... 7 F1
Greenacre Pl. Bann ... 7 F1
Greenbank Ave. Edin ... 123 D1
Greenbank Cres. Edin ... 154 A4
Greenbank Dr. Cow ... 13 D1
Greenbank Dr. Edin ... 154 A4
Greenbank Gdns. Edin ... 153 F4
Greenbank La. Edin ... 153 F4
Greenbank Loan. Edin ... 122 C1
Greenbank Pk. Edin ... 153 F4
Greenbank Pl. Edin ... 153 F4
Greenbank Pl. Falk ... 59 E2
Greenbank Rd. Edin ... 122 C1
Greenbank Rd. Falk ... 59 E2
Greenbank Rise. Edin ... 153 F4
Greenbank Row. Edin ... 153 F4
Greenbank Terr. Edin ... 123 D1
Greenbank Terr. Fau ... 193 F3
Greencraig Ave. Shi ... 81 E3
Greendykes Ave. Edin ... 124 C2
Greendykes Dr. Edin ... 124 C2
Greendykes Gdns. Edin ... 124 C2
Greendykes Loan. Edin ... 124 C2
Greendykes Rd. Brox ... 117 F3
Greendykes Rd. Edin ... 124 C1
Greendykes Terr. Edin ... 124 C2
Greenend Dr. Edin ... 155 E4
Greenend Gdns. Edin ... 155 E4
Greenend Gr. Edin ... 155 E4
Greenfield Pl. Bale ... 177 E4
Greenfield Rd. Bale ... 177 E4
Greenfield St. All ... 10 A4
Greenfield St. Bone ... 58 A3
Greenhall Rd. Gore ... 183 E1
Greenhead. Fau ... 193 E4
Greenheads Rd. N Ber ... 54 C3
Greenhill Ct. Fau ... 193 F3
Greenhill Gdns. Edin ... 123 D2
Greenhill Pk. Edin ... 123 D2

Greenhill Pk. Peni ... 203 E3
Greenhill Pl. Edin ... 123 D2
Greenhill Rd. Blac ... 142 C2
Greenhill Rd. Bon ... 58 A2
Greenhill Terr. Edin ... 123 D3
Greenhithe Terr. Madd ... 82 C4
Greenhorn's Well Ave. Falk ... 59 F2
Greenhorn's Well Cres. Falk ... 59 F2
Greenhorn's Well Dr. Falk ... 59 F2
Greenlaw Gr. Auch ... 180 A3
Greenlaw Hedge. Edin ... 153 F4
Greenlaw Rig. Edin ... 153 F4
Greenloanings. Kirk ... 16 B4
Greenmantle Loan. Edin ... 124 A1
Greenmount. Cow ... 13 D1
Greenmount Dr. Burn ... 33 F1
Greenmount Dr. Shi ... 81 E3
Greenmount Rd N. Burn ... 33 F1
Greenmount Rd S. Burn ... 34 A1
Greenpark Dr. Pol ... 61 F1
Greenrigg Cotts. Hart ... 169 D3
Greenside La. Edin ... 93 F1
Greenside Pl. Edin ... 93 F1
Greenside Pl. Rose ... 181 E1
Greenside Row. Edin ... 93 F1
Greenside St. All ... 10 A3
Greenside. Torp ... 113 F3
Greenwell Sa. Fau ... 193 F3
Greenwell Terr. Madd ... 82 C4
Greenwells Dr. Madd ... 82 C4
Greenwood Ave. Stir ... 7 D4
Greenwood Pk. Liv ... 147 E3
Greenwood St. Shot ... 191 F3
Gregory Rd. Liv ... 147 D1
Gregory Rd. W Cal ... 173 D4
Greig Cres. Arm ... 144 A3
Greig Pl. Loch ... 14 A4
Greig Rd. Ros ... 46 A1
Grendon Ct. Stir ... 7 D3
Grendon Gdns. Stir ... 7 D3
Grey Craigs. Crossf ... 27 E1
Grey School Cnr. Pres ... 96 C1
Greyfriar's Wlk. Inver ... 47 E2
Greyfriars. Edin ... 123 E4
Greygoran. N Sau ... 5 E1
Grierson Ave. Edin ... 93 D3
Grierson Cres. Cam ... 6 B3
Grierson Gdns. Edin ... 93 D3
Grierson Rd. Edin ... 92 C3
Grierson Sq. Edin ... 93 D3
Grierson Villas. Edin ... 93 D3
Grieve Ct. Auch ... 203 F4
Grieve St. Dunf ... 28 C2
Grieve St. Kirk ... 17 D3
Griffith Dr. Whit ... 170 A3
Griffiths St. Falk ... 60 A2
Grigor Ave. Edin ... 92 B2
Grigor Dr. Edin ... 92 B2
Grigor Gdns. Edin ... 92 C2
Grigor Terr. Edin ... 92 B2
Grindlay St. Edin ... 123 D4
Grindlay Street Ct. Edin ... 123 D4
Groathill Ave. Edin ... 92 B1
Groathill Gdns E. Edin ... 92 B1
Groathill Gdns W. Edin ... 92 B1
Groathill Rd N. Edin ... 92 B1
Groathill Rd S. Edin ... 92 B1
Grodwell Dr. Alva ... 4 C4
Grosvenor Gdns. Edin ... 122 C4
Grosvenor St. Edin ... 123 D4
Grove End. Bonn ... 182 A4
Grove St. Den ... 36 B1
Grove St. Edin ... 123 D4
Grove St. Muss ... 126 A3
Grove The. Muss ... 126 C3
Grundie's Well Rd. Edin ... 155 F3
Guardians Wood. Edin ... 122 B4
Guildhall St. Dunf ... 29 D2
Guildie Howes Rd N. Mid ... 207 F1
Guildiehaugh Roundabout.
  Bath ... 145 E2
Guildry Dr. Dunf ... 29 F2
Gullan's Cl. Edin ... 123 F4
Gunn Rd. Gran ... 61 E3
Gunner Rd. Gran ... 62 C4
Gurlie St. Edin ... 123 E4
Guttergates Rd. Hal ... 30 A3
Gyle Park Gdns. Edin ... 121 D3
Gylemuir Rd. Edin ... 121 E3
Gylers Rd. Dir ... 53 D2

Haddington Pl. Edin ... 93 F1
Haddington Rd. E Lin ... 103 D4
Haddington Rd. Muss ... 127 D3
Haddington Rd. N Ber ... 54 B3
Haddington Rd. Tran ... 128 C3
Haddington Station. Ind Est.
  Hadd ... 131 F4
Haddon's Ct. Edin ... 123 F4
Haddow Gr. Burn ... 50 B4
Hadfast Rd. Path ... 158 B3
Hadrian Way. B'ness ... 64 A3
Haig Ave. Kirk ... 17 E4
Haig Ave. Stir ... 2 A1
Haig Cres. Bath ... 145 E3

Haig Cres. Dunf ... 29 E3
Haig St. Gran ... 61 E3
Hailes App. Edin ... 153 D4
Hailes Ave. Edin ... 153 D4
Hailes Bank. Edin ... 153 D4
Hailes Cres. Edin ... 153 D4
Hailes Gdns. Edin ... 153 D4
Hailes Gr. Edin ... 153 D4
Hailes Loan. E Lin ... 103 D2
Hailes Pk. Edin ... 152 C4
Hailes Pl. Dunf ... 29 E2
Hailes St. Edin ... 123 D3
Hailes Terr. Edin ... 153 D4
Hailesland Gdns. Edin ... 121 F1
Hailesland Gr. Edin ... 121 F1
Hailesland Pk. Edin ... 121 F1
Hailesland Pl. Edin ... 121 F1
Hailesland Rd. Edin ... 121 F1
Hailstonegreen. For ... 215 D1
Hailstones Cres. Arm ... 143 F3
Hainburn Pk. Edin ... 153 F3
Haining Pl. Gran ... 61 F4
Haining Rd. Madd ... 83 F3
Haining Terr. Madd ... 83 F3
Hakness Cres. Tran ... 128 B3
Halbeath Dr. Dunf ... 29 F3
Halbeath Pl. Dunf ... 29 F3
Halbeath Rd. Dunf ... 29 F3
Halbeath Rd. Hal ... 30 A3
Halberts Cres. Stir ... 7 D1
Haldane Ave. B of A ... 2 A3
Haldane Ave. Hadd ... 100 C1
Haldane Gr. Bla ... 26 B4
Haldane Sq. Muri ... 173 E3
Halketshall. Lime ... 45 E2
Halkett Cres. Dunf ... 29 E1
Hall Cres. Gull ... 52 A1
Hall La. Loch ... 14 A4
Hall Rd. Brox ... 117 F3
Hall Row. Lime ... 45 E2
Hall St. Cow ... 13 E2
Hall St. Loch ... 14 A4
Hallcroft Cl. Rat ... 119 E1
Hallcroft Cres. Rat ... 119 E1
Hallcroft Gdns. Rat ... 119 E1
Hallcroft Grn. Rat ... 119 E1
Hallcroft Neuk. Rat ... 119 E1
Hallcroft Pk. Rat ... 119 E1
Hallcroft Rise. Rat ... 119 E1
Hallglen Rd. Falk ... 60 A1
Hallhead Rd. Edin ... 123 F1
Hallhill. Dunb ... 106 B4
Halliburton Terr. Dir ... 53 D2
Hallow Pk. Auch ... 204 A4
Hallpark. N Sau ... 5 E1
Hallyards Rd. Kirkl ... 119 D4
Hallyards Rd. Kirkl ... 119 E3
Halmyre St. Edin ... 94 A2
Halyard Terr. Aucht ... 15 D1
Hamburgh Pl. Edin ... 93 F3
Hamilton Ave. Lin ... 84 C3
Hamilton Cres. Gull ... 52 A1
Hamilton Cres. Newt ... 183 D3
Hamilton Cres. Madd ... 82 C3
Hamilton Dr. Edin ... 124 C4
Hamilton Dr. Falk ... 60 A2
Hamilton Dr. Stir ... 2 B2
Hamilton Dr W. Edin ... 124 C4
Hamilton Gdns. Edin ... 124 C4
Hamilton Gr. Edin ... 124 C4
Hamilton La. B'ness ... 63 F4
Hamilton La. Bath ... 144 C4
Hamilton Pk. Edin ... 124 C4
Hamilton Pl. Edin ... 93 E1
Hamilton Pl. Falk ... 60 A2
Hamilton Pl. Gran ... 125 D3
Hamilton Rd. Bath ... 144 C4
Hamilton Rd. Gran ... 61 F3
Hamilton Rd. Ros ... 46 C2
Hamilton St. Car ... 230 A1
Hamilton St. Falk ... 60 A3
Hamilton Terr. H Val ... 26 A1
Hamilton Terr. Inver ... 47 E1
Hamilton Wynd. Edin ... 93 F3
Handax. For ... 215 D1
Haney's Way. B'ness ... 64 B4
Hanover Ct. Brox ... 117 F3
Hanover Ct. Liv ... 147 D2
Hanover Grange. Gran ... 61 E3
Hanover St. Edin ... 93 E1
Harbour Dr. D Bay ... 47 F2
Harbour Pl. Burn ... 50 C4
Harbour Pl. D Bay ... 48 A2
Harbour Pl. Edin ... 95 D1
Harbour Pl. Inver ... 47 E1
Harbour Rd. B'ness ... 64 B4
Harbour Rd. Edin ... 94 A3
Harbour Rd. King ... 35 D1
Harbour Rd. Muss ... 126 A3
Harburn Ave. Liv ... 146 C3
Harburn Ave W. Liv ... 146 C4

Harburn Dr. W Cal ... 172 C2
Harburn Gdns. W Cal ... 172 C2
Harburn La. W Cal ... 172 C2
Harburn Rd. W Cal ... 172 C2
Harcourt Rd. Kirk ... 17 D3
Harden Pl. Edin ... 122 C3
Hardengreen Ind Est. Dalk ... 156 C1
Hardengreen Junc. Dalk ... 182 C4
Hardgate. Hadd ... 101 D1
Hardhill Dr. Bath ... 144 C3
Hardhill Pl. Arm ... 144 A3
Hardhill Rd. Bath ... 144 C3
Hardhill Terr. Bath ... 144 C3
Hardie Cres. Fall ... 8 B2
Hardie Ct. Stir ... 7 E2
Hardie Rd. Bog ... 146 B4
Hardie Rd. Liv ... 146 C4
Hardie Terr. E Lin ... 103 E4
Hardwell Cl. Edin ... 123 F4
Hardy Gdns. Bog ... 145 F3
Harebum Ave. Avon ... 112 A3
Harelaw Rd. Edin ... 153 D3
Hares Cl. Cocke ... 97 E2
Harestanes Rd. Arm ... 143 F2
Harewood Cres. Edin ... 124 C2
Harewood Dr. Edin ... 124 C2
Harewood Rd. Edin ... 124 C2
Harkenburn Gardens. Peni ... 203 E3
Harlaw Gr. Peni ... 203 E3
Harlaw Hill. Pres ... 96 C1
Harlaw March. Bale ... 177 E4
Harlaw Rd. Bale ... 177 F4
Harlaw Rd. Curr ... 152 B2
Harlawhill Gdns. Pres ... 97 D1
Harley Cl. Falk ... 60 A4
Harley St. Ros ... 47 D2
Harling Pl. Madd ... 82 C4
Harpenside Cres. Dir ... 53 E3
Harper's Brae. Auch ... 204 A3
Harperdean Terr. Hadd ... 100 C1
Harriebrae Pk. Dunf ... 28 C2
Harriet St. Kirk ... 17 F3
Harris Ct. All ... 10 A3
Harris Dr. Kirk ... 16 C4
Harris Pl. Dunf ... 29 F1
Harris Pl. Gran ... 61 E3
Harrison Gdns. Edin ... 122 C2
Harrison La. Edin ... 122 C3
Harrison Pl. Edin ... 122 C2
Harrison Rd. Edin ... 122 C3
Harrysmuir Cres. Pump ... 148 A4
Harrysmuir N. Pump ... 148 A4
Harrysmuir Rd. Pump ... 148 A4
Harrysmuir S. Pump ... 148 A4
Harrysmuir Terr. Pump ... 148 A4
Hart St. Edin ... 93 E1
Hart Street La. Edin ... 93 E1
Hart Wynd. Bann ... 7 F1
Hartfield Terr. Alla ... 212 A4
Harthill Rd. Blac ... 142 C3
Harthill Rd. Fau ... 193 E3
Hartington Gdns. Edin ... 123 D3
Hartington Pl. Edin ... 123 D3
Hartley Pl. Gran ... 61 D3
Hartwood Gdns. Shot ... 191 D1
Hartwood Rd. Shot ... 191 D2
Hartwood Rd. W Cal ... 172 B2
Harvest Dr. Kirkl ... 119 D3
Harvest Rd. Kirkl ... 119 D3
Harvey Ave. Pol ... 61 F1
Harvey Wynd. Stir ... 2 A1
Harvieston Villas. Gore ... 207 E4
Hatfield Pl. Bath ... 145 D4
Hatton Pl. Edin ... 123 E3
Haugh Gdns. Falk ... 39 D1
Haugh La. Falk ... 39 D1
Haugh Park. Edin ... 122 A1
Haugh Rd. Burn ... 50 B4
Haugh Rd. Stir ... 2 A1
Haugh St. Edin ... 93 D1
Haugh St. Falk ... 39 D1
Haven The. D Bay ... 48 A2
Haven's Edge. Lime ... 45 F2
Hawes Brae. Dal ... 68 B1
Hawk Brae. Liv ... 147 E3
Hawkcraig Rd. Abe ... 49 E4
Hawkhead Cres. Edin ... 155 D4
Hawkhead Gr. Edin ... 155 D4
Hawkhill Ave. Edin ... 94 A2
Hawkhill Rd. All ... 10 B3
Hawkhill. Kirk ... 23 E3
Hawkins Terr. Auch ... 204 A4
Hawkwood Terr. For ... 215 D1
Hawley Rd. Falk ... 60 B2
Hawthorn Bank. Oak ... 27 E3
Hawthorn Bank. Que ... 68 A1
Hawthorn Cres. Cow ... 12 C1
Hawthorn Cres. Fall ... 8 B2
Hawthorn Cres. May ... 183 E4
Hawthorn Dr. Shot ... 192 B2
Hawthorn Gdns. Loan ... 155 D1
Hawthorn Pl. Alla ... 212 A4

Hawthorn Pl. Edin 155 F3
Hawthorn Pl. Orm 159 E4
Hawthorn Pl. Uph 116 C2
Hawthorn Rd. Pres 97 D1
Hawthorn St. Gran 61 E3
Hawthorn Terr. Cocke 97 D2
Hawthornbank La. Edin 123 D4
Hawthornbank Pl. Edin 93 E3
Hawthornbank Rd. Hadd 100 C1
Hawthornbank Terr. Edin 93 F3
Hawthornden Ave. Bonn 182 A4
Hawthornden Gdns. Bonn 182 A4
Hawthorne Pl. Lar 38 B1
Hawthorns The. Gull 52 A2
Hawthornvale. Edin 93 E3
Hay Ave. Edin 124 C2
Hay Dr. Edin 125 D2
Hay Gr. Dunf 29 F1
Hay Pl. Edin 124 C2
Hay Rd. Edin 124 C2
Hay Terr. Edin 124 C2
Hayfield. Edin 121 D4
Hayfield. Falk 60 B4
Hayfield Pl. Kirk 17 D4
Hayfield Rd. Falk 60 B4
Hayfield Rd. Kirk 17 E4
Hayfield Terr. Bank 57 F4
Haygate Ave. Pol 82 C4
Haymarket. Edin 123 D4
Haymarket Terr. Edin 122 C4
Haypark Rd. Bank 57 E3
Hayworth Ave. Laur 61 D2
Hazel Ave. Kirk 17 D1
Hazel Cres. Duni 36 B2
Hazel Ct. Dunb 78 A1
Hazel Dr. Bonn 182 A3
Hazel Gr. Dunf 46 C4
Hazel Gr. Liv 148 A3
Hazel La. Loan 180 C4
Hazel Rd. Gran 61 E3
Hazelbank Gdns. Stir 2 A1
Hazelbank Terr. Edin 122 C2
Hazeldean Ave. B'ness 63 E3
Hazeldean Terr. Edin 124 A1
Hazelhurst. Pol 82 C4
Hazelwood Gr. Edin 124 B1
Heatheccross Rd. Shot 192 C1
Hedrig Rd. New 97 E1
Headrigg Row. Edin 124 A1
Heatherd Ave. Dunf 29 D3
Heathend Ave. Dunf 29 D3
Heaney Ave. Pump 148 A4
Heath Rd. Ros 46 C2
Heather Ave. Shi 81 E3
Heather Gr. Dunf 46 C4
Heather Gr. Madd 83 D3
Heather Pk. Black 146 A1
Heatherbank. Liv 147 E3
Heatherdale Gdns. Bank 57 F4
Heathervale Wlk. Arm 144 A3
Heatherwood Pk. Pump 148 A4
Hedge Row. Loan 180 C4
Hedges The. Falk 59 F3
Heggie's Wynd. Kirk 17 D1
Heights Rd. Blac 142 B2
Helen Pl. Inver 68 B3
Helmsdale Pk. Dunf 28 C1
Henderland Rd. Edin 122 B4
Henderson Ave. All 10 A4
Henderson Cres. Uph 117 D3
Henderson Ct. E Cal 148 C2
Henderson Gdns. Edin 93 F3
Henderson Gdns. Tran 128 B3
Henderson Pl. Alva 5 D3
Henderson Pl. Edin 93 E1
Henderson Pl. Uph 117 D3
Henderson Place La. Edin 93 D1
Henderson Row. Edin 93 D1
Henderson St. B of A 2 A4
Henderson St. Edin 93 F3
Henderson St. Hal 12 A1
Henderson St. Loch 14 A4
Henderson Terr. Edin 122 C3
Hendry Cres. Kirk 17 D3
Hendry Rd. Kirk 17 D3
Hendry St. Falk 60 A4
Hendry's Wynd. Kirk 17 D3
Hennings The. N Sau 5 E1
Henry Ross Pl. Que 68 A1
Henry St. Alva 5 D3
Henry St. B'ness 64 A4
Henry St. Gran 61 F4
Henryson Rd. Dunf 29 F2
Hepburn Dr. Dalk 157 E1
Hepburn Rd. Hadd 101 D1
Herald Rise. Muri 147 F1
Herbertshire St. Den 36 C1
Hercus Loan. Muss 126 A3
Herd Gn. Liv 147 D4
Herd Terr. Loan 181 D4
Herdmanflatt. Hadd 101 D1
Herdshill Ave. Shi 81 E3
Heriot Bridge. Edin 123 D4
Heriot Gdns. Burn 33 F1
Heriot Hill Terr. Edin 93 E2
Heriot Pl. Edin 123 E4

Heriot Row. Edin 93 E1
Heriot St. Inver 47 E1
Heriot Way. Stow 228 B1
Heritage Dr. Sten 39 D2
Hermand Cres. Edin 122 C2
Hermand St. Edin 122 C2
Hermand Terr. Edin 122 B2
Hermiston House Rd. Rat 120 C1
Hermitage Dr. Edin 123 D1
Hermitage Gdns. Edin 123 D1
Hermitage Park Gr. Edin 94 A2
Hermitage Park S. Edin 94 A2
Hermitage Pl. Edin 94 A2
Hermitage Rd. B of A 2 C3
Hermitage Terr. Edin 123 D1
Heron Ind Comlex. Liv 146 B4
Hervey St. All 10 A4
Heugh Brae. N Ber 54 C3
Heugh Rd. N Ber 54 C3
Heugh St. Falk 60 A2
Heugh The. Tran 128 B4
Heyford Pl. Cam 6 B3
Higginson Loan. May 183 F3
High Academy Gr. Arm 143 F3
High Academy St. Arm 143 F3
High Beveridgewell. Dunf 28 C3
High Brae. Torp 113 F3
High Buckstone. Edin 154 B3
High Meadow. Car 230 B1
High Mill Rd. Car 230 A1
High Park Rise. Peni 203 F2
High Port. Lin 85 D4
High Rd. E Lin 106 B2
High Rd. Madd 83 D3
High Rd. Rose 204 C3
High Riggs. Edin 123 D4
High School Yards. Edin 123 F4
High St. Abe 49 E1
High St. Aber 71 E2
High St. Air 22 B2
High St. All 10 A3
High St. Bath 145 D4
High St. Bon 58 A3
High St. Bonn 156 A1
High St. Bonn 182 A4
High St. Burn 50 C4
High St. Clack 10 C2
High St. Cocke 97 E2
High St. Cow 13 E2
High St. Dalk 157 D2
High St. Dunb 78 A1
High St. Dunb 78 B1
High St. Dunf 29 D2
High St. E Lin 103 E4
High St. Edin 123 E4
High St. Falk 60 A2
High St. Giff 163 F2
High St. Hadd 132 A4
High St. Inver 47 D1
High St. Kin 23 F2
High St. King 34 C1
High St. Kirk 17 E2
High St. Kirk 18 A4
High St. Kirkl 89 D1
High St. Lin 85 D4
High St. Loan 181 E4
High St. Loch 14 A4
High St. Muss 126 B3
High St. N Ber 54 B4
High St. Orm 159 F4
High St. Pres 96 C1
High St. Que 68 B1
High St. Shot 191 F2
High St. Slam 110 A4
High St. Tran 128 B3
High Station Rd. Falk 60 A2
High View Gr. Shi 81 E3
Highfield Ave. Lin 84 C4
Highfield Cres. Lin 84 C4
Highfield. E Lin 54 A2
Highfield. Liv 147 D2
Highfield Rd. N Ber 54 A2
Highland Dr. Lar 38 B2
Highland Dykes Cres. Bon 58 A3
Highland Dykes Dr. Bon 58 A3
Highlea Circ. Bale 177 D4
Highlea Gr. Bale 177 D4
Hill Cres. Bla 26 B4
Hill House Rd. Bank 57 F4
Hill Pl. All 10 B4
Hill Pl. Edin 123 F4
Hill Pl. Kirk 17 E2
Hill Pl. May 183 F3
Hill Pl. Shot 191 F3
Hill Rd. East 168 A3
Hill Sq. Gull 51 F1
Hill Rd. Path 185 D3
Hill Sq. Edin 123 F4
Hill St. All 10 A4
Hill St. Cow 13 E2
Hill St. Dunf 29 D2
Hill St. Edin 93 E1
Hill St. Inver 47 D1
Hill St. Kirk 17 D2
Hill St. Kirk 18 A4

Hill St. Stir 7 D2
Hill Street La N. Edin 93 E1
Hill Street La S. Edin 93 E1
Hill View. Peni 204 A3
Hillary St. Lar 38 C1
Hillbank. Inver 47 D2
Hillcoat Loan. Edin 95 D1
Hillcoat Pl. Edin 95 D1
Hillcrest Ave. Kirk 16 C3
Hillcrest. B'ness 63 F3
Hillcrest. Cow 13 D2
Hillcrest. Dr. All 10 B3
Hillcrest Pl. Bank 57 E4
Hillcrest Rd. Falk 59 F1
Hillend Rd. Inver 47 E2
Hillfield Cres. Inver 47 D2
Hillfield Rd. Inver 47 D1
Hillfoot Terr. Car 230 A1
Hillfoots Rd. B of A 2 C2
Hillhead Ave. Car 230 A1
Hillhead. Dr. Falk 59 F1
Hillhouse Ave. Bath 144 C2
Hillhouse Cres. Kir 149 F2
Hillhouse Rd. Edin 92 A1
Hillhouse Terr. Kir 149 F2
Hillhouseridge Rd. Shot 191 E3
Hillock Ave. Laur 61 E1
Hillpark Ave. Edin 91 F2
Hillpark Brae. Edin 91 F1
Hillpark Cres. Bann 7 E1
Hillpark Cres. Edin 91 F1
Hillpark Ct. Edin 91 F2
Hillpark Dr. Edin 91 F1
Hillpark Gdns. Edin 91 F1
Hillpark Gr. Edin 91 F1
Hillpark Loan. Edin 92 A1
Hillpark Rd. Edin 91 F1
Hillpark Terr. Edin 91 F1
Hillpark Way. Edin 92 A1
Hillpark Wood. Edin 92 A1
Hillside Ave. D Bay 48 A2
Hillside Camp Rd. Ros 46 C1
Hillside Cres. Edin 93 F1
Hillside Cres N. Gore 207 E4
Hillside Cres S. Gore 207 E4
Hillside Dr. Blac 142 B2
Hillside. N Sau 5 F1
Hillside Pl. Blac 142 B2
Hillside Pl. Fau 170 B1
Hillside Rd. Dal 90 B2
Hillside St. Edin 93 F1
Hillside Terr. B of A 10 A4
Hillside Terr. Dal 90 B3
Hillside Terr. Laur 61 D2
Hillview Ave. Brox 117 F3
Hillview Cotts. Rat 119 E1
Hillview. Cow 13 D2
Hillview Cres. Cross 30 C2
Hillview Cres. Edin 121 E4
Hillview Dr. B of A 2 A3
Hillview Dr. Edin 121 E4
Hillview. Edin 92 A1
Hillview. Fau 193 F3
Hillview. Oak 26 C4
Hillview Pl. Brox 117 F3
Hillview Pl. Fall 8 B2
Hillview Rd. Bon 58 B2
Hillview Rd. Edin 121 E4
Hillview Rd. Lar 38 B2
Hillview Rd. Orm 159 F4
Hillview Rd. Pol 82 B4
Hillview Terr. All 10 A3
Hillview Terr. Edin 121 E4
Hillwood Ave. Kirkl 119 E3
Hillwood Cres. Kirkl 119 E3
Hillwood Gdns. Kirkl 119 E3
Hillwood Pl. Kirkl 119 E3
Hillwood Rise. Kirkl 119 E3
Hillwood Terr. Kirkl 119 E3
Hillwood Terr. Ros 47 D2
Hilton. Cowie 20 C4
Hilton Cres. All 10 A4
Hilton Ct. Hadd 132 A4
Hilton Rd. All 10 A4
Hilton Rd. Crossf 27 F1
Hilton Rd. Ros 46 B1
Hilton Terr. Fall 8 B1
Hilton View. Loch 13 F3
Hirst Gdns. Shot 191 E2
Hirst Rd. East 168 A2
Hirst Rd. Sals 167 E2
Hirstrigg Cotts. Sals 167 D2
Hoban Sq. Brox 117 F3
Hobart St. Liv 148 A3
Hodge St. Falk 60 B3
Hogarth Ave. Gore 183 E1
Hoggan Cres. Dunf 29 E1
Hoghill Ct. E Cal 148 C2
Hoghill Pl. E Cal 148 C2
Holborn Pl. Ros 46 C3
Holbourne Pl. Men 4 A4
Holden Way. D Bay 48 A3
Holly Ave. Sten 38 C2
Holly Bank. May 183 F4

Holly Cres. Dunf 46 C4
Holly Pl. Kirk 17 E4
Holly Terr. Bonn 182 A3
Holly Wlk. Loan 180 C4
Hollybank Pl. E Cal 148 C1
Hollybank Terr. Edin 122 C2
Holmes Farm La. Uph 117 D3
Holmes Holdings. Brox 117 E2
Holmes Rd. Uph 117 D2
Holmlea Ave. Pol 82 B4
Holton Cres. N Sau 5 E1
Holton Sq. N Sau 5 E1
Holygate Pl. Brox 117 E3
Holyrood Park Rd. Edin 123 F3
Holyrood Pl. Dunf 29 D2
Holyrood Pl. Sten 38 C2
Home Farm Cotts. Den 57 F3
Home Pk. Abe 49 E4
Home St. Edin 123 D3
Homesteads The. Stir 6 B4
Honeybank Cres. Car 230 A2
Honeyman Ct. Arm 143 F4
Hookney Terr. Den 36 B1
Hope Cotts. Muir 64 B3
Hope La. Edin 125 D4
Hope Park Cres. Edin 123 F3
Hope Park Terr. Edin 123 F3
Hope Pk. Cres. Hadd 101 D1
Hope Pk Gdns. Bath 144 C3
Hope Pl. Hadd 101 D1
Hope Pl. Muss 126 C3
Hope St. B'ness 63 F4
Hope St. Car 230 A1
Hope St. Edin 123 D4
Hope St. Falk 60 A3
Hope St. Inver 47 D1
Hope St. Loch 89 D4
Hope St. Que 68 A1
Hope St. Stir 1 C1
Hope Street La. Edin 123 D4
Hope Terr. Edin 123 E2
Hopefield Dr. Black 171 E4
Hopefield Pk. Bonn 182 A3
Hopefield Pl. Black 171 E4
Hopefield Pl. Bonn 182 A3
Hopefield Rd. Black 171 E4
Hopefield Terr. Bonn 182 A3
Hopefield Terr. Edin 93 F3
Hopelands Rd. Peni 202 C3
Hopepark. Bath 144 C3
Hopepark Terr. Bon 57 F3
Hopetoun Cres. Edin 93 F1
Hopetoun Crescent La. Edin 93 F1
Hopetoun Dr. B of A 2 A4
Hopetoun Dr. Hadd 100 C1
Hopetoun La. Bath 145 D3
Hopetoun Mews. Hadd 101 D1
Hopetoun Pl. Kirk 16 B3
Hopetoun Rd. Que 68 A1
Hopetoun Rd. Ros 46 B1
Hopetoun St. Bath 145 D3
Hopetoun St. Edin 93 F2
Hopetoun Terr. Gull 52 A2
Hopetoun Terr. Orm 159 F4
Hopeward Ct. D Bay 48 B2
Hopeward Mews. D Bay 48 B2
Hoprig Pk. Cock 140 C1
Hoprig Rd. Cock 140 C1
Hoprig Rd. Cock 140 C2
Hornbeam Cres. Laur 61 D2
Horne Terr. Edin 123 D3
Horsburgh Bank. Bale 151 E2
Horsburgh Gdns. Bale 151 E2
Horsburgh Gr. Bale 151 E2
Horse Wynd. Edin 123 F4
Hoseason Gdns. Edin 91 E1
Hosie Rigg. Edin 125 D3
Hospital Hill. Dunf 29 D1
Hospital Interchange. Liv 147 E2
Hospital Rd. Hadd 100 C1
Hot Pot Wynd. Kirk 18 A4
Houldsworth Cres. Alla 212 A4
Houldsworth St. Bla 26 A4
Houliston Ave. Inver 47 D2
House O' Muir Rd. Sals 167 D1
House O'Hill Ave. Edin 92 A2
House O'Hill Brae. Edin 92 A2
House O'Hill Cres. Edin 92 A2
House O'Hill Gdns. Edin 92 A2
House O'Hill Gn. Edin 92 A2
House O'Hill Gr. Edin 92 A2
House O'Hill Pl. Edin 92 A2
House O'Hill Rd. Edin 92 A2
House O'Hill Row. Edin 92 A2
House O'Hill Terr. Edin 92 A1
Houston Ct. Dunf 28 C2
Houston Rd. Pump 117 D1
Houstoun Gdns. Uph 116 C2
Houstoun Interchange. Liv 147 F4
Houstoun Rd. Liv 147 F3
Howard Cres. Dunf 29 E1
Howard Pl. Edin 93 E2
Howard Pl. Kirk 18 A4
Howard St. Edin 93 E2
Howard St. Falk 59 F2
Howburn Cres. East 168 C3

Howburn Rd. East 168 B3
Howden East Rd. Liv 147 F2
Howden Hall Cres. Edin 154 C3
Howden Hall Ct. Edin 154 C3
Howden Hall Dr. Edin 154 C3
Howden Hall Gdns. Edin 155 D3
Howden Hall Loan. Edin 154 C3
Howden Hall Pk. Edin 154 C3
Howden Hall Rd. Edin 155 D3
Howden Hall Way. Edin 155 D3
Howden St. Edin 123 F3
Howden South Rd. Liv 147 F2
Howden South Rd. Muri 147 F2
Howden West Rd. Liv 147 F2
Howe Pk. Edin 153 F3
Howe St. Edin 93 E1
Howetown. Fish 5 E2
Howie's Pl. Falk 59 D2
Howieson Ave. B'ness 63 F3
Howieson Gn. Uph 116 C2
Howlands Rd. Stir 7 D2
Howley Ave. Liv 147 E2
Hudson Rd. Ros 46 C2
Hugh Miller Pl. Edin 93 D1
Hugh Pl. Loch 14 A4
Hugh Russell Pl. Que 89 D4
Hughes Cres. May 183 F3
Humbie Rd. Kirkl 89 D1
Humbie Terr. Abe 49 E4
Hume Cres. B of A 2 A3
Hume Ct. B of A 2 A3
Hummel Rd. Gull 51 F1
Hungerage Sq. Tran 128 B3
Hunt Cl. Dalk 157 D2
Hunt Pl. Crossf 28 A1
Huntburn Ave. Lin 85 E4
Hunter Ave. Loan 181 E4
Hunter Ct. Loan 181 E4
Hunter Gdns. Den 36 B1
Hunter Gr. Bog 145 F3
Hunter Gr. Whit 169 F3
Hunter Pl. Dunf 28 C3
Hunter Pl. Kirk 17 D2
Hunter Pl. Shot 191 F3
Hunter Pl. Sten 39 D2
Hunter Rd. Liv 147 E1
Hunter Sq. Edin 123 E4
Hunter Sq. Gore 207 E4
Hunter St. Kirk 17 D2
Hunter St. Shot 191 E3
Hunter Terr. Bonn 182 A4
Hunter Terr. Loan 181 E4
Hunter's Ct. Edin 123 E4
Hunter's La. Whit 170 A3
Hunterfield Ct. Gore 207 E4
Hunterfield Pk. Gore 183 E1
Hunterfield Rd. Gore 207 D4
Hunterfield Terr. Gore 183 D1
Hunters Hill. Peni 203 E3
Hunters Rd. Pen 160 C3
Huntly Ave. Liv 146 C3
Huntly Cres. Kirk 16 B4
Huntly St. Edin 93 E2
Huntly St. Shot 192 A2
Huron Ave. Liv 147 F2
Hursted Ave. May 183 E4
Hurworth St. Falk 59 F2
Husband Pl. Dunf 29 F1
Hutchison Ave. Edin 122 B2
Hutchison Cotts. Edin 122 B2
Hutchison Crossway. Edin 122 B2
Hutchison Gdns. Edin 122 B2
Hutchison Loan. Edin 122 B2
Hutchison Medway. Edin 122 B2
Hutchison Pk. Edin 122 B2
Hutchison Pl. Edin 122 B2
Hutchison Rd. Edin 122 B2
Hutchison Terr. Edin 122 B2
Hutchison View. Edin 122 B2
Hutton Pk. All 10 B4
Hutton Sq. Muri 173 E3
Hyndshaw Rd. Car 230 A2
Hyvot Ave. Edin 155 E3
Hyvot Bank Ave. Edin 155 F3
Hyvot Ct. Edin 155 E3
Hyvot Gdns. Edin 155 E3
Hyvot Gr. Edin 155 E3
Hyvot Loan. Edin 155 E3
Hyvot Pk. Edin 155 E3
Hyvot Terr. Edin 155 E3
Hyvot View. Edin 155 E3

Ibris Pl. N Ber 54 A4
Icehouse Brae. Laur 61 D2
Implement Rd. Dunf 77 F1
Imrie Pl. Peni 203 F3
Inch Ave. Abe 49 D3
Inch Cres. Bog 145 E3
Inch Keith Ave. King 34 C1
Inch View. King 34 C1
Inchcolm Dr. Inver 68 A3
Inchcolm Rd. Dunf 29 F2
Inchcolm Terr. Que 89 D4
Inchcorse Pl. Black 145 E1
Inches The. D Bay 48 A1
Inchgarvie Cres. Dunf 29 F2

Inchgarvie Pk. Que 68 A1
Inchgarvie Rd. Kirk 16 C4
Inchkeith Ave. Que 89 E4
Inchkeith Dr. Dunf 29 F2
Inchkeith Pl. Falk 60 A1
Inchmickery Ave. D Bay 48 B3
Inchmickery Rd. D Bay 48 B3
Inchna. Men 4 A3
Inchview Cres. Muss 127 E3
Inchview Gdns. D Bay 48 A2
Inchview N. Pres 96 C1
Inchview. Pres 96 C1
Inchview Rd. Muss 127 E3
Inchview Terr. Edin 94 C1
Inchyra Rd. Gran 61 F3
India Pl. Edin 93 D1
India St. Edin 93 D1
Industrial Rd. Edin 94 A2
Industry La. Edin 93 F3
Infirmary St. Edin 123 F4
Ingleston Ave. Dunf 36 B2
Inglewood. All 9 F4
Inglewood Pl. Edin 155 D4
Inglewood Rd. All 9 F4
Ingliston St. Liv 147 F3
Inglis Ave. Cocke 97 E2
Inglis Cres. King 34 C2
Inglis' Ct. Edin 1 C4
Inglis Gn Rd. Edin 122 A1
Inglis Pl. Pol 82 C4
Inglis St. Dunf 29 D2
Inkerman Ct. Auch 204 A4
Inn Pl. Liv 147 D1
Innerpethray Dr. Pen 4 A3
Institution St. Kirk 17 F4
Inver Ct. Falk 39 E1
Inverallan Ct. B of A 1 C4
Inverallan Dr. B of A 1 C4
Inverallan Rd. B of A 1 C4
Inveralmond Dr. Edin 91 D3
Inveralmond Gdns. Edin 91 D3
Inveralmond Gr. Edin 91 D3
Inverary Dr. Sten 38 C3
Inveravon Rd. Loan 155 D1
Inveravon Roundabout.
  B'ness 62 B3
Inveravon Terr. Muss 126 B3
Inveresk Brae. Muss 126 B3
Inveresk Ind Est. Muss 126 B3
Inveresk Rd. Muss 126 B3
Inveresk Village Rd. Muss .. 126 B4
Inverkeithing Rd. Abe 49 D4
Inverkeithing Rd. Cross 30 C3
Inverkip Dr. Shot 191 F3
Inverleith Ave. Edin 93 D2
Inverleith Ave S. Edin 93 D2
Inverleith Gr. Edin 92 C2
Inverleith Pl. Edin 93 D2
Inverleith Place La. Edin ... 93 D2
Inverleith Row. Edin 93 D2
Inverleith Terr. Edin 93 D2
Inverleith Terrace La. Edin . 93 E2
Invertiel Rd. Kirk 35 D4
Invertiel Terr. Kirk 17 D1
Inzievar Terr. Oak 27 D3
Iona Pl. Falk 60 A1
Iona Rd. Dunf 29 F2
Iona St. Edin 93 F2
Ireland Ave. Whit 169 F3
Iris Terr. Avon 82 C1
Ironmills Rd. Dalk 156 C2
Irvine Cres. Bath 144 C3
Irvine Pl. Stir 7 D4
Irving Ct. Falk 59 F3
Islands Cres. Falk 60 A1
Islay Ct. Gran 61 E3
Islay Rd. Dunf 29 F1
Ivanhoe Cres. Edin 124 A1
Ivanhoe Pl. Stir 2 A1
Ivanhoe Rise. Muri 148 A1
Ivy Cir. Dunf 46 C4
Ivy La. Kirk 18 A4
Ivy Terr. Edin 122 C3
Izatt Ave. Dunf 29 D1
Izatt St. All 10 A4
Izatt Terr. Clack 11 D2

Jacklin Gn. Liv 147 D4
Jackson Ave. Gran 61 E4
Jackson Pl. Liv 147 E2
Jackson St. Peni 203 F3
Jacob Pl. Falk 60 A2
Jail Wynd. Stir 7 D4
Jamaica Mews. Edin 93 D1
Jamaica St. Edin 93 E1
Jamaica St W. Edin 93 D1
Jamaica Street North La.
  Edin 93 D1
Jamaica Street South La.
  Edin 93 D1
James Croft Dr. Falk 59 F1
James Ct. Cow 13 E1
James Cir. Kirk 17 D1
James Hog Cres. Oak 26 C3
James Lean Ave. Dalk 157 D2
James Leary Way. Bonn 182 B4
James' Park La. Burn 33 F1
James' Pk. Burn 33 F1

James St. Alva 5 D3
James St. Arm 143 F3
James St. Bank 57 D2
James St. Bann 7 E3
James St. Cow 13 E1
James St. Dunf 29 D2
James St. Edin 125 E4
James St. Falk 60 A3
James St. Lar 38 B1
James St. Laur 60 C2
James St. Muss 126 B3
James St. Stir 2 A1
James Street La. Edin 125 E4
James Watt Ave. B'ness 64 A4
James Wilson Dr. Madd 83 D3
Jameson Pl. Edin 93 F2
Jamieson Ave. B' ness 63 F3
Jamieson Gdns. Shot 191 F3
Jane St. Edin 93 F2
Janefield. Edin 155 D2
Jarnac Ct. Dalk 157 D2
Jarvey St. Bath 145 D4
Jarvie Pl. Falk 60 A2
Jasper Ave. Laur 61 D2
Jawbanes Rd. Kirk 35 D4
Jean Armour Dr. Dalk 157 E1
Jeffrey Ave. Edin 92 A1
Jeffrey Bank. B' ness 63 F4
Jeffrey St. Edin 123 F4
Jeffrey Terr. Pol 61 F1
Jellyholm Rd. N Sau 10 C4
Jennie Rennie's Rd. Dunf 29 D1
Jessfield Pl. B' ness 63 F3
Jessfield Terr. Edin 93 E3
Jewel The. Edin 125 D3
Jock's Hill Cres. Lin 84 C4
John Bernard Way. Gore 207 E3
John Brown Ct. Hadd 132 A4
John Cres. Tran 128 B3
John Davidson Dr. Duni 36 B2
John Humble St. May 183 F3
John Knox Pl. Peni 203 F3
John Knox Rd. Long 98 C3
John Mason Ct. Que 89 E4
John Murray Dr. B of A 2 A4
John Row Pl. Oak 27 D4
John Rushforth Pl. Stir 1 C2
John St. Bank 57 D2
John St. Dunf 29 D1
John St. Edin 125 E4
John St. Falk 60 A4
John St. Kin 23 E2
John St. Kirk 17 D3
John St. Peni 203 F3
John St. Stir 7 D4
John Street La E. Edin 125 E4
John Street La. Edin 125 E4
John Street La. Peni 203 F3
John Street La W. Edin 125 E4
John Stuart Gait. Oak 26 C3
John's La. Edin 94 A3
John's Pl. Edin 94 A3
Johnnie Cope's Rd. Tran 128 A4
Johnsburn Gn. Bale 151 D1
Johnsburn Haugh. Bale 151 D1
Johnsburn Pk. Bale 177 D4
Johnsburn Rd. Bale 151 D1
Johnston Ave. Sten 38 C2
Johnston Ave. Stir 2 A2
Johnston Ave. Uph 116 C2
Johnston Cres. Dunf 29 D1
Johnston Cres. Loch 14 A4
Johnston Pk. Cow 13 E3
Johnston Pk. Inver 47 D1
Johnston Pl. Auch 203 F4
Johnston Pl. Den 36 B1
Johnston Terr. Bann 7 F1
Johnston Terr. Cocke 97 E2
Johnston Terr. Edin 123 E4
Johnstone La. Car 230 A1
Johnstone St. Alva 5 D3
Johnstone St. Men 3 F3
Jones Ave. Lar 59 E4
Jones Gn. Liv 147 D4
Joppa Gdns. Edin 125 E4
Joppa Gr. Edin 125 E4
Joppa Pk. Edin 125 E4
Joppa Rd. Edin 125 E4
Joppa Terr. Edin 125 E4
Jordan La. Edin 123 D2
Joseph Scott Gdns. Brox 117 F2
Jubilee Ave. Liv 146 C3
Jubilee Cres. Gore 183 E1
Jubilee Rd. Kirk 17 D3
Jubilee Rd. Dunf 46 A1
Jubilee Rd. Kirkl 119 F4
Jubilee Rd. Whit 170 A3
Junction Pl. Edin 93 F3
Junction Rd. Kirk 17 E4
Juner Pl. Gore 183 E1
Juniper Ave. Curr 152 B3
Juniper Gdns. Curr 152 B3
Juniper Gr. Curr 152 B3
Juniper Gr. Dunf 46 B4
Juniper Gr. Liv 148 A3
Juniper Park Rd. Curr 152 B3
Juniper Terr. Curr 152 B3

Juniperlee. Curr 152 B3
Jura. Liv 146 C3
Jura Pl. Gran 61 E3
Jura St. Gran 61 E3
Justinhaugh Dr. Lin 84 B4

Kaemuir Ct. West 112 C3
Kaim Cres. Bog 145 E3
Kaimes Ave. Kir 149 F2
Kaimes Cres. Kir 149 F2
Kaimes Gdns. Kir 149 F2
Kaimes Gr. Kir 149 F2
Kaimes Pl. Kir 149 F2
Kaimes Rd. Edin 121 F4
Kaimes View. Dan 156 A4
Karnes Pl. Dunf 29 E3
Karnes Rd. Shot 191 F3
Katesmill Rd. Edin 153 D4
Katherine St. Kirk 17 D3
Katherine St. Liv 148 A3
Katrine Cres. Kirk 16 C4
Katrine Ct. All 10 B3
Katrine Dr. Crossf 28 A1
Katrine Pl. Bank 57 E3
Katrine Rd. Shot 191 F3
Katrine Rd. Whit 170 B4
Kay Gdns. Cocke 97 E2
Keavil Pl. Crossf 28 A1
Kedslie Pl. Edin 154 C4
Kedslie Rd. Edin 154 C4
Keilarsbrae. N Sau 5 E1
Keir Ave. Stir 2 A1
Keir Gdns. B of A 2 A4
Keir Hardie Ave. Laur 61 D2
Keir Hardie Dr. May 183 F3
Keir Hardie Rd. Alva 5 E4
Keir Hardie Terr. Dunf 29 D1
Keir St. B of A 2 A4
Keir St. Cow 13 D2
Keir St. Edin 123 E4
Keirsbeath Ct. Hal 12 A1
Keith Ave. Stir 2 A1
Keith Cres. Edin 92 A1
Keith Gdns. Brox 117 E3
Keith Pl. Dunf 29 E2
Keith Pl. Inver 47 F2
Keith Rd. Ros 46 B1
Keith Row. Edin 92 B1
Keith St. Kin 23 F2
Keith Terr. Edin 92 A1
Kekewich Ave. Edin 94 C1
Kellie Pl. All 10 A4
Kelliebank. All 9 F3
Kelly Dr. Den 36 C2
Kelly's La. Car 230 A1
Kellywood Cres. Kin 23 F2
Kelso Dr. Car 230 B4
Kelso Pl. Kirk 17 D3
Kelso St. Uph 117 D3
Kelty Ave. B'ness 64 A4
Kelvin Dr. Shot 192 A2
Kelvin Sq. Pump 148 A4
Kelvin St. Gran 40 A1
Kemp Pl. Edin 93 D1
Kemper Ave. Falk 60 B2
Kendieshill Ave. Madd 83 D3
Kenilworth Dr. Edin 155 D4
Kenilworth Dr. Laur 60 C2
Kenilworth La. Gran 61 E3
Kenilworth Rd. B of A 2 A4
Kenilworth Rise. Muri 147 F1
Kenilworth St. Gran 61 E3
Kenmore Ave. Liv 146 C4
Kenmore Ave. Pol 62 A1
Kenmore Terr. Kirk 16 C4
Kenmuir St. Falk 59 E3
Kenmure Ave. Edin 124 B4
Kenmure Pl. Dunf 29 E3
Kenmure Pl. Sten 38 C2
Kennard Rd. Pol 82 B4
Kennard St. Falk 60 B3
Kennard St. Loch 14 A4
Kennedie Pk. E Cal 148 B2
Kennedy Cres. Dunf 29 E1
Kennedy Cres. Kirk 17 D3
Kenningknowes Rd. Stir 6 C3
Kennington Ave. Loan 181 D4
Kennington Terr. Loan 181 D4
Kent Rd. Falk 60 A4
Kent St. Dunf 29 D1
Kentigern Mall. Peni 203 F3
Keppel Rd. N Ber 54 A3
Kepscaith Cres. Whit 170 A3
Kepscaith Gr. Whit 170 A3
Kepscaith Rd. Whit 170 A3
Kerr Ave. Dalk 156 C1
Kerr Pl. Den 36 B1
Kerr Pl. Dunf 29 E1
Kerr St. Edin 93 D1
Kerr's Wynd. Muss 126 B3
Kerrisk Dr. Dunf 29 F1
Kerse Gdns. Falk 60 C3
Kerse Gn Rd. Clack 10 C3
Kerse La. Falk 60 B3
Kerse Pl. Falk 60 B3
Kerse Rd. Gran 61 F4
Kerse Rd. Stir 7 F3

Kerse Rd. Gran 61 E4
Kerse Rd. Stir 7 E3
Kersebonny Rd. Cam 6 B4
Kersie Rd. Fall 8 C2
Kersie Terr. All 9 F2
Kersiebank Ave. Gran 61 F3
Kestrel Brae. Liv 147 E3
Kestrel Dr. Madd 82 C4
Kettil'stoun Gr. Lin 84 B3
Kettil'stoun Mains. Lin 84 B3
Kettlestoun Rd. Lin 84 B4
Keverkae. All 9 F3
Kevock Rd. Bonn 181 F4
Kidd St. Kirk 17 E4
Kilbagie St. Kin 23 E2
Kilbean Dr. Falk 59 F1
Kilbirnie Terr. Den 36 B2
Kilbrennan Dr. Falk 59 D2
Kilburn Rd. Crossf 28 A1
Kilchurn Ct. Edin 121 D4
Kilcruik Rd. King 34 C2
Kildonan Pk. Dunf 28 C1
Kildrummy Ave. Sten 38 C2
Kilduthie Pl. Kin 23 F2
Kilfinan Rd. Shot 191 E3
Kilgour Ave. Kirk 17 E4
Kilgraston Rd. Edin 123 E2
Killin Ct. Dunf 28 C1
Killin Dr. Pol 62 A1
Kilmachan Way. Dunf 29 E3
Kilmartin Way. Dunf 29 E3
Kilmaurs Rd. Edin 124 A2
Kilmaurs Terr. Edin 124 A2
Kilmory Ct. Falk 59 E2
Kilmundy Dr. Burn 33 E1
Kilncadzow Rd. Car 230 B1
Kilmun Rd. Kirk 16 B4
Kilmundy Dr. Burn 33 E1
Kilncraigs Ct. All 10 B3
Kilncraigs Rd. All 10 B3
Kilncroft Side. Edin 154 A4
Kilns Pl. Falk 59 F3
Kilns Rd. Falk 60 A3
Kilpair St. Hadd 132 A4
Kilpunt View. Brox 118 A3
Kilrie Cotts. Auch 202 A4
Kilrymont. For 215 D1
Kilspindie Ct. Aber 71 E2
Kilsyth Rd. Bann 57 D2
Kilwinning Pl. Muss 126 B3
Kilwinning St. Muss 126 B3
Kilwinning Terr. Muss 126 B3
Kinacres Gr. B'ness 64 B4
Kincairne Ct. Kin 23 F2
Kincardine Rd. Sten 39 E2
Kincraig Pl. Dunf 28 C1
Kinellan Gdns. Edin 122 B4
Kinellan Rd. Edin 122 B4
King Cres. W Cal 172 B2
King Edwards Way. Kirkl 89 D1
King James IV Rd. Ros 46 B1
King O' Muirs Ave. Men 4 C2
King St. Arm 144 A3
King St. Bath 145 D3
King St. Cow 13 E2
King St. Edin 93 F3
King St. Falk 60 B3
King St. Fall 8 B2
King St. Inver 47 E1
King St. Kirk 17 D3
King St. Muss 126 B3
King St. Shot 191 F2
King St. Sten 38 C2
King St. Stir 7 D4
King's Ave. Long 98 B2
King's Court. Long 98 B2
King's Cramond. Edin 91 D2
King's Cres. Car 230 A2
King's Cres. Ros 46 C2
King's Dr. King 34 C2
King's Gr. Long 98 B2
King's Park Rd. N Ber 54 B3
King's Park Rd. Stir 7 D4
King's Pk. Pk. Long 98 B3
King's Pl. Ros 46 C2
King's Rd. Edin 95 D1
King's Rd. Long 98 B3
King's Rd. Ros 46 C3
King's Rd. Tran 128 B3
King's Rd. Whit 170 A3
King's Stables La. Edin 123 E4
King's Stables Rd. Edin 123 E4
King's Terr. Edin 94 C1
Kinghorn Pl. Burn 33 F1
Kinghorn Pl. Edin 93 E3
Kinghorn Rd. Burn 34 A1
Kinghorn Rd. Burn 50 C4
Kinghorn Rd. Kirk 35 D3
Kinglass Ave. B'ness 64 A4
Kings Ct. All 10 B3
Kings Ct. Falk 60 A2
Kings Gdns. Liv 122 C3
Kings Haugh. Edin 124 B2
Kings Rd. Gran 61 F4
Kingsburgh Ct E. Lin 103 E4
Kingsburgh Gdns. E Lin 103 E4

Kingsburgh Rd. Edin 122 B4
Kingseat Ave. Gran 61 E3
Kingseat Pl. Falk 59 F2
Kingsfield. Lin 85 E4
Kingsfield Rd. Dunf 29 E3
Kingsfield. Lin 85 E4
Kinghill Rd. Alla 212 A4
Kingsknowe Ave. Edin 122 A1
Kingsknowe Cres. Edin 122 A1
Kingsknowe Ct. Edin 121 F1
Kingsknowe Dr. Edin 122 A1
Kingsknowe Gdns. Edin 122 A1
Kingsknowe Gr. Edin 153 D4
Kingsknowe Pk. Edin 153 D4
Kingsknowe Pl. Edin 121 F1
Kingsknowe Rd N. Edin 122 A1
Kingsknowe Rd S. Edin 122 A1
Kingsknowe Terr. Edin 122 A1
Kingslaw Farm Cotts. Tran .. 128 C3
Kingsley Ave. Sten 38 C2
Kingsport Ave. Liv 147 F2
Kingstables La. Stir 7 D4
Kingston Ave. Edin 124 B1
Kingston Cotts. E Lin 53 F1
Kingswell Pl. All 10 B4
Kinimmonth St. Kirk 17 F4
Kinloch Pl. Gran 61 F3
Kinloss Ct. H Val 26 A1
Kinnaird Ave. Sten 39 D2
Kinnaird Dr. Sten 38 C2
Kinnaird Park. Edin 125 E2
Kinnaird Pl. Dunf 29 E3
Kinnear Rd. Edin 93 D2
Kinneil Dr. B' ness 63 E3
Kinneil Rd. B' ness 63 E4
Kinneil Rd. Inver 47 D1
Kinnis Ct. Dunf 29 F1
Kinnonmonth Ave. Burn 33 E1
Kintyre Pl. Falk 59 E2
Kippielaw Dr. Dalk 157 E1
Kippielaw Gdns. Dalk 157 E1
Kippielaw Medway. Dalk 157 E1
Kippielaw Pk. May 183 E4
Kippielaw Rd. Dalk 157 E1
Kippielaw Wlk. Dalk 157 E1
Kippithill. Hum 187 D1
Kirk Ave. Sten 38 C3
Kirk Brae. E Lin 106 A1
Kirk Brae. Edin 155 D4
Kirk Brae. Fau 170 B1
Kirk Brae. Kin 23 F3
Kirk Cramond. Edin 91 E3
Kirk La. Liv 147 D1
Kirk Loan. Edin 121 F3
Kirk Path. Alia 212 A4
Kirk Pk. Dunb 78 A1
Kirk Pk. Edin 155 D4
Kirk Ports. N Ber 54 B4
Kirk Rd. Aber 71 E2
Kirk Rd. Bath 145 E3
Kirk Rd. Shot 191 F2
Kirk St. Cul 25 E1
Kirk St. Edin 93 F2
Kirk St. Kin 23 F2
Kirk St. Pres 96 C1
Kirk View. Hadd 132 B4
Kirk Wynd. Clack 11 D3
Kirk Wynd. Falk 60 A2
Kirk Wynd. Kirk 17 D3
Kirk Wynd. Stir 7 D2
Kirkbank Rd. Burn 33 F1
Kirkbrae. Clack 10 C2
Kirkbride Terr. Plea 20 B2
Kirkburn. Slam 110 A4
Kirkcaldy Rd. Burn 33 F1
Kirkcaldy Rd. King 35 D2
Kirkfield E. Liv 147 D2
Kirkfield View. Liv 147 E2
Kirkfield W. Liv 147 D2
Kirkflat. Uph 117 D3
Kirkford Ct. Cow 13 D2
Kirkgate. All 10 A3
Kirkgate. Burn 50 C4
Kirkgate. Curr 152 A2
Kirkgate. Dunf 29 D2
Kirkgate. Edin 155 D4
Kirkgate. Inver 47 D2
Kirkgate. Lin 85 D4
Kirkgate. W Cal 172 B2
Kirkgate. Liv 147 D2
Kirkhall Ct. Dunf 29 D1
Kirkhill Dr. Edin 124 A3
Kirkhill Gdns. Edin 124 A3
Kirkhill Gdns. Peni 203 F3
Kirkhill Pk. Brox 117 E3
Kirkhill Rd. Brox 117 E3
Kirkhill Rd. Edin 124 A3
Kirkhill Terr. Brox 117 E3
Kirkhill Terr. Gore 183 E1
Kirkhill Terr. Gore 124 A3
Kirkland Dr. Dunf 29 D1
Kirklands. Dunf 29 D1
Kirklands. Edin 121 E2
Kirklands Pk. Que 203 F3
Kirkliston Rd. Que 89 D4
Kirksap. Den 29 D1
Kirkstyle Gdns. Kirkl 89 D1

Kirkton Ave. Bath ... 145 E3
Kirkton Bank. Peni ... 203 E3
Kirkton N. Liv ... 147 D2
Kirkton Pl. Cow ... 13 D3
Kirkton Pl. Sten ... 39 E2
Kirkton Rd. Burn ... 33 F1
Kirkton S Rd. Murl ... 147 E1
Kirkway. Air ... 22 B2
Kirkwood Ave. Laur ... 61 E1
Kirkwood Cres. Crossf ... 28 A1
Kisimul Ct. Edin ... 121 D4
Kitchener Cres. Long ... 98 C3
Kittle Yards. Edin ... 123 F2
Knights Way. Den ... 36 B1
Knightsbridge Rd. Dech ... 116 B1
Knightsbridge Rd. Liv ... 147 E4
Knightslaw Pl. Peni ... 203 E3
Knightsridge Ct. Dech ... 116 B1
Knightsridge E. Liv ... 147 E4
Knightsridge Rd. Dech ... 116 B1
Knightsridge Roundabout.
  Liv ... 147 E4
Knightsridge W. Liv ... 147 D4
Knockenhair Rd. Dunb ... 78 A1
Knockhill Ct. Loch ... 14 A4
Knockhouse Gdns. Crossf ... 28 A1
Knockhouse Rd. Crossf ... 28 A1
Knoll Croft Rd. Shot ... 192 A2
Knowe Park Rd. Ston ... 171 D1
Knowe The. D Bay ... 48 B2
Knowe The. N Sau ... 5 E1
Knowefaulds Rd. Tull ... 4 A2
Knowehead Rd. Laur ... 61 E1
Knowes Rd. Hadd ... 131 E4
Knowetop. Muri ... 173 E4
Knowetop Pl. Rosl ... 180 C2
Knowhead Rd. Crossf ... 28 A1
Knox Pl. Hadd ... 132 A4
Komarom Pl. Dalk ... 157 E2
Kyle Ave. Crowe ... 20 C4
Kyle Pl. Edin ... 93 F1
Kyles The. Kirk ... 17 F3

La Porte Prec. Gran ... 61 E4
Labrador Ave. Liv ... 147 F2
Laburnum Dr. Kirk ... 17 E4
Laburnum Gr. Burn ... 33 F1
Laburnum Gr. Stir ... 6 C3
Laburnum Pl. May ... 183 F3
Laburnum Rd. Burn ... 33 F1
Laburnum Rd. Whit ... 170 B3
Lade Braes D Bay ... 48 A2
Lade Ct. Lin ... 84 C4
Lade Dr. Lar ... 59 E4
Lade Dr. D Bay ... 48 A2
Lade Rd. Bon ... 58 A3
Ladehead. Edin ... 93 E2
Ladeside Ave. Black ... 171 E4
Ladeside Cres. Lar ... 38 C1
Ladeside Dr. Black ... 171 E4
Ladeside Rd. Black ... 171 E4
Lademeadow. Edin ... 121 F3
Lady Anne Ct. Cross ... 30 C3
Lady Brae. Gore ... 207 E4
Lady Brae Pl. Gore ... 207 F4
Lady Helen Cottages. Card ... 15 D4
Lady Helen St. Kirk ... 17 D1
Lady Jane Gdns. N Ber ... 54 B3
Lady Jane Rd. N Ber ... 54 B3
Lady Lawson St. Edin ... 123 E4
Lady Menzies Pl. Edin ... 94 A1
Lady Nairn Ave. Kirk ... 17 F3
Lady Nairne Cres. Edin ... 124 B4
Lady Nairne Gr. Edin ... 124 B4
Lady Nairne Loan. Edin ... 124 B4
Lady Nairne Pl. Edin ... 124 B4
Lady Nairne Rd. Dunf ... 28 C3
Lady Pl. Liv ... 147 D3
Lady Rd. Edin ... 124 A2
Lady Road Pl. Newt ... 183 D3
Lady Victoria Bsns Ctr.
  Newt ... 183 D2
Lady Wood Pl. Liv ... 147 D3
Lady Wynd. Edin ... 123 E4
Ladyburn Pl. King ... 35 D2
Ladycroft. Bale ... 151 E1
Ladysgate Ct. Sten ... 39 D2
Ladysmill. Falk ... 60 B3
Ladysmith Rd. Edin ... 123 F1
Ladysneuk Rd. Stir ... 2 B1
Ladywell Ave. Edin ... 121 E3
Ladywell Ct. Edin ... 121 E3
Ladywell Ct. Lar ... 4 A2
Ladywell Dr. Tull ... 4 A2
Ladywell E. Liv ... 147 E3
Ladywell East Rd. Liv ... 147 F3
Ladywell Gdns. Edin ... 121 E3
Ladywell Gr. Clack ... 11 D2
Ladywell. Muss ... 126 B3
Ladywell Pl. Tull ... 4 A2
Ladywell Rd. Edin ... 121 E3
Ladywell View. B'ness ... 63 E3
Ladywell Way. Muss ... 126 B3
Ladywell West Rd. Liv ... 147 E3
Ladywood. Clack ... 11 E2
Legan Rd. Car ... 230 A1
Laggan Ave. Shot ... 192 A2
Laggan Path. Shot ... 191 F3

Lichfield. Edin ... 122 A2
Laichpark Pl. Edin ... 122 A2
Laichpark Rd. Edin ... 122 A2
Laing Gdns. Brox ... 117 E3
Laing Terr. Edin ... 125 E4
Laing Terr. Peni ... 203 F4
Laird Terr. Bonn ... 182 B3
Laird's Entry. Path ... 185 E2
Lakeside Rd. Kirk ... 16 C2
Lamb's Cl. Edin ... 123 F3
Lamb's Pend. Peni ... 203 F2
Lamberton Ave. Stir ... 7 E2
Lambert Dr. Dunf ... 29 E2
Lambert Terr. All ... 10 B4
Lambertons Ave. Stir ... 7 E2
Lamberton Ct. Pen ... 160 C3
Lambie St. Whit ... 170 A4
Lamer St. Dunb ... 78 C2
Lamington Rd. Glad ... 130 C4
Lammerlaws Rd. Burn ... 50 C4
Lammermoor Gdns. Tran ... 128 A3
Lammermoor Terr. Edin ... 124 B1
Lammermoor Terr. Tran ... 128 A3
Lammermuir Cres. Dunb ... 78 B1
Lammermuir Cres. Hadd ... 132 B4
Lammermuir Ct. Gull ... 52 A1
Lammermuir Pl. Kirk ... 16 C3
Lammermuir. Glad ... 130 B4
Lammerview. Tran ... 128 B3
Lamond View. Lar ... 38 B1
Lamont Cres. Fall ... 8 B3
Lamont Way. Liv ... 147 E4
Lampacre Rd. Edin ... 121 F3
Lanark Ave. Liv ... 147 D3
Lanark Rd. Curr ... 152 C3
Lanark Rd. Edin ... 122 A1
Lanark Rd. Edin ... 152 C3
Landale Gdns. Burn ... 33 F1
Landale. Burn ... 33 F1
Landale St. Loch ... 14 A4
Lane The. White ... 126 C1
Lang Loan. Edin ... 155 E2
Langfauld Gdns. Bath ... 144 C3
Langhill Pl. Den ... 36 B1
Langlaw Rd. May ... 183 E4
Langlees St. Falk ... 39 F1
Langrigg. Hadd ... 132 A4
Langside Cres. W Cal ... 173 D3
Langside Dr. Blac ... 142 A2
Langside. E Lin ... 103 E4
Langside Gdns. W Cal ... 173 D3
Langton Ave. E Cal ... 148 C2
Langton Gdns. E Cal ... 148 C2
Langton Rd. Edin ... 123 F2
Langton Rd. E Cal ... 148 C2
Langton View. E Cal ... 148 C2
Lanrigg Ave. Fau ... 193 F4
Lanrigg Rd. Fau ... 193 F4
Lansbury Ct. Dalk ... 157 D2
Lansbury St. Kirk ... 17 F4
Lansdowne Cres. Edin ... 123 D4
Lansdowne Cres. Kin ... 23 F2
Lansdowne Cres. Shot ... 192 A2
Lapicide Pl. Edin ... 93 F3
Larbert Ave. Liv ... 147 D4
Larbert Rd. Bon ... 58 A3
Larbourfield. Edin ... 121 E1
Larch Cres. May ... 183 F3
Larch Dr. Whit ... 170 B3
Larch Gr. Dunf ... 46 B4
Larch Gr. Sten ... 38 C2
Larch St. Gran ... 61 E3
Larchbank. Liv ... 147 F3
Larches The. All ... 10 A4
Larchfield. Bale ... 151 E1
Larchfield La. Shot ... 192 A1
Larchfield Neuk. Bale ... 151 E1
Largo Pl. Edin ... 93 F3
Larkfield Dr. Dalk ... 156 C1
Larkfield Rd. Dalk ... 156 C1
Lasswade Bank. Edin ... 155 E3
Lasswade Gr. Edin ... 155 E3
Lasswade Rd. Bonn ... 156 A1
Lasswade Rd. Dalk ... 156 C1
Lasswade Rd. Edin ... 155 E3
Lasswade Rd. Loan ... 155 F1
Lasswade Rd. Loan ... 181 D4
Latch Rd. Dunb ... 78 C1
Latch The. Crossf ... 27 E1
Lathallan Dr. Pol ... 61 F1
Lauder Loan. Edin ... 123 F2
Lauder Lodge. Dalk ... 157 D2
Lauder Pl. E Lin ... 103 E4
Lauder Pl. Edin ... 93 F1
Lauder Rd. Dalk ... 157 E1
Lauder Rd. Edin ... 123 E2
Lauder Rd. Kirk ... 17 E3
Lauder St. Dunf ... 28 B1
Lauderdale St. Edin ... 123 E3
Laurel Bank. Dalk ... 157 E1
Laurel Bank Pl. May ... 183 F3
Laurel Bank Rd. May ... 183 F3
Laurel Cres. Kirk ... 17 D4
Laurel Cres. Falk ... 59 F1
Laurel Gr. Bon ... 57 F2
Laurel Gr. Laur ... 61 D1
Laurel Pl. Bon ... 57 F2
Laurel Rd. Ros ... 46 B1

Laurel Terr. Edin ... 122 C3
Laurelbank Ave. Bon ... 58 A2
Laurelbank Ct. E Cal ... 148 C1
Laureihill Gdns. Stir ... 6 C3
Laureihill Pl. Stir ... 7 D3
Laurels The. Tull ... 4 A1
Laurence Croft Rd. Stir ... 2 A1
Laurie St. Edin ... 94 A2
Laurieston Rd. Gran ... 61 D3
Lauriston Dr. Dunf ... 29 E3
Lauriston Farm Rd. Edin ... 91 F2
Lauriston Gdns. Edin ... 123 E3
Lauriston Pk. Edin ... 123 E4
Lauriston Pl. Edin ... 123 E4
Lauriston St. Edin ... 123 E4
Lauriston Terr. Edin ... 123 E4
Laurmont Ct. Laur ... 61 D2
Laverock Dr. Peni ... 203 E3
Laverock Pk. Lin ... 85 D3
Laverockbank Ave. Edin ... 93 E3
Laverockbank Cres. Edin ... 93 E3
Laverockbank Gdns. Edin ... 93 E3
Laverockbank Gr. Edin ... 93 E3
Laverockbank Rd. Edin ... 93 E3
Laverockbank Terr. Edin ... 93 E3
Laverockdale Cres. Edin ... 153 D3
Laverockdale Loan. Edin ... 153 D3
Laverockdale Pk. Edin ... 153 D3
Law Pl. Edin ... 95 D1
Law Rd. Dunf ... 29 F2
Law Rd. N Ber ... 54 B4
Lawers Cres. Pol ... 62 A1
Lawers Pl. Gran ... 61 F3
Lawers Sq. Peni ... 204 A4
Lawfield Rd. May ... 183 E4
Lawhead Cotts. E Lin ... 75 F2
Lawhead Pl. Peni ... 203 E3
Lawnmarket. Edin ... 123 E4
Lawrence St. Hadd ... 131 F4
Lawrie Terr. Peni ... 203 F4
Lawson Cres. Que ... 89 E4
Lawson Gdns. Kirk ... 17 F4
Lawson Pl. Dunb ... 78 B1
Lawson Pl. Madd ... 83 D3
Lawson St. Kirk ... 17 F4
Lawswell. Fish ... 5 F2
Laxdale Dr. Bank ... 57 E4
Laxford Cres. D Bay ... 48 A2
Laxburn Ave. Dunf ... 29 D4
Leadervale Rd. Edin ... 154 C4
Leadervale Terr. Edin ... 154 C4
Leadside Cres. Dunf ... 29 D4
Leamington Pl. Edin ... 123 D4
Leamington Rd. Edin ... 123 D3
Leamington Terr. Edin ... 123 D3
Learmonth Ave. Edin ... 92 C1
Learmonth Cres. Edin ... 92 C1
Learmonth Cres. W Cal ... 172 B2
Learmonth Ct. Edin ... 92 C1
Learmonth Gardens Mews.
  Edin ... 93 D1
Learmonth Gdns. Edin ... 92 C1
Learmonth Gr. Edin ... 92 C1
Learmonth Pk. Edin ... 93 D1
Learmonth Pl. Edin ... 92 C1
Learmonth Rd. Edin ... 93 D1
Learmonth St. Falk ... 60 A2
Learmonth Terr. Edin ... 93 D1
Learmonth Terrace La. Edin ... 93 D1
Ledi Ave. Tull ... 4 A1
Ledi Terr. Peni ... 204 A4
Ledi View. Stir ... 2 A2
Ledmore Pl. Falk ... 60 C1
Lee Cres. Edin ... 125 D4
Leighton Cres. May ... 183 E4
Leighton St. H Val ... 26 A1
Leith Ave. Burn ... 33 F1
Leith Pl. Bank ... 57 E3
Leith St. Edin ... 93 E1
Leith Wlk. Edin ... 93 F2
Lempockwells Rd. Pen ... 160 C3
Lendrick Ave. Falk ... 59 F1
Lennel Ave. Edin ... 122 C4
Lenniemuir. Kirkl ... 90 A1
Lennox Ave. Stir ... 7 D2
Lennox Gdns. Lin ... 84 B4
Lennox Milne Ct. Hadd ... 132 B4
Lennox Rd. Hadd ... 132 B4
Lennox Row. Edin ... 93 D3
Lennox St. Edin ... 93 D1
Lennox Street La. Edin ... 93 D1
Lennox Terr. Gran ... 61 F3
Lennoxlove Acredales. Giff ... 132 A4
Lenny Pl. Dunf ... 29 D3
Lenzie Ave. Liv ... 147 D3
Leopold Pl. Edin ... 93 F1
Leslie Pl. Edin ... 93 D1
Leslie Rd. Ros ... 46 B3
Leslie St. Kirk ... 35 D4
Lestrange Terr. Alva ... 5 D3
Letham Ave. Pump ... 148 A4
Letham Cotts. Air ... 39 E4
Letham Cres. Pump ... 148 A4
Letham Dr. Hadd ... 131 F4
Letham Gdns. Pump ... 148 A4
Letham Gr. Pump ... 148 A4
Letham Hill Ave. D Bay ... 47 F2
Letham Pk. Dunb ... 78 B1
Letham Pk. Pump ... 148 A4

Letham Pl. Dunb ... 78 B2
Letham Pl. Pump ... 148 A4
Letham Rd. Dunb ... 78 B1
Letham Rd. Liv ... 148 A4
Letham Rise. D Bay ... 47 F2
Letham Terr. Pump ... 148 A4
Letham Terr. Air ... 22 B1
Letham Way. D Bay ... 47 F2
Leuchatsbeath Dr. Cow ... 13 D3
Leven Cl. All ... 10 B3
Leven Pl. Shot ... 191 F3
Leven St. Edin ... 123 D3
Leven St. Falk ... 60 A4
Leven Terr. Edin ... 123 E3
Leven Wlk. Liv ... 148 A2
Leving Pl. Liv ... 147 E2
Lewis Ct. All ... 10 A3
Lewis Ct. Falk ... 60 A1
Lewis Rd. Pol ... 61 F1
Lewisvale Ave. Muss ... 126 C3
Lewisvale Ct. Muss ... 126 C3
Leyden Pl. Bonn ... 182 A4
Leyden Pl. Bonn ... 182 A4
Leys Park Rd. Dunf ... 29 D2
Liberton Brae. Edin ... 155 D4
Liberton Dr. Edin ... 154 C4
Liberton Gdns. Edin ... 155 D4
Liberton Pl. Edin ... 155 D4
Liberton Rd. Edin ... 124 A1
Library La. Gran ... 40 B1
Liddesdale Pl. Edin ... 93 D1
Liddle Dr. B'ness ... 63 F3
Lidgate Street. Rat ... 119 F1
Liggar's Pl. Dunf ... 28 C1
Liggat Pl. Brox ... 117 E3
Liggat Syke Pl. Brox ... 118 A3
Lighton Terr. Edin ... 171 D1
Lilac Ave. May ... 183 F3
Lilac Cres. Kirk ... 17 E4
Lilac Gr. Dunf ... 46 B4
Lillies La. Giff ... 163 F3
Lily's La. Dunf ... 29 D1
Lily Terr. Edin ... 122 C2
Lilybank Ct. N Ber ... 54 B4
Lilyhill Terr. Edin ... 94 B1
Lime Ave. New ... 66 C1
Lime Gr. Dunf ... 29 F1
Lime Gr. May ... 183 F3
Lime Gr. N Ber ... 54 C3
Lime Gr. Pol ... 61 F1
Lime Gr. Bonn ... 182 A3
Lime Rd. Falk ... 59 D2
Lime St. Gran ... 61 D3
Limebank Pk. E Cal ... 148 C1
Limefield Ave. W Cal ... 173 D3
Limefield Cres. Bog ... 145 F3
Limefield Gdns. W Cal ... 173 D3
Limefield Rd. W Cal ... 173 D3
Limefield Pl. Bog ... 145 E3
Limefield Rd. Bath ... 145 E4
Limefield Rd. W Cal ... 173 D3
Limekilns Gr. E Cal ... 149 D2
Limekilns. Pen ... 161 D3
Limekilns Rd. Dunf ... 28 C2
Limes The. Edin ... 123 D2
Limetree Wlk. E Lin ... 103 F4
Limeylands Cres. Orm ... 159 E4
Limeylands Rd. Orm ... 159 E4
Lina St. Kirk ... 17 D3
Linburn Gr. Dunf ... 29 F2
Linburn Pk. E Cal ... 150 A3
Linburn Pl. Dunf ... 29 F2
Linburn Rd. Dunf ... 29 F2
Lindean Pl. Edin ... 94 A2
Lindean Terr. E Cal ... 149 F3
Linden Ave. Dunf ... 46 C4
Linden Ave. Stir ... 7 E3
Linden Gr. Liv ... 148 A3
Linden Pl. Loan ... 181 E4
Lindores Dr. Kirk ... 16 C4
Lindores Dr. Tran ... 128 B3
Lindsay Dr. Stir ... 2 A2
Lindsay Pl. Edin ... 93 F3
Lindsay Rd. Edin ... 93 F3
Lindsay Sq. Liv ... 146 B3
Lindsay St. Edin ... 93 F3
Lindsay Way. Liv ... 147 E4
Lindsay's Wynd. Oak ... 26 C3
Lingerwood Farm Cotts.
  Newt ... 183 D2
Lingerwood Rd. Newt ... 183 D2
Lingerwood Wlk. Newt ... 183 D2
Linhouse Dr. E Cal ... 148 C2
Linhouse Rd. E Cal ... 148 C2
Linkfield Ct. Muss ... 126 C3
Linkfield Rd. Muss ... 126 C3
Links Ave. Muss ... 126 A4
Links Ct. Cocke ... 97 E2
Links Gardens. Edin ... 94 A3
Links Gardens La. Edin ... 94 A3
Links Gdns. Edin ... 94 A3
Links Pl. B'ness ... 63 F4
Links Pl. Burn ... 50 C4
Links Pl. Cocke ... 97 F2
Links Pl. Edin ... 94 A3
Links Pl. B'ness ... 64 A4

Links Rd. Cocke ... 97 F2
Links Rd. Long ... 98 C3
Links Rd. N Ber ... 54 A4
Links St. Kirk ... 17 D1
Links View. Cocke ... 97 F2
Links View. Muss ... 126 B4
Links View. Cocke ... 97 F2
Linlithgow Pl. Sten ... 38 C2
Linlithgow Rd. B' ness ... 63 F3
Linlithgow Terr. Orm ... 159 F4
Linmill Rd. Avon ... 112 A3
Linn Mill. Que ... 67 F1
Linn Pl. Brox ... 117 F2
Linsay Macdonald Ct. Dunf ... 29 E2
Lint Riggs. Falk ... 60 A3
Linton La. Kirk ... 16 C3
Linton Pl. Ros ... 46 C2
Linty La. Peni ... 203 E3
Lion Well Wynd. Lin ... 84 C4
Lionthorn Rd. Falk ... 59 F1
Lipney. Men ... 4 A3
Lismore Ave. Edin ... 94 B1
Lismore Ave. Kirk ... 16 C4
Lismore Cres. Edin ... 94 B1
Lismore Ct. Falk ... 60 A1
Lismore Pl. Kirk ... 16 C4
Lister Ct. B of A ... 2 A3
Lister Rd. Liv ... 147 D1
Listloaning Pl. Lin ... 84 B4
Listloaning Rd. Lin ... 84 B4
Liston Dr. Kirkl ... 89 D1
Liston Pl. Kirkl ... 89 D1
Liston Rd. Kirkl ... 89 D1
Little Acre. May ... 183 E4
Little Carriden. Muir ... 64 B3
Little Cswy. Cul ... 42 B4
Little Denny Rd. Den ... 36 B1
Little France Mills. Edin ... 124 B1
Little King St. Edin ... 93 E1
Little Rd. Edin ... 155 D4
Livery St. Bath ... 145 D4
Livesay Rd. Ros ... 46 B1
Livesey Terr. Auch ... 204 A4
Livilands Ct. Stir ... 7 D3
Livilands Gate. Stir ... 7 D3
Livilands La. Stir ... 7 D3
Livingston Rd. Liv ... 147 F3
Livingstone Cres. Falk ... 60 A2
Livingstone Dr. B'ness ... 63 E3
Livingstone Dr. Burn ... 33 F1
Livingstone Dr. Laur ... 61 D1
Livingstone La. Abe ... 49 E4
Livingstone Pl. Edin ... 123 E3
Livingstone Quadrant. East ... 168 B2
Livingstone St. Add ... 171 F1
Livingstone Terr. Laur ... 61 D1
Lixmount Ave. Edin ... 93 E3
Lixmount Gdns. Edin ... 93 E3
Lizzie Brice's Interchange.
  E Cal ... 148 A1
Llynallan Rd. East ... 168 A3
Loan Pl. East ... 168 C3
Loan The. B'ness ... 63 E3
Loan The. Loan ... 181 D4
Loan The. Path ... 184 B4
Loan The. Oak ... 68 A1
Loan The. Torp ... 113 F3
Loanburn Ave. Peni ... 203 F3
Loanburn. Peni ... 203 F3
Loanfoot Cres. Uph ... 117 D3
Loanfoot Gdns. Plea ... 20 B2
Loanfoot Rd. Uph ... 117 D2
Loanhead Ave. Bank ... 57 E3
Loanhead Ave. Gran ... 61 E4
Loanhead Pl. Kirk ... 17 D3
Loanhead Rd. Edin ... 155 D1
Loaning Cres. Edin ... 94 B1
Loaning Rd. Edin ... 94 B1
Loaninghill Pk. Uph ... 117 D3
Loaninghill Rd. Uph ... 117 D2
Loch Awe Way. Whit ... 170 B4
Loch Earn Way. Whit ... 170 B4
Loch Fyne Way. Whit ... 170 B4
Loch Linnhe Ct. Whit ... 170 B4
Loch Maree Way. Whit ... 170 B4
Loch Pl. Que ... 68 A1
Loch Rd. Edin ... 92 A1
Loch Rd. Que ... 68 A1
Loch Rd. Tran ... 128 B3
Loch Sq. Tran ... 128 B3
Loch Trool Way. Whit ... 170 B4
Lochaber Cres. Shot ... 192 A2
Lochaber Dr. Sten ... 38 C2
Lochbank. Liv ... 147 F3
Lochbridge Rd. N Ber ... 54 B3
Lochend Ave. Dunb ... 78 C1
Lochend Ave. Edin ... 94 A2
Lochend Castle Barns. Edin ... 94 A1
Lochend Cl. Edin ... 123 F4
Lochend Cres. Dunb ... 78 B1
Lochend Cres. Edin ... 94 B1
Lochend Dr. Edin ... 94 A1
Lochend Gdns. Edin ... 94 A1
Lochend Gr. Edin ... 94 B1
Lochend Ind Est. Kirkl ... 119 D3

Lochend Pk. Edin 94 A2
Lochend Quadrant. Edin 94 B1
Lochend Rd. Dunb 78 C1
Lochend Rd. Edin 94 A2
Lochend Rd. Kirki 119 D4
Lochend Rd N. Muss 126 A3
Lochend Rd S. Muss 126 A3
Lochend Rd S. Edin 94 A1
Lochend Sq. Edin 94 A2
Lochgelly Rd. Cow 13 E3
Lochgreen Rd. Falk 59 F1
Lochhead Ave. Den 36 C1
Lochhill Cotts. Ath 99 F4
Lochies Rd. Burn 34 A1
Lochies Rd. Clack 11 D2
Lochinvar Pl. Bon 58 B2
Lochinvar Rd. Ros 46 B1
Lochlands Ind Est. Falk 59 D4
Lochmaben Dr. Sten 38 C2
Lochpark Pl. Den 36 C1
Lochridge Pl. Den 36 B1
Lochrin Pl. Edin 123 D3
Lochside Cres. Laur 61 D1
Lochside Rd. Slam 110 B1
Lock Rd. Ros 47 D2
Lock Sixteen. Falk 59 E3
Lockerby Cotts. Edin 155 E3
Lockerby Cres. Edin 155 E3
Lockerby Gr. Edin 155 E3
Locknart Terr. Rosl 180 D2
Lockharton Ave. Edin 122 C1
Lockharton Cres. Edin 122 C1
Lockharton Gdns. Edin 122 C2
Lodge Dr. Sten 38 C1
Lodge St. Hadd 132 B4
Logan St. Edin 93 E1
Logan Way. Liv 147 E4
Loganlea Ave. Edin 94 B3
Loganlea Cres. Add 171 E1
Loganlea Dr. Edin 94 B3
Loganlea Gdns. Edin 94 B1
Loganlea Loan. Edin 94 B3
Loganlea Pl. Edin 94 B1
Loganlea Rd. Add 171 E1
Loganlea Rd. Edin 94 B3
Loganlea Terr. Add 171 E1
Loganlea Terr. Edin 94 B1
Logie Dr. Lar 38 A2
Logie Green Gdns. Edin 93 E2
Logie Green Loan. Edin 93 E2
Logie Green Rd. Edin 93 E2
Logie La. B of A 2 B2
Logie Mill. Edin 93 E2
Logie Pl. Dunf 28 B3
Logie St. Stir 2 B2
Lomond Cres. Dunf 29 F1
Lomond Cres. Sten 38 C2
Lomond Cres. Stir 2 A2
Lomond Cres. Whit 170 A3
Lomond Ct. All 10 B3
Lomond Dr. Bann 7 F1
Lomond Dr. Falk 39 E1
Lomond Gdns. Kirk 16 C3
Lomond Rd. Edin 93 D3
Lomond Rd. Gran 61 F3
Lomond Rd. Shot 191 F3
Lomond St. All 10 A4
Lomond Vale. Peni 204 A4
Lomond View. West 112 C2
Lomond Way. Bank 57 E3
Lomond Wlk. Edin 155 D1
London Rd. Dalk 157 D2
London Rd. Edin 94 A1
London St. Edin 93 E1
Loney Cres. Den 57 F4
Long Byres. Brox 117 F3
Long Craigs. Cocke 97 F2
Long Craigs Terr. King 35 D2
Long Cram. Hadd 131 F4
Long Crook. Que 89 D4
Long Dalmahoy Rd. Bale 150 B2
Long Dalmahoy Rd. Kir 150 B2
Long Dalmahoy Rd. Rat 150 B2
Long Row. Hal 30 A4
Long Row. Men 4 A4
Longannet Cotts. Kin 24 A1
Longbraes Gdns. Kirk 16 B3
Longcroft Gdns. Lin 84 C4
Longdales Ave. Falk 60 A4
Longdales Ct. Falk 60 A4
Longdales Pl. Falk 60 A4
Longdales Rd. Falk 60 A4
Longdyke Pl. Sten 39 E2
Longdykes Rd. Pres 97 D1
Longfort. For 215 D1
Longformacus Rd. Edin 155 D3
Longhill Gdns. D Bay 48 A2
Longridge Rd. Whit 170 A3
Longstone Ave. Edin 122 B2
Longstone Cres. Edin 122 A2
Longstone Gdns. Edin 121 F2
Longstone Gr. Edin 122 A1
Longstone Pk. Edin 122 A1
Longstone Rd. Edin 122 A1
Longstone St. Edin 122 A1
Longstone Terr. Edin 121 F2
Longstone View. Edin 121 F2
Lonsdale Cres. Burn 33 F1

Lonsdale Terr. Edin 123 E3
Lookaboutye Brae. Clack 11 D2
Loom Rd. Kirk 17 D3
Lord President Rd. N Ber 54 A4
Loretto Ct. Muss 126 A2
Lorimar Pl. Sten 39 D1
Lorne Gdns. Laur 60 C2
Lorne Gr. Edin 155 D1
Lorne Pl. Edin 93 F2
Lorne St. Edin 93 F2
Lorne St. Lar 38 B1
Lorne Sq. Edin 93 F2
Lorne Sq. N Ber 54 B4
Lorne St. Edin 93 F2
Lorne St. Kirk 17 F4
Lornshill Cres. All 9 F4
Losshill. Men 4 A3
Lothian Bank. Edin 156 C1
Lothian Cres. B'ness 64 A3
Lothian Cres. Stir 2 B2
Lothian Ct. Inver 47 E1
Lothian Dr. May 183 E4
Lothian Rd. Dalk 157 D2
Lothian Rd. Edin 123 D4
Lothian St. B'ness 64 A3
Lothian St. Bath 145 D4
Lothian St. Bonn 182 B4
Lothian St. Burn 50 C4
Lothian St. Dalk 157 D2
Lothian St. Rose 181 E1
Lothian Terr. Kirk 17 D4
Lothianburn. Edin 154 B2
Lothianbridge. Newt 183 D2
Lothians View. Ros 47 D1
Louburn. Blac 142 B2
Loudens Wlk. Duni 36 B3
Loughborough Rd. Kirk 17 F4
Louisa Sq. Rose 181 E1
Louise St. Dunf 29 E1
Lovedale Ave. Bale 151 D1
Lovedale Cres. Bale 151 D1
Lovedale Gdns. Bale 151 E1
Lovedale Gr. Bale 151 D1
Lovedale Rd. Bale 151 E1
Lovells Glen. Lin 84 B4
Lovers La. Que 89 E4
Lovers Loan. Alva 5 D4
Lovers Loan. Dunf 28 C1
Lovers Wlk. Stir 2 A1
Low Brae. Torp 113 F3
Low Causewayside. Cul 42 B4
Low Causewayside. Torr 26 B1
Low Cswy. Cul 25 F1
Low Cswy. Torr 26 B1
Low Doors The. Kir 149 F1
Lower Alderston Rd. Hadd 100 C1
Lower Bathville. Arm 144 A3
Lower Bridge St. Bath 145 D3
Lower Bridge St. Stir 2 A1
Lower Broomieknowe.
  Bonn 182 A4
Lower Castlehill. Stir 2 A1
Lower Gilmore Pl. Edin 123 D3
Lower Glebe. Abe 49 E4
Lower Granton Rd. Edin 93 D3
Lower Joppa. Edin 125 E4
Lower London Rd. Edin 94 A1
Lower Wellheads. Lime 45 E2
Lowrie Ave. Peni 203 E3
Lowry Pl. Ros 46 C2
Ludgate. All 10 A3
Luffness Ct. Aber 71 E2
Luffness Mains Cotts. Aber 72 A2
Lugton Brae. Dalk 156 C2
Lumley Ct. Gran 61 E4
Lumley Pl. Gran 61 E4
Lumley St. Gran 61 E4
Lumphinnans Rd. Loch 14 A4
Lumsdaine Dr. D Bay 48 A1
Lumsden Ct. Rat 119 E1
Lundin Rd. Crossf 28 A2
Lussielaw Rd. Edin 123 F2
Lutton Pl. Edin 123 F3
Lyall Pl. Pol 61 F1
Lyars Rd. Long 98 C3
Lyarthall. Uph 117 E3
Lychgate La. Brox 117 E3
Lychgate Rd. Tull 4 A1
Lydgait Gdns. Hadd 101 D1
Lydgait. Hadd 101 D1
Lygon Rd. Edin 123 F1
Lyle Gn. Liv 147 D4
Lyne Gr. Crossf 28 B3
Lyne St. Edin 94 A1
Lyne Terr. Peni 204 A4
Lyneburn Cres. Hal 30 A3
Lynedoch Pl. Edin 123 D4
Lynedoch Place La. Edin 123 D4
Lyness Ct. Pol 61 F1
Lynn Lea Ave. Hadd 132 B4
Lyon Cres. B of A 2 A3
Lyon Ct. B'ness 63 E3

Mac Cormick Terr. Auch 203 F4
Macadam Place. Falk 59 E3
Macbeth Cres. Madd 82 C3
Macbeth Moir Rd. Muss 127 D4
Macbeth Rd. Dunf 29 E2
Macdonald Ave. Arm 143 F3
Macdonald Dr. Stir 7 D2

Macdonald Pl. Burn 34 A1
Macdonald Sq. Hal 30 A3
Macdowall Rd. Edin 123 F2
Macduff Cres. King 34 C1
Mace Ct. Bann 7 E2
Macfarlane Cres. Falk 60 A3
Macfarlane Pl. Uph 116 C2
Machrie Ct. Falk 59 E2
Macindoe Cres. Kirk 17 E4
Macintosh Rd. Liv 146 C1
Mackenzie Cres. Loch 14 B4
Mackenzie Pl. Edin 93 D1
Mackenzie Terr. Gran 61 E3
Mackie Pl. Dunf 29 F1
Maclachlan Ave. Den 36 B1
Maclardy Ct. Uph 116 C2
Maclaren Terr. Sten 39 D1
Maclean Cres. Alva 5 E4
Maclean St. Stir 7 E2
Maclean Terr. Blac 142 B2
Macmerry Ind Est. Glad 129 F3
Macmillan Rd. Muri 147 E1
Macnair Ave. N Ber 54 B3
Mactaggart Loan. Newt 183 D2
Maddiston Rd. Pol 82 C4
Madeira Pl. Edin 93 F3
Madeira St. Edin 93 F3
Madill Pl. Sten 38 C2
Maesterton Pl. Newt 183 D2
Mag's Bank. Giff 133 D1
Magdala Cres. Edin 122 C4
Magdala Mews. Edin 122 C4
Magdalene Ave. Edin 125 D3
Magdalene Ct. Edin 125 D3
Magdalene Dr. Edin 125 D3
Magdalene Gdns. Edin 125 D3
Magdalene Loan. Edin 125 D3
Magdalene Medway. Edin 125 D3
Magdalene Pl. Edin 125 D3
Maggie Wood's Loan. Falk 59 F3
Magnus Rd. B'ness 62 B3
Maidencraig Cres. Edin 92 B1
Maidencraig Gr. Edin 92 B1
Maidenpark Pl. B'ness 63 F3
Maidlands. Lin 85 E4
Main Rd. Glad 129 E2
Main Rd. Gran 62 A4
Main Rd. Lime 44 C4
Main St. Abe 49 E4
Main St. All 10 B4
Main St. Auch 204 A4
Main St. Avon 112 A3
Main St. B'ness 64 A4
Main St. Bale 151 E1
Main St. Bann 7 E1
Main St. Bla 26 A4
Main St. Blac 142 B2
Main St. Bon 58 A3
Main St. Brid 86 B4
Main St. Cali 81 F3
Main St. C 6 B3
Main St. Camb 9 D4
Main St. Clack 11 D2
Main St. Cow 13 D1
Main St. Cowie 20 B4
Main St. Cross 30 C3
Main St. Crossf 27 E1
Main St. Crossf 28 B1
Main St. Cul 25 F1
Main St. D Bay 48 B2
Main St. Dal 89 F4
Main St. Dech 116 B1
Main St. Dunf 29 E4
Main St. E Cal 148 C2
Main St. E Cal 148 C2
Main St. E. Men 4 A3
Main St. Edin 91 F2
Main St. Edin 93 E4
Main St. Elph 128 A1
Main St. Fau 193 E3
Main St. Fau 159 F3
Main St. Fau 170 B1
Main St. Fau 160 A1
Main St. Fau 193 E4
Main St. For 215 D1
Main St. Gift 163 F3
Main St. Gore 207 E4
Main St. Gull 52 A1
Main St. Hal 30 A3
Main St. Inver 68 B3
Main St. Kir 149 F1
Main St. Kirkl 89 D2
Main St. Lar 38 B1
Main St. Laur 61 D1
Main St. Lime 45 E2
Main St. Liv 146 B3
Main St. Liv 147 E1
Main St. Loch 13 F3
Main St. Loch 14 A4
Main St. Long 98 C3
Main St. N Sau 5 E1
Main St. New 88 A1
Main St. Newt 183 D3
Main St. Newt 206 B3

Main St. Oak 27 E4
Main St. Orm 159 F4
Main St. Path 184 B3
Main St. Path 185 D3
Main St. Pen 161 F2
Main St. Plea 20 B2
Main St. Pol 61 F1
Main St. Rat 119 E1
Main St. Rosl 181 D2
Main St. Shi 81 E3
Main St. Shot 192 A2
Main St. Slam 110 A4
Main St. Sten 39 D1
Main St. Stir 7 D2
Main St. Stir 2 B2
Main St. Ston 171 D1
Main St. Torr 26 B1
Main St. Tull 4 A1
Main St W. Cal 172 B2
Main St W. Men 3 F3
Main St. Whit 170 B4
Main St. Winch 87 F2
Mains Of Craigmillar. Edin 124 B4
Mains Rd. Beat 168 C3
Mains St. Lin 84 C3
Maitland Ave. Bann 7 E1
Maitland Ave. Muss 126 A3
Maitland Cres. Stir 7 D2
Maitland Hog La. Kirkl 89 D1
Maitland Park Rd. Muss 126 A3
Maitland Pl. Kirkl 89 D1
Maitland Rd. Ros 67 D4
Maitland St. Dunf 28 C2
Maitland St. Muss 126 A3
Majors Loan. Falk 60 A2
Majors Pl. Falk 60 A2
Malcolm Ct. Bath 144 C3
Malcolm Dr. Sten 38 C2
Malcolm St. Dunf 29 D3
Mall Ave. Muss 126 B3
Mallens Brae. Torp 114 A3
Mallery Millgate. Bale 177 E4
Malplaquet Ct. Car 230 A1
Malta Gn. Edin 93 D1
Malta Terr. Edin 93 D1
Maltings The. Aucht 15 D1
Maltings The. Lin 84 B3
Mamre Dr. Cali 81 F3
Man O' War Way. B'ness 64 A4
Mandela Ave. Falk 60 B4
Manderston St. Edin 93 F2
Mandora Ct. Car 230 A1
Manitoba Ave. Liv 147 F2
Mannan Dr. Clack 11 D2
Mannering Pl. Edin 155 D4
Mannfield Ave. Bon 57 F2
Manor Cres. Tull 4 A1
Manor Loan. B of A 3 D3
Manor Pl. Edin 123 D4
Manor Powis Cotts. B of A 3 D2
Manor Rd. Brid 116 C4
Manor Wynd. Madd 83 D3
Manse Ave. Arm 143 F3
Manse Ave. Whit 170 A3
Manse Cres. Stir 7 D2
Manse Ct. E Cal 148 A1
Manse Gr. Ston 171 E1
Manse La. Burn 33 F1
Manse La. Cocke 97 E2
Manse La. Muss 126 B3
Manse Pk. Uph 116 C3
Manse Pl. Bann 7 F1
Manse Pl. Bog 145 F3
Manse Pl. Falk 60 A2
Manse Pl. Inver 47 D1
Manse Pl. Slam 110 A4
Manse Rd. Cross 30 C3
Manse Rd. Dir 53 D3
Manse Rd. Edin 121 E3
Manse Rd. For 215 D1
Manse Rd. Inver 47 D1
Manse Rd. Kin 23 F2
Manse Rd. King 34 C2
Manse Rd. Kirkl 89 D1
Manse Rd. Lin 85 D3
Manse Rd. Newt 206 B3
Manse Rd. Rosl 180 C2
Manse Rd. Shot 192 A2
Manse Rd. Whit 170 A3
Manse St. Abe 49 E4
Manse St. Edin 121 E3
Manse View. Arm 143 F3
Manse View. E Lin 107 F1
Mansefield Ct. Bath 145 D4
Mansefield Ct. Liv 147 E2
Mansefield. E Cal 148 B2
Mansefield Gr. Bath 145 D4
Mansefield St. Bath 145 D4
Mansewood Cres. Whit 170 A3
Mansfield Ave. Muss 126 B3
Mansfield Ave. N Sau 5 E1
Mansfield Ave. Newt 183 D3
Mansfield Ct. Muss 126 B3
Mansfield Pl. Edin 93 E1
Mansfield Pl. Muss 126 B3
Mansfield Pl. Newt 183 D3

Mansfield Rd. Bale 177 E4
Mansfield Rd. Muss 126 B3
Mansfield Rd. Newt 183 D3
Mansionhouse Rd. Edin 123 E3
Mansionhouse Rd. Falk 59 E3
Manson Sq. Liv 146 B3
Manuel Terr. Madd 83 F3
Maple Ave. Sten 38 C2
Maple Ct. All 10 A3
Maple Gr. Liv 148 A3
Maple Pl. Duni 36 B2
Maple St. Kirk 17 D4
Mar Pl. All 10 A4
Mar Pl. N Sau 5 E1
Mar Pl. Stir 7 D4
Mar St. All 10 A3
Mar Terr. Clack 11 D2
Maranatha Cres. Pol 82 B4
March Gr. Edin 92 A3
March Pines. Edin 91 F1
March Rd. Edin 92 A1
Marchbank Dr. Bale 177 E4
Marchbank Gdns. Bale 177 E4
Marchbank Gr. Bale 177 E4
Marchbank Pl. Bale 177 E4
Marchbank Way. Bale 151 E1
Marchburn Dr. Peni 203 E3
Marches Dr. Arm 144 A3
Marches The. Arm 144 A3
Marchfield Gr. Edin 92 A2
Marchfield Park La. Edin 91 F2
Marchfield Pk. Edin 91 F2
Marchfield Terr. Edin 92 A2
Marchglen. Fish 5 F3
Marchhall Cres. Edin 124 A3
Marchhall Pl. Edin 124 A3
Marchhall Rd. Edin 124 A3
Marchlands Ave. B'ness 64 A4
Marchlands La. B'ness 64 A4
Marchmont Ave. Pol 61 F1
Marchmont Cres. Edin 123 E3
Marchmont Rd. Edin 123 E3
Marchmont St. Edin 123 E3
Marchside Ct. N Sau 5 E1
Marchwood Ave. Bath 145 E3
Marchwood Cres. Bath 145 E3
Mardale Cres. Edin 123 D2
Maree Ct. All 10 B3
Maree Pl. Crossf 28 A1
Maree Pl. Kirk 16 C4
Marefield Ct. B'ness 64 A4
Marette Wlk. Liv 148 A2
Margaret Ave. Bank 57 D2
Margaret Ave. Bog 145 F3
Margaret Ct. Bann 36 C1
Margaret Dr. Bon 58 A3
Margaret Pl. Bann 7 E1
Margaret Terr. Sten 38 C2
Maria St. Kirk 17 E3
Marina Rd. Bog 145 F3
Marine Dr. Edin 92 A3
Marine Espl. Edin 94 B3
Marine Par. N Ber 54 C4
Marine Rd. Dunb 78 B2
Marine Rd. Gull 52 A2
Mariner Terr. Gull 52 A2
Mariner Ave. Falk 59 D3
Mariner Gdns. Falk 59 E3
Mariner Rd. Falk 59 E3
Mariner St. Falk 59 D3
Mariners St. Kirk 17 D3
Mariners Wlk. D Bay 47 F2
Marion St. Kirk 17 D3
Marionville Ave. Edin 94 B1
Marionville Cres. Edin 94 B1
Marionville Dr. Edin 94 B1
Marionville Gr. Edin 94 B1
Marionville Pk. Edin 94 A1
Marionville Rd. Edin 94 A1
Marischal Dr. Edin 124 C2
Maritime La. Edin 94 A3
Maritime St. Edin 94 A3
Marjoribanks St. Bath 145 D3
Market Ct. Hadd 101 D1
Market La. Lin 85 D4
Market Pl. N Ber 54 B4
Market Pl. Whit 170 A4
Market St. B'ness 64 A3
Market St. Dunf 29 D2
Market St. E Cal 148 B2
Market St. Edin 123 E4
Market St. Hadd 132 A4
Market St. Muss 126 B3
Marketgate. Orm 159 F4
Markfield Rd. D Bay 48 B2
Markle Steading. E Lin 103 D4
Marlborough Dr. Stir 2 B2
Marlborough St. Edin 125 D4
Marly Gn. N Ber 54 A3
Marly Rise. N Ber 54 A3
Marmion Ave. Rosl 180 C2
Marmion Cres. Edin 124 A1
Marmion Cres. N Ber 54 A4
Marmion Rd. Bath 144 C4
Marmion Rd. Gran 61 E3
Marmion Rd. N Ber 54 A4
Marmion St. Falk 60 A4

Marquis Dr. Clack 11 D2
Marrifield Rd. Pump 117 D1
Marrfield Terr. Pump 117 D1
Marschal Ct. Bann 7 E2
Marshall Pl. Dunf 29 D2
Marshall Rd. Kirk 89 D1
Marshall St. Cocke 97 D2
Marshall St. Gran 13 E2
Marshall St. Edin 123 E4
Marshall St. Gran 8 E4
Marshall's Ct. Edin 93 F1
Marshill. All 10 A3
Martin Brae. Liv 147 E3
Martin Gr. Bonn 182 B4
Martin Pl. Dalk 156 C1
Mary Pl. Clack 7 D2
Mary Pl. Dunf 29 D1
Mary Sq. Laur 61 D2
Mary St. Laur 60 C2
Mary Stevenson Dr. All 10 A4
Mary's Pl. Edin 123 D4
Maryburn Rd. May 183 E4
Maryfield. Edin 93 F1
Maryfield. Edin 95 D1
Maryfield Pk. E Cal 148 B1
Maryfield Pl. Bonn 182 B4
Maryfield Pl. Edin 94 A1
Maryfield Pl. Falk 59 D2
Maryflats Pl. Gran 61 F4
Maryhall St. Kirk 17 E3
Marywell. Kirk 17 E3
Mason Pl. Bonn 181 F3
Masserene Rd. Kirk 16 C3
Masterton Rd. Dunf 47 D4
Mathar Terr. Laur 60 C2
Mathers Ave. Whit 169 F3
Matheson Pl. Dunf 29 F1
Matthew St. Kirk 17 D3
Maukeshill Ct. Liv 147 E1
Maulsford Ave. Dan 156 A4
Maurice Ave. Bann 7 E2
Maurice Pl. Edin 123 E1
Mauricewood Ave. Peni 203 F4
Mauricewood Bank. Peni 203 F4
Mauricewood Gr. Peni 203 F4
Mauricewood Pk. Peni 203 F4
Mauricewood Rd. Auch 203 F4
Mauricewood Rise. Peni 203 F4
Mavisbank Ave. Shi 81 E3
Mavisbank. Loan 181 E4
Mavisbank Pl. Bonn 181 F3
Maxton Cres. Alva 5 E4
Maxton Ct. Dalk 157 D2
Maxton Pl. Ros 46 C2
Maxwell Cres. Cow 13 D1
Maxwell Pl. Stir 7 D4
Maxwell Rd. Stir 53 D2
Maxwell Sq. Muri 173 E3
Maxwell St. Edin 123 D2
May Terr. N Ber 54 A4
Maybank Villas. Edin 121 E4
Mayburn Ave. Loan 155 D1
Mayburn Bank. Loan 181 D4
Mayburn Cres. Loan 155 D1
Mayburn Ct. Loan 181 D4
Mayburn Dr. Loan 155 D1
Mayburn Gr. Loan 181 D4
Mayburn Hill. Loan 181 D4
Mayburn Loan. Loan 155 D1
Mayburn Terr. Loan 155 D1
Mayburn Vale. Loan 181 D4
Mayburn Wlk. Loan 181 D4
Maybury Rd. Edin 121 D4
Mayfeld Ave. Muss 126 C3
Mayfield Cres. Clack 11 D3
Mayfield Cres. Loan 181 E4
Mayfield Ct. Arm 143 F2
Mayfield Ct. Loan 181 E4
Mayfield Ct. Stir 2 C2
Mayfield Dr. Arm 143 F3
Mayfield Dr. Bank 57 D2
Mayfield Gardens La. Edin 123 F2
Mayfield Gdns. Edin 123 F2
Mayfield Ind Est. Newt 183 E3
Mayfield News. Falk 59 F2
Mayfield Pk. Muss 126 A2
Mayfield Pl. May 183 E3
Mayfield Pl. Muss 126 A2
Mayfield Pl. Ros 46 B1
Mayfield Rd. Laur 61 E1
Mayfield Rd. May 183 D4
Mayfield St. Stir 7 D2
Mayfield Terr. Edin 123 F2
Mayfield Terr. Dunf 29 E4
Maygate. Dunf 29 D2
Mayne Ave. B of A 2 A3
Mayshade Rd. Loan 155 D1
Mayville Bank. Muss 127 D3
Mayville Gdns E. Edin 93 E3
Mayville Gdns. Edin 93 E3
Mayville Pk. Dunb 78 B2
Mc Call Gdns. E Lin 103 E4
Mc Kinnon Rd. Fau 193 F4
Mc Leod St. Brox 117 F3
McAdam Sq. Muri 173 E3
McAley Ct. B of A 1 C4
McAllister Ct. Bann 7 E1

McCallum Ct. Arm 143 F4
McCann Ave. Uph 117 D3
McCathie Dr. Newt 183 D3
McClelland Cres. Dunf 29 D1
McDiarmid Gr. Newt 183 D2
McDonald Pl. Edin 93 F2
McDonald Rd. Edin 93 F2
McDonald St. Edin 93 F2
McDouall Stuart Pl. Kirk 18 A4
McGregor Ave. Loch 14 A4
McGrigor Rd. Ros 46 B1
McGrigor Rd. Stir 7 D2
McIntosh Ct. Brox 117 E3
McKane Pl. Dunf 28 C1
McKay Dr. Dunf 29 F1
McKenzie St. Kirk 17 F4
McKinlay Cres. All 10 B4
McKinlay Terr. Loan 181 D4
McKinnon Dr. May 183 F3
McLachlan Ave. Stir 7 D1
McLachlan St. Lar 38 B1
McLaren Ave. Madd 84 A3
McLaren Ct. Lar 38 B1
McLaren Rd. Edin 124 A2
McLaren Terr. Stir 7 D2
McLauchlan Rise. Abe 49 D4
McLean Pl. Bonn 181 F3
McLean Pl. Gore 207 E4
McLean Wlk. Newt 183 D2
McLeod Cres. Pres 96 C1
McLeod St. Edin 122 C3
McNeil Cres. Arm 144 A3
McNeil Path. Tran 128 B3
McNeil Way. Tran 128 B3
McNeil Wlk. Tran 128 B3
McNeill Ave. Loan 181 D4
McNeill Pl. Loan 181 D4
McNeill St. Edin 123 D3
McNeill Terr. Loan 181 D4
McPhail Sq. Tran 128 B3
McPherson Dr. Stir 2 A1
McQuade St. Bonn 182 B4
McRae Cres. Burn 33 F1
McVean Pl. Bank 57 D2
Meadow Cres. Fau 193 F3
Meadow Ct. Burn 33 F1
Meadow Ct. Car 230 B1
Meadow Gr. Shot 171 D1
Meadow Gn. N Sau 5 D1
Meadow La. Edin 123 F3
Meadow Pk. Alva 5 D3
Meadow Pl. Dunf 29 F2
Meadow Pl. Edin 123 E3
Meadow Pl. Rosl 180 C3
Meadow Pl. Stir 2 B1
Meadow Pl. Stenh 171 D1
Meadow Place Rd. Edin 121 E3
Meadow Rd. Rat 151 F4
Meadow Rd. Ston 171 D1
Meadow St. Falk 60 B2
Meadowbank Ave. Edin 94 A1
Meadowbank Cres. Edin 94 A1
Meadowbank Cres. Orm 159 E4
Meadowbank. Edin 94 A1
Meadowbank. Liv 147 F3
Meadowbank. Pen 159 F4
Meadowbank Rd. Orm 159 F4
Meadowbank View. Kir 149 F2
Meadowend. Crossf 28 B1
Meadowfield Ave. Edin 124 C4
Meadowfield. Cow 13 E3
Meadowfield Ct. Edin 124 B4
Meadowfield. D Bay 48 A2
Meadowfield Dr. Edin 124 B4
Meadowfield Gdns. Edin 124 B3
Meadowfield Rd. Edin 120 C4
Meadowfield Terr. Edin 124 B3
Meadowforth Rd. Stir 7 E4
Meadowhead Ave. Add 171 F1
Meadowhead Cres. Add 171 F1
Meadowhead Gdns. Add 171 F1
Meadowhead Gr. Add 171 F1
Meadowhead Loan. Add 171 F1
Meadowhead Pl. Add 171 F1
Meadowhead Rd. Add 171 F1
Meadowhead Terr. Add 171 F1
Meadowhouse Rd. Edin 121 F3
Meadowland Rd. B of A 2 A3
Meadowpark. Hadd 132 A4
Meadowpark Rd. Bath 144 C3
Meadowside. Tran 128 C3
Meadowspot. Crossf 122 C1
Meadowview. Crossf 28 A1
Mearenside. Edin 121 D4
Medwyn Pl. All 9 F3
Meeks Rd. Falk 60 A3
Meeting House Dr. Tran 128 B3
Meggat Pl. Peni 204 A4
Meggetland Terr. Edin 122 C2
Meikle Rd. Liv 147 E1
Melbourne Pl. N Ber 54 B4
Melbourne Rd. Brox 117 F3
Melbourne Rd. N Ber 54 B4
Melbourne St. Liv 148 A3
Meldrum Cres. Burn 33 E1
Meldrum Ct. Dunf 29 F1
Meldrum Rd. Kirk 17 D3
Melford Ave. Shot 192 A2

Melfort Dr. Stir 7 D2
Melgund Pl. Loch 14 A4
Melgund Terr. Edin 93 E1
Mellerstain Rd. Kirk 16 B3
Mellock Gdns. Falk 59 F1
Mellor Ct. Ros 46 C2
Melrose Cres. Kirk 17 E3
Melrose Dr. Gran 61 F3
Melrose Pl. Falk 60 A2
Melville Cotts. Dalk 156 B2
Melville Cres. Edin 123 D4
Melville Dykes Rd. Dalk 156 B1
Melville Gate. Dalk 156 B2
Melville Gate Rd. Dalk 156 C2
Melville Pl. B of A 2 A4
Melville Pl. Kirk 16 B3
Melville Rd. Dalk 156 C1
Melville St. Edin 123 D4
Melville St. Loch 14 A4
Melville Street La. Edin 123 D4
Melville Terr. Dalk 156 C1
Melville Terr. Edin 123 F3
Melville Terr. Stir 7 D3
Melville View. Bonn 182 A4
Menstrie Pl. Men 4 A3
Menteith Ct. All 10 B3
Menteith Dr. Dunf 29 F1
Menteith Rd. Stir 2 A2
Mentone Ave. Edin 95 D1
Mentone Gdns. Edin 123 F2
Mentone Terr. Edin 123 F2
Menzies Cres. Kirk 16 C3
Menzies Dr. Stir 2 A1
Menzies Rd. Bath 145 D3
Mercat Pl. Clack 11 D2
Mercat The. Kirk 17 E2
Mercer Pl. Dunf 29 F2
Mercer St. Dunf 29 E2
Merchant St. Edin 123 E4
Merchiston Ave. Edin 123 D3
Merchiston Bank Ave. Edin 123 D2
Merchiston Bank Gdns.
 Edin 123 D2
Merchiston Gdns. Edin 122 C2
Merchiston Gr. Edin 122 C2
Merchiston Mews. Edin 123 D3
Merchiston Pk. Edin 123 D3
Merchiston Pl. Edin 123 D3
Merchiston Rd. Edin 60 A4
Merchiston Terr. Falk 60 A4
Meredith Dr. Sten 38 C2
Merker Terr. Lin 85 D4
Merkland Cres. D Bay 48 A2
Merkland Dr. Falk 60 C1
Merlin Way. D Bay 48 B3
Merryon Way. Peni 203 E4
Merrick Rd. Gran 61 F3
Merrick Way. Gran 61 F3
Merryfield Ave. Glad 129 E3
Mertoun Pl. Edin 122 C3
Merville Cres. Call 81 F3
Merville Terr. Call 81 F3
Methven Dr. Dunf 29 D3
Methven Pl. Dunf 29 D3
Methven Terr. Bonn 181 F3
Mouse La. Edin 123 E4
Mid Beveridgewell. Dunf 28 C3
Mid Brae. Dunf 28 C3
Mid Cswy. Cul 42 B4
Mid Liberton. Edin 124 A1
Mid New Cultins. Edin 121 D1
Mid Rd. King 34 C2
Mid St. Bath 145 D3
Mid St. Kirk 17 E3
Mid St. Liv 146 C3
Mid St. Loch 14 A4
Middle Street La. Gran 40 B1
Middlebank St. Ros 46 C3
Middleby St. Edin 123 F2
Middlefield. Edin 93 F2
Middlefield Rd. Falk 60 B3
Middlemass Ct. Falk 60 B3
Middlemuir Rd. Stir 7 F3
Middleshot Rd. Gull 52 B1
Middleshot Sq. Pres 97 D1
Middleton Ave. Uph 117 D2
Middleton. Men 4 A3
Middleton Rd. Uph 117 D2
Middlewood Pk. Liv 146 C3
Midhope Pl. Winch 88 A1
Midmar Ave. Edin 123 E1
Midmar Dr. Edin 123 E1
Midmar Gdns. Edin 122 C1
Midthorn Cres. Falk 60 C3
Midtown. Men 3 F3
Milburn Cres. Arm 143 E3
Milburn Cres. Arm 143 E4
Mill Farm Rd. Abe 49 D4
Mill Hill. Edin 6 B3
Mill La. Edin 93 F3

Mill Lade. Lin 84 C4
Mill Rd. All 10 A3
Mill Rd. Arm 143 F3
Mill Rd. Bath 145 D4
Mill Rd. Black 171 E4
Mill Rd. Cam 6 B3
Mill Rd. Clack 11 D3
Mill Rd. Duni 36 B2
Mill Rd. E Lin 104 B1
Mill Rd. East 168 C3
Mill Rd. Lin 84 B4
Mill Rd. Sten 39 D2
Mill Road Ind Est. Lin 84 B4
Mill Roundabout. Liv 147 D2
Mill St. All 10 A3
Mill St. Dunf 28 C2
Mill St. Kirk 17 D1
Mill Wynd. Hadd 132 A4
Mill Wynd. E Lin 103 F4
Mill Wynd. Pres 96 C1
Millar Cres. Edin 123 D2
Millar Pl. Bon 58 A2
Millar Pl. Edin 123 D2
Millar Pl. Sten 39 D3
Millar Pl. Stir 2 B1
Millar Rd. Tran 128 B3
Millars Wynd. N Sau 5 E1
Millbank. Uph 116 C2
Millbank Sq. Whit 170 A4
Millbank Terr. Madd 82 C4
Millbrae. Liv 148 B3
Millbrook Pl. Men 3 F3
Millburn Rd. Bath 144 C3
Millburn Rd. West 112 C3
Millburn St. Falk 60 B3
Milldean Gr. Dunf 29 E3
Miller Ave. Crossf 28 A1
Miller Cres. Muir 64 B3
Miller Pk. Pol 61 F1
Miller Pl. Air 22 C2
Miller Row. Edin 123 D4
Miller Rd. Dunf 28 C3
Millerfield. Liv 148 A4
Millerfield Pl. Edin 123 E3
Millerhill Gdns. Edin 125 D1
Millerhill Rd. Dan 156 B4
Millfield Dr. Pol 61 F1
Millfield. Hadd 132 A4
Millfield. Liv 147 D1
Millflats St. Falk 39 D1
Millgate. Winch 87 F1
Millhall Rd. Stir 7 E3
Millhaugh La. Bath 145 D4
Millhill La. Muss 126 B3
Millhill. Muss 126 B3
Millington St. Dunf 29 D1
Millside. Stir 7 E3
Millway. Pen 161 D3
Milne-acre. Edin 93 E2
Milne Cres. Cow 13 E2
Milne Rd. Ros 46 C1
Milnepark Rd. Bann 7 D1
Milton Cl. Duni 36 B2
Milton Cres. Bann 7 E1
Milton Cres. Edin 125 D4
Milton Dr. Edin 125 E3
Milton Gdns. Bann 7 D1
Milton Gdns N. Edin 125 D3
Milton Gdns S. Edin 125 D3
Milton Glen. Edin 125 E3
Milton Gr. Edin 125 F4
Milton Link. Edin 125 E3
Milton Pl. Duni 36 B2
Milton Pl. Bann 7 E1
Milton Rd E. Edin 125 E4
Milton Rd. Bann 7 D1
Milton Rd. Bon 125 D3
Milton Rd W. Edin 124 C3
Milton Row. Duni 36 C2
Milton St. Edin 94 A1
Milton Terr. Bann 7 D1
Milton Terr. Edin 125 F4
Minard Rd. Shot 191 E3
Mine Rd. B of A 2 A4
Miner's Terr. Muss 127 D3
Mingle Pl. B'ness 64 A4
Minorca Ct. Rosl 181 D2
Minthill Pl. East 168 B3
Minto Ct. Alva 5 D3
Minto Gdns. Alva 5 D3
Minto Pl. Edin 123 F2
Minto St. Loch 14 A4
Mission La. Falk 60 A2
Mitchell Cres. All 9 F4
Mitchell Cres. Cow 13 D1
Mitchell St. Falk 59 F1
Mitchell Pl. Kirk 17 E3
Mitchell Rd. Ros 46 B1
Mitchell St. Dalk 156 C2

Mitchell St. Edin 94 A3
Mitchell St. Kirk 17 E2
Mitchell Wlk. Ros 46 C2
Mitchellhall Brae. Giff 132 C3
Moat Dr. Edin 122 B2
Moat Pl. Edin 122 B2
Moat St. Edin 122 B2
Moat Terr. Edin 122 B2
Moat View. Rosl 180 C2
Mochrum Dr. Crossf 45 D4
Modan Rd. Stir 7 D2
Moffat Ave. Bonn 182 A3
Moffat Ave. Sten 39 E2
Moffat Cres. Loch 14 A4
Moffat Rd. Orm 159 E3
Moidart Rd. Whit 170 B4
Moir Ave. Muss 127 D3
Moir Cres. Muss 127 D3
Moir Ct. Kel 12 C4
Moir Dr. Muss 127 D3
Moir Pl. Muss 127 D3
Moir St. All 10 A4
Moir Terr. Muss 127 D3
Moira Pk. Edin 94 C1
Moira Terr. Edin 94 C1
Mollison Ave. East 168 C3
Monar Ct. D Bay 48 A2
Monastery St. Dunf 29 D2
Moncks Rd. Falk 60 B2
Moncreiff Terr. Edin 123 F3
Moncrieff Way. Liv 147 E4
Moncur St. Dunf 29 E4
Monkbarns Gdns. Edin 155 D4
Monkland Rd. Bath 144 C3
Monkmains Rd. Hadd 132 B4
Monkrigg Pl. Hadd 132 B4
Monksrig Rd. Peni 203 E3
Monkswood Rd. Newt 183 D2
Monktonhall Pl. Muss 126 A2
Monktonhall Terr. Muss 126 A2
Monkwood Ct. Edin 123 E2
Monmouth Terr. Edin 93 D2
Montagu Terr. Edin 93 D2
Montague St. Edin 123 F3
Monteith Wlk. Shot 191 F3
Montfort Pl. Falk 60 A2
Montgomery St. Edin 93 F1
Montgomery St. Falk 60 C3
Montgomery St. Gran 61 E3
Montgomery St. Kirk 17 D3
Montgomery Street La. Edin 93 F1
Montgomery Way. Stir 2 A2
Montpelier. Edin 123 D3
Montpelier Pk. Edin 123 D3
Montpelier Terr. Edin 123 D3
Montrose Rd. Pol 62 A1
Montrose Rd. Stir 2 B2
Montrose Terr. Edin 93 F1
Moodie St. Dunf 29 D2
Moor Pl. Rath 185 E2
Moor Rd. Path 210 B3
Moor Rd. Pen 186 A3
Moreland Gdns. Add 171 E1
Moorelands. Add 171 E1
Moorfield Cotts. Dan 156 B4
Moorfoot Ct. Bonn 182 A4
Moorfoot Pl. Bonn 182 A3
Moorfoot Pl. Peni 203 F3
Moorfoot View. Bonn 182 A3
Moorfoot View. Rosl 180 C3
Moorside St. Car 230 A1
Morar Ct. Gran 61 E3
Morar Ct. Stir 2 A2
Morar Pl. Gran 61 E3
Morar Rd. Crossf 28 A1
Morar Way. Shot 192 A2
Morar St. Auch 15 D1
Moray Ct. D Bay 48 A2
Moray Ct. D Bay 84 C3
Moray Dr. Lin 84 C3
Moray Pk. D Bay 48 A2
Moray Pl. Edin 93 D1
Moray Pl. Gran 61 F4
Moray Pl. Lin 84 C3
Moray Way N. D Bay 48 B2
Moray Way S. D Bay 48 A1
Morayvale. Abe 49 E4
Moredun Dykes Rd. Edin 155 E3
Moredun Park Ct. Edin 155 E4
Moredun Park Dr. Edin 155 E4
Moredun Park Gdns. Edin 155 E4
Moredun Park Gr. Edin 155 E4
Moredun Park Loan. Edin 155 E4
Moredun Park Rd. Edin 155 E4
Moredun Park St. Edin 155 E4
Moredun Park View. Edin 155 E4
Moredun Park Way. Edin 155 E4
Moredun Park Wlk. Edin 155 E4
Moredunvale Bank. Edin 155 E4
Moredunvale Gn. Edin 155 E4
Moredunvale Gr. Edin 155 E4
Moredunvale Loan. Edin 155 E4
Moredunvale Pk. Edin 155 E4
Moredunvale Pl. Edin 155 E4
Moredunvale Rd. Edin 155 E4
Moredunvale View. Edin 155 E4
Moredunvale Way. Edin 155 E4
Morgan Ct. Stir 7 E2

Morison Gdns. Que 68 A1
Morison Ct. Gran 61 F2
Morley Cres. Stir 7 D2
Morlich Cres. D Bay 48 A1
Morlich Ct. D Bay 48 A1
Morlich Gr. D Bay 48 A1
Morlich Pk. D Bay 48 A1
Morlich Pl. D Bay 48 A1
Morlich Rd. D Bay 48 A1
Mornay Way. Shot 191 E3
Morningside Ct. Edin 123 D1
Morningside Dr. Edin 123 D1
Morningside Gdns. Edin . 123 C1
Morningside Gr. Edin 122 C1
Morningside Pk. Edin 123 D2
Morningside Pl. Edin 123 D2
Morningside Rd. Edin 123 D2
Morningside Terr. Edin ... 123 D2
Morris Ct. Inver 47 E1
Morris Rd. Newt 183 E3
Morris Terr. Stir 7 D4
Morrison Ave. Bon 57 F3
Morrison Ave. Tran 128 C3
Morrison Dr. Bann 7 E1
Morrison Dr. Dunf 46 C4
Morrison St. Edin 123 D4
Morrison Street La. Edin . 123 D4
Morrison Way. Liv 147 E4
Mortimer Ct. D Bay 48 A1
Morton St. Edin 125 E4
Mortonhall Gate. Edin ... 154 C3
Mortonhall Park Ave. Edin 155 D3
Mortonhall Park Bank. Edin 155 D3
Mortonhall Park Cres. Edin 155 D3
Mortonhall Park Dr. Edin 155 D3
Mortonhall Park Gdns. Edin 155 D3
Mortonhall Park Terr. Edin 155 D3
Mortonhall Park Pl. Edin . 155 D3
Mortonhall Park Terr. Edin 155 D3
Mortonhall Park Way. Edin 154 C3
Mortonhall Rd. Edin 123 E2
Morven Ct. Falk 60 B1
Morven Dr. Pol 61 E1
Morven Gr. Kirk 16 C4
Morven Pl. D Bay 48 A2
Morven St. Edin 91 E1
Moss Interchange. Liv 147 E3
Moss Rd. Fall 8 B2
Moss Rd. Liv 147 E4
Moss Way. D Bay 48 A3
Moss-side Rd. Cow 13 D2
Mossband La. Shot 191 F3
Mossbank. Cow 13 D1
Mossbank. Liv 147 F3
Mossbank. Ros 46 C3
Mossburn Ave. East 168 B3
Mosscastle Rd. Slam 110 A4
Mossend Terr. Cow 13 D1
Mossgiel Ave. Cowie 20 B4
Mossgiel Ave. Stir 2 A1
Mossgiel Cotts. Liv 146 B4
Mossgiel St. Falk 59 D2
Mossgiel Terr. Laur 61 D2
Mosshat Rd. Auc 216 C2
Mosside Dr. Black 145 E1
Mosside Rd. Black 145 E1
Mosside Terr. Black 145 E1
Moston Terr. Edin 123 F2
Motion St. Loch 14 A4
Moubray Gr. Que 89 E4
Moubray Rd. D Bay 48 B3
Moulin Way. Dunf 29 F3
Mound Pl. Edin 123 E4
Mound The. Edin 123 E4
Mount Grange. Edin 123 E2
Mount Hooly Cres. Inver . 68 B3
Mount Hope. B of A 2 B2
Mount Lodge Pl. Edin 125 D4
Mount Oliphant. Cowie .. 20 B4
Mount Pleasant. Arm 143 F3
Mount Vernon Rd. Edin . 155 D4
Mount William. N Sau 5 F1
Mountbatten Pl. Ros 46 C2
Mountbatten St. Gran 61 E3
Mountcastle Bank. Edin . 124 C4
Mountcastle Cres. Edin . 124 C4
Mountcastle Dr N. Edin . 124 C4
Mountcastle Dr S. Edin . 124 C3
Mountcastle Gdns. Edin . 124 C4
Mountcastle Gn. Edin 94 C1
Mountcastle Gr. Edin 124 C4
Mountcastle Loan. Edin . 124 C4
Mountcastle Pk. Edin 94 C1
Mountcastle Pl. Edin 94 C1
Mountcastle Terr. Edin .. 124 C4
Mountfair Pl. Glad 129 E3
Mounthooly Loan. Edin . 154 B3
Mountjoy Terr. Muss 126 A4
Mowbray Ct. Bann 7 E2
Mowbray Gdns. Cross 30 C3
Mowbray Rise. Muri 147 F1
Moy Ct. Gran 61 E3
Muckle Hill Pk. Inver 47 D1
Mucklets Ave. Muss 126 A2
Mucklets Cres. Muss 126 A2
Mucklets Ct. Muss 126 A2
Mucklets Dr. Muss 126 A2
Mucklets Pl. Muss 126 A2

Mucklets Rd. Muss 125 F2
Mudale Ct. Falk 60 B1
Muir Ct. Cross 30 C3
Muir Rd. Bath 144 C4
Muir Rd. Dunf 29 E2
Muir Rd. Liv 148 A4
Muir St. Lar 38 B1
Muir Wood Cres. Curr 152 A3
Muir Wood Dr. Curr 152 A3
Muir Wood Gr. Curr 152 A3
Muir Wood Pl. Curr 152 A3
Muir Wood Rd. Curr 152 A3
Muiralehouse Rd. Bann .. 19 F4
Muirdyke Ave. Sten 39 E2
Muiredge And Jersy Rd.
    Shot 191 D4
Muirend Ave. Edin 152 C4
Muirend Ct. B'ness 64 A3
Muirend Rd. Stir 7 D3
Muirepark Ct. B'ness 64 A3
Muirfield Cres. Gull 52 A1
Muirfield Dr. Gull 52 A1
Muirfield Dr. Uph 116 C2
Muirfield Gdns. Loan 181 E1
Muirfield Pk. Gull 52 A2
Muirfield Rd. Lar 38 C1
Muirfield Steading. Gull . 52 B2
Muirfield Terr. Gull 52 A1
Muirhall Way. Liv 146 C3
Muirhall Pl. Lar 38 B2
Muirhall Rd. Lar 38 B2
Muirhead Pl. Auch 203 F4
Muirhead Pl. East 168 B2
Muirhead Rd. Sten 38 C2
Muirhouse Ave. Edin 92 A4
Muirhouse Bank. Edin 92 A3
Muirhouse Cres. Edin 92 A3
Muirhouse Dr. Edin 92 A4
Muirhouse Gdns. Edin 92 A3
Muirhouse Gn. Edin 92 A3
Muirhouse Gr. Edin 92 A3
Muirhouse Loan. Edin 92 A3
Muirhouse Medway. Edin 92 A3
Muirhouse Parkway. Edin 92 A3
Muirhouse Pk. Edin 92 A2
Muirhouse Pl E. Edin 92 A2
Muirhouse Pl W. Edin 92 A2
Muirhouse Terr. Edin 92 A2
Muirhouse View. Edin 92 A3
Muirhouse Way. Edin 92 A3
Muirkirk Dr. Falk 59 D3
Muirlee Rd. Car 215 D1
Muirlea Rd. Car 215 D1
Muirpark Ct. Tran 128 C3
Muirpark. Dalk 156 C1
Muirpark Dr. Shi 81 E3
Muirpark Gr. Tran 128 C3
Muirpark Gdns. Men 4 C2
Muirpark Gdns. Tran 128 C3
Muirpark Pl. Tran 128 C3
Muirpark Rd. Tran 128 C3
Muirpark Terr. Tran 128 C3
Muirpark Wynd. Tran 128 C3
Muirside Gr. Tran 128 C3
Muirside Gr. Crossf 27 E1
Muirside La. Lime 44 B4
Muirside Rd. Tull 4 A1
Muirton Rd. Fal 7 F3
Muirton Way. D Bay 48 A3
Mulberry Dr. Dunf 29 F1
Mulberry Pl. Edin 93 E3
Mulberry Terr. Shot 192 A1
Mull Ct. All 10 A3
Mull Ct. Gran 61 E3
Mungalend. Falk 60 A4
Mungale St W Cal 172 B2
Mungle St. Falk 60 A4
Munro Dr. Edin 153 D3
Munro Gdns. Laur 60 C2
Munro Pl. All 9 F3
Munro Rd. Fal 17 D1
Munro Rd. Stir 38 C2
Munro Way. Liv 147 E4
Murano Pl. Edin 93 F1
Murderdean Rd. Newt ... 183 D3
Murdoch Terr. Edin 123 D3
Murdock Rd. Liv 146 C2
Mudostoun Cres. East ... 168 C3
Murieston Cres. Edin 122 C3
Murieston Cres La. Edin . 122 C3
Murieston Ct. Muri 174 A3
Murieston Dr. Muri 174 A3
Murieston E. Muri 174 A4
Murieston Gdns. Muri ... 174 A4
Murieston Gn. Muri 173 F3
Murieston La. Edin 122 C3
Murieston Pk. Muri 173 F3
Murieston Pl. Edin 122 C3
Murieston Rd. Edin 122 C3
Murieston Rd. Muri 174 A3
Murieston Terr. Edin 122 C3
Murieston Valw. Muri 174 A3
Murieston Valley. Muri ... 173 F3
Murieston W. Muri 173 F4
Murieston Way. Muri 174 A4

Murieston Wlk. Muri 173 F2
Murieston Wood. Muri ... 173 F3
Murnin Ct. Stir 7 E2
Murnin Rd. Bon 58 A2
Murray Cotts. Edin 121 E3
Murray Cres. Madd 83 D3
Murray Pl. Cam 6 B3
Murray Pl. Stir 7 D4
Murray Rd. Ros 46 B1
Murray Wlk. Dunf 29 F2
Murrayburn App. Edin ... 121 E1
Murrayburn Dr. Edin 121 E1
Murrayburn Gate. Edin . 152 B4
Murrayburn Gdns. Edin . 121 F1
Murrayburn Gn. Edin 121 F1
Murrayburn Gr. Edin 121 F1
Murrayburn Pl. Edin 121 F1
Murrayburn Rd. Edin 121 E1
Murrayfield Ave. Edin ... 122 B4
Murrayfield Dr. Black 171 E4
Murrayfield Dr. Edin 122 B4
Murrayfield Gdns. Edin . 122 B4
Murrayfield Pl. Bann 7 E1
Murrayfield Pl. Edin 122 B4
Murrayfield Rd. Edin 122 B4
Murrayfield Terr. Bann 7 E1
Murrayfield Terr. Black .. 171 E4
Murrays Brae The. Edin . 155 E2
Murrays Brae The. Edin . 155 E2
Murrays The. Edin 155 E2
Murraysgate Cres. Whit . 169 F3
Murraysgate Ind Est. Whit 169 F3
Murrayshall Rd. Stir 7 D2
Murrel Rd. Aber 49 E4
Murrel Terr. Abe 49 E4
Music Hall La. Dunf 29 D2
Musselburgh Rd. Dalk ... 157 D2
Musselburgh Rd. Edin ... 125 F4
Myers Ct. Dunf 29 D2
Myine Pl. Sten 39 D1
Mylnebum Gdns. Lime ... 45 E2
Myothill Rd. Bank 57 E4
Myre Cres. King 35 D2
Myre Dale. Bonn 182 B3
Myreside Ct. Edin 122 C1
Myreside Rd. Edin 122 C2
Myreton Dr. Bann 19 F4
Myreton. Men 4 A3
Myreton Rd. Gran 61 E3
Myreton Way. Falk 59 F2
Myretoungate. Alva 4 C2
Myrtle Cres. Kirk 17 D4
Myrtle Cres. Rosl 180 C3
Myrtle Gr. May 183 E4
Myrtle Terr. Edin 122 C3

Nailer Rd. Falk 59 F3
Nailer Rd. Stir 7 D3
Nairn Ct. Falk 60 B1
Nairn Rd. Liv 146 C4
Nairn St. Kirk 17 F3
Naismith Ct. Gran 40 C1
Namayo Ave. Laur 61 D3
Namur Rd. Auch 204 A4
Nantwich Dr. Edin 94 C2
Napier Ave. Bath 145 E3
Napier Cres. Falk 60 A4
Napier Pl. Falk 60 A4
Napier Rd. Edin 123 D2
Napier Rd. Ros 46 B1
Napier Sq. Liv 148 A4
Napier St. Kirk 17 F4
Nasmyth Ct. Liv 148 A3
Nasmyth Rd. Ros 46 A1
Nasmyth Sq. Liv 148 A3
Natal Pl. Cow 13 E2
Navar Ct. Shot 192 A2
Nebit The. Alva 4 C3
Neidpath Ct. Edin 121 D4
Neidpath Ct. Leng 98 C3
Neidpath Dr. Sten 38 C2
Neidpath Pl. Dunf 29 E3
Neilson Gr. Burn 33 F1
Neilson Park Rd. Hadd ... 132 A4
Neilson Sq. Liv 146 B3
Neilson St. Falk 60 A4
Nellburn. Liv 146 C3
Nellfield. Edin 155 D4
Nelson Ave. Liv 147 E2
Nelson Gdns. Gran 40 C1
Nelson Pl. Stir 7 E3
Nelson St. Edin 93 E1
Nelson St. Gran 61 F4
Nelson St. Kirk 17 D3
Nelson St. Ros 46 C3
Ness The. Torr 26 C1
Nether Craigour. Edin ... 124 B1
Nether Currie Cres. Curr 152 A3
Nether Currie Pl. Curr ... 152 A3
Nether Currie Rd. Curr .. 152 A3
Nether Dechmont Cotts.
    Liv 147 D4
Nether St. Kirk 18 A4
Netherbank. Edin 154 C3
Netherbeath Rd. Cross ... 30 C4

Netherby Rd. Air 22 B2
Netherby Rd. Edin 93 D3
Netherfield Rd. Pol 61 E1
Nethergate. King 35 D1
Nethergate Tha. Alva 4 C3
Netherlaw. N Ber 54 A3
Nethermost Rd. Den 36 B1
Nethershot Rd. Pres 97 D1
Nethergr. Whit 170 A2
Netherton Pl. Whit 170 A2
Netherton St. East 168 B3
Nethertown Broad St. Dunf 29 D1
Netherwood Pk. Liv 147 D4
Nethfield Dr. Pump 116 C1
Nettlehill Dr. Liv 147 F4
Nethill Rd. Liv 147 F4
Nettlehill Rd. Pump 117 D1
Neucks The. Slam 111 D3
Nevis Cres. All 10 A4
Nevis Gdns. Peni 204 A4
Nevis Pl. Falk 60 B1
Nevis Pl. Gran 61 F3
Nevis Pl. Shot 192 A2
New Arthur Pl. Edin 123 F4
New Broompark. Edin 92 C4
New Broughton. Edin 93 E1
New Halfglen Rd. Falk 60 B1
New Halls Rd. Que 68 B1
New Holygate. Brox 117 E3
New Houses. Ath 74 B2
New Hunterfield. Gore ... 183 D1
New John's Pl. Edin 123 F3
New La. Edin 93 E3
New Line Rd. Bann 19 D4
New Liston Rd. Kirkl 89 D1
New Market Rd. Edin 122 B2
New Murt Rd. Edin 122 C1
New Meadowspott. Dalk . 157 D1
New Orchardfield. Edin ... 93 F2
New Row. Ath 74 A4
New Row. Dunf 29 D2
New Row. Kin 24 A4
New Row. Tran 128 B3
New Skinners Cl. Edin ... 123 F4
New St. B of A 1 C4
New St. Cocke 97 E2
New St. Edin 123 F4
New St. Muss 126 A3
New St. Pres 96 C1
New St. Slam 110 A4
New St. Tran 128 B4
New Swanston. Edin 153 F3
New Tower Pl. Edin 95 D1
New Well Wynd. Lin 84 C3
Newbattle Abbey Cres.
    Dalk 182 C4
Newbattle Terr. Edin 123 D2
Newbiggin Cres. Tull 4 B1
Newbiggin Rd. Gran 61 F3
Newbiggin. Auch 15 E1
Newbiggin. Muss 126 B3
Newbiggin Terr. Auch 15 E1
Newbyres Ave. Gore 183 E1
Newbyres Cres. Gore ... 207 E4
Newcraighall Dr. Edin ... 125 E2
Newcraighall Rd. Edin .. 125 E2
Newcraighall Rd. Edin .. 125 E2
Newhailes Ave. Muss 126 A3
Newhailes Cres. Muss ... 126 A3
Newhailes Rd. Muss 125 F3
Newhaven Pl. Edin 93 E4
Newhaven Rd. Edin 93 E3
Newhouse Ave. Dunb 78 C1
Newhouse Dr. Falk 59 F1
Newhouse Pl. Dunb 78 C1
Newhouse Rd. Gran 61 E4
Newhouse. Stir 7 D2
Newhouses Rd. Brox 118 A2
Newington Rd. Edin 123 F3
Newland Ave. Bath 145 D3
Newlands Pk. Dunf 29 D3
Newlands Pk. Edin 123 F2
Newlands Pl. Tull 4 B2
Newlands Rd. Bann 19 E4
Newlands Rd. Gran 61 D3
Newlands Rd. Pol 62 B4
Newliston Dr. Kirk 16 B4
Newmains Farm La. Kirkl . 89 D1
Newmains Rd. Kirkl 89 D1
Newmarket. Bann 7 F1
Newmarket St. Falk 60 A3
Newmill And Canthill Rd.
    Shot 191 D3
Newmill-Canthill Rd. Shot 191 D3
Newmills Ave. Curr 151 E2
Newmills Cres. Curr 151 E2
Newmills Gr. Curr 151 E2
Newmills Rd. Bale 151 D2
Newmills Rd. Dalk 157 D2
Newmills Rd. Rat 151 D2
Newmills Terr. Dalk 157 D2
Newmills. Tull 4 A2
Newpark Roundabout.

Muri 173 E4
Newtoft St. Edin 155 F3
Newton Ave. Gran 40 A2
Newton Church Rd. Dan . 156 B4
Newton Cres. Ros 47 D2
Newton Pl. Ros 46 C2
Newton Port. Hadd 101 D1
Newton Rd. Gran 40 A1
Newton St. Edin 122 C3
Newton St. May 183 E4
Newtonshaw. N Sau 5 E1
Newtown. B' ness 63 F3
Newtown St. B' ness 63 F3
Newyearfield Roundabout.

Muri 147 E4
Nicholson Way. Liv 147 E4
Nicklaus Gn. Liv 147 E4
Nicol St. Kirk 17 D2
Nicolson Sq. Edin 123 F4
Nicolson St. Edin 123 F4
Nicolton Ave. Madd 82 C4
Nicolton Rd. Pol 82 B1
Niddrie Farm Gr. Edin .. 124 C2
Niddrie House Ave. Edin 124 C2
Niddrie House Dr. Edin . 125 D2
Niddrie House Gdns. Edin 124 C2
Niddrie House Gr. Edin . 125 D2
Niddrie House Sq. Edin . 124 C2
Niddrie Mains Ct. Edin . 125 D2
Niddrie Mains Dr. Edin . 124 C2
Niddrie Mains Rd. Edin 124 C2
Niddrie Mains Terr. Edin 124 C2
Niddrie Marischal Cres.

Edin 124 C2
Niddrie Marischal Dr. Edin 124 C2
Niddrie Marischal Gdns.

Edin 124 C2
Niddrie Marischal Gn. Edin 124 C2
Niddrie Marischal Gr. Edin 125 D2
Niddrie Marischal Loan.

Edin 124 C2
Niddrie Marischal Pl. Edin 124 C2
Niddrie Marischal Rd. Edin 125 D2
Niddrie Marischal St. Edin 125 D2
Niddrie Mill Ave. Edin .. 125 D2
Niddrie Mill Cres. Edin . 125 D2
Niddrie Mill Dr. Edin 125 D2
Niddrie Mill Gr. Edin 125 D2
Niddrie Mill Pl. Edin 125 D2
Niddrie Mill Terr. Edin .. 125 D2
Niddry Rd. Winch 87 F1
Niddry St. Edin 123 E4
Niddry Street S. Edin 123 F4
Niddry View. Winch 87 F1
Nidrie Cotts. Edin 125 E2
Nielson Ct. Black 171 D4
Nigel Loan. Edin 155 D4
Nigel Rise. Muri 147 F1
Nile Gr. Edin 123 D2
Nile St. Kirk 17 D3
Nimmo Ave. Pres 97 D1
Ninian Rd. B'ness 62 C3
Ninth St. Newt 183 D3
Nisbet Dr. Den 36 B1
Nisbet Rd. Gull 51 F1
Nith St. Dunf 29 F1
Nithsdale St. Shot 191 E3
Niven Rd. Inver 47 E2
Niven's Knowe Rd. Loan 180 C4
Nivensknowe Pk. Loan .. 180 C4
No 7 Pit Rd. Cow 13 E2
Nobel Pl. Rosl 180 C2
Nobel View. Shi 82 A4
Noble Pl. Edin 94 A2
Norman Rise. Muri 147 F1
Normand Brae. Kirk 18 A4
Normand Rd. Kirk 18 A4
North App Rd. Kin 23 F2
North Ave. Madd 83 D4
North Bank Rd. Pres 127 F4
North Bank St. Edin 123 E4
North Bridge. Edin 123 E4
North Bridge St. Bath ... 145 D3
North Bridge St. Gran 40 B1
North Bughtlin Bank. Edin 91 D1
North Bughtlin Brae. Edin 91 D1
North Bughtlin Gate. Edin 91 D1
North Bughtlin Neuk. Edin 91 D1
North Bughtlin Pl. Edin .. 91 D1
North Bughtlin Rd. Edin . 91 D1
North Bughtlin Rig. Edin . 91 D1
North Bughtlinside. Edin . 91 D1
North Cairntow. Edin 124 B3
North Castle St. All 10 A3
North Charlotte St. Edin . 93 D1
North Clyde Street La. Edin 93 E1
North Cres. Dunf 46 C4
North Cres. Pres 97 D1
North East Circus Pl. Edin 93 D1
North East Cumberland Street La.

Edin 93 E1
North East Thistle Street La.

Edin 93 E1
North-East Rd. Ros 46 B1
North Fort St. Edin 93 F3
North Gate. Torr 113 F3
North Grange Ave. Pres .. 96 C1

251

North Grange Gr. Pres — Parkhead Terr. Edin

North Grange Gr. Pres 96 C1
North Grange Rd. Pres 96 C1
North Greendykes Rd. Brox 117 F4
North Greens. Edin 125 D3
North Gyle Ave. Edin 121 D3
North Gyle Dr. Edin 121 D4
North Gyle Farm Ct. Edin 121 D3
North Gyle Farm La. Edin 121 D3
North Gyle Gr. Edin 121 D3
North Gyle Loan. Edin 121 D4
North Gyle Pk. Edin 121 D4
North Gyle Rd. Edin 121 D4
North Gyle Terr. Edin 121 D3
North High St. Muss 126 A3
North Hillhousefield. Edin 93 F3
North Junction St. Edin 93 F3
North Leith Sands. Edin 93 F3
North Loanhead. Lime 45 F2
North Lorimer Pl. Cocke 97 D2
North Main St. Sten 39 E2
North Meggetland. Edin 122 C2
North Overgate. King 34 C2
North Park Terr. Edin 93 D1
North Peffer Pl. Edin 124 B2
North Rd. Dunb 78 B2
North Rd. Fau 193 F4
North Rd. Inver 47 E2
North Reeves Pl. Whit 170 A3
North Richmond St. Edin 123 F4
North Roundall. Lime 45 F2
North Row. Lime 45 D2
North Seton Pk. Cocke 97 E2
North Shore Rd. Gran 40 C1
North St. All 10 A4
North St Andrew La. Edin 93 E1
North St Andrew St. Edin 93 E1
North St. Arm 143 F3
North St. B' ness 63 F4
North St. Clack 11 D2
North St David St. Edin 93 E1
North St. Dunb 78 A1
North St. Falk 60 A4
North St. Loch 14 A4
North St. Rat 119 E1
North St. Stir 2 B1
North View. Burn 50 C4
North View. W Cal 172 B2
North Way. D Bay 48 B3
North Werber Pk. Edin 92 C2
North West Circus Pl. Edin 93 D1
North West Cumberland Street La. Edin 93 E1
North West Thistle Street La. Edin 93 E1
North Wood Rd. Tull 4 B1
North Wynd. Dalk 157 D2
Northbank Ct. B'ness 64 A3
Northbank Dr. B'ness 64 A3
Northbank Pk. B' ness 63 F3
Northbank Rd. Crossf 27 E1
Northend. Cam 6 B3
Northfield Ave. Edin 124 B4
Northfield Ave. Shot 192 A1
Northfield Broadway. Edin 124 C4
Northfield Cir. Edin 124 B4
Northfield Cotts. W Cal 172 B2
Northfield. Cow 13 E3
Northfield Cres. Edin 124 C4
Northfield Cres. Fau 170 B1
Northfield Ct. Pres 127 F4
Northfield Dr. Edin 124 C4
Northfield E. Tran 128 C3
Northfield Farm Ave. Edin 124 C4
Northfield Farm Rd. Edin 124 C4
Northfield Gdns. Clack 11 D2
Northfield Gdns. Edin 124 C4
Northfield Gdns. Pres 127 F4
Northfield Gr. Edin 124 C4
Northfield Meadows. Fau 170 B1
Northfield Park Gr. Edin 124 C4
Northfield Pk. Edin 124 C4
Northfield Rd. Duni 36 B2
Northfield Rd. Edin 124 B4
Northfield Sq. Edin 124 C4
Northfield Terr. Edin 124 B4
Northfield Terr. Fau 170 B1
Northfield. Tran 128 C3
Northlawn Ct. Edin 91 F2
Northlawn Terr. Edin 91 F2
Northrig Cotts. Giff 133 D4
Northumberland Place La. Edin 93 E1
Northumberland St. Edin 93 E1
Northumberland Street North East La. Edin 93 E1
Northumberland Street North West La. Edin 93 E1
Northumberland Street South East La. Edin 93 E1
Northumberland Street South West La. Edin 93 E1
Northwood Pk. Liv 146 C4
Norton Pk. Edin 94 A1
Norton Pl. Dunf 29 F1
Norton St. Alva 5 D4
Norval Pl. Ros 46 C2
Norwood Ave. All 9 F4
Norwood Ave. Bon 58 A4
Norwood Ave. Whit 170 A3
Norwood Cres. All 9 F4
Norwood Ct. Whit 170 A3
Norwood Gr. All 9 F4
Norwood Pl. Bon 58 A4
Nottingham Pl. Edin 93 F1
Novar Cres. Kirk 17 D1
Nungate Rd. N Ber 54 A4
Nursery Rd. Falk 59 F2

Oak Ave. Loan 180 C4
Oak Bank. Laur 61 D1
Oak Cres. May 183 F3
Oak Cres. Plea 20 B2
Oak Dr. Fall 8 B2
Oak Dr. Lar 38 B1
Oak Gr. Dunf 46 C4
Oak Gr. Liv 148 A3
Oak Hill View. Madd 83 D3
Oak La. Edin 91 F1
Oak Pl. May 183 F3
Oak St. Stir 1 C1
Oakbank Ave. E Cal 148 C1
Oakbank Cotts. Ston 172 B3
Oakbank Pl. Winch 88 A1
Oakbank Rd. E Cal 148 C1
Oakfield Pl. Edin 123 F4
Oakfield St. Kel 12 C4
Oaktree Ct. Kirk 17 E4
Oaktree Sq. Kirk 17 E4
Oakville Terr. Edin 94 A2
Oatlands Pk. Lin 85 D3
Oberon. All 9 F4
Observatory Gn. Edin 123 F1
Observatory Rd. Edin 123 F1
Ochil Ave. Kirk 16 C3
Ochil Cres. Stir 2 A1
Ochil Ct. Que 89 E4
Ochil Ct. Tull 4 B2
Ochil Dr. Madd 83 D3
Ochil Dr. Sten 38 C2
Ochil La. Whit 169 F3
Ochil Rd. Alva 5 D4
Ochil Rd. Men 4 A4
Ochil Rd. Stir 2 B2
Ochil St. All 10 A4
Ochil St. Fall 8 B2
Ochil St. Gran 61 E4
Ochil St. Tull 4 A2
Ochil Terr. Dunf 29 F1
Ochil View. Den 57 E4
Ochil View. Kin 23 E2
Ochil View. Shi 81 E4
Ochilmount. Bann 7 F1
Ochiltree Cres. E Cal 148 A1
Ochiltree Ct. E Cal 148 A1
Ochiltree Dr. E Cal 148 A1
Ochiltree Gdns. Edin 124 B1
Ochiltree Terr. Falk 59 D3
Ochilview. Alva 5 D4
Ochilview. Cowie 20 C3
Ochilview Dr. H Val 26 A1
Ochilview. Loch 13 F3
Ochilview Pl. B' ness 63 F3
Ochilview Rd. B' ness 63 F3
Ochilview Terr. B' ness 63 F3
Ochville Terr. Fish 5 E2
Octavia St. Kirk 17 D3
Ogilface Cres. Blac 142 B1
Ogilvie Pl. B of A 2 A3
Ogilvie Rd. Stir 7 D3
Ogilvie Terr. Edin 122 C2
Ogilvie Way. Liv 147 E4
Ogilvy Cres. Fau 193 F3
Old Abbey Rd. N Ber 54 A4
Old Bellsdyke Rd. Lar 38 A2
Old Bridge St. All 10 A3
Old Broughton. Edin 93 E1
Old Burdiehouse Rd. Edin 155 D2
Old Church La. Edin 124 B3
Old Craighall Junc. White 126 A1
Old Craighall Rd. Dan 156 C4
Old Dalkeith Rd. Edin 156 B3
Old Dean Rd. Long 98 B2
Old Denny Rd. Lar 38 A2
Old Drove Rd. Cam 6 B3
Old Drove Rd. W Lin 219 D2
Old Eastfield St. East 168 B3
Old Edinburgh Rd. Dalk 156 C2
Old Farm Ave. Edin 153 E4
Old Farm Pl. Edin 153 D4
Old Fishmarket Cl. Edin 123 E4
Old Forge Gr. Bla 26 C4
Old Hillview Pl. Cross 30 C3
Old Kirk Pl. Dunf 29 E2
Old Kirk Rd. Dunf 29 E2
Old Kirk Rd. Edin 121 F4
Old Kirk Rd. Inver 68 B3
Old Linbun Rd. Dunf 29 F2
Old Liston Rd. Kirkl 119 D3
Old Mill Courtyard The. Dunf 29 D1
Old Mill Ct. Whit 170 C4
Old Mill Gr. Whit 170 C4
Old Mill La. Edin 124 A1
Old Mill La. Oak 26 C3
Old Mill Rd. Alla 191 D1
Old Mill Rd. Brox 117 F3
Old Newmills Rd. Curr 151 E2
Old Orch The. Lime 45 E2
Old Perth Rd. Cow 13 D2
Old Redding Rd. Laur 60 C2
Old Refinery Rd. Gran 62 A4
Old School Ct. Tull 4 A1
Old Tolbooth Wynd. Edin 123 F4
Old Town. Bann 7 E1
Old Town. Brox 117 F3
Oldwalls Pl. Gran 61 F4
Oldwalls Rd. Gran 62 B4
Oldwood Pl. Liv 147 D2
Olive Bank Rd. Muss 126 A3
Oliver Rd. Falk 60 B2
Olympia Arc. Kirk 17 D2
Onich Pl. Shot 192 A2
Onslow St. Liv 148 A3
Orchard Bank. Edin 92 C1
Orchard Brae Ave. Edin 92 C1
Orchard Brae. Edin 92 C1
Orchard Brae Gdns. Edin 92 C1
Orchard Brae Gdns W. Edin 92 C1
Orchard Brae W. Edin 92 C1
Orchard Cres. Edin 92 B1
Orchard Cres. Pres 96 C1
Orchard Ct. E Lin 103 F4
Orchard Ct. King 35 D2
Orchard Ct. Long 98 B2
Orchard Dr. Edin 92 B1
Orchard Gr. Edin 92 C1
Orchard Gr. Hadd 101 D1
Orchard Gr. Kin 23 F2
Orchard Gr. Pol 61 F1
Orchard La. Dunf 29 E1
Orchard La. Kirk 18 A4
Orchard Pl. Edin 92 C1
Orchard Pl. Kirk 18 A4
Orchard Pl. Liv 147 D3
Orchard Rd. B of A 2 A3
Orchard Rd. Edin 92 C1
Orchard Rd. Gran 62 B4
Orchard Rd. King 34 C2
Orchard Rd S. Edin 92 B1
Orchard Sq. Lime 45 E2
Orchard St. Falk 60 A3
Orchard St. Gran 61 E4
Orchard Terr. Clack 11 E1
Orchard Terr. Edin 92 C1
Orchard Terr. Torr 26 C1
Orchard The. Crossf 28 A1
Orchard The. Orm 159 F4
Orchard The. Pol 82 B4
Orchard The. Tran 128 B4
Orchard The. Tull 4 A1
Orchard Toll. Edin 92 C1
Orchard View. Dalk 156 C1
Orchardcroft. Stir 7 D4
Orchardfield Ave. Edin 121 E3
Orchardfield. E Lin 103 E4
Orchardfield Terr. E Cal 150 A3
Orchardhead Loan. Edin 155 D4
Orchardhead Rd. Edin 155 D4
Ordnance Rd. Lime 44 B4
Oriel Cres. Kirk 17 D2
Oriel Rd. Kirk 16 C3
Orkney Ct. All 10 A3
Orkney Pl. Falk 60 A1
Orkney Pl. Kirk 17 F4
Orlit Cotts. Ath 74 B2
Ormelie Terr. Edin 125 E4
Ormidale Terr. Edin 122 B4
Ormiston Ave. Tran 128 C3
Ormiston Cres E. Tran 128 C3
Ormiston Cres W. Tran 128 C3
Ormiston Dr. All 4 C1
Ormiston Dr. E Cal 149 D2
Ormiston Pk. Dunf 29 E3
Ormiston Pl. Pres 96 C1
Ormiston Rd. Tran 128 B3
Orr Terr. East 168 B2
Orrin Gr. D Bay 48 A2
Orrock Dr. Burn 33 F1
Orrok Pk. Edin 124 A1
Orwell Pl. Dunf 29 E2
Orwell Pl. Edin 122 C3
Orwell Terr. Edin 122 C3
Osborne Ct. Cocke 97 E2
Osborne Dr. Kin 23 F2
Osborne Gdns. Falk 59 F2
Osborne St. Falk 59 F2
Osborne Terr. Cocke 97 E2
Osborne Terr. Edin 122 C4
Oswald Ave. Gran 61 F4
Oswald Ct. Edin 123 E2
Oswald Rd. Edin 123 E2
Oswald St. Falk 60 A2
Oswald Terr. Edin 121 E3
Oswalds Wynd. Kirk 17 E2
Otterburn Pk. Edin 153 D4
Otterston Gr. D Bay 48 A2
Otterston Pl. Kirk 16 C4
Oudenarde Ct. Car 230 A1
Overhaven. Lime 45 F2
Overton Cres. Den 36 B1
Overton Cres. E Cal 149 D2
Overton Cres. Laur 61 D1
Overton Mains. Kirk 17 F4
Overton Rd. Gran 61 F3
Overton Rd. Gran 62 A4
Overton Rd. Kirk 17 E4
Owen sq. Muri 147 F1
Oxcars Dr. D Bay 48 A2
Oxcraig St. Edin 92 C4
Oxenfoord Ave. Path 185 D3
Oxenfoord Dr. Path 185 D3
Oxford St. Edin 123 F3
Oxford Terr. Edin 93 D1
Oxgang Rd. Gran 61 F4
Oxgangs Ave. Edin 153 F4
Oxgangs Bank. Edin 153 F3
Oxgangs Brae. Edin 153 F3
Oxgangs Broadway. Edin 153 F3
Oxgangs Cres. Edin 153 F4
Oxgangs Dr. Edin 153 F4
Oxgangs Farm Ave. Edin 153 F3
Oxgangs Farm Dr. Edin 153 F3
Oxgangs Farm Gdns. Edin 153 F3
Oxgangs Farm Gr. Edin 153 F3
Oxgangs Farm Loan. Edin 153 F3
Oxgangs Farm Terr. Edin 153 F3
Oxgangs Gdns. Edin 153 F4
Oxgangs Gn. Edin 153 F4
Oxgangs Gr. Edin 153 F4
Oxgangs Hill. Edin 153 F4
Oxgangs House. Edin 153 F4
Oxgangs Loan. Edin 153 F4
Oxgangs Medway. Edin 153 F3
Oxgangs Path. Edin 153 F3
Oxgangs Pk. Edin 153 F3
Oxgangs Pl. Edin 153 F4
Oxgangs Rd. Edin 154 A3
Oxgangs Rd N. Edin 153 F4
Oxgangs Rise. Edin 153 F4
Oxgangs Row. Edin 153 F3
Oxgangs St. Edin 153 F3
Oxgangs Terr. Edin 153 F3
Oxgangs View. Edin 153 F3

Paddock The. Gull 52 A1
Paddock The. Muss 126 B4
Paddockholm The. Edin 121 F3
Page St. Loch 14 A4
Paisley Ave. Edin 124 B4
Paisley Cres. Edin 124 B4
Paisley Dr. Edin 124 B4
Paisley Gdns. Edin 124 B4
Paisley Gr. Edin 124 B4
Paisley Terr. Edin 124 B4
Palmer Pl. Curr 151 F2
Palmer Rd. Curr 151 F2
Palmer Rise. Muri 147 F1
Palmerston Pl. Edin 123 D4
Palmerston Place La. Edin 123 D4
Palmerston Rd. Edin 123 E3
Pan Ha'. Kirk 18 A3
Panbrae Rd. B' ness 63 F4
Pankhurst Loan. Dalk 157 E2
Panmure Pl. Edin 123 E3
Pannie Rd. Kirk 17 E4
Panstead St. Gran 61 F4
Panton Gn. Liv 147 D4
Papana Cotts. Giff 134 B1
Papple Farm Cotts. E Lin 134 B3
Paradise La. Kin 23 F2
Paradykes Ave. Loan 181 D4
Pardovan Cres. Brid 86 B4
Pardovan Pl. Falk 59 F3
Pariothall. Edin 93 D1
Paris Ave. Den 36 C1
Paris St. Gran 61 F4
Park Ave. Bank 57 F3
Park Ave. Cow 13 E2
Park Ave. Dunb 78 B1
Park Ave. Dunf 29 D2
Park Ave. Edin 125 D4
Park Ave. Gore 183 E1
Park Ave. Lar 38 B1
Park Ave. Laur 60 C2
Park Ave. Loan 181 D4
Park Ave. Muss 126 C3
Park Ave. Pol 82 B4
Park Ave. Rosl 180 B3
Park Ave. Stir 7 D3
Park Cres. Bann 7 E1
Park Cres. Bonn 182 A4
Park Cres. Edin 155 D4
Park Cres. Giff 163 F3
Park Cres. Laur 61 D2
Park Cres. Loan 181 D4
Park Cres. May 183 E4
Park Cres. N Sau 5 E1
Park Cres. Sten 39 D1
Park Ct. Muss 126 C3
Park Dr. Bann 7 E1
Park Dr. Lar 38 B1
Park Dr. Pol 82 B4
Park Dr. W Cal 173 D3
Park Gdns. Bann 7 E1
Park Gdns. Edin 155 D4
Park Gr. Edin 155 D4
Park Gr. Uph 117 D3
Park Grove Pl. Muss 126 C3
Park Grove Terr. Muss 126 C3
Park Hill. Gore 183 D1
Park La. Abe 49 D4
Park La. B'ness 64 A4
Park La. Edin 125 D4
Park La. Hadd 131 F4
Park La. Muss 126 C3
Park La. Stir 7 D4
Park Lea. Ros 47 D3
Park Par. Fau 193 F3
Park Pl. All 10 B4
Park Pl. Clack 11 D2
Park Pl. Dunf 29 D2
Park Pl. Edin 93 E3
Park Pl. King 34 C1
Park Pl. Kirk 17 D2
Park Pl. Liv 147 D3
Park Pl. Stir 6 C3
Park Rd. Blac 142 C2
Park Rd. Bonn 182 A4
Park Rd. Brox 117 F3
Park Rd. Cocke 97 E2
Park Rd. Cow 13 D2
Park Rd. Dalk 156 C1
Park Rd. Edin 93 E3
Park Rd. Falk 39 D1
Park Rd. Giff 163 F2
Park Rd. Gore 183 E1
Park Rd. Gran 61 E4
Park Rd. Hart 169 D3
Park Rd. Kirk 17 F4
Park Rd. Men 4 A3
Park Rd. Newt 183 D3
Park Rd. Orm 159 E3
Park Rd. Ros 46 C3
Park Rd. Shot 191 E3
Park Rd W. Ros 46 B3
Park St. Alva 5 D4
Park St. Bon 58 B2
Park St. Cow 13 E2
Park St. Cowie 20 C4
Park St. Falk 60 A3
Park St. Loch 14 A4
Park Terr. Edin 125 F2
Park Terr. Kir 149 F1
Park Terr. Pol 82 B4
Park Terr. Stir 7 D3
Park Terr. Tull 4 A1
Park Terr. Uph 117 D3
Park View E. Cocke 97 E2
Park View. Fau 193 F4
Park View. Kirk 16 C3
Park View. Loan 181 D4
Park View. Muss 126 C3
Park View. Pen 160 C4
Park View. Pol 82 C4
Park View. Pres 97 D1
Park View. Ston 171 E1
Park View Terr. Inver 47 D1
Park View. Uph 117 D3
Park View W. Cocke 97 E2
Park View. West 112 C2
Park View. Whit 170 A4
Park-View. Long 98 C3
Parkandarroch Cres. Car 230 A1
Parkdyke. Stir 6 C3
Parkend Cres. Shi 81 E3
Parker Ave. Edin 94 C1
Parker Rd. Edin 94 C1
Parker Terr. Edin 94 C1
Parkfoot Ct. Falk 60 A2
Parkgate. Alva 4 C3
Parkgate. Ros 46 C2
Parkgrove Ave. Edin 91 E1
Parkgrove Bank. Edin 91 E1
Parkgrove Cres. Edin 91 E1
Parkgrove Dr. Edin 91 E1
Parkgrove Gdns. Edin 91 E1
Parkgrove Gn. Edin 91 E1
Parkgrove Loan. Edin 91 E1
Parkgrove Neuk. Edin 91 E1
Parkgrove Path. Edin 91 E1
Parkgrove Pl. Edin 91 E1
Parkgrove Rd. Edin 91 E1
Parkgrove Row. Edin 91 E1
Parkgrove St. Edin 91 E1
Parkgrove Terr. Edin 91 E1
Parkgrove View. Edin 91 E1
Parkhall Dr. Madd 83 D3
Parkhead Ave. Edin 121 F1
Parkhead Cotts. W Cal 172 C1
Parkhead Cres. Edin 121 F1
Parkhead Cres. W Cal 172 C2
Parkhead Ct. N Sau 10 B4
Parkhead Dr. Edin 121 F1
Parkhead Gdns. Edin 121 F1
Parkhead Gdns. W Cal 172 C2
Parkhead Gr. Edin 121 F1
Parkhead Loan. Edin 121 F1
Parkhead Pk. May 183 E4
Parkhead Pl. Edin 121 F1
Parkhead Pl. May 183 E4
Parkhead Rd. Falk 60 A1
Parkhead Rd. Lin 84 C4
Parkhead Rd. N Sau 10 B4
Parkhead St. Edin 121 F1
Parkhead Terr. Edin 121 F1

Parkhead View. Edin

Parkhead View. Edin 121 F1
Parkland Gr. Bla 26 B4
Parkland Gr. Ston 170 C1
Parklands. Brox 117 E2
Parkneuk Rd. Dunf 28 B3
Parkside Ct. Plea 20 B2
Parkside. Kirk 119 D3
Parkside Pl. Dalk 157 D2
Parkside Rd. Shot 191 E2
Parkside Sq. Ros 47 D2
Parkside St. Edin 123 F3
Parkside St. Ros 46 C2
Parkside Terr. Edin 123 F3
Parkvale Pl. Edin 94 A2
Parkview Ave. Falk 59 F1
Parkway. All 10 A4
Parkwood Cres. Brox 117 E2
Parkwood Gdns. Brox 117 E3
Parliament Sq. Edin 123 E4
Parliament St. Edin 93 F3
Parnishes. Brox 117 E2
Parsonage The. Muss 126 B3
Parsons Green Terr. Edin 94 B1
Parsonspool. Bonn 182 B3
Parsonspool. Dunb 78 B1
Paterson Dr. Shi 81 E3
Paterson Pl. B of A 2 A3
Paterson Pl. Bon 58 B3
Paterson Way. Dunf 29 D1
Paterson's Ct. Brox 117 F3
Path Brae. Kirl 89 D1
Path The. Bann 7 F1
Path The. Kirk 17 E3
Pathfoot Ave. B of A 2 B4
Pathfoot Dr. B of A 2 B4
Pathfoot Rd. B of A 2 B3
Paton's Rd. Edin 153 E4
Paton St. All 10 A4
Paton St. Dunf 29 E3
Patrick Dr. Shi 81 F4
Patterson La. Cow 13 E2
Patterson Pl. Kirk 17 D3
Patterson Pl. Kirk 17 D3
Pattison St. Edin 94 A3
Pattle Ct. N Ber 54 A4
Paul Dr. Air 22 C2
Paul Pl. Cow 13 E2
Paul St. Loch 14 A3
Pavilion View. All 9 F4
Paxstone Cres. East 168 C3
Paxstone Dr. East 168 C3
Paxton Cres. Loch 14 A4
Peachdales. Hadd 131 F4
Peacock Ct. Edin 93 E4
Peacocktail Cl. Edin 125 D2
Pearce Ave. Edin 121 E4
Pearce Gr. Edin 121 E4
Pearce Rd. Edin 121 E4
Pearson Pl. Bank 57 E3
Peathill Rd. Bon 58 A3
Peatville Gdns. Edin 122 A1
Peatville Terr. Edin 122 A1
Peddie Pl. Gran 61 F4
Peden St. East 168 B3
Peebles Rd. Peni 203 F2
Peebles St. Kirk 35 D4
Peel Roundabout. Liv 147 E2
Peel Terr. Edin 123 F2
Peffer Bank. Edin 124 B2
Peffer Pl. Edin 124 B2
Peffer St. Edin 124 B2
Peffer's Pl. Hadd 132 A4
Peffermill Ind Est. Edin 124 B2
Peffermill Rd. Edin 124 B2
Peggy's Mill Rd. Edin 91 D2
Peirson Rd. Dunf 29 F2
Pelstream Ave. Stir 7 D2
Pembroke Pl. Edin 122 C4
Pembroke St. Lar 38 B2
Pencraig Brae. E Lin 103 E3
Pendreich La. Edin 60 A3
Pendreich Ave. Bonn 182 B4
Pendreich Dr. Bonn 182 B4
Pendreich Gr. Bonn 182 B4
Pendreich Terr. Bonn 182 B4
Pendreich View. Bonn 182 B4
Pendreich Way. Stir 2 A2
Penicuik Rd. Rosl 180 C2
Pennelton Pl. B'ness 63 F3
Pennyschool Pl. Clack 11 D2
Pennywell Ct. Edin 92 A3
Pennywell Gdns. Edin 92 A3
Pennywell Gr. Edin 92 A3
Pennywell Medway. Edin 92 A3
Pennywell Pl. Edin 92 A3
Pennywell Rd. Edin 92 A3
Pennywell Villas. Edin 92 A3
Pentland Ave. Bog 145 F3
Pentland Ave. Curr 151 F2
Pentland Ave. Edin 153 D2
Pentland Ave. Gore 183 D2
Pentland Ave. Peni 203 F3
Pentland Cres. Edin 154 A4
Pentland Cres. Rose 181 E2
Pentland Ct. D Bay 48 A2
Pentland Ct. Rosl 180 C3
Pentland Dr. Edin 153 F3
Pentland Dr. Whit 170 B3
Pentland Gr. Edin 154 A4
Pentland Ind Est. Loan 181 D4
Pentland Pk. Liv 148 A2
Pentland Pk. Loan 180 C4
Pentland Pl. Curr 151 F2
Pentland Pl. Kirk 16 C3
Pentland Rd. Bonn 182 A4
Pentland Rd. Edin 153 D4
Pentland Rd. Rose 154 B1
Pentland Rise. D Bay 48 B3
Pentland Terr. Dunf 29 F1
Pentland Terr. Edin 154 A4
Pentland Terr. H Val 26 A1
Pentland Terr. Peni 203 F3
Pentland View. Ct. Liv 147 D3
Pentland View. Curr 151 F2
Pentland View. Dalk 157 E1
Pentland View. Edin 154 A3
Pentland View Pl. Rosl 180 C2
Pentland View Rd. Kirkl 89 D1
Pentland View Rd. Rosl 180 C2
Pentland View Terr. Rosl 180 C2
Pentland View. Uph 117 D3
Pentland Way. Gran 61 F3
Pentland Wk. Whit 170 B3
Pentlands Gdns. Edin 154 A4
Percival St. Kirk 17 D3
Perdieus Mount. Dunf 28 C3
Perdrixknowe. Edin 122 B1
Perth Rd. Cow 13 E3
Perth St. Edin 93 D1
Petershill Gdns. Bath 145 E4
Pettigrew's Cl. Dalk 157 D2
Pettycur Bay. King 34 C1
Pettycur Rd. King 34 C1
Peveril Rise. Muri 173 F4
Peveril Terr. Edin 155 D4
Phantassie Sq. E Lin 103 F4
Philip Ave. Bog 145 F3
Philip Ave. Lin 84 C4
Philip Dr. Lar 38 B1
Philip Pl. Peni 203 F4
Philip St. Falk 60 A4
Philpingstone La. B'ness 64 B4
Philpingstone Rd. B'ness 64 B4
Phoenix La. Dunf 28 C2
Picardy Pl. Edin 93 E1
Pier Pl. Edin 93 E4
Pier Rd. B'ness 64 B4
Pierhead Bldgs. Inver 68 B3
Piersfield Gr. Edin 94 B1
Piersfield Pl. Edin 94 B1
Piersfield Terr. Edin 94 B1
Piershill La. Edin 94 B1
Piershill Pl. Edin 94 B1
Piershill Sq E. Edin 94 B1
Piershill Square W. Edin 94 B1
Piershill Terr. Edin 94 B1
Pilgrims Hill. Lin 85 E4
Pilkham Ct. Cow 13 E2
Pilmuir St. Dunf 29 D3
Pilrig Gdns. Edin 93 F2
Pilrig House Cl. Edin 93 F2
Pilrig St. Edin 93 F2
Pilton Ave. Edin 92 C3
Pilton Cres. Edin 92 C3
Pilton Dr. Edin 92 C3
Pilton Dr N. Edin 92 C3
Pilton Gdns. Edin 92 C3
Pilton Loan. Edin 92 C3
Pilton Pk. Edin 92 C3
Pilton Pl. Edin 92 C3
Pine Gn. B'ness 63 E2
Pine Gr. All 10 B3
Pine Gr. Dunf 46 C4
Pine Gr. Laur 61 D1
Pine Gr. Liv 148 A3
Pine St. Dunb 78 A1
Pine Wlk. Lar 38 B1
Pinebank. Liv 147 F3
Pines The. Gull 52 A2
Pinewood Dr. D Bay 48 A2
Pinewood Pk. Liv 146 C4
Pinewood Pl. May 183 F3
Pinewood Rd. May 183 F3
Pinewood View. May 183 F3
Pinkerton Pl. Ros 46 C3
Pinkhill. Edin 121 F3
Pinkie Ave. Muss 126 C3
Pinkie Dr. Muss 126 C3
Pinkie Hill Cres. Muss 126 C3
Pinkie Pl. Muss 126 C3
Pinkie Rd. Muss 126 C3
Pinkie Terr. Muss 126 C3
Pinkie Wlk. Tran 128 B3
Pinnel Pl. D Bay 48 B2
Pipe La. Edin 95 D1
Pipe St. Edin 95 D1
Piper Cres. Burn 33 E1
Pirig Cotts. Edin 93 F2
Pirleyhill Dr. Shi 81 E3
Pirleyhill Gdns. Falk 60 A1
Pirnhall Rd. Bann 19 E4
Pirniefield Bank. Edin 94 B2
Pirniefield Gdns. Edin 94 B2
Pirniefield Gr. Edin 94 B2
Pirniefield Pl. Edin 94 B2

Pirniefield Terr. Edin 94 B2
Pirrie St. Edin 93 F2
Pitbauchlie Bank. Dunf 29 E1
Pitcairn St. Dunf 29 E1
Pitcorthie Dr. Dunf 46 C4
Pitcorthie Rd. Dunf 29 E1
Pitdinnie Pl. Crossf 27 E1
Pitdinnie Rd. Crossf 27 E1
Pitfairn Rd. Fish 5 F2
Pitfirrane Pk. Crossf 28 A1
Pitlour Pl. Kirk 16 B4
Pittochry Pl. Edin 94 A1
Pitsligo Rd. Edin 123 D2
Pitt St. Edin 93 F3
Pitt Terr. Stir 7 D3
Pittencrieff Ct. Muss 126 C3
Pittencrieff St. Dunf 28 C2
Pittville St. Edin 125 E4
Pittville Street La. Edin 125 D4
Place Charente. Dalk 157 E1
Plane St. Dunf 46 C4
Plane St. Dunb 78 A1
Plantation St. Loch 14 A4
Player Gn. Liv 147 D4
Pleasance Brae. Crossf 27 F1
Pleasance Ct. Falk 60 A2
Pleasance Ct. Hal 30 A4
Pleasance. Edin 123 F4
Pleasance. Falk 60 A2
Pleasance Gdns. Falk 60 A2
Pleasance Rd. Falk 60 A2
Pleasance Rd. Hal 30 A3
Pleasance Row. For 215 D2
Pleasance Sq. Falk 60 A2
Pleasance The. Aber 71 D2
Plewlandcroft. Que 68 A1
Plewlands Ave. Edin 122 C1
Plewlands Gdns. Edin 122 C1
Plewlands Pl. Que 89 D4
Plewlands Terr. Edin 122 C1
Pleydell Pl. Edin 155 D4
Poachers Gn. Clack 11 D3
Pointgarry Rd. N Ber 54 A4
Polbeth Ave. W Cal 172 C3
Polbeth Cres. W Cal 172 C3
Polbeth Gdns. W Cal 172 C3
Polbeth Pl. W Cal 172 C3
Polbeth Rd. W Cal 172 C3
Poldrate. Hadd 132 A4
Polkemmet Dr. Hart 169 D3
Polkemmet La. Hart 168 C3
Polkemmet Rd. Hart 168 C3
Polkemmet Rd. Whit 169 F3
Pollock Wlk. Dunf 29 D2
Polmaise Ave. Stir 7 D2
Polmaise Cres. Fall 8 B3
Polmaise Ct. Stir 7 D2
Polmaise Rd. Cam 6 C2
Polmaise Rd. Stir 7 D2
Polmont House Gdns. Pol 61 F1
Polmont Pk. Pol 61 F2
Polmont Rd. Laur 61 D2
Polson Gdns. Tran 128 A3
Polton Avenue Rd. Bonn 182 A3
Polton Bank. Bonn 181 F3
Polton Bank Rd. Bonn 181 F3
Polton Bank Terr. Bonn 181 F3
Polton Cotts. Rose 181 E3
Polton Ct. Bonn 182 A4
Polton Gdns. Bonn 182 A4
Polton Rd. Bonn 182 A4
Polton Rd. Loan 181 E4
Polton Rd W. Bonn 181 F3
Polton St. Bonn 182 A3
Polton Terr. Bonn 182 A4
Polwarth Ave. Pol 82 B4
Polwarth Cres. Edin 123 D3
Polwarth Cres. Pres 97 D1
Polwarth Gdns. Edin 122 C3
Polwarth Gr. Edin 122 C3
Polwarth Pk. Edin 122 C3
Polwarth Pl. Edin 122 C3
Polwarth Terr. Edin 122 C3
Polwarth Terr. Pres 97 D1
Polworth Pl. Cow 13 E2
Pomathorn Bank. Peni 203 F2
Pomathorn Rd. How 203 F2
Pompee Rd. N Sau 5 D1
Ponton St. Edin 123 D3
Poolewe Dr. Laur 61 E1
Poplar Cres. Kirk 17 E4
Poplar Gr. Dunf 46 C4
Poplar Gr. Liv 148 A3
Poplar La. Edin 94 A3
Poplar St. Dunb 78 A1
Poplar St. Gran 61 F4
Poplar St. May 183 F3
Poplar Terr. Bonn 182 A3
Poplars The. Tull 4 A1
Port Buchan. Brox 117 E3
Port St. Clack 11 D2
Port St. Inver 47 E1
Port St. Stir 7 D4
Portal Rd. Gran 61 E3
Portdownie. Falk 59 E3
Porterfield. Bla 26 C4
Porterfield Rd. Edin 92 C2

Portgower Pl. Edin 93 D1
Portland Pl. Edin 93 F3
Portland Pl. Fau 193 E3
Portland St. Edin 93 F3
Portobello Rd. Edin 94 C1
Portree Cres. Pol 62 A1
Post Office La. Inver 68 B3
Posthill. N Sau 5 E1
Potter Pl. Gran 39 F2
Potterrow. Edin 123 E4
Pottery St. Kirk 17 F4
Pottery The. Edin 95 D1
Pottery The. Pres 96 C1
Pottis Rd. Bann 7 E2
Pottishaw Pl. Black 145 E1
Povert Rd. Gore 182 C1
Powdermill Brae. Gore 207 E3
Powdrake Rd. Gran 61 F4
Pratt St. Kirk 17 D1
President Kennedy Dr. Plea .. 20 B2
Preston Ave. Lin 84 C3
Preston Ave. Pres 97 D1
Preston Cres. Inver 47 E1
Preston Cres. Lin 84 C3
Preston Cross Cotts. Pres 97 D1
Preston Ct. Lin 84 C3
Preston Ct. Pres 127 F4
Preston Pk. Lin 84 C3
Preston Pl. Path 185 D2
Preston Rd. E Lin 103 F4
Preston Rd. Lin 84 C3
Preston Rd. Pres 97 D1
Preston St. H Val 26 A1
Preston St. Rose 181 E1
Preston Terr. Inver 47 E1
Preston Terr. Lin 84 C3
Preston Terr. Pres 97 D1
Preston Tower. Pres 97 D1
Prestonfield Ave. Edin 124 A2
Prestonfield Bank. Edin 124 A2
Prestonfield Cres. Edin 124 A2
Prestonfield Gdns. Edin 124 A2
Prestonfield Rd. Edin 124 A2
Prestonfield Terr. Edin 124 A2
Prestongrange Rd. Pres 127 F4
Prestongrange Terr. Pres 96 C1
Prestonhall Cres. Rose 181 E1
Prestonhall Rd. Rose 181 E1
Pretoria Pl. Cow 13 D2
Pretoria Pl. Pol 61 F1
Pretoria Rd. Lar 38 A1
Priest Bank. Giff 134 B1
Priestfield Ave. Edin 124 A2
Priestfield Cres. Edin 124 A2
Priestfield Gdns. Edin 124 A2
Priestfield Gr. Edin 124 A3
Priestfield Rd. Edin 124 A3
Priestfield Rd N. Edin 124 A3
Prime Gilt Box St. Kirk 17 D3
Primmer Pl. Cow 13 E1
Primrose Ave. Gran 61 D3
Primrose Ave. Ros 46 B3
Primrose Bank Rd. Edin 93 D3
Primrose Cres. Dalk 157 E1
Primrose Ct. Brox 117 F3
Primrose Cres. Dal 89 D2
Primrose Dr. Dal 90 B2
Primrose Gdns. Newt 206 B3
Primrose Gdns. Que 89 E4
Primrose La. Cow 13 E3
Primrose La. Kin 23 F2
Primrose La. Ros 46 B3
Primrose Pl. All 10 A4
Primrose Rd. Lime 45 D3
Primrose St. All 10 A4
Primrose St. Bon 58 A3
Primrose St. Edin 94 A2
Primrose Terr. Dalk 157 E1
Primrose Terr. Edin 122 C3
Prince Regent St. Edin 93 F3
Princes St. Call 81 F3
Princes St. Edin 123 E4
Princes St. Falk 60 A3
Princes St. Gran 61 F4
Princes St. Stir 7 D4
Princess Mary Pl. Hadd 101 D1
Princess Mary Rd. Hadd 101 D1
Princess St. Bon 58 A3
Priora Grange. Torp 113 F3
Priorscroft. Torp 113 F3
Priory Gr. Que 89 D2
Priory La. Dunf 29 D2
Priory Rd. Lin 84 C3
Priory Rd. Madd 83 D3
Priory Sq. Kin 23 F2
Priory Wlk. Hadd 101 D1
Promenade. Edin 95 D2
Promenade. Lime 45 E2
Promenade. Muss 126 A4
Prospect Bank Cres. Edin 94 B2
Prospect Bank Gdns. Edin 94 B2
Prospect Bank Gr. Edin 94 B2
Prospect Bank Pl. Edin 94 B2
Prospect Bank Rd. Edin 94 B2
Prospect Bank Terr. Edin 94 B2

Queensferry Street La. Edin

Prospect St. Cow 13 D2
Prospect St. Falk 59 F3
Prospecthill Rd. Falk 60 A1
Providence Brae. B' ness 63 F4
Provost Hunter Ave. Alva 5 E4
Provost Milne Gr. Que 89 E4
Provost Rd. B' ness 63 E3
Provost Rd. Lin 85 D4
Pryde Ave. Bonn 182 A4
Pryde Terr. Bonn 182 A4
Puir Wife's Brae. Bog 145 E3
Pullar Ave. B of A 2 A3
Pullar Ct. B of A 2 A3
Pumpherston Rd. E Cal 148 B3
Pumpherston Rd. Pump 148 B3
Pyothall Rd. Brox 117 E3
Pypers Wynd. Pres 96 C1

Quadrant La. N Ber 54 B4
Quadrant. N Ber 54 B4
Quakerfield. Bann 201 F3
Quakerfield. Bann 7 F1
Quality St. Edin 91 F2
Quality St. Kirk 18 A4
Quality St. N Ber 54 B4
Quality Street La. Edin 91 F2
Quarrywood Cl. Liv 147 E2
Quarrybank Cres. Stet 39 D2
Quarrole Brae. Pol 82 C4
Quarry Brae. Pol 82 C4
Quarry Cl. Edin 123 F3
Quarry Cotts. Edin 125 D2
Quarry Ct. Cow 13 D2
Quarry Howe. Bale 151 E1
Quarry Knowe. Bann 19 F4
Quarry Pl. N Sau 10 B4
Quarry Pl. Shot 191 E3
Quarry Rd. Cam 6 B3
Quarry Rd. Fau 193 F3
Quarry Rd. Shot 191 E3
Quarry St. Shot 191 E3
Quarryfoot Gdns. Bonn 182 B4
Quarryfoot Gn. Bonn 182 B4
Quarryfoot Pl. Bonn 182 A4
Quarryford Farm Cotts.
  Giff 190 C4
Quarryknowes The. B' ness ... 63 E3
Quarryside Ct. Dunf 28 B3
Quayside St. Edin 93 F3
Quebec Ave. Liv 147 F2
Queen Anne Dr. Kirkl 119 D3
Queen Anne Pk. Kirkl 119 D3
Queen Anne St. Dunf 29 D2
Queen Charlotte La. Edin 94 A3
Queen Charlotte St. Edin 94 A3
Queen Margaret Cl. Edin 154 B3
Queen Margaret Dr. Que 89 E4
Queen Margaret St. King 34 C1
Queen Margaret's Pl. Inver ... 68 B3
Queen St. All 10 A4
Queen St. Alva 5 D4
Queen St. Bann 7 E1
Queen St. Edin 93 E1
Queen St. Falk 60 B3
Queen St. Fall 8 B2
Queen St. Gran 61 F4
Queen St. Inver 47 D1
Queen St. Stir 7 D4
Queen Street Gdns W. Edin .. 93 E1
Queen's Ave. B of A 2 A3
Queen's Ave. Edin 92 B1
Queen's Ave S. Edin 92 B1
Queen's Bay Cres. Edin 125 E4
Queen's Bldgs. Ros 46 C3
Queen's Cres. Car 230 A1
Queen's Cres. Edin 123 F2
Queen's Cres. Falk 59 F3
Queen's Ct. B of A 2 A3
Queen's Dr. Edin 124 B3
Queen's Dr. Lar 38 B1
Queen's Dr. Pen 160 C3
Queen's Gdns. Edin 92 B1
Queen's La. B of A 2 A3
Queen's Park Ave. Edin 94 A1
Queen's Park Ct. Edin 124 B4
Queen's Rd. Brox 117 F2
Queen's Rd. Dunb 78 B1
Queen's Rd. Edin 92 B1
Queen's Rd. Stir 2 A2
Queen's St. Call 81 F3
Queen's Wlk. Edin 124 C2
Queen's Ave. Hadd 100 C1
Queens Cres. King 34 C1
Queens Ct. Dunf 36 C2
Queens Dr. Falk 59 F3
Queens Gdns. E Cal 148 C2
Queens Rd. Falk 59 F3
Queens Terr. E Cal 148 C2
Queens Way. Ros 46 A1
Queensferry Rd. Dunf 46 B3
Queensferry Rd. Edin 91 D2
Queensferry Rd. Kirl 89 D1
Queensferry Rd. Ros 46 C3
Queensferry St. Edin 123 D4
Queensferry Street La.
  Edin 123 D4

Queensferry Terr. Edin 92 C1
Queenshaugh Dr. Stir 2 B1
Queensway. Peni 203 F4
Quench Rd. B'ness 62 A3
Quentin Rise. Muri 147 F1
Quidenham Ct. N Ber 54 A3
Quills The. Edin 93 F3
Quilts Wynd. Edin 93 F3

Race Rd. Bath 144 C4
Rae St. Cow 13 E1
Rae St. Sten 38 B2
Raeburn Cres. Kirk 17 D2
Raeburn Cres. Whit 170 A3
Raeburn Mews. Edin 93 D1
Raeburn Pl. Edin 93 D1
Raeburn Rigg. Liv 147 D3
Raeburn St. Edin 93 D1
Raes Gdns. Bonn 182 B4
Rainhill Ave. Madd 82 C3
Raith Ave. Cow 13 E2
Raith Cres. Kirk 17 D2
Raith Dr. Kirk 17 D2
Raith Gdns. Kirk 16 C2
Raleigh Ct. Falk 59 F3
Ramage Rd. Car 230 A1
Ramillies Ct. Auch 204 A4
Ramillies Ct. Car 230 A1
Ramsay Ave. Laur 61 D2
Ramsay Cotts. Newt 182 C2
Ramsay Cres. Bath 145 E3
Ramsay Cres. Burn 34 A1
Ramsay Cres. May 183 F3
Ramsay Ct. Liv 148 B3
Ramsay Gdns. Kin 23 F2
Ramsay La. Lime 45 E2
Ramsay Pl. Edin 95 D1
Ramsay Pl. Stir 2 A2
Ramsay Rd. Kirk 17 D1
Ramsay Terr. Bonn 181 F3
Ramsay Wlk. May 183 F3
Ramsay La. Kin 23 F2
Ramsay Pl. Edin 123 E4
Ramsay La. Edin 123 E4
Ramsay Pl. Peni 203 E3
Ramsay Pl. Ros 46 C2
Ramsay Tullis Ave. Tull 4 B1
Ramsey Tullis Dr. Tull 4 B1
Randolph Cres. Barn 7 F1
Randolph Cres. Edin 123 D4
Randolph Cres. Pol 82 B4
Randolph Gdns. Den 36 B1
Randolph La. Edin 123 D4
Randolph Pl. Barn 7 E1
Randolph Pl. Edin 123 D4
Randolph Pl. Kirk 18 A4
Randolph Rd. Stir 7 D3
Randolph St. Cow 13 E2
Randolph Terr. Stir 7 D2
Randyford Rd. Falk 60 B3
Randyford St. Falk 60 C3
Randy Rd. Gran 62 B4
Rankeillor St. Edin 123 F3
Rankin Ave. Edin 123 F1
Rankin Dr. Edin 123 F1
Rannoch Ct. All 10 B3
Rannoch Dr. Crossf 28 A1
Rannoch Dr. Whit 170 B4
Rannoch Pl. Edin 91 E1
Rannoch Pl. Edin 91 E1
Rannoch Pl. Shi 81 F4
Rannoch Pl. Shot 191 F3
Rannoch Pl. Sten 38 C2
Rannoch Rd. Edin 91 E1
Rannoch Rd. Gran 61 E2
Rannoch Rd. Kirk 16 C4
Rannoch Rd. Ros 46 C1
Rannoch Rd. Whit 170 B4
Rannoch Terr. Edin 91 E1
Rannoch Wlk. Liv 148 A2
Rannoch Wlk. Whit 170 B4
Ransome Gdns. Edin 91 E1
Rappoch Rd. Stir 1 C1
Rashiehill Cres. Add 194 C3
Rashiehill Rd. Slam 110 A3
Rashiehill Terr. Add 194 C3
Rashiemuir. For 215 D1
Rashwing. Ugin 117 D3
Ratcliffe Terr. Edin 123 F2
Rathbone Pl. Edin 95 D1
Ratho Park Rd. Rat 119 F1
Ratho Pl. Dunf 29 E2
Rattray Gdns. Black 171 F4
Rattray St. B'ness 64 A4
Rattray Terr. Loch 14 A4
Ravelrig Hill. Bale 151 D1
Ravelrig Pk. Bale 151 D1
Ravelrig Rd. Bale 151 D2
Ravelston Dykes. Edin 122 B4
Ravelston Dykes La. Edin 122 B4
Ravelston Dykes Rd. Edin ... 122 A4
Ravelston Gdn. Edin 122 B4
Ravelston Heights. Edin 92 B1
Ravelston House Gr. Edin ... 92 B1
Ravelston House Loan. Edin . 92 B1

Ravelston House Pk. Edin 92 B1
Ravelston House Rd. Edin 92 B1
Ravelston Pk. Edin 122 C4
Ravelston Rise. Edin 122 B4
Ravelston Terr. Edin 92 C1
Ravelsykes Rd. Peni 203 E3
Ravendean Gdns. Peni 203 E3
Ravens Craig. Kirk 17 E3
Ravenscraig St. Kirk 17 F3
Ravenscroft Gdns. Edin 155 F3
Ravenscroft Pl. Edin 155 F3
Ravenscroft St. Edin 155 F3
Ravenshaugh Cres. Muss ... 127 D3
Ravenshaugh Rd. Muss 127 D4
Ravenswood Ave. Edin 124 B1
Ravenswood Rise. Muri 173 F4
Rectory La. Kirk 18 A4
Red Craigs. Kirk 16 B4
Red Fox Cres. Auch 180 A1
Red Row. Lime 45 E2
Redbrae Ave. B'ness 64 A3
Redbraes Gr. Edin 93 E2
Redbraes Pl. Edin 93 E2
Redburn Rd. Blac 142 A1
Redburn Rd N. Pres 96 C1
Redburn Rd. Pres 96 C1
Redburn Wynd. Kirk 17 D2
Redcraig Rd. E Cal 148 C1
Redcroft Pl. Ston 171 D1
Redcroft St. Dan 156 A4
Redcroft St. Ston 171 D1
Redding Rd. La ur 61 D1
Redding Rd. Pol 82 B4
Reddingmuirhead Rd. Shi 61 D1
Reddoch Rd. Gran 62 A3
Reddoch Rd. Pol 62 A2
Redford Ave. Edin 153 E4
Redford Bank. Edin 153 E3
Redford Cres. Edin 153 E3
Redford Dr. Edin 153 D3
Redford Gdns. Edin 153 E3
Redford Gr. Edin 153 E3
Redford Loan. Edin 153 E3
Redford Neuk. Edin 153 E3
Redford Pl. Edin 153 E3
Redford Rd. Edin 153 E3
Redford Terr. Edin 153 E3
Redford Wlk. Edin 153 E3
Redgauntlet Terr. Edin 124 B1
Redhall Ave. Edin 122 A1
Redhall Bank Rd. Edin 122 A1
Redhall Cres. Edin 122 A1
Redhall Dr. Edin 122 A1
Redhall Gdns. Edin 122 A1
Redhall Gr. Edin 122 A1
Redhall House Dr. Edin 122 A1
Redhall Pl. Edin 122 A1
Redhall Rd. Edin 122 A1
Redhall View. Edin 122 A1
Redheughs Rd. Shot 192 A2
Redheugh Loan. Gore 183 E1
Redheughs Ave. Edin 121 D2
Redheughs Rigg. Edin 121 D2
Redholm Pk. N Ber 54 C3
Redhouse Cotts. Winch 86 C2
Redhouse Ct. Black 171 F4
Redhouse Pl. Black 145 E1
Redhouse Rd. Black 172 A4
Redlands Ct. Whit 170 C4
Redlands Rd. Tull 4 A2
Redmill Cotts. Whit 170 C4
Redmill Ct. Whit 170 C4
Redmill View. Whit 170 C4
Redmire Cres. Alla 212 A4
Redpath Dr. Sten 39 D2
Redwell Pl. All 9 F4
Reed Dr. Newt 183 D4
Reedlands Dr. Den 57 E4
Regent Pl. Edin 94 A1
Regent Rd. Edin 93 F1
Regent Sq. Lin 85 D4
Regent St. Edin 125 D4
Regent St. Kin 23 F2
Regent Street La. Edin 125 D4
Regent Terr. Edin 93 F1
Regent Terrace Mews. Edin . 93 F1
Regents Way. D Bay 48 A3
Regis Ct. Edin 91 D2
Register Pl. Edin 93 E1
Register St. Edin 93 E1
Reid Ave. Cross 30 C3
Reid St. Dunf 29 D2
Reid St. Loch 14 A4
Reid Terr. Edin 93 D1
Reid's Cl. Edin 123 F4
Reilly Rd. Bon 58 A2
Relugas Gdns. Edin 123 F2
Relugas Pl. Edin 123 F2
Relugas Rd. Edin 123 F2
Rendall Gdns. Brox 117 F3
Rennie Pl. Lin 103 E4
Rennie Sq. Muri 173 E3
Rennie St. Falk 60 B2
Research Ave 1. Rat 151 F4
Research Ave 2. Rat 151 F4
Research Ave N. Rat 120 C1
Research Park Rd. Rat 151 F4
Restalrig Ave. Edin 94 B1

Restalrig Cir. Edin 94 B2
Restalrig Cres. Edin 94 B2
Restalrig Dr. Edin 94 B1
Restalrig Gdns. Edin 94 B1
Restalrig Pk. Edin 94 A2
Restalrig Rd. Edin 94 A2
Restalrig Rd S. Edin 94 B1
Restalrig Sq. Edin 94 B2
Restalrig Terr. Edin 94 A2
Reveston La. Whit 170 A3
Reynard Gdns. Madd 84 A3
Rhodders Gr. Alva 5 D4
Rhodes St. Dunf 29 D1
Riccarton Ave. Curr 152 A3
Riccarton Cres. Curr 152 A2
Riccarton Dr. Curr 152 A2
Riccarton Gr. Curr 152 A2
Riccarton Mains Rd. Curr ... 152 A3
Riccarton Mains Rd. Rat 152 A3
Riccarton Rd. Lin 84 C3
Richmond Dr. Pol 82 B4
Richmond La. Edin 123 F4
Richmond Pl. Edin 123 F4
Richmond Pl. Loch 14 A4
Richmond Terr. B'ness 63 F4
Riddochhill Cres. Black 171 E4
Riddochhill Ct. Black 171 E4
Riddochhill Dr. Black 171 E4
Riddochhill Rd. Black 171 E4
Riddochhill View. Black 171 E4
Ridge Way. D Bay 48 A3
Riding Pk. Edin 91 D2
Ridley Dr. Ros 46 C2
Rifle Rd. Gran 62 B4
Rig Pl. Aber 71 E2
Rig St. Aber 71 E2
Rigg Pk. Dunb 78 B1
Riggs View. Crossf 27 E1
Rigley Terr. Pres 127 F4
Rillbank Cres. Edin 123 E3
Rillbank Terr. Edin 123 E3
Rimmon Cres. Shot 191 F3
Ring Rd. All 10 A4
Ringwood Pl. Edin 155 D4
Rintoul Ave. Bla 26 A4
Rintoul Pl. Bla 26 A4
Rintoul Pl. Edin 93 D1
Riselaw Cres. Edin 154 A4
Riselaw Pl. Edin 154 A4
Riselaw Rd. Edin 154 A4
Riselaw Terr. Edin 154 A4
Ritchie Pl. B'ness 64 A3
Ritchie Pl. Edin 122 C3
Ritchie Pl. Gran 61 E3
Rivaldsgreen Cres. Lin 85 D3
River St. Falk 39 D1
River View. D Bay 48 A1
River Wlk. D Bay 48 A1
Riverbank View. Stir 7 E4
Riversdale Cres. Edin 122 B4
Riversdale Gr. Edin 122 B4
Riversdale Rd. Edin 122 B4
Riverside Ct. Liv 147 E2
Riverside Dr. Hadd 101 D1
Riverside. Edin 91 E4
Riverside Gdns. Muss 126 A3
Riverside. Kirkl 118 C3
Riverside Pl. Hadd 101 E1
Riverside Rd. B'ness 62 A2
Riverside Rd. Dal 90 C2
Riverside Terr. Kin 23 F2
Riverside View. All 10 A2
Road 10. Gran 62 B3
Road 11. Gran 62 B3
Road 13. Gran 62 B3
Road 15. Gran 62 B3
Road 24. Gran 62 A3
Road 25. Gran 62 A3
Road 27. Gran 62 A3
Road 28. Gran 62 A3
Road 30. Gran 62 A3
Road 30b. Gran 62 A3
Road 30c. Gran 62 A3
Road 31. Gran 62 A3
Road 32. Gran 62 A3
Road 33. B'ness 62 A3
Road 4. Gran 62 B3
Road 4a. Gran 62 B3
Road 4b. Gran 62 B3
Road 6. Gran 62 B3
Road 7. Gran 62 B3
Road 9. Gran 62 B3
Roanhead Terr. Kin 23 F3
Roanshead Rd. May 183 E4
Robb's Loan. Edin 122 B2
Robb's Loan Gr. Edin 122 B2
Robert Bruce Ct. Lar 38 A1
Robert Burns Dr. Edin 124 A1
Robert Burns Mews. Dalk .. 157 E2
Robert Dick Ct. Tull 4 B1
Robert Kinmond Ave. Tull 4 B1
Robert Knox Ave. Tull 4 B1
Robert Smilie Ave. May 183 F3
Robert Smith Ct. Loch 13 F3
Roberts Ave. Pol 61 E1
Roberts St. Shot 191 F2

Roberts St. Kirk 17 F4
Robertson Ave. Bath 144 C3
Robertson Ave. Bon 58 A3
Robertson Ave. Edin 122 B3
Robertson Ave. Pres 97 D1
Robertson Ave. Tran 128 B3
Robertson Bank. Gore 207 E3
Robertson Dr. Tran 128 B4
Robertson Pl. Stir 7 D2
Robertson Rd. Dunf 29 E3
Robertson St. Alva 5 D4
Robertson Way. Liv 147 E4
Robertson's Cl. Dalk 157 D2
Robertson's Cl. Edin 123 F4
Robertsons Bank. Gore 207 E4
Robins Neuk. Glad 129 E3
Rocheid Pk. Edin 92 C2
Rochester Terr. Edin 123 D2
Rocks Rd. Lime 45 D2
Rockville Gr. Lin 85 D3
Rockville Terr. Bonn 182 A4
Roddinglaw Rd. Kirkl 120 B2
Rodel Dr. Pol 61 F1
Rodney St. Edin 93 E1
Rodney St. Gran 61 E3
Roebuck Pl. B'ness 63 F3
Rolland St. Dunf 29 D2
Roman Camp Cotts. Pump . 117 E1
Roman Camp. Path 185 D2
Roman Camp Way. Path ... 185 D2
Roman Dr. Falk 59 F3
Roman Rd. Bon 58 A2
Roman Rd. Inver 47 D1
Roman Way. B'ness 63 E3
Romero Pl. Edin 123 F3
Romyn Rd. Ros 46 B1
Ronades Rd. Falk 60 A4
Ronald Cres. Lar 38 A1
Ronald Pl. Stir 7 D4
Ronaldsay Cres. Gran 61 F4
Ronaldson Gr. Dunf 29 D3
Ronaldson's Wharf. Edin 93 F3
Rood Well Cotts. E Lin 104 C1
Roods Cres. Inver 47 D2
Roods Gr. Inver 47 D1
Roods Sq. Inver 47 E2
Roomlin Gdns. Kirk 17 F4
Roosevelt Rd. Kir 149 F2
Rope Wlk. Pres 96 C1
Ropeway. Ros 46 A1
Rosabelle Rd. Rosl 180 C2
Rosabelle St. Kirk 17 F4
Rose Cres. Dunf 29 D2
Rose Ct. Edin 91 F2
Rose Gdns. Crossf 27 E1
Rose La. Loch 14 A4
Rose La. Que 68 A1
Rose La. Torr 26 C2
Rose Pk. Edin 93 D3
Rose St. All 4 C1
Rose St. Bon 58 A3
Rose St. Cow 13 E2
Rose St. Dunf 29 D2
Rose St. Edin 123 E4
Rose Street North La. Edin . 123 E4
Rose Street South La. Edin . 123 E4
Rose Terr. Den 36 C2
Rose Terr. Sten 38 C2
Rosebank Ave. Falk 59 F3
Rosebank Cotts. Edin 123 D4
Rosebank. Cow 13 E2
Rosebank. Dunf 29 E1
Rosebank Gdns. Dunf 29 E1
Rosebank Gdns. Edin 93 D3
Rosebank Gdns. Kin 23 F2
Rosebank Gr. Edin 93 D3
Rosebank. N Sau 5 E1
Rosebank Pl. Falk 59 F3
Rosebank Rd. Edin 93 D3
Rosebank Roundabout.
      W Cal 173 D4
Roseberry Ct. Que 89 E4
Roseberry Pl. Que 89 E4
Rosebery Ave. Que 89 E4
Rosebery Cres. Bath 145 D3
Rosebery Cres. Edin 122 C4
Rosebery Cres. Gore 207 E3
Rosebery Crescent La.
      Edin 122 C4
Rosebery Ct. D Bay 47 F1
Rosebery Gr. D Bay 47 F1
Rosebery Pl. D Bay 47 F1
Rosebery Rd. D Bay 47 F1
Rosebery Terr. Edin 2 A1
Rosebery Terr. Kirk 17 D3
Rosebery View. D Bay 47 F1
Roseburn Ave. Edin 122 B4
Roseburn Cliff. Edin 122 B4
Roseburn Cres. Edin 122 B4
Roseburn Dr. Edin 122 B4
Roseburn Gdns. Edin 122 B4
Roseburn Pl. Edin 122 B4
Roseburn St. Edin 122 B3
Roseburn Terr. Edin 122 B4
Rosecourt. Dunf 29 E2
Rosefield Ave. Edin 125 D4
Rosefield Avenue La. Edin . 125 D4

Rosefield La. Edin 125 D4
Rosefield Pl. Edin 125 D4
Rosefield St. Edin 125 D4
Rosehall Rd. Bath 144 B1
Rosehall Pl. Hadd 131 F4
Rosehall Rd. Shot 191 E2
Rosehall Terr. Falk 60 A2
Rosehill Cres. Cow 13 D2
Rosehill Terr. Dal 89 E4
Roseleta Dr. Pol 82 B4
Rosemead Terr. Cali 81 F3
Rosemill Ct. Torr 26 B1
Rosemount Ave. Kirk 17 D2
Rosemount Bldgs. Edin 123 D4
Rosemount Ct. Bath 145 D3
Rosemount Dr. Uph 116 C2
Rosemount Pl. Edin 123 E3
Roseneath Pl. Edin 123 E3
Roseneath Terr. Edin 123 E3
Rosevale Pl. Edin 94 A2
Rosevale Terr. Edin 94 A2
Roseville Gdns. Edin 93 E3
Rosewell Rd. Bonn 181 F2
Ross Ave. D Bay 48 A1
Ross Cres. Falk 59 E3
Ross Cres. Tran 128 B3
Ross Ct. Stir 7 F2
Ross Gdns. Edin 123 F2
Ross Gdns. Kirk 17 F4
Ross La. Dunf 28 C2
Ross Pl. Edin 123 F2
Ross Pl. King 34 C1
Ross Pl. Newt 183 D3
Ross Rd. Edin 123 F1
Ross St. Dunf 29 D3
Rossend Terr. Burn 50 B4
Rossie Pl. Edin 94 A1
Rossland Pl. King 34 C1
Rosslyn Cres. Edin 93 F2
Rosslyn St. Kirk 17 F4
Rosslyn Terr. Edin 93 F2
Rossness Dr. King 34 C1
Rothesay Mews. Edin 122 C4
Rothesay Pl. Edin 123 D4
Rothesay Pl. Muss 126 B3
Rothesay Terr. Edin 123 D4
Roughburn Rd. B of A 2 A4
Roughlands Cres. Sten 39 D2
Roughlands Dr. Sten 39 D2
Roull Gr. Edin 121 E3
Roull Pl. Edin 121 F3
Roull Rd. Edin 121 E3
Round The. Dunf 60 B4
Roundel The. Falk 60 B4
Roundelwood. N Sau 5 D1
Rowallan Ct. Edin 121 D4
Rowallen Dr. Bann 19 F4
Rowan Cres. Falk 59 D2
Rowan Ct. Bann 7 F1
Rowan Dr. Black 145 F1
Rowan Dr. Dunf 29 E1
Rowan Gr. Liv 148 A3
Rowan Rd. Black 145 E1
Rowan St. Dunb 78 A1
Rowan Terr. Black 171 E4
Rowan Terr. Cow 13 E2
Rowan Tree Ave. Curr 151 F2
Rowan Tree Gr. Curr 151 F2
Rowans The. Gull 52 A2
Rowans The. N Sau 5 E1
Rowantree Rd. May 183 F4
Roxburgh Pl. Edin 123 F4
Roxburgh Pl. Sten 38 C2
Roxburgh St. Edin 123 F4
Roxburgh Terr. Gran 61 F4
Roxburghe Pk. Dunb 78 C1
Roxburghe Terr. Dunb 78 C1
Royal Cir. Edin 93 E1
Royal Cres. Edin 93 E1
Royal Ct. Peni 203 E4
Royal Gdns. Stir 7 D4
Royal Park Terr. Edin 94 A1
Royal Scot Way. Dunf 29 D3
Royal Terr. Edin 93 F1
Royal Terr. Lin 84 C3
Royston Mains Ave. Edin 92 C3
Royston Mains Cl. Edin 92 C3
Royston Mains Cres. Edin ... 92 C3
Royston Mains Gdns. Edin .. 92 C3
Royston Mains Gn. Edin 92 C3
Royston Mains Pl. Edin 92 B3
Royston Mains Rd. Edin 92 C3
Royston Mains St. Edin 92 B3
Royston Rd. Liv 146 C4
Royston Terr. Edin 93 D2
Rulley View. Duni 36 B2
Rullion Green Ave. Peni ... 203 E4
Rullion Green Cres. Peni .. 203 E4
Rullion Green Gr. Peni 203 E3
Rullion Rd. Peni 203 E3
Rumblingwell. Dunf 28 B3
Rumlie The. Slam 110 A3
Run The. B'ness 64 B4
Runciman Pl. Kirk 17 E4
Rushbank. Liv 147 F3
Ruskie Rd. Stir 2 A2
Ruskin Pl. May 183 F3
Russel Ct. Loch 14 A4

254

Russel Pl. Edin

Silverknowes Pl. Edin

Russel Pl. Edin 93 D3
Russel St. Falk 60 A3
Russell Ave. Arm 143 F4
Russell Ct. Dunf 29 F1
Russell Gr. Burn 33 F1
Russell Pl. Kirk 17 E3
Russell Pl. Oak 26 C4
Russell Rd. Edin 122 C3
Russell St. Cow 13 D2
Russell St. Loch 14 A4
Rutherford Ct. B of A 2 A4
Rutherford Ct. Kirk 17 F4
Rutherford Dr. Edin 124 A1
Rutherford Sq. Muri 173 E3
Ruthven Rd. Dir 53 D2
Rutland Court La. Edin 123 D4
Rutland Sq. Edin 123 D4
Rutland St. Edin 123 D4
Ryebank. Liv 147 F3
Ryehill Ave. Edin 94 A2
Ryehill Gdns. Edin 94 A2
Ryehill Gr. Edin 94 A2
Ryehill Pl. Edin 94 A2
Ryehill Terr. Edin 94 A2

Saddletree Loan. Edin 124 B1
Sailors' Wlk. Burn 50 B4
Sainford Cres. Falk 39 D1
St Alban's Rd. Edin 123 F2
St Andrew Pl. Edin 94 A2
St Andrew Sq. Edin 93 E1
St Andrew St. Dalk 157 D2
St Andrew St. Dunf 29 E1
St Andrew St. N Ber 54 B4
St Andrew's Ct. Lar 38 A2
St Andrew's Dr. Air 22 A4
St Andrew's Dr. Arm 143 F4
St Andrew's Dr. Uph 116 C2
St Andrew's Way. Liv 146 C3
St Andrews Pl. Falk 60 A2
St Ann's Ave. Bonn 181 F3
St Ann's Path. Bonn 181 F3
St Anne's Cres. Bann 7 F1
St Anne's Ct. Newt 183 D3
St Anthony La. Edin 93 F3
St Anthony Pl. Edin 93 F3
St Anthony St. Edin 93 F3
St Baldred's Cres. N Ber 54 B4
St Baldred's Rd. N Ber 54 B3
St Bernard's Cres. Edin 93 D1
St Bernard's Row. Edin 93 D1
St Bridgets Brae. D Bay 48 B2
St Brycedale Ave. Kirk 17 D2
St Brycedale Rd. Kirk 17 D2
St Catherine. Madd 82 C4
St Catherine's Gdns. Edin 122 A3
St Catherine's Pl. Edin 123 F3
St Catherine's Wynd. Dunf 28 C2
St Catherines Cres. Shot 191 F3
St Clair Ave. Edin 94 A2
St Clair Cres. Rosl 181 D2
St Clair Pl. Edin 94 A2
St Clair Rd. Edin 94 A2
St Clair St. Edin 94 A2
St Clair St. Kirk 17 F4
St Clair Terr. Edin 122 C1
St Clement's Cres. Muss 127 D2
St Clement's Gdns N. Muss 127 D2
St Clement's Gdns S. Muss 127 D2
St Clement's Terr. Muss 127 D2
St Colme Ave. Abe 49 D3
St Colme Cres. Abe 49 D4
St Colme Dr. D Bay 48 B3
St Colme Rd. D Bay 48 B2
St Colme St. Edin 93 D1
St Crispin's Pl. Falk 60 A2
St David's Ct. D Bay 48 A2
St David's Ct. Lar 38 A1
St David's Pl. Edin 123 D4
St David's Terr. Edin 123 D4
St Davids. Newt 183 D3
St Fillan's Terr. Edin 123 D1
St Fillans Cres. Abe 49 E4
St Fillans Gr. Abe 49 E4
St Fillans Pl. Kirk 16 B4
St Fillans Rd. Kirk 16 B4
St George's Ct. Lar 38 A1
St Germains Terr. Glad 129 E3
St Giles Sq. Falk 59 D3
St Giles St. Edin 123 E4
St Giles Way. Falk 59 D3
St James' Orch. Stir 2 B1
St James' Pl. Edin 93 E1
St James Pl. King 35 D1
St James Sq. Edin 93 E1
St James's Gdns. Peni 203 F2
St James's View. Peni 203 F2
St John St. E Lin 106 B2
St John St. Edin 123 F4
St John St. Stir 7 D4
St John's Ave. Edin 121 F3
St John's Ave. Falk 60 B3
St John's Ave. Lin 84 C3
St John's Cres. Edin 121 F3
St John's Ct. Inver 47 E2
St John's Dr. Dunf 29 E2
St John's Gate. Den 36 B1
St John's Gdns. Den 36 B1
St John's Gdns. Edin 121 F3
St John's Gr. Den 36 B1
St John's Hill. Edin 123 F4
St John's Pl. Dunf 29 E2
St John's Pl. Torp 113 F3
St John's Rd. Brox 117 F2
St John's Rd. Edin 121 E3
St John's Terr. Edin 121 F3
St John's Way. B' ness 63 F3
St Joseph's Cotts. Tran 128 B4
St Katharine's Cres. Edin 155 D3
St Katharine's Loan. Edin 155 D3
St Katherine's Brae. Edin 155 D3
St Kentigern Rd. Peni 203 E3
St Kilda Cres. Kirk 16 C4
St Laurence Cres. Slam 110 A3
St Lawrence St. Dunf 29 E1
St Leonard's Bank. Edin 123 F3
St Leonard's Ct. King 35 D2
St Leonard's. Edin 123 F3
St Leonard's Hill. Edin 123 F3
St Leonard's La. Edin 123 F3
St Leonard's Pl. Dunf 29 D1
St Leonard's Pl. King 34 C2
St Leonard's St. Dunf 29 D1
St Leonard's St. Edin 123 F3
St Magdalene's. Lin 85 D4
St Margaret St. Dunf 29 D2
St Margaret's Cres. Pol 61 F1
St Margaret's Dr. Arm 143 F3
St Margaret's Rd. Edin 123 D2
St Margaret's Rd. N Ber 54 B4
St Margarets Ct. N Ber 54 B4
St Margarets Dr. Dunf 29 D2
St Mark's La. Edin 125 D4
St Mark's La. Edin 125 D4
St Mark's Pl. Edin 125 D4
St Martin's Ct. Hadd 132 B4
St Martin's Gate. Hadd 132 A4
St Martin's Pl. Hadd 132 B4
St Mary's Pl. Edin 125 E4
St Mary's Pl. Kirk 17 E3
St Mary's Place La. Edin 125 E4
St Mary's Rd. Kirk 17 E3
St Mary's St. Edin 123 F4
St Mary's Wynd. Stir 7 D4
St Marys Pl. Gran 61 F4
St Michael's Ave. Muss 126 B3
St Michael's Wynd. Lin 85 D4
St Modans Ct. Falk 60 A2
St Mungo's View. Peni 203 F3
St Ninian's Ave. Lin 84 C4
St Ninian's Dr. Edin 121 E4
St Ninian's Rd. Edin 121 E4
St Ninian's Rd. Lin 84 C4
St Ninian's Row. Edin 93 E1
St Ninian's Terr. Edin 122 C1
St Ninian's Way. Lin 84 C4
St Ninians Rd. Stir 6 C3
St Ninians Rd. Stir 7 D3
St Ninians Way. Muir 65 F2
St Patrick Sq. Edin 123 F3
St Patrick St. Edin 123 F3
St Paul's Dr. Arm 144 A3
St Peter's Ct. Inver 47 E2
St Ronan's Terr. Edin 123 D1
St Serf's Pl. Tull 4 A2
St Serf's Rd. Tull 4 A2
St Serf's Wlk. Alva 4 C3
St Serfs Gr. Clack 11 D2
St Stephen Pl. Edin 93 D1
St Stephen St. Edin 93 D1
St Teresa Pl. Edin 122 C2
St Thomas Rd. Edin 123 F2
St Thomas's Pl. Stir 6 C3
St Thomas's Well. Stir 6 B4
St Valery Dr. Stir 7 D2
St Vincent St. Edin 93 D1
Sainthill Ct. N Ber 54 A4
Salamanca Cres. Auch 204 A4
Salamander Pl. Edin 94 A3
Salamander St. Edin 94 A3
Salen Loan. Shot 192 A2
Salisbury Pl. Edin 123 F3
Salisbury Rd. Edin 123 F3
Salisbury St. Kirk 17 D3
Salisbury View. May 183 E3
Salmon Dr. Falk 59 F1
Salmon Inn Rd. Laur 61 E1
Salmon Inn Rd. Pol 61 E1
Salmond Pl. Edin 94 A1
Salt Preston Pl. Pres 96 C1
Saltcoats Dr. Gran 61 F4
Saltcoats Rd. Gran 62 A4
Saltcoats Rd. Gull 52 A1
Salter's Rd. Dalk 157 E3
Salter's Rd. Muss 127 D2
Salter's Rd. Path 186 A1
Salter's Rd. White 127 E3
Salters' Gr. Dalk 157 E2
Salters' Rd. Dalk 157 E2
Salters' Rd. Path 185 F1
Salters' Terr. Dalk 157 E2
Saltire Gdns. Ath 101 F4
Saltpans. Lime 45 D2
Salvage Rd. Ros 46 B1
Salvesen Cres. Edin 92 A3
Salvesen Gdns. Edin 92 A3
Salvesen Gr. Edin 92 A3
Salvesen Terr. Edin 92 A3
Samoa Terr. Auch 204 A4
Sand Port. Edin 94 A3
Sandeman Ct. Kin 23 F2
Sanderson Terr. Aucht 15 D1
Sanderson's Gr. Tran 128 B4
Sandersons Wynd. Tran 128 B4
Sandford Gdns. Edin 125 D4
Sandiland Dr. E Cal 148 A1
Sandilands. Lime 45 E2
Sandport Pl. Edin 93 F3
Sandport St. Edin 93 F3
Sands The. Hadd 132 A4
Sandy Loan. Gull 52 A1
Sandy Loan. Laur 61 D2
Sandy Rd. Abe 32 B3
Sandyford Ave. Madd 84 A3
Sandyhill Ave. Shot 192 A2
Sandyloan Cres. Laur 61 D2
Sandyvale Pl. Shot 192 A2
Sang Pl. Kirk 17 D2
Sang Rd. Kirk 17 D2
Sarazen Gn. Liv 147 D4
Sauchenbush Rd. Kirk 16 C3
Sauchie Ct. Bann 7 F1
Sauchiebank. Edin 122 C3
Saughbank. Uph 117 D3
Saughs The. Newt 183 D2
Saughton Ave. Edin 122 B2
Saughton Cres. Edin 122 A3
Saughton Gdns. Edin 122 A3
Saughton Gr. Edin 122 A3
Saughton Loan. Edin 122 A3
Saughton Mains Ave. Edin 121 F2
Saughton Mains Bank. Edin 122 A2
Saughton Mains Dr. Edin 121 F2
Saughton Mains Gdns. Edin 121 F2
Saughton Mains Gr. Edin 122 A2
Saughton Mains Loan. Edin 121 F2
Saughton Mains Pk. Edin 121 F2
Saughton Mains Pl. Edin 121 F2
Saughton Mains St. Edin 122 A2
Saughton Mains Terr. Edin 121 F2
Saughton Pk. Edin 122 A3
Saughton Rd. Edin 121 F2
Saughton Rd N. Edin 121 F3
Saughtonhall Ave. Edin 122 B3
Saughtonhall Ave W. Edin 122 A3
Saughtonhall Cir. Edin 122 B3
Saughtonhall Cres. Edin 122 A3
Saughtonhall Dr. Edin 122 A3
Saughtonhall Gdns. Edin 122 B3
Saughtonhall Gr. Edin 122 B3
Saughtonhall Pl. Edin 122 B3
Saughtonhall Terr. Edin 122 B3
Saunders St. Edin 93 D1
Saunders St. Kirk 17 D1
Savile Pl. Edin 123 F2
Savile Terr. Edin 123 F2
Sawers Ave. Den 36 B1
Saxe Coburg Pl. Edin 93 D1
Saxe Coburg St. Edin 93 D1
Schaw Ct. N Sau 5 E1
Schaw Rd. Pres 97 D1
Schawpark Ave. N Sau 5 E1
Schiltron Way. Bann 7 E2
Scholars' Brae. Burn 50 C4
School Brae. B' ness 63 F4
School Brae. Bonn 156 A1
School Brae. Dunb 105 F4
School Brae. Edin 91 D3
School Brae. Kirk 18 A4
School Gn. Bonn 156 A1
School Gn. Long 98 C3
School La. Alla 212 A4
School La. Bath 145 D3
School La. Cocke 97 E2
School La. E Cal 148 B2
School La. Men 4 A4
School Pl. Uph 116 C2
School Rd. Aber 71 E2
School Rd. E Lin 103 F4
School Rd. Fau 170 B1
School Rd. Laur 61 D1
School Rd. Laur 61 D2
School Rd. N Ber 54 B4
School Rd. Tull 4 A1
School Row. Dunf 28 B3
School St. Cow 13 E2
School St. Shot 191 F2
School Wlk. Sten 38 B2
School Wynd. Kirk 17 D1
Sciennes. Edin 123 F3
Sciennes Gdns. Edin 123 F3
Sciennes Hill Pl. Edin 123 F3
Sciennes House Pl. Edin 123 F3
Sciennes Pl. Edin 123 F3
Sciennes Rd. Edin 123 E3
Sclandersburn Rd. Den 57 E4
Scobie Pl. Dunf 29 E2
Scollon Ave. Bonn 182 B4
Scone Gdns. Edin 94 B1
Scotia Pl. Falk 60 B3
Scotland Dr. Dunf 29 F2
Scotland St. Edin 93 E1
Scotlands Cl. B' ness 63 F4
Scotmill Way. Inver 47 E2
Scotstoun Ave. Que 89 E4
Scotstoun Gn. Que 89 D4
Scotstoun Pk. Que 89 E4
Scotstoun Rd. Cowie 20 C4
Scott Ave. Pol 61 F1
Scott Cres. All 10 A3
Scott Ct. Liv 148 B3
Scott Pl. Fau 193 F3
Scott Rd. Peni 203 F4
Scott St. Dunf 28 C3
Scott St. Gran 61 E3
Scott St. Kirk 17 D1
Scott St. Stir 2 A1
Scott Terr. Bath 145 E3
Seabegs Cres. Bon 58 A2
Seabegs Pl. Bon 57 F2
Seabegs Rd. Bon 57 F2
Seacliff. E Lin 56 A3
Seacot. Edin 94 B2
Seafield Ave. Edin 94 B2
Seafield Cres. Dunb 78 A1
Seafield Ct. Falk 59 F1
Seafield Moor Rd. Rosl 180 B3
Seafield Pl. D Bay 48 A1
Seafield Pl. Edin 94 B2
Seafield Rd. Black 171 F4
Seafield Rd. Edin 94 B2
Seafield Rd. Kirk 35 D4
Seafield Rd. Rosl 180 C3
Seafield Road E. Edin 94 C2
Seafield Rows. Black 146 A1
Seafield St. Edin 94 B2
Seafield View. King 35 D2
Seafield View. Kirk 35 D4
Seafield Way. Edin 94 C2
Seaforth Dr. Edin 92 B1
Seaforth Pl. Burn 50 C4
Seaforth Pl. Kirk 17 F4
Seaforth Pl. Stir 7 D4
Seaforth Rd. Falk 39 E1
Seaforth Terr. Bonn 181 F3
Sealcar St. Edin 92 C4
Sealock Ct. Gran 61 E3
Sealstrand. D Bay 48 B2
Seaport St. Edin 94 A3
Seaside Pl. Abe 49 E4
Seaton Pl. Falk 60 B2
Seaview Cres. Edin 125 F4
Seaview Pl. B' ness 63 F4
Seaview Terr. Edin 125 F4
Seco Pl. Cow 13 E2
Second Gait. Rat 151 F4
Second St. Newt 183 D2
Sedgebank. Liv 147 F3
Seggarsdean Ct. Hadd 132 B4
Seggarsdean Pk. Hadd 132 B4
Seggarsdean Terr. Hadd 132 B4
Selkirk Ave. Cow 13 E1
Selkirk Rd. Ros 67 D4
Selm Pk. Liv 148 A2
Selvage Pl. Ros 47 D2
Selvage St. Ros 47 D2
Semple St. Edin 123 D4
Seton Ct. Cocke 97 F2
Seton Ct. Tran 128 B3
Seton Dr. Stir 7 E2
Seton Mains. Cocke 98 A2
Seton Pl. Cocke 97 E2
Seton Pl. D Bay 48 B3
Seton Pl. Edin 123 F3
Seton Pl. Kirk 16 B4
Seton Rd. Long 98 C3
Seton Terr. B'ness 64 A4
Seton View. Cocke 97 F2
Seton Wynd. Cocke 97 F2
Seventh St. Newt 183 D3
Shadepark Cres. Dalk 157 D2
Shadepark Dr. Dalk 157 D2
Shadepark Gdns. Dalk 157 D2
Shaftesbury Pk. Edin 122 C2
Shaftesbury St. All 10 A4
Shafto Pl. B' ness 63 F3
Shamrock Pl. Cow 13 D2
Shamrock St. Dunf 29 D3
Shandon Cres. Edin 122 C2
Shandon Pl. Edin 122 C2
Shandon Rd. Edin 122 C2
Shandon St. Edin 122 C2
Shandon Terr. Edin 122 C2
Shandwick Pl. Edin 123 D4
Shanks Ave. Den 57 F4
Shanks Rd. Whit 170 A4
Shannon Dr. Falk 59 F2
Sharp Terr. Gran 61 E3
Sharpdale Loan. Edin 124 A2
Shaw Ave. Arm 143 F3
Shaw Cres. Loch 14 A4
Shaw Pl. Arm 143 F3
Shaw Pl. Gran 61 E3
Shaw Pl. May 183 E4
Shaw St. Dunf 29 E1
Shaw's Pl. Edin 93 F2
Shaw's Sq. Edin 93 F1
Shaw's St. Edin 93 F
Shaw's Terr. Edin 93 F
Shaws Ct. Auch 180 A
Sheephousehill. Fau 193 F
Sheperdlands Gr. Bla 26 B
Shepherd Cres. Burn 50 B
Sherbrooke Rd. Ros 46 B
Sheriff Bank. Edin 93 F
Sheriff Brae. Edin 93 F
Sheriff Pk. Edin 93 F
Sheriffhall Junction. Dan 156 B
Sheriffmuir Rd. B of A 2 B
Sheriffmuirlands. Stir 2 B
Sheriffs Pk. Lin 85 F
Sherriff Hall Cotts. E Lin 74 C
Sherriff La. Sten 38 C
Sherwood Ave. Bonn 182 B
Sherwood Cres. Bonn 182 B
Sherwood Ct. Bonn 182 B
Sherwood Dr. Bonn 182 B
Sherwood Gr. Bonn 182 B
Sherwood Ind Est. Bonn 182 B
Sherwood Loan. Bonn 182 B
Sherwood Pk. Bonn 182 B
Sherwood Pl. Bonn 182 B
Sherwood Terr. Bonn 182 B
Sherwood View. Bonn 182 B
Sherwood Way. Bonn 182 B
Sherwood Wlk. Bonn 182 B
Shetland Ct. All 10 A3
Shetland Pl. Kirk 17 F4
Shiel Ct. Gran 61 E2
Shiel Gdns. Falk 39 E1
Shiel Gdns. Shot 192 A2
Shiel Wlk. Liv 148 A3
Shields Rd. Dunf 29 F2
Shieling The. Crossf 27 F1
Shillinghill. All 10 A3
Shinwell Pl. Ros 46 C2
Shiphaugh Pl. Stir 2 B1
Shire Way. All 9 F3
Shirra's Brae Rd. Stir 7 E2
Shoestanes Rd. Stow 228 B1
Shoestanes Terr. Stow 228 B1
Shore. Edin 94 A3
Shore Pl. Edin 94 A3
Shore Rd. Abe 49 E4
Shore Rd. Air 22 B2
Shore Rd. Kirk 18 A3
Shore Rd. Que 68 A1
Shore Rd. Stir 7 D4
Shore St. Dunb 78 C2
Shore The. All 10 A3
Shorthope St. Muss 126 B3
Shotts Rd. Fau 193 E2
Shotts Rd. Sals 167 F1
Shottsburn Rd. Sals 167 D2
Shottskirk Rd. Shot 191 E3
Shrub Mount. Edin 95 D1
Shrub Place La. Edin 93 F1
Sibbald Pl. Liv 147 D3
Sibbalds Brae. Bath 144 B3
Sidegate. Hadd 132 A4
Sidehead Rd. East 168 C3
Sidlaw Pl. Gran 61 F3
Sidlaw St. Kirk 16 C4
Sienna Gdns. Edin 123 F3
Sighthill Ave. Edin 121 F1
Sighthill Bank. Edin 121 E1
Sighthill Cres. Edin 121 E1
Sighthill Ct. Edin 121 E1
Sighthill Dr. Edin 121 E1
Sighthill Gdns. Edin 121 E1
Sighthill Gn. Edin 121 E1
Sighthill Gr. Edin 121 F1
Sighthill Ind Est. Edin 121 D2
Sighthill Loan. Edin 121 E1
Sighthill Neuk. Edin 121 E1
Sighthill Pk. Edin 121 F1
Sighthill Pl. Edin 121 E1
Sighthill Rd. Edin 121 E1
Sighthill Rise. Edin 121 E1
Sighthill St. Edin 121 E1
Sighthill Terr. Edin 121 E1
Sighthill View. Edin 121 E1
Sighthill Wynd. Edin 121 E1
Silver St. Dunb 78 B1
Silver St. Kin 23 F2
Silverbarton Terr. Burn 33 E1
Silverburn Dr. Peni 203 E3
Silverdale Rd. Pol 82 C4
Silverknowes Ave. Edin 91 F2
Silverknowes Bank. Edin 91 F2
Silverknowes Brae. Edin 92 A2
Silverknowes Cres. Edin 91 F2
Silverknowes Ct. Edin 91 F2
Silverknowes Dell. Edin 91 F2
Silverknowes Dr. Edin 91 F2
Silverknowes Eastway. Edin 91 F2
Silverknowes Gdns. Edin 92 A2
Silverknowes Gn. Edin 92 A2
Silverknowes Gr. Edin 91 F2
Silverknowes Hill. Edin 91 F2
Silverknowes Loan. Edin 91 F2
Silverknowes Midway. Edin 92 A2
Silverknowes Neuk. Edin 92 A2
Silverknowes Parkway. Edin 91 F3
Silverknowes Pl. Edin 91 F3

255

Silverknowes Rd E. Edin

Stoneyhill Dr. Muss

Silverknowes Rd E. Edin 92 A2
Silverknowes Rd. Edin 91 F3
Silverknowes Rd S. Edin 91 F2
Silverknowes Southway. Edin 92 A2
Silverknowes Terr. Edin 91 F2
Silverknowes View. Edin 92 A2
Simon Sq. Edin 123 F4
Simpson Cres. Bath 145 E3
Simpson Dr. Madd 83 D3
Simpson Parkway. Liv 147 D1
Simpson Parkway. W Cal 173 D4
Simpson Rd. Brox 118 A3
Simpson St. Falk 59 F3
Simpson Wlk. Dunf 29 F1
Sinclair Cres. Den 36 B1
Sinclair Ct. Aber 71 E2
Sinclair Ct. Bann 7 F1
Sinclair Dr. Cow 13 D1
Sinclair Dr. Fall 8 B2
Sinclair Way. Liv 147 E3
Sir George Bruce Rd. Oak 26 C4
Sir Harry Lauder Rd. Edin 125 D4
Sir James Black Gait. Loch 14 A4
Sir Walter Scott Pend. Pres 96 C1
Sir William Fraser Homes. Edin 153 D4
Sixth St. Newt 183 D3
Skaithmuir Ave. Sten 39 D2
Skaithmuir Cres. Sten 39 D2
Skelmorlie Pl. Sten 38 C2
Skeltie Muir Ave. Bonn 182 A3
Skeltiemuir Ct. Bonn 182 A3
Skeltiemuir Gr. Bonn 182 A3
Skene St. Bon 58 A3
Skibo Ct. Dunf 29 D2
Skibo Pl. Kirk 16 B3
Skye Ct. Gran 61 E3
Skye Dr. Pol 61 F1
Skye Rd. Dunf 29 F1
Skylaw Terr. For 215 D1
Skythorn Way. Falk 59 F1
Slaeside. Bale 151 E1
Slamannan Rd. Avon 112 A3
Slamannan Rd. Falk 60 A1
Slamannan Rd. Slam 110 A1
Slateford Rd. Edin 122 B2
Sleigh Dr. Edin 94 B1
Sleigh Gdns. Edin 94 B1
Sligo St. Oak 26 C4
Sloan St. Edin 93 F2
Small St. Loch 14 A3
Smallburn Pl. Gran 61 F3
Smeaton Gdns. Kirk 17 E3
Smeaton Gr. Muss 126 B2
Smeaton Rd. Kirk 17 E3
Smith Ave. Cow 13 D2
Smith Pl. Den 36 B1
Smith St. Falk 60 A4
Smith's Pl. Edin 93 F2
Smith's Terr. Kirk 17 E3
Smithfield Loan. All 9 F3
Smithfield St. Edin 122 B3
Smithy Brae. Kir 149 F1
Smithy Gn Ave. Dan 156 A4
Smithy Row. Ath 74 A2
Snab Brae. B' ness 63 E3
Snab La. B' ness 63 E4
Snowdon Pl. Stir 7 D3
Snowdon Place La. Stir 7 D3
Society La. W Cal 172 B2
Society Pl. W Cal 172 B2
Society Rd. Que 67 F1
Solway Dr. Bank 57 E4
Somerset Pl. Edin 94 A2
Somerville Rd. Ros 46 B1
Somerville Sq. Burn 50 C4
Somerville St. Burn 50 C4
Sommers Pk. E Cal 148 B1
Sommerville Gdns. Que 89 E4
Somnerfield Ave. Hadd 131 F4
Somnerfield Cres. Hadd 131 F4
Somnerfield Ct. Hadd 131 F4
Somnerfield Gr. Hadd 131 F4
Somnerfield Pk. Hadd 131 F4
Souillac Dr. Den 36 B1
South Approach Rd. Air 23 D1
South Ave. Bla 26 A4
South Ave. Madd 83 D4
South Bantaskine Rd. Falk 60 A2
South Barnton Ave. Edin 91 F2
South Beechwood. Edin 122 A3
South Brae. Madd 83 D3
South Bridge. Edin 123 E4
South Bridge St. Bath 145 D3
South Bridge St. Gran 40 B1
South Broomage Ave. Lar 38 B1
South Charlotte St. Edin 123 D4
South Clerk St. Edin 123 F3
South College St. Edin 123 E4
South Craigs Rd. Madd 82 C4
South Cres. Pres 97 D1
South Dewar St. Dunf 28 C2
South Doors. Cocke 97 E2
South Dr. Dunf 46 C3
South Drummond St. Edin 123 F4
South East Circus Pl. Edin 93 D1
South East Cumberland Street La. Edin 93 E1
South East Thistle Street La. Edin 93 E1
South Ettrick Rd. Edin 122 C2
South Fergus Pl. Kirk 17 D2
South Fort St. Edin 93 F3
South Gait. N Ber 53 F4
South Gayfield La. Edin 93 F1
South Gillsland Rd. Edin 122 C2
South Grange Ave. Pres 127 F4
South Gray St. Edin 123 F2
South Gray's Cl. Edin 123 F4
South Green Dr. Air 22 C2
South Groathill Ave. Edin 92 B1
South Gyle Access. Edin 121 E2
South Gyle Broadway. Edin 121 D2
South Gyle Broadway. Kirkl 120 C3
South Gyle Cres. Edin 121 D2
South Gyle Cres La. Edin 121 D2
South Gyle Gdns. Edin 121 D3
South Gyle Loan. Edin 121 D3
South Gyle Mains. Edin 121 D3
South Gyle Pk. Edin 121 D3
South Gyle Rd. Edin 121 D3
South Gyle Wynd. Edin 121 E2
South Hill St. Burn 50 C4
South Hirst Rd. Sals 167 E2
South Lauder Rd. Edin 123 F2
South Laverockbank Ave. Edin 93 E3
South Learmonth Ave. Edin 92 C1
South Loanhead. Lime 45 F2
South Loch Pk. Bath 145 D3
South Lodge Ave. E Cal 148 B1
South Lorimer Pl. Cocke 97 E2
South Lorne Pl. Edin 93 F2
South Lumley St. Gran 61 E4
South Marshall St. Gran 61 E4
South Maybury. Edin 121 D3
South Mellis Pk. Edin 124 C4
South Melville La. Falk 60 A3
South Mid St. Bath 145 D3
South Morton St. Edin 125 E4
South Oswald Rd. Edin 123 E2
South Overgate. King 35 D2
South Oxford St. Edin 123 F3
South Park. Arm 143 F2
South Philpingstone La. B'ness 64 B4
South Pilmuir Rd. Clack 11 D2
South Pk. Edin 93 E3
South Pleasance Ave. Falk 60 A2
South Rd. B'ness 62 A3
South Rd. Fau 193 F4
South Riggs Acres. Crossf 27 E1
South Roundall. Lime 45 F2
South Row. Kirk 17 F4
South Row. Lime 45 D2
South Scotstoun. Que 89 E4
South Seton Pk. Cocke 97 E2
South Shore Rd. Gran 41 D1
South Sloan St. Edin 93 F2
South St Andrew St. Edin 93 E1
South St. Arm 143 F3
South St. B' ness 63 F4
South St. Camb 9 D4
South St. Cow 13 E1
South St. Dalk 157 D2
South St David St. Edin 123 E4
South St. Dunb 78 A1
South St. Loch 14 A3
South St. Muss 126 A3
South St. Stir 2 B1
South Trinity Rd. Edin 93 D3
South View. Burn 50 C4
South View. Lar 38 B1
South Village. Pump 148 B3
South West Cumberland Street La. Edin 93 E1
South West Thistle Street La. Edin 93 E1
Southbank Ct. Edin 91 F2
Southcroft. Alva 4 C3
Southerton Cres. Kirk 16 C2
Southerton Gdns. Kirk 16 C2
Southerton Rd. Kirk 16 C2
Southfield Ave. Shot 192 A2
Southfield Bank. Edin 124 C3
Southfield. Cow 13 E3
Southfield Cres. Shot 192 A2
Southfield Cres. Stir 7 D3
Southfield Dr. Slam 110 A3
Southfield Farm Gr. Edin 124 C4
Southfield Gdns E. Edin 124 C4
Southfield Gdns W. Edin 124 C3
Southfield Loan. Edin 124 C3
Southfield Pl. Edin 125 D4
Southfield Rd E. Edin 124 C3
Southfield Rd. Path 158 B3
Southfield Rd. Shot 192 A2
Southfield Rd W. Edin 124 C3
Southfield Sq. Edin 124 C3
Southfield Terr. Edin 124 C3
Southhouse Ave. Edin 155 D3
Southhouse Broadway. Edin 155 D2
Southhouse Cres. Edin 155 E2
Southhouse Gdns. Edin 155 D2
Southhouse Gr. Edin 155 D2
Southhouse Loan. Edin 155 D3
Southhouse Medway. Edin 155 D3
Southhouse Rd. Edin 155 D2
Southhouse Sq. Edin 155 D3
Southhouse Terr. Edin 155 E3
Southlawn Ct. Edin 91 F2
Spa Pl. Edin 95 D1
Spalding Cres. Dalk 157 D2
Speedwell Ave. Dan 156 A4
Spence Ave. Burn 33 F1
Spence St. Bon 58 A3
Spence St. Edin 123 F3
Spencer Pl. Edin 93 D3
Spencer Pl. Kirk 17 F4
Spencerfield Rd. Inver 47 E1
Spencerfield Steadings. Inver 47 F2
Spens La. Ros 46 B1
Spey Ct. Gran 61 E3
Spey Ct. Stir 7 E3
Spey Dr. Liv 148 A2
Spey St. Edin 93 F2
Spey Street La. Edin 93 F2
Spey Terr. Edin 93 F2
Spier's Pl. Edin 93 F3
Spinkhill. Laur 60 C1
Spinner's Ct. Crossf 27 E1
Spinney The. Edin 155 E3
Spinneys The. D Bay 48 B2
Spittal Hill. B of A 2 B2
Spittal St. Edin 123 D4
Spittal St. Stir 7 D4
Spittalfield Cres. Inver 47 E1
Spittalfield Rd. Inver 47 E1
Spott Ave. E Lin 106 B2
Spott Loan. E Lin 106 B2
Spott Rd. Dunb 78 C1
Spottiswoode Gdns. E Cal 148 B1
Spottiswoode Rd. Edin 123 E3
Spottiswoode St. Edin 123 E3
Sprig Way. East 168 C3
Spring Gdns. Edin 94 A1
Springbank Gdns. Falk 60 B3
Springbank Rd. Shot 191 E3
Springbank Rd. Stir 7 E3
Springbank Terr. Dunf 29 D3
Springfield Cres. N Ber 54 A4
Springfield Cres. Que 67 F1
Springfield Ct. Lin 85 E4
Springfield Dr. Falk 59 F3
Springfield. Dunb 105 F4
Springfield. Edin 93 F2
Springfield Gdns. N Ber 54 A4
Springfield Lea. Que 67 F1
Springfield Pl. Gore 207 E4
Springfield Pl. Que 67 F1
Springfield Pl. Rosl 181 D2
Springfield Rd. All 10 B4
Springfield Rd. Den 36 C1
Springfield Rd. How 222 C3
Springfield Rd. Lin 85 E4
Springfield Rd. Que 67 F1
Springfield Rd. Stir 7 E3
Springfield St. Edin 93 F2
Springfield Terr. Dunb 77 F1
Springfield Terr. Que 67 F1
Springfield View. Que 68 A1
Springhead Rd. Alla 212 A4
Springhill And Leadloch Rd. Shot 192 C1
Springhill Brae. Cross 30 C3
Springhill Rd. Shot 192 A2
Springkerse Rd. Stir 7 E3
Springvalley Gdns. Edin 123 D2
Springvalley Terr. Edin 123 D2
Springwell Pl. Edin 122 C3
Springwood Ave. Stir 6 C3
Springwood Pk. Edin 155 D4
Sprinty Ave. Orm 159 E4
Sprinty Dr. Orm 159 E4
Sprotwell Terr. N Sau 5 E1
Spruce Dr. Whit 170 B3
Spruce Gr. Dunf 46 B4
Spruce Gr. Liv 148 A3
Spylaw Ave. Edin 152 C4
Spylaw Bank Rd. Edin 153 D4
Spylaw Pk. Edin 152 C4
Spylaw Rd. Edin 122 C2
Spylaw St. Edin 153 D4
Square The. Cock 140 C2
Square The. Dan 156 A4
Square The. E Lin 103 F4
Square The. E Lin 106 B2
Square The. Fall 8 B2
Square The. Giff 163 F3
Square The. Kirkl 89 D1
Square The. Newt 183 D3
Square The. Peni 203 F2
Square The. Torp 113 F3
Stable La. Edin 123 D2
Stable Rd. Shot 192 A3
Stables Rd. Ros 46 B1
Staffa. Liv 146 C3
Staffa Pl. Falk 60 A1
Stafford St. Edin 123 D4
Stair Pk. Edin 122 B4
Stair Pk. Tran 128 A4
Standalane. Kin 23 F2
Standing Stone Wlk. Dunf 29 F1
Standingstane Rd. Dal 89 F3
Standingstane Rd. Que 89 F3
Standrigg Rd. Cali 82 A3
Standrigg Rd. Shi 82 A3
Stane Rd. Shot 192 A1
Stanedykehead. Edin 154 C3
Stanhope Pl. Edin 122 C4
Stanhope St. Edin 122 C4
Stanistone Rd. Car 230 A1
Stankards Rd. Uph 116 C2
Stanley Ave. Rosl 180 C3
Stanley Dr. B of A 2 A4
Stanley Dr. Hart 169 D3
Stanley Pl. Edin 94 A1
Stanley Pl. Orm 159 F4
Stanley Rd. Edin 93 E3
Stanley Rd. Hart 169 D3
Stanley St. Edin 125 D4
Stanley Terr. Oak 27 D3
Stanton Ave. All 9 F3
Stanwell St. Edin 93 F2
Stapeley Ave. Edin 94 C1
Starbank Rd. Edin 93 E3
Stark Ave. Falk 59 E3
Stark's Brae. B'ness 64 A4
Starlaw Ave. Bog 145 F3
Starlaw Cres. Bog 145 F3
Starlaw Gdns. Bog 145 F3
Starlaw Rd. Black 146 B2
Starlaw Rd. Liv 146 C2
Starlaw Terr. Bog 145 F3
Starlaw West Roundabout. Black 146 A2
Starlaw Walk. Bog 145 F3
Starryshaw Rd. Shot 191 F3
Station Ave. Hadd 131 F4
Station Brae. Edin 125 D4
Station Brae. King 34 C1
Station Ct. Hadd 131 F4
Station Ct. N Ber 54 A4
Station Hill. N Ber 54 A4
Station Loan. Bale 151 E2
Station Rd. Add 171 F1
Station Rd. Arm 143 F2
Station Rd. B of A 1 C4
Station Rd. Bann 7 F1
Station Rd. Blac 142 B1
Station Rd. Brox 116 C2
Station Rd. Brox 117 F3
Station Rd. Camb 4 A1
Station Rd. Cow 13 E2
Station Rd. Cowie 20 B3
Station Rd. Dal 89 E4
Station Rd. Dalk 156 C1
Station Rd. Dir 53 E3
Station Rd. Dunb 78 C1
Station Rd. E Lin 53 E2
Station Rd. E Lin 103 F4
Station Rd. Edin 121 F3
Station Rd. Giff 163 F3
Station Rd. Gore 207 E4
Station Rd. Gran 40 B1
Station Rd. Gull 52 A1
Station Rd. Kin 23 E2
Station Rd. Kir 149 E2
Station Rd. Kirk 17 D2
Station Rd. Kirk 18 A4
Station Rd. Kirkl 89 D1
Station Rd. Kirkl 119 E3
Station Rd. Lin 85 D4
Station Rd. Loan 181 E4
Station Rd. Loch 14 A4
Station Rd. Madd 83 F3
Station Rd. Muss 126 B3
Station Rd. N Ber 54 A4
Station Rd. Newt 183 D3
Station Rd. Oak 26 C3
Station Rd. Pol 61 F1
Station Rd. Pol 82 C4
Station Rd. Pres 128 A4
Station Rd. Pump 117 D1
Station Rd. Que 68 B1
Station Rd. Rosl 181 D2
Station Rd. Shot 191 F2
Station Rd. Slam 110 A3
Station Rd. Stir 7 D4
Station Rd. Tull 4 A1
Station Rd. Uph 116 C2
Station Row. Slam 110 A3
Station Terr. Kirkl 89 D1
Staunton Rise. Muri 173 E4
Stead's Pl. Edin 93 F2
Steading The. Glad 98 B1
Steadings The. Pol 84 A4
Steel Gr. Bla 26 B4
Steel's Pl. Edin 123 D2
Steele Ave. May 183 F3
Steelyard The. Bath 145 D3
Steeple Cres. D Bay 48 A2
Steil Gr. Tran 128 B3
Steils The. Edin 122 C1
Stein Sq. Bann 7 F1
Stein's Pl. Cow 13 E2
Stenhouse Ave. Edin 122 A2
Stenhouse Ave W. Edin 122 A2
Stenhouse Cotts. Edin 122 A2
Stenhouse Cres. Edin 122 A2
Stenhouse Cross. Edin 122 A2
Stenhouse Dr. Burn 33 E1
Stenhouse Dr. Edin 122 A2
Stenhouse Gdns. Edin 122 A2
Stenhouse Gdns N. Edin 122 A2
Stenhouse Gr. Edin 122 A2
Stenhouse Mill Cres. Edin 122 A2
Stenhouse Mill La. Edin 122 A2
Stenhouse Mill Wynd. Edin 122 A2
Stenhouse Pl E. Edin 122 A2
Stenhouse Pl W. Edin 122 A2
Stenhouse Rd. Edin 122 A2
Stenhouse Rd. Sten 38 C1
Stenhouse St. Cow 13 D2
Stenhouse St E. Edin 122 A2
Stenhouse St W. Edin 121 F2
Stenhouse Terr. Edin 122 A2
Stennis Gdns. Edin 155 E4
Stenton Loan. E Lin 104 C1
Stenton Loan. E Lin 135 F4
Stenton Rd. Dunb 105 F4
Stephen Pl. Loch 14 A4
Stephen's Dr. Inver 47 E2
Steps St. Sten 38 C2
Steuart Rd. B of A 1 C4
Stevenlaw's Cl. Edin 123 E4
Stevenson Ave. Edin 122 B3
Stevenson Ct. B of A 2 A3
Stevenson Ct. Liv 148 B3
Stevenson Ct. Long 98 B2
Stevenson Dr. Edin 122 A2
Stevenson Gr. Edin 122 B3
Stevenson La. Newt 183 D2
Stevenson Pk. Long 98 B2
Stevenson Pl. Rose 181 E3
Stevenson Rd. Auch 204 A4
Stevenson Rd. Edin 122 B3
Stevenson St. Gran 61 E3
Stevenson Terr. Bath 145 E3
Stevenson Terr. Edin 122 B3
Stevenson Way. Long 98 B2
Stewart Ave. B' ness 63 F4
Stewart Ave. Curr 151 F2
Stewart Ave. Lin 84 C3
Stewart Clark Ave. Que 89 E4
Stewart Cres. Curr 151 F2
Stewart Cres. Loch 14 A4
Stewart Dr. Whit 169 F4
Stewart Gdns. Curr 151 F2
Stewart Gr. East 168 C3
Stewart Pk. Path 158 B3
Stewart Pl. Curr 151 F2
Stewart Pl. Kirkl 89 D1
Stewart Rd. Curr 151 F2
Stewart Rd. Falk 60 B3
Stewart Sq. Stir 2 A1
Stewart St. Bon 57 F3
Stewart St. Cam 6 B3
Stewart St. Dunf 29 E4
Stewart St. Kirk 18 A4
Stewart St. W Cal 172 B1
Stewart Terr. Edin 122 C3
Stewart Terr. Que 68 A1
Stewart Way. Liv 147 E3
Stewartfield Cres. Brox 117 F3
Stewartfield. Edin 93 E2
Stewartfield Rd. Brox 117 F3
Stirling Rd. All 9 F4
Stirling Rd. Alva 4 C4
Stirling Rd. Edin 93 D3
Stirling Rd. Falk 59 E4
Stirling Rd. Fall 8 B2
Stirling Rd. Lar 38 A1
Stirling Rd. Tor 37 F3
Stirling Rd. Tull 4 A2
Stirling St. Alva 5 D4
Stirling St. Den 36 C1
Stirling St. Duni 36 B2
Stobhill Rd. Gore 183 D2
Stobhill Rd. Newt 183 D2
Stobie Pl. Oak 26 C4
Stobs Pl. Kirk 16 B4
Stone Ave. May 183 E3
Stone Pl. May 183 E3
Stonebank. Liv 147 F3
Stonedyke Cres. Car 230 A2
Stonedyke Rd. Car 230 A2
Stonelaws Cotts. E Lin 75 D3
Stoneybank Ave. Muss 126 A2
Stoneybank Cres. Muss 126 A2
Stoneybank Ct. Muss 126 A3
Stoneybank Dr. Muss 126 A3
Stoneybank Gdns. Muss 126 A3
Stoneybank Gdns N. Muss 126 A3
Stoneybank Gdns S. Muss 126 A3
Stoneybank Gr. Muss 126 A2
Stoneybank Pl. Muss 126 A2
Stoneybank Rd. Muss 126 A2
Stoneybank Terr. Muss 126 A2
Stoneyflatts Cres. Que 89 D4
Stoneyflatts. Que 89 D4
Stoneyhill Ave. Muss 126 A3
Stoneyhill Cres. Muss 126 A3
Stoneyhill Ct. Muss 126 A3
Stoneyhill Dr. Muss 126 A3

Stoneyhill Farm Rd. Muss.

Stoneyhill Farm Rd. Muss . 126 A3
Stoneyhill Gr. Muss 126 A3
Stoneyhill Pl. Muss 126 A3
Stoneyhill Rd. Muss 126 A3
Stoneyhill Rise. Muss 126 A3
Stoneyhill Steadings. Muss 126 A3
Stoneyhill Ter. Muss 126 A3
Stoneyhill Wynd. Muss 126 A3
Stoneywood Pk. Duni 36 A1
Stony Brae. Kin 2 B1
Stony Croft Rd. Que 68 B1
Stories Pk. E Lin 103 F4
Strachan Gdns. Edin 92 A1
Strachan Rd. Edin 92 A1
Strachan St. Falk 59 F2
Straehouse Wynd. Car 230 A1
Straiton Mains. Edin 155 D1
Straiton Pl. Edin 125 D4
Straiton Rd. Edin 155 D1
Straiton Rd. Loan 180 C4
Strang's Pl. Cal 81 F3
Strathallan Ct. B of A 2 A3
Strathallan Dr. Kirk 16 C3
Strathallan Rd. B of A 2 A3
Strathalmond Ct. Edin 90 C2
Strathalmond Gn. Edin 90 C2
Strathalmond Pk. Edin 90 C2
Strathalmond Rd. Edin 90 C2
Strathavon Terr. West 112 C3
Strathbeg Dr. D Bay 47 F2
Strathbrock Pl. Brox 117 F3
Strathbrock Pl. Uph 116 C2
Strathearn Pl. Edin 123 D2
Strathearn Rd. Edin 123 D2
Strathearn Rd. Kirk 17 F4
Strathearn Rd. N Ber 53 F4
Strathesk Gr. Peni 204 A3
Strathesk Pl. Peni 204 A3
Strathfillan Rd. Edin 123 E2
Strathkinnes Rd. Kirk 17 D2
Strathlachlan Ave. Car 230 A1
Strathlogie. West 112 C3
Strathmiglo Pl. Sten 38 C2
Strathmore Cres. Stir 2 A2
Strathmore Dr. Dunf 29 E3
Strathmore Dr. Stir 2 A2
Strathmore St. King 34 C1
Strathyre Dr. Ston 171 E1
Strawberry Bank. Dalk 156 C1
Strawberry Bank. Lin 85 D3
Streets Pl. Dunf 29 E4
Stripehead. All 10 A3
Striven Dr. Falk 39 E1
Striven Pl. Kirk 16 C4
Strowan Rd. Gran 61 F4
Strowan Sq. Gran 61 F4
Struan Dr. Inver 47 D2
Struan Pl. Inver 47 D2
Strude Howe. Alva 5 D4
Strude Mill. Alva 5 D4
Strude St. Alva 5 D4
Stuart Cres. Edin 121 D4
Stuart Ct. Edin 121 D4
Stuart Gn. Edin 121 D4
Stuart Pk. Edin 121 D4
Stuart Pl. Cow 13 E3
Stuart Rd. Ros 46 B1
Stuart Sq. Edin 121 D4
Stuart Terr. Bath 145 D3
Stuart Wynd. Edin 121 D4
Succoth Ave. Edin 122 B4
Succoth Ct. Edin 122 B4
Succoth Gdns. Edin 122 B4
Succoth Pk. Edin 122 B4
Suffolk Rd. Edin 123 F2
Sulven Hts. Laur 61 E2
Summer Bank. Edin 93 E1
Summer Pl. Edin 93 E1
Summerfield Gdns. Edin 94 A2
Summerfield Pk. Dunb 78 A1
Summerfield Rd. Dunb 78 B1
Summerford. Falk 59 E2
Summerford Gdns. Falk 59 E2
Summerford Rd. Falk 59 E2
Summerhall. Edin 123 F3
Summerhall Pl. Edin 123 F3
Summerhall Sq. Edin 123 F3
Summerlee. Pres 96 C1
Summerside Pl. Edin 93 E3
Summerside St. Edin 93 E3
Summertrees Ct. Edin 124 A1
Summerville Ct. Pump 148 A4
Suna Path. West 192 A2
Sunart Pl. Gran 61 E3
Sunbury Mews. Edin 122 C4
Sunbury Pl. Edin 122 C4
Sunningdale La. Dunf 28 B3
Sunnybank Pl. Edin 94 A1
Sunnybank Rd. Stir 7 D2
Sunnybrae. For 5 D1
Sunnydale Dr. Blac 142 C2
Sunnydale Rd. Blac 142 C2
Sunnylaw Pl. Falk 59 F2
Sunnylaw Rd. B of A 2 A4
Sunnyside Ave. Bath 145 E4
Sunnyside Ct. All 10 A4

Sunnyside Pl. Loch 14 A3
Sunnyside Rd. All 10 A4
Sunnyside Rd. Falk 59 F3
Sunnyside Rd. Pol 82 B4
Sunnyside St. Falk 59 F3
Sunnyside. Stir 7 D2
Sunnyside. Ston 171 D1
Sutherland Ave. All 10 B4
Sutherland Ave. Stir 2 B1
Sutherland Cres. Bath 145 D3
Sutherland Dr. Den 57 E4
Sutherland Pl. Kirk 17 F4
Sutherland St. Edin 122 C4
Sutherland Way. Liv 147 E3
Suttieslea Cres. Newt 183 E3
Suttieslea Dr. Newt 183 E3
Suttieslea Pl. Newt 183 E3
Suttieslea Rd. Newt 183 E3
Suttieslea Wlk. Newt 183 E3
Sutton Pk Cres. Sten 38 C2
Sutton Pl. Falk 60 B3
Swallow Craig. D Bay 48 A1
Swallowdrum Rd. Dunf 28 B3
Swan Cres. Gore 207 E4
Swan Pl. Gran 61 E3
Swan Rd. Kirk 17 D2
Swan Rd. Tran 128 B3
Swan Spring Ave. Edin 154 A4
Swanfield. Edin 93 F3
Swanston Ave. Edin 154 A3
Swanston Cres. Edin 154 A3
Swanston Dr. Edin 154 A3
Swanston Gdns. Edin 154 A3
Swanston Gn. Edin 154 A3
Swanston Gr. Edin 154 A2
Swanston Loan. Edin 154 A3
Swanston Muir. Edin 153 F3
Swanston Pk. Edin 154 A3
Swanston Pl. Edin 154 A3
Swanston Row. Edin 154 A3
Swanston Terr. Edin 154 A3
Swanston View. Edin 154 A3
Swanston Way. Edin 154 A3
Swintons Pl. Cow 12 C1
Sword's Way. Falk 60 B4
Sycamore Ave. B' ness 63 E3
Sycamore Ave. Kirk 17 E4
Sycamore Cres. Loch 13 E3
Sycamore Dr. Whit 170 B3
Sycamore Gdns. Edin 121 E3
Sycamore Gr. Dunf 46 B4
Sycamore Gr. Winch 87 F1
Sycamore Pl. Stir 6 C3
Sycamore Rd. May 183 F3
Sycamore Wlk. Black 171 E4
Sycamores The. Tull 4 A1
Sydney Pk. Edin 94 C1
Sydney Pl. Edin 94 C1
Sydney St. Liv 148 A3
Sydney Terr. Edin 94 C1
Sylvan Gr. B' ness 63 E3
Sylvan Pl. Edin 123 E3
Sylvan Way. Bath 144 C3
Syme Pl. Ros 46 B3
Symington St. Falk 39 D2

Ta-Verne La. Dunf 29 E1
Tailend Roundabout. Liv .. 146 B2
Tait Dr. Lar 59 E4
Tait Dr. Peni 203 F3
Tait St. Dalk 157 D2
Talbot St. Gran 61 E4
Talisman Pl. Edin 124 A1
Talman Gdns. Pol 61 F1
Tam O'Shanter Dr. Cowie ... 20 B4
Tamfourhill Ave. Falk 59 E2
Tamfourhill Rd. Falk 59 D2
Tamhouse Brae. Cul 42 B4
Tanners Rd. Falk 60 A2
Tannery La. Stir 2 A1
Tantallon Dr. Sten 39 D2
Tantallon Pl. Edin 123 E3
Tantallon Rd. N Ber 54 C4
Tantallon Terr. N Ber 54 C4
Tantera Ct. Falk 60 A1
Tapitlaw Gr. Bla 26 B4
Tappoch Pl. Lar 38 A2
Taransay Dr. Pol 61 F1
Tarbert Pl. Pol 61 F1
Tarbert Terr. Kin 23 F2
Tarbet Ct. Lar 230 A1
Tarbrax Path. Shot 192 A2
Tarbrax Rd. Auc 217 F1
Tarduff Dr. Madd 83 D3
Tarduff Pl. Duni 36 A1
Targate Rd. Dunf 28 B3
Target Rd. Gran 62 B4
Tartraven Pl. Brox 117 E4
Tarvit St. Edin 123 E3
Tashieburn Rd. For 215 F1
Tavern Cotts. Cow 31 D4
Taxi Way. D Bay 48 B3
Tay Pl. Shot 191 F3
Tay St. Edin 122 C3
Tay St. Falk 39 E1
Tay St. Gran 40 A1

Tay Terr. Dunf 29 F1
Tay Wlk. Liv 148 A2
Taylor Ave. Cow 13 E2
Taylor Gdns. Edin 93 F3
Taylor Pl. Dalk 157 E1
Taylor Pl. Dunf 29 F1
Taylor's Rd. Lar 38 B1
Taymouth Rd. Pol 62 A1
Tedder St. Gran 61 E3
Telferton. Edin 94 C1
Telford Dr. Bann 7 E1
Telford Dr. Edin 92 B2
Telford Gdns. Edin 92 B2
Telford Pl. Edin 92 B2
Telford Pl. Lin 84 B4
Telford Rd. Edin 92 B2
Telford Sq. Falk 59 F3
Telford Sq. Liv 147 F4
Telford View. Lin 84 B3
Telny Pl. Abe 49 E4
Templar Gait. Edin 52 A1
Templar La. Gull 52 A1
Templar Pl. Gull 52 A1
Templar Rise. Muri 173 E4
Templars Cres. King 34 C2
Temple Ave. Arm 144 A3
Temple Denny Rd. Den 36 B1
Temple Pk Cres. Edin 122 C3
Temple Pk. Newt 206 B1
Templedean Pk. Hadd 101 D1
Templehall Ave. Kirk 16 C4
Templeland Gr. Edin 121 E4
Templeland Rd. Edin 121 E4
Ten Acres. N Sau 5 D1
Tenacres Pl. Gran 61 F3
Tenacres Rd. Gran 62 A4
Tenant's March. W Cal 172 B2
Tennant St. Edin 93 F3
Tennent Pk. E Cal 148 B1
Tenth St. Newt 183 D3
Tern Brae. Liv 147 E3
Terrace St. Kirk 18 A4
Terrace The. White 126 C1
Terragles. Peni 203 E3
Terris St. Cow 13 E2
Teviot Gr. Peni 203 F4
Teviot Pl. Edin 123 E4
Teviot St. Falk 59 F2
Teviotdale Pl. Edin 93 D1
Thane Pl. Dunf 29 E2
Thimblehall Dr. Dunf 29 E2
Thimblehall Pl. Dunf 29 E2
Thimblehall Rd. Dunf 29 F2
Third Gait. Rat 151 F4
Third St. Newt 183 D3
Thirlestane. B'ness 64 A4
Thirlestane La. Edin 123 E2
Thirlestane Pl. B'ness 64 A4
Thirlestane Rd. Edin 123 E3
Thistle Ave. Duni 36 B2
Thistle Ave. Gran 61 D3
Thistle Pl. Edin 123 D3
Thistle St. All 10 B3
Thistle St. Burn 50 C4
Thistle St. Cow 13 E2
Thistle St. Dunf 29 D3
Thistle St. Falk 60 B3
Thistle St. Kirk 17 E2
Thompson Pl. Slam 110 A2
Thomson Cres. Cow 97 E2
Thomson Cres. Curr 152 A3
Thomson Ct. Uph 116 C2
Thomson Ct. Curr 92 B3
Thomson Gn. Liv 147 D4
Thomson Gr. Curr 152 A3
Thomson Gr. Uph 116 C2
Thomson Pl. Cam 6 B3
Thomson Pl. Ros 46 B3
Thomson Rd. Curr 152 A3
Thomson Terr. Shot 191 E3
Thorburn Gr. Edin 153 E3
Thorburn Rd. Edin 153 D3
Thorn Gr. Dunf 46 C4
Thorn Tree Pl. Oak 26 C3
Thornbridge Gdns. Falk 60 C2
Thornbridge Rd. Falk 60 C3
Thornbridge Sq. Falk 60 C3
Thornden Gdns. Bon 57 D1
Thornden Ct. Falk 59 F1
Thorne Ct. N Ber 54 A3
Thorne Rd. All 4 C1
Thornhill Dr. Kirk 17 D3
Thornhill Pl. Falk 60 B3
Thornhill Rd. Falk 60 B3
Thornton Ave. Bon 57 F2
Thornton Rd. Ros 46 A2
Thornton Pl. Fau 193 E3
Thornton Rd. Rose 181 E1
Thorntree Cres. Pres 97 D1
Thorntree St. Edin 94 A2
Thorntreeside. Edin 94 A2
Thornville Terr. Edin 94 A2
Thorny Bank. Dalk 157 E2
Thornybauk. Edin 123 D3
Thornyhaugh. Dunf 28 C3
Threipmuir Ave. Bale 177 E4
Threipmuir Gdns. Bale 177 E4
Threipmuir Pl. Bale 177 E4
Thrums The. Laur 61 D2
Thurston Pl. Liv 147 E3

Timber Bush. Edin 94 A3
Timmeryetts. Uph 117 E3
Timmons Pk. Loch 14 A4
Timmons Pl. Den 36 B1
Tinian Cres. Torr 26 B1
Tinto Dr. Cow 13 D1
Tinto Dr. Gran 61 F3
Tinto Pl. Edin 93 F2
Tipperlinn Rd. Edin 123 D2
Tippet Knowes Ct. Winch 87 F2
Tippet Knowes Pk. Winch 87 F2
Tippet Knowes Rd. Winch 87 F1
Tiree Cres. Pol 61 E1
Tiree Pk. Falk 16 C4
Titania. All 10 B4
Todd Sq. Liv 116 C1
Toddshill Rd. Kirkl 89 D1
Tolbooth St. Falk 60 A2
Tolbooth St. Kirk 17 E2
Tolbooth Wynd. Edin 94 A3
Toll Rd. Kin 23 F2
Toll Roundabout. Liv 146 C2
Toll View. Cock 140 C2
Tollgate. Dunf 29 D1
Tolmount Dr. Dunf 29 E2
Tolsta Cres. Pol 61 F1
Tonbain. Kin 16 B4
Torbain. Kin 16 A3
Torbain Rd. Kirk 16 A3
Torbane Ave. Whit 170 C4
Torbane Dr. Whit 170 C4
Torbeith Gdns. Cow 12 C1
Torbothie Rd. Shot 192 A2
Torbrex Farm Rd. Stir 7 D2
Torbrex La. Stir 7 D3
Torbrex Rd. Stir 7 D3
Torburn Ave. Plea 20 B2
Torduff Rd. Edin 153 D2
Toronto Ave. Liv 147 F2
Torosay Ave. Madd 82 C3
Torphichen Ave. E Cal 148 A1
Torphichen Pl. Edin 123 D4
Torphichen Rd. Bath 145 D4
Torphichen St. Bath 145 D4
Torphichen St. Edin 123 D4
Torrance Pk. Edin 91 E1
Torridon Ave. Falk 39 E1
Torridon Ct. All 10 B3
Torridon Dr. Ros 46 C1
Torridon La. Ros 46 C1
Torridon Pl. Kirk 16 C4
Torridon Rd. Whit 170 B4
Torridon Wlk. Liv 148 A2
Torrin Loan. Shot 192 A2
Torry Dr. Alva 4 C4
Torsonce Rd. Dalk 156 C1
Torvean Pl. Dunf 29 E1
Torwood Ave. Gran 61 F3
Torwood Ave. Lar 38 A1
Torwood Pl. Dunf 29 E3
Touch Rd. Cam 6 A3
Touch Wards. Dunf 29 D2
Touchhill Cres. Plea 20 B2
Toward Ct. Edin 121 D4
Tower Gdns. B'ness 64 B4
Tower Pl. Clack 10 C3
Tower Pl. Edin 94 A3
Tower St. All 10 A4
Tower St. Edin 94 A3
Tower Street La. Edin 94 A3
Tower Terr. Kirk 17 F4
Tower View. N Sau 5 F1
Towers Ct. Falk 60 A2
Towers Pl. Stir 2 B2
Town House St. Den 36 C1
Townhall St. Inver 47 E1
Townhead Gdns. Whit 170 B2
Townhead. King 34 C2
Townhead. Kirk 18 A4
Townhill Rd. Dunf 29 D3
Townsend Cres. Kirk 17 E2
Townsend Pl. Kirk 17 E2
Trafalgar La. Edin 93 F3
Trafalgar St. Edin 93 F3
Train Terr. Ros 46 A3
Tranent Rd. Elph 128 A1
Transy Gr. Dunf 29 E2
Transy Pl. Dunf 29 E2
Traprain Cres. Bath 144 C4
Traprain Terr. Hadd 101 D1
Traprain Terr. Loan 181 E4
Traquair Pk E. Edin 121 F3
Traquair Pk W. Edin 121 F3
Trelawney Terr. Auch 204 A4
Tremayne Pl. Dunf 28 C2
Trench Knowes Edin 154 A3
Trenchard Pl. Dunf 28 C3
Tressilian Gdns. Edin 124 A1
Trevelyan Cres. Pen 160 C3
Trevelyan Pl. Pen 160 C3
Trinity Cres. Edin 93 D3
Trinity Ct. Edin 93 D3
Trinity Gr. Edin 93 D3

Upper Gray St. Edin

Trinity Rd. Edin 93 D3
Tron Ct. Tull 4 A1
Trondheim Parkway. Dunf 29 F1
Trondheim Pl. Dunf 29 F1
Trongate. King 35 D2
Troup Ct. Gran 61 E4
Tryst Pk. Edin 153 F3
Tryst Rd. Sten 38 B2
Tryst Way. Sten 38 B1
Tudor Cr. Laur 61 E1
Tuke St. Dunf 29 D1
Tullallan Pl. Sten 39 D2
Tulliallan Terr. Kin 23 F2
Tullibody Rd. All 9 F4
Tullibody Rd. Tull 4 C1
Tulligarth Pk. All 10 A4
Tulloch Ct. Cow 13 E3
Tulloch Rd. Shot 192 A2
Tummel Dr. Kirk 16 B4
Tummel Pl. Sten 38 C2
Tummel Pl. Sten 38 C2
Turnbull Gr. Dunf 29 F1
Turner Ave. Bale 151 E2
Turner Pk. Bale 151 E2
Turner St. Bath 145 D4
Turnhigh Rd. Whit 170 A2
Turnhouse Farm Rd. Kirkl 90 B1
Turnhouse Rd. Edin 120 B4
Turnhouse Rd. Kirkl 120 B4
Turret Ct. Pol 62 A1
Turret Dr. Pol 62 A1
Turret Gdns. Pres 127 F4
Turret Rd. Gran 61 E3
Turret Pl. Kirk 16 C4
Twain Ave. Sten 39 D2
Tweed Dr. Liv 148 A3
Tweed St. Dunf 29 F1
Tweed St. Gran 40 A1
Tweedale Cres. Giff 163 F3
Tweeddale Ave. Giff 163 F3
Tweeddale Ct. Edin 29 F3
Tweeddale Gr. Giff 163 F2
Tweeddale Gr. Giff 163 F2
Tyhmebank. Liv 147 E3
Tyler's Acre Ave. Edin 121 F3
Tyler's Acre Gdns. Edin 121 F3
Tyler's Acre Rd. Edin 121 F3
Tyndrum Pl. Kirk 16 C4
Tyne Cl. Lin 103 F4
Tyne Ct. Edin 132 A4
Tynecastle La. Edin 122 C3
Tynecastle Terr. Edin 122 C3
Tynemount Ave. Orm 159 E3
Tynemount Rd. Orm 159 F4
Tyneview. Pen 159 F4
Tyrwhitt Pl. Ros 46 C2

Ugston Cotts. Hadd 100 B1
Ulg Way. Shot 192 A2
Ulster Cres. Edin 124 B4
Ulster Dr. Edin 124 B4
Ulster Gdns. Edin 124 B4
Ulster Gr. Edin 124 B4
Ulster Terr. Edin 124 B4
Underwood Cotts. Cam 6 B3
Underwood Rd. Cam 6 B3
Union Dr. Whit 170 A3
Union Pk. Bonn 182 A3
Union Pl. Edin 93 F1
Union Pl. Lar 38 B1
Union Rd. Bath 145 D3
Union Rd. Brox 117 E3
Union Rd. Falk 59 E3
Union Rd. Gran 40 B1
Union Rd. Lin 84 C3
Union Rd. Whit 170 A3
Union St. All 10 A3
Union St. B of A 2 A4
Union St. B'ness 64 A4
Union St. Burn 50 C4
Union St. Cow 13 E2
Union St. Edin 93 F1
Union St. Falk 60 A4
Union St. Kirk 17 E3
Union St. Loch 14 A4
Union St. Shot 191 E3
Union St. Sten 38 C2
Unity Pk. Shot 191 E3
Universal Rd. Gran 60 C4
University Rd W. B of A 2 A3
Uphall Station Rd. Pump 148 A4
Upper Bathville. Arm 143 F2
Upper Bow. Edin 123 E4
Upper Bridge St. Stir 2 A1
Upper Broomieknowe.
    Bonn 182 A4
Upper Castlehill. Stir 2 A1
Upper Coltbridge Terr.
    Edin 122 B4
Upper Craigour. Edin 155 F4
Upper Craigour Way. Edin ... 124 B1
Upper Craigs. Stir 7 D1
Upper Cramond Ct. Edin 91 D2
Upper Dean Terr. Edin 93 D1
Upper Gilmore Pl. Edin 123 D3
Upper Gilmore Terr. Edin 123 D3
Upper Gray St. Edin 123 F3

Upper Grove Pl. Edin 123   D3
Upper Millhill St. Dunf 29   D2
Upper Newmarket St. Falk ... 60   A3
Upper Wellheads. Lime 45   F2
Ure Cres. Bon 58   A3
Ure Ct. Gran 60   C3
Urquhart Cres. Dunf 28   C2
Urquhart Cut. Dunf 28   C2
Urquhart Farm Cotts.
    Crossf 28   B1

Vale Pl. Duni 36   C2
Valeview. Lar 38   B1
Valley Field View. Peni ... 203   F2
Valley Gdns. Kirk 16   C3
Valley Gdns S. Kirk 16   C3
Valley View. Kirk 16   C3
Valleyfield Ave. H Val 26   A1
Valleyfield Pl. Cow 13   E3
Valleyfield Pl. Stir 7   E3
Valleyfield Rd. Peni 203   F2
Valleyfield St. Edin 123   E3
Valleyview Dr. Falk 60   A4
Vancouver Ave. Liv 147   F2
Vandeleur Ave. Edin 94   C1
Vandeleur Gr. Edin 94   C1
Vandeleur Pl. Edin 94   C1
Vardon Rd. Gull 52   A2
Vaucluse Pl. Peni 203   F2
Veere Pk. Cul 25   F1
Veitch's Sq. Edin 93   D1
Vellore Rd. Madd 83   D1
Venachar Pl. Crossf 28   A1
Vennachar St. Shot 191   F3
Vennel The. Den 36   C1
Vennel The. Dunb 78   C1
Vennel The. Lin 85   D4
Ventnor Pl. Edin 124   A2
Ventnor Terr. Edin 123   F2
Venturefair Ave. Dunf 29   D3
Veronica Cres. Kirk 17   E4
Vetch Pk. Hadd 101   D1
Vexhim Pk. Edin 125   D3
Vicar St. Falk 60   A3
Viceroy St. Kirk 17   D3
Victor Park Terr. Edin 121   E4
Victoria Gdns. Kirk 17   D2
Victoria Gdns. Newt 182   C3
Victoria Pk. Fau 193   F4
Victoria Pk. Hadd 101   D1
Victoria Pk. B'ness 64   A4
Victoria Pl. Dunb 78   B2
Victoria Pl. Pol 61   E1
Victoria Pl. Stir 7   D4
Victoria Rd. East 168   C3
Victoria Rd. Falk 60   B3
Victoria Rd. Fau 193   F4
Victoria Rd. Gran 61   E4
Victoria Rd. Hadd 132   A4
Victoria Rd. Kirk 17   D3
Victoria Rd. Lar 38   A1
Victoria Rd. N Ber 54   B4
Victoria Rd. Newt 182   C3
Victoria Rd. Stir 7   D4
Victoria Rd. Stir 7   D4
Victoria St. All 10   A4
Victoria St. Dunb 78   B2
Victoria St. Dunf 29   D3
Victoria St. Gran 61   E4
Victoria St. East 168   C3
Victoria St. Edin 123   E4
Victoria St. Gore 183   D1
Victoria St. Kirk 18   A4
Victoria St. Liv 148   A2
Victoria St. Rose 181   E1
Victoria Terr. Dunf 29   D3
Victoria Terr. Hadd 132   A4
Victoria Terr. Men 4   A3
Victoria Terr. Muss 126   C3
Viewbank Dr. Bonn 182   B4
Viewbank Rd. Bonn 182   A4
Viewbank View. Bonn 182   B4
Viewcraig Gdns. Edin 123   F4
Viewcraig St. Edin 123   F4
Viewfield Ave. Bonn 182   B4
Viewfield Dr. Alva 4   C3
Viewfield Pl. Auc 217   F2
Viewfield Rd. Edin 152   C4
Viewfield St. East 168   C3
Viewfield St. Stir 7   D4
Viewfield Terr. Dunf 29   D2
Viewfield Terr. Loch 13   F3
Viewforth Ave. Kirk 17   F4
Viewforth. B'ness 64   A4
Viewforth. Cocke 97   E2
Viewforth. Dunf 61   D2
Viewforth. Dunb 78   B2
Viewforth. Edin 123   D3
Viewforth Gdns. Edin 123   D3
Viewforth Gdns. Kirk 17   F4
Viewforth Gdns. Tran 128   B3
Viewforth. N Ber 54   B4
Viewforth Pl. Que 89   D4
Viewforth Rd. Que 89   D4
Viewforth Sq. Edin 123   D3
Viewforth St. Kirk 17   F4
Viewforth Terr. Edin 123   D3
Viewforth Terr. Kirk 17   F4

Viewforth Terr. Tran 128   B3
Viewpark Gdns. Bonn 182   A4
Villa Bank. Den 36   C1
Villa Rd. Que 68   A1
Village La. Liv 147   D2
Vinefields. Pen 160   C3
Violet Terr. Edin 122   C3
Vivian Terr. Edin 92   A1
Vogrie Cres S. Gore 207   E4
Vogrie Pl. Gore 207   E4
Vogrie Rd. Gore 207   E4
Voil Rd. Stir 2   A2
Volunteer's Gn. Kirk 17   E2
Vorlich Cres. Peni 204   A4
Vorlich Dr. Shi 81   F4
Vorlich Pl. Stir 2   A2

Waddell St. Sten 39   E1
Wadingburn La. Bonn 155   F1
Wadingburn Rd. Bonn 181   F4
Waggon Rd. B'ness 63   F4
Waggon Rd. Crosf 28   A1
Waggon Rd. Falk 60   A4
Waggon Rd. Inver 47   E1
Waggon Rd. Lime 45   E4
Waggon Rd. Stir 82   B4
Wakefield Ave. Edin 94   C1
Walden Dr. Giff 163   F3
Walden Pl. Giff 163   F2
Walden Terr. Giff 163   F2
Waldie Ave. Lin 85   D3
Walk The. All 10   A3
Walk The. Kirk 18   A4
Walker Cres. Dalk 156   C1
Walker Dr. Que 68   A1
Walker Pl. Bonn 181   F3
Walker Pl. Dunf 29   F1
Walker Rd. Fau 193   E3
Walker St. Cow 13   D2
Walker St. Edin 123   D4
Walker St. Kin 23   F2
Walker St. Kirk 17   D3
Walker St. Loch 14   A3
Walker Terr. E Lin 103   E4
Walkers Ct. Edin 121   F1
Walkers Rig. Edin 121   F1
Walkers Wynd. Edin 121   F1
Wall Gdns. Falk 59   E3
Wall St. Falk 59   E3
Wallace Cres. Den 36   B1
Wallace Cres. Plea 20   B2
Wallace Cres. Rosl 180   C2
Wallace Cres. Rosi 181   D2
Wallace Ct. Gran 61   E4
Wallace Ct. Stir 2   A1
Wallace Gdns. Stir 2   A2
Wallace Mill Gdns. E Cal ... 148   B2
Wallace Pl. Cam 6   B3
Wallace Pl. Falk 60   B3
Wallace Pl. Fall 8   B2
Wallace Cres. Rosl 181   D2
Wallace Ct. Stir 2   A1
Wallace St. Barn 7   F1
Wallace St. Cow 13   E2
Wallace St. Dunf 29   E1
Wallace St. Falk 60   A2
Wallace St. Gran 61   E4
Wallace St. Stir 2   A1
Wallace View. B'ness 63   E3
Wallace View. Shi 81   E4
Wallace View. Tull 4   B2
Wallace Wlk. Ston 171   D1
Wallacelea. Pol 61   F1
Wallacestone Brae. Shi 82   A4
Walls Pl. Dunf 29   F1
Wallsend Ct. Dunf 28   B3
Wallstale Rd. Stir 7   D2
Walmer Dr. Dunf 29   D2
Walnut Gr. Dunf 46   C4
Walter Hay Ct. Ros 46   C2
Walter Scott Ave. Edin ... 124   A1
Ward Ave. Laur 61   E1
Ward St. All 10   A3
Wardie's Cl. Edin 123   D3
Wardie Ave. Edin 93   D3
Wardie Cres. Edin 93   D3
Wardie Dell. Edin 93   D3
Wardie Gr. Edin 92   C3
Wardie House La. Edin ... 93   D3
Wardie Pk. Edin 93   D3
Wardie Rd. Edin 93   D3
Wardie Sq. Edin 93   D3
Wardieburn Dr. Edin 92   C3
Wardieburn Pl E. Edin 92   C3
Wardieburn Pl N. Edin 92   C3
Wardieburn Pl S. Edin 92   C3
Wardieburn Pl W. Edin 92   C3
Wardieburn Rd. Edin 92   C3
Wardieburn St E. Edin 92   C3
Wardieburn St W. Edin 92   C3
Wardieburn Terr. Edin 92   C3
Wardiefield. Edin 93   D3
Wardlaw Cres. Dunf 29   E1
Wardlaw Cres. Oak 26   C4
Wardlaw Pl. Edin 122   C3
Wardlaw St. Cow 13   E2
Wardlaw St. Edin 122   C3

Wardlaw Terr. Edin 122   C3
Wardlaw Way. Oak 26   C4
Wardrop Cres. Arm 143   F3
Ware Rd. Dir 53   E3
Ware Rd. N Ber 54   A4
Warrender Cres. Dunb 78   C1
Warrender Ct. N Ber 54   A3
Warrender Park Cres. Edin   123   E3
Warrender Park Rd. Edin ... 123   E3
Warrender Park Terr. Edin   123   E3
Warriston Ave. Edin 93   E2
Warriston Cres. Edin 93   E2
Warriston Dr. Edin 93   E2
Warriston Gdns. Edin 93   E2
Warriston Gr. Edin 93   D2
Warriston Rd. Edin 93   E2
Warriston Terr. Edin 93   D2
Washington La. Edin 122   C3
Water St. Edin 94   A3
Water Yett. Lin 84   C4
Waterfall Wlk. Dalk 157   D1
Waterlands Gdns. Car 230   A2
Waterloo Pl. Edin 93   E1
Waterloo Pl. Elph 128   A1
Waters' Cl. Edin 94   B3
Waterside. Hadd 132   A4
Watertoun Rd. Edin 123   F2
Watling Ave. Falk 59   E3
Watling Dr. Falk 59   E3
Watling Gdns. Falk 59   E3
Watling St. Falk 59   E3
Watson Cres. Edin 122   C3
Watson Pl. Arm 144   A3
Watson Pl. Bank 57   E2
Watson Pl. Dunf 29   D3
Watson St. Cow 13   E2
Watson St. Falk 60   A3
Watson St. Peni 203   F3
Watt Ave. Arm 144   A3
Watt Gdns. Falk 59   E3
Watt Gr. May 183   F3
Watt Pk. Newt 183   D2
Watt Rd. Ros 46   A1
Watt St. Kirk 18   A4
Watt's Cl. Muss 126   A3
Watters Cres. Loch 14   A3
Wauchope Ave. Edin 124   C2
Wauchope Cres. Edin 124   C2
Wauchope Pl. Edin 124   C2
Wauchope Sq. Edin 124   C2
Wauchope Terr. Edin 124   C2
Waugh Path. Bonn 182   B4
Waughton Cotts. E Lin 74   C3
Waulkmill Dr. Peni 204   A3
Waulkmill Loan. Curr 151   F2
Waulkmill View. Peni 203   F3
Waulkmill St. Gran 61   E3
Waverley Bridge. Edin 123   E4
Waverley Cres. Bon 58   A2
Waverley Cres. Bonn 182   B4
Waverley Cres. Gran 61   E3
Waverley Cres. Stir 2   B1
Waverley Dr. Bonn 182   B4
Waverley Park Terr. Edin ... 94   A1
Waverley Pk. Bonn 182   B4
Waverley Pk. Edin 94   A1
Waverley Pl. Kirk 61   D1
Waverley Pk. May 183   E3
Waverley Pk. Tran 128   B3
Waverley Rd. Bonn 182   B4
Waverley Rd. Dalk 156   C1
Waverley Rd. Lar 38   B1
Waverley St. Bath 145   D4
Waverley St. Falk 60   A2
Waverley St Ind Units.
    Bath 145   D4
Waverley St. May 183   E3
Waverley Terr. Bonn 182   B4
Waverley Terr. Lar 38   B1
Waverley Terr. May 183   E3
Weaver Pl. Bath 145   D4
Weaver's Knowe Cres.
    Curr 151   F3
Weavers Cres. Kirk 17   F3
Weavers La. Whit 170   A3
Weavers Wk. Dunf 29   F2
Webster Ave. Sten 39   D2
Webster Ct. Brox 117   F3
Webster Pl. Ros 46   B3
Wedderburn Cres. Dunf ... 29   F1
Wedderburn Pl. Dunf 29   F1
Wedderburn Pl N. Kirk 16   B4
Wedderburn St. Dunf 29   F1
Wedderburn Terr. Muss ... 126   B2
Wee Brae. Bonn 156   A1
Wee Row. Falk 60   A3
Weir Ave. Cow 13   D1
Weir Cres. Dalk 156   C1
Weir Dr. Fall 8   B2
Weir St. Falk 60   A3
Weir St. Stir 7   C1
Well Pl. B of A 2   A4
Well Rd. B of A 2   A4
Well Rd. Loch 14   A4

Well Wynd. Tran 128   B3
Wellflats Rd. Kirkl 89   D1
Wellgate Dr. B of A 2   B4
Wellgreen. Stir 7   D3
Wellington Pl. Edin 94   A3
Wellington St. Edin 93   F1
Wellmyre. Clack 11   D2
Welpark. Brid 116   C4
Welpark Cres. Stir 6   C2
Welpark Terr. Bon 58   A3
Wellside. Hadd 131   F4
Wellside Pl. Falk 60   A3
Welsh Gdns. B of A 2   A4
Welsh Rd. Whit 169   F3
Wemyss Ct. Ros 46   C3
Wemyss Gdns. Muss 127   E3
Wemyss Pl. Cocke 97   E2
Wemyss Pl. Edin 93   D1
Wemyss Place Mews. Edin   93   D1
Wemyss Rd. Long 98   C3
Wemyss St. Cow 13   E2
Wemyss St. Ros 46   C3
Wemyss Terr. Long 98   C3
Wemysfield. Kirk 17   D2
Wesley Pl. Shi 82   A4
West Adam St. Edin 123   F4
West Albert Rd. Kirk 17   D2
West Annandale St. Edin ... 93   E2
West Approach Rd. Edin ... 123   D4
West Baldridge Rd. Dunf ... 28   C3
West Bankton. Muri 173   F4
West Bay Rd. N Ber 54   A4
West Benhar Rd. East 168   A2
West Boreland Rd. Den ... 36   B1
West Bow. Edin 123   E4
West Bowling Green St.
    Edin 93   F3
West Bridge St. Falk 60   A3
West Brighton Cres. Edin ... 125   D4
West Broomhill Rd. Burn ... 50   C4
West Bryson Rd. Edin 122   C3
West Burnside. Brox 117   F3
West Cairn Cres. Peni 203   F3
West Caiystane Rd. Edin ... 154   A3
West Carmuirs Loan. Bon ... 58   C3
West Carnethy Ave. Edin ... 153   D3
West Castle Rd. Edin 123   D3
West Catherine Pl. Edin ... 122   C4
West Church Dr. Gran 40   A1
West Clifton Farm Cotts.
    Rat 149   E2
West Coates. Edin 122   C4
West Colinton House. Edin 153   D3
West College St. Edin 123   E4
West Craigs Ave. Edin 120   C3
West Craigs Cres. Edin 120   C4
West Cres. Peni 161   F2
West Croft. Rat 119   F1
West Cromwell St. Edin ... 93   F3
West Crosscauseway.
    Edin 123   F3
West Ct. Edin 92   C2
West Ct. Edin 124   C2
West Dr. Dunf 29   D2
West Dr. Lar 38   B1
West End Gdns. All 10   A3
West End Pl. Edin 122   C3
West End. W Cal 172   B1
West Fenton Cotts. Gull ... 72   C4
West Fergus Pl. Kirk 17   D2
West Ferryfield. Edin 92   C2
West Fountain Pl. Edin 122   C3
West Gate Rd. Gran 62   A4
West Glen Ave. Liv 146   C3
West Gorgie Pk. Edin 122   B2
West Gorgie Pl. Edin 122   B2
West Grange Gdns. Edin ... 123   E2
West Granton Cres. Edin ... 92   A3
West Granton Dr. Edin 92   A3
West Granton Gdns. Edin ... 92   A3
West Granton Gr. Edin 92   A3
West Granton Pl. Edin 92   B3
West Granton Rd. Edin 92   B3
West Granton Row. Edin ... 92   B3
West Granton Terr. Edin ... 92   B3
West Granton View. Edin ... 92   B3
West Harbour Rd. Cocke ... 97   C4
West Harbour Rd. Edin 92   C4
West Harbour Rd. Lime ... 45   D2
West Holmes Gdns. Muss 126   A3
West James St. Alva 5   D3
West Johnstone St. Alva ... 5   D3
West La. Cow 13   D1
West Leven St. Burn 50   C4
West Link Rd. B of A 2   B3
West Links Rd. Gull 51   F1
West Loan Ct. Pres 127   F4
West Loan. Pres 96   C1
West Lodge Gdns. All 9   F4
West Lorimer Pl. Cocke ... 97   D2
West Main St. Arm 143   F3
West Main St. Black 171   E4
West Main St. Brox 117   E3
West Main St. East 168   C3
West Main St. Uph 116   C2
West Main St. Uph 117   E3
West Main St. Uph 169   F3
West Mains Rd. Edin 123   F1

West Mains Rd. Gran 60   C4
West Mains St. Aber 71   E2
West Maitland St. Edin 123   D4
West March St. Kirk 17   E4
West Mayfield. Edin 123   F2
West Mill La. Edin 123   D4
West Mill Rd. Edin 152   C3
West Montgomery Pl. Edin   93   F1
West Muir Pl. W Cal 172   B1
West Murrayfield. Bann 7   E1
West Nethertown St. Dunf ... 29   D1
West Newington Pl. Edin ... 123   F3
West Nicolson St. Edin 123   F4
West Norton Pl. Edin 93   F1
West Park Gr. Uph 117   E3
West Park Pl. Edin 122   C3
West Pilton Ave. Edin 92   B2
West Pilton Bank. Edin 92   B3
West Pilton Cres. Edin 92   A3
West Pilton Crossway. Edin 92   B3
West Pilton Dr. Edin 92   B3
West Pilton Gdns. Edin 92   B3
West Pilton Gn. Edin 92   B3
West Pilton Gr. Edin 92   B3
West Pilton Lea. Edin 92   B3
West Pilton Loan. Edin 92   B3
West Pilton Pk. Edin 92   B3
West Pilton Pl. Edin 92   B3
West Pilton Rd. Edin 92   B3
West Pilton Rise. Edin 92   B3
West Pilton St. Edin 92   B3
West Pilton Terr. Edin 92   B3
West Pilton View. Edin 92   B2
West Pk. Loch 14   A4
West Pk. Oak 27   E3
West Port. Dunb 78   B1
West Port. Edin 123   E4
West Port. Kirk 18   A4
West Port. Lin 84   C4
West Powburn. Edin 123   F2
West Preston St. Edin 123   F3
West Quality St. Kirk 18   A4
West Rd. Hadd 131   F4
West Rd. Lime 45   D2
West Register St. Edin 93   E1
West Register Street La.
    Edin 93   E1
West Relugas Rd. Edin 123   E2
West Richmond St. Edin ... 123   F4
West Savile Rd. Edin 123   F2
West Savile Terr. Edin 123   F2
West Scotland Street La.
    Edin 93   E1
West Seaside. Pres 96   C1
West Shore Rd. Edin 92   B4
West Silvermills La. Edin ... 93   D1
West Sq. Dunf 46   C3
West St. Pent 203   F2
West Stirling St. Alva 4   C4
West Telferton. Edin 94   C1
West Tollcross. Edin 123   D3
West Torbain. Kirk 16   A4
West Vennel. All 10   A3
West Way. D Bay 48   A3
West Werberside. Edin 92   C2
West Windygoul. Tran 128   A3
West Winnelstrae. Edin 92   C2
West Woods. Edin 92   C2
West Works. Edin 117   E3
Westbank Ct. Glad 129   E3
Westbank Gdns. Glad 129   E3
Westbank Loan. Edin 95   D1
Westbank Pl. Edin 95   D1
Westbank Rd. Glad 129   E3
Westbank St. Edin 95   D1
Westbank Terr. Glad 129   E3
Westburn Ave. Cow 13   D1
Westburn Ave. Edin 152   B4
Westburn Ave. Falk 59   F2
Westburn Gdns. Edin 152   B4
Westburn Gr. Edin 152   B4
Westburn Middlefield. Edin 152   B4
Westburn Pk. Curr 152   B4
Westburn Pk. Edin 61   F3
Westcraigs Pk. Blac 142   B2
Westcraigs Rd. Blac 142   B2
Westcraigs Rd. East 168   C3
Westend Pl. N Ber 54   A4
Wester Bankton. Muri 174   A4
Wester Bogie Rd. Kirk 16   A4
Wester Broom Ave. Edin ... 121   E3
Wester Broom Dr. Edin 121   E3
Wester Broom Gdns. Edin 121   E3
Wester Broom Gr. Edin 121   E3
Wester Broom Pl. Edin 121   E3
Wester Broom Terr. Edin ... 121   E3
Wester Coates Ave. Edin ... 122   C4
Wester Coates Gdns. Edin 122   C4
Wester Coates Pl. Edin 122   C4
Wester Coates Rd. Edin ... 122   C4
Wester Coates Terr. Edin ... 122   C4
Wester Drylaw Ave. Edin ... 92   A2
Wester Drylaw Dr. Edin 92   A2
Wester Drylaw Pk. Edin 92   B2
Wester Drylaw Pl. Edin 92   A2
Wester Drylaw Row. Edin ... 92   B1
Wester Hailes Pk. Edin 152   B4
Wester Hailes Pk. Edin 152   C4

Wester Hailes Rd. Edin 152 B4
Wester Row. Rat 120 C1
Wester Steil. Edin 122 C1
Westerdunes Pk. N Ber 53 E4
Westerglen Rd. Falk 60 A1
Westerlands Dr. Stir 7 D3
Westerlea Ct. B of A 2 A3
Westerlea Dr. B of A 2 A3
Westermains. Arm 143 F3
Western Ave. Crossf 26 A1
Western Ave. Falk 60 A3
Western Gdns. Edin 122 B4
Western Pl. Edin 122 B4
Western Terr. Edin 122 B4
Westerton. Cowie 20 B4
Westerton Dr. B of A 2 A4
Westerton Rd. Brox 118 A3
Westerton Rd. Gran 61 F4
Westerton Terr. Sten 39 E2
Westfield Ave. Edin 122 B3
Westfield Ct. Dalk 156 C1
Westfield Dr. Dalk 156 C1
Westfield Gr. Cross 30 C3
Westfield Gr. Dalk 156 C1
Westfield. Kin 24 A2
Westfield Pk. Dalk 156 C1
Westfield Pl. Den 36 C1
Westfield Rd. Edin 122 B3
Westfield St. Edin 122 B3
Westfield St. Falk 60 A2
Westgarth Ave. Edin 153 D3
Westgate. Dunb 78 B2
Westgate. E Cal 148 A2
Westgate. N Ber 54 A4
Westhall Cres. Crossf 27 E1
Westhall Gdns. Uph 117 D2
Westhall Rd. Brox 117 F2
Westhouse Ave. May 183 F3
Westhouse Dr. May 183 F3
Westhouse St. May 183 F3
Westhouses Rd. May 183 F3
Westmill Rd. Bonn 182 A4
Westmill Wynd. Bonn 182 A4
Westminster Pl. Stir 38 C2
Westpoint. Dunb 78 B1
Westquarter Ave. Laur 61 D1
Westray Terr. Falk 60 A1
Westview Cres. Tull 4 B1
Westview. Lin 84 B4
Westwater St. Loch 14 A4
Westwood Ave. Kirk 17 F4
Westwood Pk. Liv 146 C3
Westwood Pl. Edin 29 F2
Westwood View. W Cal 172 B2
Wharry Rd. Alva 4 C4
Wheatfield Pl. Edin 122 B3
Wheatfield Rd. Edin 122 B3
Wheatfield St. Edin 122 C3
Wheatfield Terr. Edin 122 B3
Wheatlands Ave. Bon 58 A3
Wheatsheaf La. Dalk 157 D2
Whim Rd. Gull 51 F1
Whin Park Ind Est. Cocke 97 D2
Whin Pk. Cocke 97 D2
Whinbank. Liv 147 F3
Whinhill. Dunf 29 E2
Whinneyknowe. Inver 68 B3
Whinniehill Terr. Oak 27 E3
Whinny Hill Cres. Inver 47 D1
Whinnyburn Pl. Ros 46 B3
Whinnig. Uph 117 E3
Whins Pl. Edin 95 D1
Whins Rd. All 10 B4
Whins Rd. Stir 7 D1
Whinwell Rd. Stir 2 A1
Whirlbut Cres. Dunf 29 D1
Whirlbut St. Dunf 29 D1
Whitburn Rd. Bath 144 C2
Whitburn Rd. Liv 147 E2
White Hart St. Dalk 157 D2
White St. Whit 170 A3
White's Cl. Dalk 157 D2
Whitecraig Ave. White 126 C1
Whitecraig Cres. White 126 C1
Whitecraig Gdns E. White . 126 C1
Whitecraig Gdns. White ... 126 C1
Whitecraig Rd. White 126 C1
Whitedalehead Rd. Whit ... 170 B3
Whitedales. Edin 154 B3
Whitefield Rd. Dunf 29 F3
Whitegates Pl. Falk 59 E2
Whitehead Gr. Que 89 E4
Whitehill Ave. Muss 126 A2
Whitehill Dr. Black 171 E4
Whitehill Dr. Dalk 157 E1
Whitehill Farm Rd. Muss .. 126 A2
Whitehill Gdns. Muss 126 A2
Whitehill Gr. Dalk 157 E1
Whitehill Ind Est. Black ... 145 E1
Whitehill Pl. Rose 181 E1
Whitehill Pl. Stir 7 D3
Whitehill Rd. Black 145 E1
Whitehill Rd. Dan 125 E2
Whitehill Rd. Edin 125 E2
Whitehill St. Edin 125 E2
Whitehill View. Black 171 E4
Whitehouse Loan. Edin 123 E3

Whitehouse Rd. Edin 91 D2
Whitehouse Rd. Stir 7 E4
Whitelaw Cres. Dunf 29 E1
Whitelaw Dr. Bog 145 F3
Whitelaw Pl. Dunf 29 E1
Whitelaw Rd. Dunf 29 E1
Whitelaw St. Blac 142 B1
Whitelea Cres. Bale 177 E4
Whitelea Rd. Bale 177 E4
Whiteloch Rd. Glad 129 E3
Whitemoss Rd. Kir 149 F1
Whitemyre Ct. Dunf 28 B3
Whites Quay. D Bay 47 F1
Whiteside. Bath 144 C3
Whiteside Ind Est. Bath ... 144 C2
Whitesideloan. Pol 82 C4
Whitestone Pl. Black 145 E1
Whitingford. Edin 93 E3
Whitson Cres. Edin 122 A3
Whitson Gr. Edin 122 A3
Whitson Pl E. Edin 122 A3
Whitson Pl W. Edin 122 A3
Whitson Rd. Edin 122 A3
Whitson Terr. Edin 122 A3
Whitson Way. Edin 122 A3
Whitson Wlk. Edin 122 A3
Whitten La. Liv 84 C4
Whittingehame Dr. Hadd .. 132 A4
Whittinghame Dr. Hadd ... 132 B4
Wholeflats Rd. B'ness 62 A2
Wholeflats Rd. Gran 61 F2
Wholequarter Ave. Laur 61 E1
Whyte Pl. Edin 94 A1
Whyte St. East 168 C3
Whyte St. Loch 14 A4
Whyte Wlk. Dunf 29 F2
Whytehouse Ave. Kirk 17 D2
Whyteman's Brae. Kirk 17 E4
Whytescauseway. Kirk 17 D2
Wilderness The. Air 22 B2
Wildridge Way. Loch 14 A4
Wilfred Terr. Edin 94 B1
Wilkieston Rd. Rat 119 E1
William Black Pl. Que 89 E4
William Booth Pl. Stir 7 D2
William Jameson Pl. Edin .. 95 D1
William St. Dunf 28 C2
William St. Edin 123 D4
William St. Kirk 17 D1
William Street La NE. Edin 123 D4
William Street La NW. Edin 123 D4
William Street La SE. Edin 123 D4
William Street La SW. Edin 123 D4
Williamfield Ave. Stir 7 D2
Williamfield Sq. Edin 95 D4
Williamson Ave. Falk 39 D1
Williamson Pl. Falk 60 B4
Williamson St. Falk 60 A2
Williamston Interchange.
  Mur 148 A1
Willow Ave. Bonn 182 A3
Willow Brae. Fau 193 F3
Willow Dell. B'ness 63 E3
Willow Gr. Dunf 46 C4
Willow Gr. Liv 148 A2
Willow Pk. Fau 193 F3
Willow Rd. May 183 F3
Willowbank. Liv 147 F3
Willowbank Row. Edin 93 E3
Willowbrae Ave. Edin 124 B4
Willowbrae Gdns. Edin 124 B4
Willowbrae. Pol 82 B4
Willowbrae Rd. Edin 124 B4
Willowdean. Brid 86 B2
Willows The. Tull 4 A1
Wilson Ave. Dalk 157 E2
Wilson Ave. Den 36 B1
Wilson Ave. Falk 59 E3
Wilson Ave. Kirk 17 D3
Wilson Ave. Pol 61 F1
Wilson Ave. Pres 96 C1
Wilson Dr. Bann 7 E1
Wilson Dr. Falk 59 E3
Wilson Gdns. Falk 59 E3
Wilson Pl. Bon 58 B2
Wilson Rd. Alla 212 A4
Wilson Rd. Falk 59 E3
Wilson Rd. Gore 183 E1
Wilson St. Bla 26 A4
Wilson St. Cow 13 E2
Wilson St. Dunf 29 E4
Wilson St. Gran 61 E3
Wilson St. Peni 203 F3
Wilson Terr. Ston 171 D1
Wilson Wlk. Tran 128 B3
Wilson's Cl. Dunf 29 D2
Wilson's Pk. Edin 95 D1
Wilsontown Rd. For 215 E1
Wilton Rd. Car 230 A1
Wilton Rd. Edin 123 F2
Winchburgh Cotts. Winch ... 87 F1
Winchester Ave. Den 36 C2
Windlebrook. Dunf 47 D4
Windmill Gn. Kirk 17 F4
Windmill Knowe. Cross 30 C3

Windmill La. Edin 123 F3
Windmill Pl. Kirk 18 A4
Windmill Rd. Kirk 17 F4
Windsor Ave. Falk 59 F2
Windsor Cres. Falk 59 F2
Windsor Cres. Madd 83 D3
Windsor Cres. Peni 204 A3
Windsor Dr. Duni 36 B2
Windsor Dr. Falk 59 F2
Windsor Dr. Peni 204 A3
Windsor Gdns. All 9 F4
Windsor Gdns. Falk 59 F2
Windsor Gdns. Muss 126 C3
Windsor Park Dr. Muss 126 C3
Windsor Park Pl. Muss 126 C3
Windsor Park Terr. Muss . 126 C3
Windsor Pk. Muss 126 C3
Windsor Pl. Edin 125 D4
Windsor Pl. Shot 191 F3
Windsor Pl. Stir 7 D4
Windsor Rd. Falk 59 F2
Windsor Rd. Peni 204 A3
Windsor Sq. Peni 204 A3
Windsor St. Edin 93 F1
Windsor St. Men 3 F3
Windsor St. Shot 191 F3
Windsor Street La. Edin 93 F1
Windsor Terr. Peni 204 A3
Windygate. Kirk 16 C1
Windygates Rd. N Ber 54 A3
Windygoul Cres. Tran 128 C3
Windyhill Ave. Kin 23 E3
Windyknowe Cres. Bath .. 144 C3
Windyknowe Pk. Bath 144 C3
Wingate Cres. Dunb 78 B1
Winifred Cres. Kirk 17 D3
Winifred St. Kirk 17 D3
Winton Cl. Tran 128 C2
Winton Ct. Orm 129 D2
Winton Ct. Tran 128 C2
Winton Dr. Edin 154 B2
Winton Gdns. Edin 154 B2
Winton Gr. Edin 154 A3
Winton Gr. Tran 128 C2
Winton Loan. Edin 154 B2
Winton Loan. Glad 129 D3
Winton Pk. Cocke 97 E2
Winton Pk. Edin 154 A2
Winton Pl. Tran 128 B3
Winton Terr. Edin 154 A3
Winton Terr. Orm 129 D2
Winton Way. Tran 128 B2
Wishart Ave. Bonn 182 B4
Wishart Ave. N Ber 54 B3
Wishart Dr. Stir 7 E2
Wishart Pl. Dalk 156 C1
Wishart Pl. Kirk 17 F3
Wishaw Terr. Edin 94 A1
Wisp Gn. Edin 125 D2
Wisp The. Dan 125 D1
Wisp The. Edin 125 D2
Witchbrae. Dunf 29 D2
Wolfe Rd. Falk 60 B1
Wolrige Rd. Edin 155 D4
Wolseley Cres. Edin 94 B1
Wolseley Pl. Edin 94 B1
Wolsey Ave. Bonn 182 B3
Wood Avens. Tull 4 B1
Wood Dr. Whit 169 F3
Wood Lea. Kin 23 F3
Wood Pl. Liv 147 E2
Wood Pl. Ros 46 C3
Wood Rd. Ros 46 B1
Wood St. Gran 61 E4
Woodbank. Cow 13 D1
Woodbank Gr. Bla 26 B4
Woodbine Terr. Edin 94 A2
Woodburn Ave. Dalk 157 E1
Woodburn Ave. Laur 61 D1
Woodburn Bank. Dalk 157 E1
Woodburn Dr. Dalk 157 E1
Woodburn Gdns. Dalk 157 E2
Woodburn Gdns. Falk 60 C3
Woodburn Gr. Dalk 157 E1
Woodburn Loan. Dalk 157 E1
Woodburn Medway. Dalk . 157 E2
Woodburn Pk. Dalk 157 E2
Woodburn Pl. Dalk 157 E2
Woodburn Pl. Edin 157 E2
Woodburn Rd. Dalk 157 E2
Woodburn Rd. Falk 60 B3
Woodburn St. Dalk 157 E1
Woodburn Terr. Dalk 157 E2
Woodburn Terr. Edin 123 D2
Woodburn View. Dalk 157 E2
Woodburn Way. Alva 5 D3
Woodbush Ct. Dunb 78 C1
Woodbush Cross. Dunb 78 C1
Woodbush. Dunb 78 C1
Woodend Pk. Rosl 180 C2
Woodend Pl. Cow 13 D1
Woodend Rd. Car 230 A1
Woodend Wlk. Arm 143 F3

Woodfield Ave. Edin 152 C3
Woodfield Pk. Edin 152 C3
Woodfield Pk. Edin 153 D3
Woodfield Pk. Rosl 180 B3
Woodhall Ave. Curr 152 B3
Woodhall Bank. Edin 152 C3
Woodhall Dr. Curr 152 B3
Woodhall Gr. Edin 152 C3
Woodhall Millbrae. Edin .. 152 C3
Woodhall Pl. Pen 160 C3
Woodhall Rd. Pen 160 B3
Woodhall Terr. Curr 152 B3
Woodhead Farm Rd. Cul ... 25 F1
Woodhead Pl. Bath 144 C3
Woodhead St. H Val 26 A1
Woodhill Ct. Gran 61 E3
Woodhill Gr. Crossf 28 A1
Woodhill Rd. Blac 142 A2
Woodland Way. Den 57 E4
Woodlands Bank. D Bay 48 A2
Woodlands Cotts. Arm 144 A3
Woodlands Cres. Falk 60 A2
Woodlands Dr. B' ness 63 E3
Woodlands Dr. Crossf 28 A1
Woodlands Dr. Pol 82 C4
Woodlands Gr. Arm 144 A3
Woodlands Gr. Edin 124 C3
Woodlands. N Sau 5 F1
Woodlands Pk. Liv 146 C4
Woodlands Rd. Kirk 16 B3
Woodlands Terr. Bla 26 A4
Woodlands The. Ros 46 C3
Woodlea Pk. N Sau 10 A4
Woodmill Cres. Dunf 29 E2
Woodmill Pl. Dunf 29 F2
Woodmill Rd. Dunf 29 E2
Woodmill St. Dunf 29 D2
Woodmill Terr. Dunf 29 D2
Woodmuir Pl. Add 194 C3
Woodmuir Rd. Add 194 C3
Woodmuir Rd. Whit 170 B3
Woodrow. Gore 183 E1
Woodside Ave. Ros 46 C3
Woodside. Cow 13 E2
Woodside Ct. Cam 6 B3
Woodside Dr. Peni 203 F3
Woodside Gdns. Muss 126 C3
Woodside Pl. Pol 82 C4
Woodside Pl. Brid 86 B2
Woodside Pl. Fall 8 B2
Woodside Rd.' All 9 F3
Woodside Rd. Cald 141 D2
Woodside Rd. Stir 2 A2
Woodside Rd. Tull 4 A1
Woodside St. Ros 46 C3
Woodside Terr. Auc 217 F2
Woodside Terr. Brid 86 B2
Woodside Terr. Clack 10 C2
Woodside Terr. Edin 125 E4
Woodside Terr. Falk 60 A2
Woodstock Pl. Edin 124 A1
Woodville Terr. Edin 94 A2
Wooer St. Falk 60 A2
Woofords Cotts. Auc 217 D4
Woolmet Cres. Dan 156 A4
Wotherspoon Cres. Arm ... 143 F3
Wotherspoon Dr. B' ness ... 63 E3
Wright Pl. Kirk 17 E4
Wright St. Falk 60 A3
Writers Ct. Dunb 78 B2
Wynd The. Aber 71 E3
Wynd The. Alva 5 D4
Wynd The. D Bay 48 B2
Wynd The. Gill 163 F3
Wynd The. Orm 159 F4
Wyndford Ave. Uph 117 D3
Wyndford Pl. Uph 117 D3
Wyvern Pk. Edin 123 E2
Wyvis Pk. Peni 204 A4
Wyvis Pl. Shot 192 A2

Yardheads. Edin 93 F3
Yardley Pl. Falk 39 D1
Yarrow Ct. Peni 204 A4
Yarrow Pl. Gran 61 F3
Yeaman La. Edin 122 C3
Yeaman Pl. Edin 122 C3
Yester Pl. Hadd 100 C1
Yetholm Pk. Dunf 28 C1
Yetts The. Cam 6 B3
Yew La. Liv 148 A3
Yew Terr. Laur 61 D1
Yewlands Cres. Edin 155 D4
Yewlands Gdns. Edin 155 D4
Yieldshields Rd. Car 231 E2
York Arc. Gran 40 B1
York Ct. Falk 60 B3
York La. Edin 93 E1
York La. Gran 40 B1
York Pl. Dunf 29 E3
York Pl. Edin 93 E1
York Pl. Kirk 17 E3
York Rd. Edin 93 E3
York Rd. N Ber 54 A4
York Sq. Gran 40 B1
York St. Falk 60 B3
Young Ave. Tran 128 B3

Young Cres. Bath 144 C3
Young St. Cow 13 E2
Young Sq. Muri 173 E3
Young Sq. W Cal 173 D3
Young St. Edin 123 D4
Young St. W Cal 172 B1
Young Street La N. Edin .. 123 D4
Young Street La S. Edin .. 123 D4
Young Terr. Cow 13 D2
Young's Terr. Kirk 17 E3
Youngs Rd. Brox 118 A3
Yule Pl. Black 145 E1
Yule Terr. Black 171 E4

Zealandia Rd. Ros 46 A3
Zetland Dr. Laur 61 D2
Zetland Pl. Edin 93 D3
Zetland Pl. Gran 39 F2
Zetland Pl. Loch 14 A4
Zetland St. Clack 11 D2
Zetland Terr. Pol 61 F1

O S STREET ATLASES ORDER FORM

T511N99CO1	Hardback QUANTITY	TOTAL	Softback QUANTITY	TOTAL	Pocket QUANTITY	TOTAL	
	£12.99		£8.99		£4.99		
Berkshire	ISBN 0-540-05992-7		ISBN 0-540-05993-5		ISBN 0-540-05994-3		➤
Buckinghamshire	ISBN 0-540-05989-7		ISBN 0-540-05990-0		ISBN 0-540-05991-9		➤
East Essex	ISBN 0-540-05848-3		ISBN 0-540-05866-1		ISBN 0-540-05850-5		➤
West Essex	ISBN 0-540-05849-1		ISBN 0-540-05867-X		ISBN 0-540-05851-3		➤
North Hampshire	ISBN 0-540-05852-1		ISBN 0-540-05853-X		ISBN 0-540-05854-8		➤
South Hampshire	ISBN 0-540-05855-6		ISBN 0-540-05856-4		ISBN 0-540-05857-2		➤
Hertfordshire	ISBN 0-540-05995-1		ISBN 0-540-05996-X		ISBN 0-540-05997-8		➤
East Kent	ISBN 0-540-06026-7		ISBN 0-540-06027-5		ISBN 0-540-06028-3		➤
West Kent	ISBN 0-540-06029-1		ISBN 0-540-06031-3		ISBN 0-540-06030-5		➤
Nottinghamshire	ISBN 0-540-05858-0		ISBN 0-540-05859-9		ISBN 0-540-05860-2		➤
Oxfordshire	ISBN 0-540-05986-2		ISBN 0-540-05987-0		ISBN 0-540-05988-9		➤
East Sussex	ISBN 0-540-05875-0		ISBN 0-540-05874-2		ISBN 0-540-05873-4		➤
West Sussex	ISBN 0-540-05876-9		ISBN 0-540-05877-7		ISBN 0-540-05878-5		➤
	£12.99		£9.99		£4.99		
Bristol and Avon	ISBN 0-540-06140-9		ISBN 0-540-06141-7		ISBN 0-540-06142-5		➤
Cardiff	ISBN 0-540-06186-7		ISBN 0-540-06187-5		ISBN 0-540-06207-3		➤
Cheshire	ISBN 0-540-06143-3		ISBN 0-540-06144-1		ISBN 0-540-06145-X		➤
Derbyshire	ISBN 0-540-06137-9		ISBN 0-540-06138-7		ISBN 0-540-06139-5		➤
Edinburgh	ISBN 0-540-06180-8		ISBN 0-540-06181-6		ISBN 0-540-06182-4		➤
Glasgow	ISBN 0-540-06183-2		ISBN 0-540-06184-0		ISBN 0-540-06185-9		➤
Staffordshire	ISBN 0-540-06134-4		ISBN 0-540-06135-2		ISBN 0-540-06136-0		➤
	£10.99		£8.99		£4.99		
Surrey	ISBN 0-540-05983-8		ISBN 0-540-05984-6		ISBN 0-540-05985-4		➤
Warwickshire	ISBN 0-540-05642-1						➤ ⬇

Name _____

Address _____

_____ Postcode

◆ Free postage and packing ◆ All available titles will normally be dispatched within 5 working days of receipt of order but please allow up to 28 days for delivery
☐ Please tick this box if you do not wish your name to be used by other carefully selected organisations that may wish to send you information about other products and services

I enclose a cheque / postal order, for a **total** of ☐

made payable to **Reed Book Services**, or please debit my

☐ Access ☐ American Express ☐ Visa

account by ☐

Account no ☐☐☐☐ ☐☐☐☐ ☐☐☐☐ ☐☐☐☐

Expiry date ☐☐ ☐☐

Signature _____